G. S. Morris.

THE

PROSE WORKS

OF

RALPH WALDO EMERSON.

NEW AND REVISED EDITION.

IN TWO VOLUMES.

VOL. II.

BOSTON:
FIELDS, OSGOOD, & CO.
1870.

University Press: Welch, Bigelow, & Co.,
Cambridge.

REPRESENTATIVE MEN.

CONTENTS OF VOL. II.

REPRESENTATIVE MEN.

ENGLISH TRAITS.

CONDUCT OF LIFE.

I.

USES OF GREAT MEN.

USES OF GREAT MEN.

IT is natural to believe in great men. If the companions of our childhood should turn out to be heroes, and their condition regal, it would not surprise us. All mythology opens with demigods, and the circumstance is high and poetic; that is, their genius is paramount. In the legends of the Gautama, the first men ate the earth, and found it deliciously sweet.

Nature seems to exist for the excellent. The world is upheld by the veracity of good men: they make the earth wholesome. They who lived with them found life glad and nutritious. Life is sweet and tolerable only in our belief in such society; and actually, or ideally, we manage to live with superiors. We call our children and our lands by their names. Their names are wrought into the verbs of language, their works and effigies are in our houses, and every circumstance of the day recalls an anecdote of them.

The search after the great men is the dream of youth, and the most serious occupation of manhood. We travel into foreign parts to find his works, — if possible, to get a glimpse of him. But we are put off with fortune instead. You say, the English are practical; the Germans are hospitable; in Valencia, the climate is delicious; and in the hills of the Sacramento, there is gold for the gathering. Yes, but I do not travel to find comfortable, rich, and hospitable people, or clear sky, or ingots that cost too much. But if there were any magnet that would point to the countries and houses where are the persons who are intrinsically rich and powerful, I would sell all, and buy it, and put myself on the road to-day.

The race goes with us on their credit. The knowledge that in the city is a man who invented the railroad, raises the credit of all the citizens. But enormous populations, if they be beggars, are disgusting, like moving cheese, like hills of ants, or of fleas, — the more, the worse.

Our religion is the love and cherishing of these patrons. The gods of fable are the shining moments of great men. We run all our vessels into one mould. Our colossal theologies of Judaism, Christism, Buddhism, Mahometism, are the necessary and structural action of the human mind. The student of history is like a man going into a warehouse to buy cloths or carpets. He fancies he has a new article. If he go to the factory, he shall find that his new stuff still repeats the scrolls and rosettes which are found on the interior walls of the pyramids of Thebes. Our theism is the purification of the human mind. Man can paint, or make, or think nothing but man. He believes that the great material elements had their origin from his thought. And our philosophy finds one essence collected or distributed.

If now we proceed to inquire into the kinds of service we derive from others, let us be warned of the danger of modern studies, and begin low enough. We must not contend against love, or deny the substantial existence of other people. I know not what would happen to us. We have social strengths. Our affection towards others creates a sort of vantage or purchase which nothing will supply. I can do that by another which I cannot do alone. I can say to you what I cannot first say to myself. Other men are lenses through which we read our own minds. Each man seeks those of different quality from his own, and such as are good of their kind; that is, he seeks other men, and the *otherest*. The stronger the nature, the more it is reactive. Let us have the quality pure. A little genius let us leave alone. A main difference betwixt men is, whether they attend their own affair or not. Man is that noble endogenous plant which grows, like the palm, from within outward. His own affair, though impossible to others, he can open with celerity and in sport. It is easy to sugar to be sweet, and to nitre to be salt. We take a great deal of pains to waylay and entrap that which of itself will fall into our hands. I count him a great man who inhabits a higher sphere of thought, into which other men rise with labor and difficulty; he has but to open his eyes to see things in a true light, and in large relations; whilst they must make painful corrections, and keep a vigilant eye on many sources of error. His service to us is of like sort. It costs a beautiful person no exertion to paint her image on our eyes; yet how splendid is that benefit! It costs no more for a wise soul to convey his quality to other men. And every one can do his best thing easiest. "*Peu de moyens, beaucoup d'effét.*" He is great who is what he is from nature, and who never reminds us of others.

But he must be related to us, and our life receive from him some promise of explanation. I cannot tell what I would know; but I have observed there are persons who, in their character and actions, answer questions which I have not skill to put. One man answers some question which none of his contemporaries put, and is isolated. The past and passing religions and philosophies answer some other question. Certain men affect us as rich possibilities, but helpless to themselves and to their times, — the sport, perhaps, of some instinct that rules in the air; — they do not speak to our want. But the great are near; we know them at sight. They satisfy expectation, and fall into place. What is good is effective, generative; makes for itself room, food, and allies. A sound apple produces seed, — a hybrid does not. Is a man in his place, he is constructive, fertile, magnetic, inundating armies with his purpose, which is thus executed. The river makes its own shores, and each legitimate idea makes its own channels and welcome, — harvests for food, institutions for expression, weapons to fight with, and disciples to explain it. The true artist has the planet for his pedestal; the adventurer, after years of strife, has nothing broader than his own shoes.

Our common discourse respects two kinds of use or service from superior men. Direct giving is agreeable to the early belief of men; direct giving of material or metaphysical aid, as of health, eternal youth, fine senses, arts of healing, magical power, and prophecy. The boy believes there is a teacher who can sell him wisdom. Churches believe in imputed merit. But, in strictness, we are not much cognizant of direct serving. Man is endogenous, and education is his unfolding. The aid we have from others is mechanical, compared with the discoveries of nature in us. What is thus learned is delightful in the doing, and the effect remains. Right ethics are central, and go from the soul outward. Gift is contrary to the law of the universe. Serving others is serving us. I must absolve me to myself. 'Mind thy affair,' says the spirit: — 'coxcomb, would you meddle with the skies, or with other people?' Indirect service is left. Men have a pictorial or representative quality, and serve us in the intellect. Behmen and Swedenborg saw that things were representative. Men are also representative; first, of things, and secondly, of ideas.

As plants convert the minerals into food for animals, so each man converts some raw material in nature to human use. The inventors of fire, electricity, magnetism, iron, lead, glass, linen, silk, cotton; the makers of tools; the inventor of decimal notation; the geometer; the engineer; the musician, — severally make an easy way for all, through unknown and impossible confusions. Each man is, by secret liking, connected with some district of nature, whose agent and interpreter he is, as Linnæus, of plants; Huber, of bees; Fries, of lichens; Van Mons, of pears; Dalton, of atomic forms; Euclid, of lines; Newton, of fluxions.

A man is a centre for nature, running out threads of relation through everything, fluid and solid, material and elemental. The earth rolls; every clod and stone comes to the meridian: so every organ, function, acid, crystal, grain of dust, has its relation to the brain. It waits long, but its turn comes. Each plant has its parasite, and each created thing its lover and poet. Justice has already been done to steam, to iron, to wood, to coal, to loadstone, to iodine, to corn, and cotton: but how few materials are yet used by our arts! The mass of creatures and of qualities are still hid and expectant. It would seem as if each waited, like the enchanted princess in fairy tales, for a destined human deliverer. Each must be disenchanted, and walk forth to the day in human shape. In the history of discovery, the ripe and latent truth seems to have fashioned a brain for itself. A magnet must be made man, in some Gilbert, or Swedenborg, or Oersted, before the general mind can come to entertain its powers.

If we limit ourselves to the first advantages; — a sober grace adheres to the mineral and botanic kingdoms, which, in the highest moments, comes up as the charm of nature, — the glitter of the spar, the sureness of affinity, the veracity of angles. Light and darkness, heat and cold, hunger and food, sweet and sour, solid, liquid, and gas, circle us round in a wreath of pleasures, and, by their agreeable quarrel, beguile the day of life. The eye repeats every day the first eulogy on things, — "He saw that they were good." We know where to find them; and these performers are relished all the more, after a little experience of the pretending races. We are entitled, also, to higher advantages. Something is wanting to science, until it has been humanized. The table of logarithms is one thing, and its vital play in botany, music, optics, and architecture, another. There are advancements to numbers, anatomy, architecture, astronomy, little suspected at first, when, by union with intellect and will, they ascend into the life, and reappear in conversation, character, and politics.

But this comes later. We speak now only of our acquaintance with them in their own sphere, and the way in which they seem to fascinate and draw to them some genius who occupies himself with one thing, all his life long. The possibility of interpretation lies in the identity of the observer with the observed. Each material thing has its celestial side; has its translation, through humanity, into the spiritual and necessary sphere, where it plays a part as indestructible as any other. And to these, their ends, all things continually ascend. The gases gather to the solid firmament: the chemic lump arrives at the plant, and grows; arrives at the quadruped, and walks; arrives at the man, and thinks. But also the constituency determines the vote of the representative. He is not only representative, but participant. Like can only be known by like. The reason why he knows about them is, that he is of them; he has just come out of nature, or from being a part of that thing. Animated chlorine knows of chlorine, and incarnate zinc, of zinc. Their quality makes his career; and he can variously publish their virtues, because they compose him. Man, made of the dust of the world, does not forget his origin; and all that is yet inanimate will one day speak and reason. Unpublished nature will have its whole secret told. Shall we say that quartz mountains will pulverize into innumerable Werners, Von Buchs, and Beaumonts; and the laboratory of the atmosphere holds in solution I know not what Berzeliuses and Davys?

Thus, we sit by the fire, and take hold on the poles of the earth. This *quasi* omnipresence supplies the imbecility of our condition. In one of those celestial days, when heaven and earth meet and adorn each other, it seems a poverty that we can only spend it once: we wish for a thousand heads, a thousand bodies, that we might celebrate its immense beauty in many ways and places. Is this fancy? Well, in good faith, we are multiplied by our proxies. How easily we adopt their labors! Every ship that comes to America got its chart from Columbus. Every novel is a debtor to Homer. Every carpenter who shaves with a foreplane borrows the genius of a forgotten inventor. Life is girt all round with a zodiac of sciences, the contributions of men who have perished to add their point of light to our sky. Engineer, broker, jurist, physician, moralist, theologian, and every man, inasmuch as he has any science, is a definer and map-maker of the latitudes and longitudes of our condition. These road-makers on every hand enrich us. We must extend the area of life, and multiply our relations. We are as much gainers by finding a new property in the old earth, as by acquiring a new planet.

We are too passive in the reception of these material or semi-material aids. We must not be sacks and stomachs. To ascend one step,— we are better served through our sympathy. Activity is contagious. Looking where others look, and conversing with the same things, we catch the charm which lured them. Napoleon said, "You must not fight too often with one enemy, or you will teach him all your art of war." Talk much with any man of vigorous mind, and we acquire very fast the habit of looking at things in the same light, and, on each occurrence, we anticipate his thought.

Men are helpful through the intellect and the affections. Other help, I find a false appearance. If you affect to give me bread and fire, I perceive that I pay for it the full price, and at last it leaves me as it found me, neither better nor worse: but all mental and moral force is a positive good. It goes out from you, whether you will or not, and profits me whom you never thought of. I cannot even hear of personal vigor of any kind, great power of performance, without fresh resolution. We are emulous of all that man can do. Cecil's saying of Sir Walter Raleigh, "I know that he can toil terribly," is an electric touch. So are Clarendon's portraits, — of Hampden; "who was of an industry and vigilance not to be tired out or wearied by the most laborious, and of parts not to be imposed on by the most subtle and sharp, and of a personal courage equal to his best parts," — of Falkland; "who was so severe an adorer of truth, that he could as easily have given himself leave to steal, as to dissemble." We cannot read Plutarch, without a tingling of the blood; and I accept the saying of the Chinese Mencius: "A sage is the instructor of a hundred ages. When the manners of Loo are heard of, the stupid become intelligent, and the wavering, determined."

This is the moral of biography; yet it is hard for departed men to touch the quick like our own companions, whose names may not last as long. What is he whom I never think of? whilst in every solitude are those who succor our genius, and stimulate us in wonderful manners. There is a power in love to divine another's destiny better than that other can, and, by heroic encouragements, hold him to his task. What has friendship so signal as its sublime attraction to whatever virtue is in us? We will never more think cheaply of ourselves, or of life. We are piqued to some purpose, and the industry of the diggers on the railroad will not again shame us.

Under this head, too, falls that homage, very pure, as I think, which all ranks pay to the hero of the day, from Coriolanus and Gracchus, down to Pitt, Lafayette, Wellington, Webster, Lamartine. Hear the shouts in the street! The people cannot see him enough. They delight in a man. Here is a head and a trunk! What a front! what eyes! Atlantean shoulders, and the whole carriage heroic, with equal inward force to guide the great machine! This pleasure of full expression to that which, in their private experience, is usually cramped and obstructed, runs, also, much higher, and is the secret of the reader's joy in literary genius. Nothing is kept back. There is fire enough to fuse the mountain of ore. Shakespeare's principal merit may be conveyed, in saying that he, of all men, best understands the English language, and can say what he will. Yet these unchoked channels and floodgates of expression are only health or fortunate constitution. Shakespeare's name suggests other and purely intellectual benefits.

Senates and sovereigns have no compliment, with their medals, swords, and armorial coats, like the addressing to a human being thoughts out of a certain height, and presupposing his intelligence. This honor, which is possible in personal intercourse scarcely twice in a lifetime, genius perpetually pays; contented, if now and then, in a century, the proffer is accepted. The indicators of the values of matter are degraded to a sort of cooks and confectioners, on the appearance of the indicators of ideas. Genius is the naturalist or geographer of the supersensible regions, and draws their map; and, by acquainting us with new fields of activity, cools our affection for the old. These are at once accepted as the reality, of which the world we have conversed with is the show.

We go to the gymnasium and the swimming-school to see the power and beauty of the body; there is the like pleasure, and a higher benefit, from witnessing intellectual feats of all kinds; as, feats of memory, of mathematical combination, great power of abstraction, the transmutings of the imagination, even versatility, and concentration, as these acts expose the invisible organs and members of the mind, which respond, member for member, to the parts of the body. For, we thus enter a new gymnasium, and learn to choose men by their truest marks, taught, with Plato, "to choose those who can, without aid from the eyes, or any other sense, proceed to truth and to being." Foremost among these activities, are the summersaults, spells, and resurrections wrought by the imagination. When this wakes, a man seems to multiply ten times or a thousand times his force. It opens the delicious sense of indeterminate size, and inspires an audacious mental habit. We are as elastic as the gas of gunpowder, and a sentence in a book, or a word dropped in conversation, sets free our fancy, and instantly our heads are bathed with galaxies, and our feet tread the floor of the Pit. And this benefit is real, because we are entitled to these enlargements, and, once having passed the bounds, shall never again be quite the miserable pedants we were.

The high functions of the intellect are so allied, that some imaginative power usually appears in all eminent minds, even in arithmeticians of the first class, but especially in meditative men of an intuitive habit of thought. This class serve us, so that they have the perception of identity and the perception of reaction. The eyes of Plato, Shakespeare, Swedenborg, Goethe, never shut on either of these laws. The perception of these laws is a kind of metre of the mind. Little minds are little, through failure to see them.

Even these feasts have their surfeit. Our delight in reason degenerates into idolatry of the herald. Especially when a mind of powerful method has instructed men, we find the examples of oppression. The dominion of Aristotle, the Ptolemaic astronomy, the credit of Luther, of Bacon, of Locke, — in religion, the history of hierarchies, of saints, and the sects which have taken the name of each founder, are in point. Alas! every man is such a victim. The imbecility of men is always inviting the impudence of power. It is the delight of vulgar talent to dazzle and to blind the beholder. But true genius seeks to defend us from itself. True genius will not impoverish, but will liberate, and add new senses. If a wise man should appear in our village, he would create, in those who conversed with him, a new consciousness of wealth, by opening their eyes to unobserved advantages; he would establish a sense of immovable equality, calm us with assurances that we could not be cheated; as every one would discern the checks and guaranties of condition. The rich would see their mistakes and poverty, the poor their escapes and their resources.

But nature brings all this about in due time. Rotation is her remedy. The soul is impatient of masters, and eager for change. Housekeepers say of a domestic who has been valuable, She had lived with me long enough. We are tendencies, or rather, symptoms, and none of us complete. We touch and go, and sip the foam of many lives. Rotation is the law of nature. When nature removes a great man, people explore the horizon for a successor; but none comes, and none will. His class is extinguished with him. In some other and quite different field, the next man will appear; not Jefferson, not Franklin, but now a great salesman; then a road-contractor; then a student of fishes; then a buffalo-hunting explorer; or a semi-savage Western general. Thus we make a stand against our rougher masters; but against the best there is a finer remedy. The power which they communicate is not theirs. When we are exalted by ideas, we do not owe this to Plato, but to the idea, to which also Plato was debtor.

I must not forget that we have a special debt to a single class. Life is a scale of degrees. Between rank and rank of our great men are wide intervals. Mankind have, in all ages, attached themselves to a few persons, who, either by the quality of that idea they embodied, or by the largeness of their reception, were entitled to the position of leaders and lawgivers. These teach us the qualities of primary nature, — admit us to the constitution of things. We swim day by day on a river of delusions, and are effectually amused with houses and towns in the air, of which the men about us are dupes. But life is a sincerity. In lucid intervals we say, 'Let there be an entrance opened for me into realities; I have worn the fool's cap too long.' We will know the meaning of our economies and politics. Give us the cipher, and, if persons and things are scores of a celestial music, let us read off the strains. We have been cheated of our reason; yet there have been sane men, who enjoyed a rich and related existence. What they know, they know for us. With each new mind, a new secret of nature transpires; nor can the Bible be closed, until the last great man is born. These men correct the delirium of the animal spirits, make us considerate, and engage us to new aims and powers. The veneration of mankind selects these for the highest place. Witness the multitude of statues, pictures, and memorials which recall their genius in every city, village, house, and ship: —

> "Ever their phantoms arise before us,
> Our loftier brothers, but one in blood;
> At bed and table they lord it o'er us,
> With looks of beauty, and words of good."

How to illustrate the distinctive benefit of ideas, the service rendered by those who introduce moral truths into the general mind? — I am plagued, in all my living, with a perpetual tariff of prices. If I work in my garden and prune an apple-tree, I am well enough entertained, and could continue indefinitely in the like occupation. But it comes to mind that a day is gone, and I have got this precious nothing done. I go to Boston or New York, and run up and down on my affairs: they are sped, but so is the day. I am vexed by the recollection of this price I have paid for a trifling advantage. I remember the *peau d'ane*, on which whoso sat should have his desire, but a piece of the skin was gone for every wish. I go to a convention of philanthropists. Do what I can, I cannot keep my eyes off the clock. But if there should appear in the company some gentle soul who knows little of persons or parties, of Carolina or Cuba, but who announces a law that disposes these particulars, and so certifies me of the equity which checkmates every false player, bankrupts every self-seeker, and apprises me of my independence on any conditions of country, or time, or human body, that man liberates me; I forget the clock; I pass out of the sore relation to persons; I am healed of my hurts; I am made immortal by apprehending my possession of incorruptible goods. Here is great competition of rich and poor. We live in a market, where is only so much wheat, or wool, or land; and if I have so much more, every other must have so much less. I seem to have no good, without breach of good manners. Nobody is glad in the gladness of another, and our system is one of war, of an injurious superiority. Every child of the Saxon race is educated to wish to be first. It is our system; and a man comes to measure his greatness by the regrets, envies, and hatreds of his competitors. But in these new fields there is room: here are no self-esteems, no exclusions.

I admire great men of all classes, those who stand for facts, and for thoughts; I like rough and smooth, "Scourgers of God," and "Darlings of the human race." I like the first Cæsar; and Charles V., of Spain; and Charles XII., of Sweden; Richard Plantagenet; and Bonaparte, in France. I applaud a sufficient man, an officer equal to his office; captains, ministers, senators. I like a master standing firm on legs of iron, well-born, rich, handsome, eloquent, loaded with advantages, drawing all men by fascination into tributaries and supporters of his power. Sword and staff, or talents sword-like or staff-like, carry on the work of the world. But I find him greater, when he can abolish himself, and all heroes, by letting in this element of reason, irrespective of persons; this subtilizer, and irresistible upward force, into our thought, destroying individualism; the power so great, that the potentate is nothing. Then he is a monarch, who gives a constitution to his people; a pontiff, who preaches the equality of souls, and releases his servants from their barbarous homages; an emperor, who can spare his empire.

But I intended to specify, with a little minuteness, two or three points of service. Nature never spares the opium or nepenthe; but, wherever she mars her creature with some deformity or defect, lays her poppies plentifully on the bruise, and the sufferer goes joyfully through life, ignorant of the ruin, and incapable of seeing it, though all the world point their finger at it every day. The worthless and offensive members of society, whose existence is a social pest, invariably think themselves the most ill-used people alive, and never get over their astonishment at the ingratitude and selfishness of their contemporaries. Our globe discovers its hidden virtues, not only in heroes and archangels, but in gossips and nurses. Is it not a rare contrivance that lodged the due inertia in every creature, the conserving, resisting energy, the anger at being waked or changed? Altogether independent of the intellectual force in each, is the pride of opinion, the security that we are right. Not the feeblest grandame, not a mowing idiot, but uses what spark of perception and faculty is left, to chuckle and triumph in his or her opinion over the absurdities of all the rest. Difference from me is the measure of absurdity. Not one has a misgiving of being wrong. Was it not a bright thought that made things cohere with this bitumen, fastest of cements? But, in the midst of this chuckle of self-gratulation, some figure goes by, which Thersites too can love and admire. This is he that should marshal us the way we were going. There is no end to his aid. Without Plato, we should almost lose our faith in the possibility of a reasonable book.

We seem to want but one, but we want one. We love to associate with heroic persons, since our receptivity is unlimited; and, with the great, our thoughts and manners easily become great. We are all wise in capacity, though so few in energy. There needs but one wise man in a company, and all are wise, so rapid is the contagion.

Great men are thus a collyrium to clear our eyes from egotism, and enable us to see other people and their works. But there are vices and follies incident to whole populations and ages. Men resemble their contemporaries, even more than their progenitors. It is observed in old couples, or in persons who have been housemates for a course of years, that they grow alike; and, if they should live long enough, we should not be able to know them apart. Nature abhors these complaisances, which threaten to melt the world into a lump, and hastens to break up such maudlin agglutinations. The like assimilation goes on between men of one town, of one sect, of one political party; and the ideas of the time are in the air, and infect all who breathe it. Viewed from any high point, this city of New York, yonder city of London, the Western civilization, would seem a bundle of insanities. We keep each other in countenance, and exasperate by emulation the frenzy of the time. The shield against the stingings of conscience, is the universal practice, or our contemporaries. Again; it is very easy to be as wise and good as your companions. We learn of our contemporaries what they know, without effort, and almost through the pores of the skin. We catch it by sympathy, or, as a wife arrives at the intellectual and moral elevations of her husband. But we stop where they stop. Very hardly can we take another step. The great, or such as hold of nature, and transcend fashions, by their fidelity to universal ideas, are saviors from these federal errors, and defend us from our contemporaries. They are the exceptions which we want, where all grows alike. A foreign greatness is the antidote for cabalism.

Thus we feed on genius, and refresh ourselves from too much conversation with our mates, and exult in the depth of nature in that direction in which he leads us. What indemnification is one great man for populations of pygmies? Every mother wishes one son a genius, though all the rest should be mediocre. But a new danger appears in the excess of influence of the great man. His attractions warp us from our place. We have become underlings and intellectual suicides. Ah! yonder in the horizon is our help; — other great men, new qualities, counterweights and checks on each other. We cloy of the honey of each peculiar greatness. Every hero becomes a bore at last. Perhaps Voltaire was not bad-hearted, yet he said of the good Jesus, even, "I pray you, let me never hear that man's name again." They cry up the virtues of George Washington, — "Damn George Washington!" is the poor Jacobin's whole speech and confutation. But it is human nature's indispensable defence. The centripetence augments the centrifugence. We balance one man with his opposite, and the health of the state depends on the see-saw.

There is, however, a speedy limit to the use of heroes. Every genius is defended from approach by quantities of unavailableness. They are very attractive, and seem at a distance our own; but we are hindered on all sides from approach. The more we are drawn, the more we are repelled. There is something not solid in the good that is done for us. The best discovery the discoverer makes for himself. It has something unreal for his companion, until he too has substantiated it. It seems as if the Deity dressed each soul which he sends into nature in certain virtues and powers not communicable to other men, and, sending it to perform one more turn through the circle of beings, wrote "*Not transferable,*" and "*Good for this trip only,*" on these garments of the soul. There is somewhat deceptive about the intercourse of minds. The boundaries are invisible, but they are never crossed. There is such good-will to impart, and such good-will to receive, that each threatens to become the other; but the law of individuality collects its secret strength; you are you, and I am I, and so we remain.

For nature wishes everything to remain itself; and, whilst every individual strives to grow and exclude, and to exclude and grow, to the extremities of the universe, and to impose the law of its being on every other creature, Nature steadily aims to protect each against every other. Each is self-defended. Nothing is more marked than the power by which individuals are guarded from individuals, in a world where every benefactor becomes so easily a malefactor, only by continuation of his activity into places where it is not due; where children seem so much at the mercy of their foolish parents, and where almost all men are too social and interfering. We rightly speak of the guardian angels of children. How superior in their security from infusions of evil persons, from vulgarity and second thought! They shed their own abundant beauty on the objects they behold. Therefore, they are not at the mercy of such poor educators as we adults. If we huff and chide them, they soon come not to mind it, and get a self-reliance; and if we indulge them to folly, they learn the limitation elsewhere.

We need not fear excessive influence. A more generous trust is permitted. Serve the great. Stick at no humiliation. Grudge no office thou canst render. Be the limb of their body, the breath of their mouth. Compromise thy egotism. Who cares for that, so thou gain aught wider and nobler? Never mind the taunt of Boswellism: the devotion may easily be greater than the wretched pride which is guarding its own skirts. Be another: not thyself, but a Platonist; not a soul, but a Christian; not a naturalist, but a Cartesian; not a poet, but a Shakespearian. In vain, the wheels of tendency will not stop, nor will all the forces of inertia, fear, or of love itself, hold thee there. On, and forever onward! The microscope observes a monad or wheel-insect among the infusories circulating in water. Presently, a dot appears on the animal, which enlarges to a slit, and it becomes two perfect animals. The ever-proceeding detachment appears not less in all thought, and in society. Children think they cannot live without their parents. But, long before they are aware of it, the black dot has appeared, and the detachment taken place. Any accident will now reveal to them their independence.

But *great men*:—the word is injurious. Is there caste? is there fate? What becomes of the promise to virtue? The thoughtful youth laments the superfœtation of nature. 'Generous and handsome,' he says, 'is your hero; but look at yonder poor Paddy, whose country is his wheelbarrow; look at his whole nation of Paddies.' Why are the masses, from the dawn of history down, food for knives and powder? The idea dignifies a few leaders, who have sentiment, opinion, love, self-devotion; and they make war and death sacred; but what for the wretches whom they hire and kill? The cheapness of man is every day's tragedy. It is as real a loss that others should be low, as that we should be low; for we must have society.

Is it a reply to these suggestions, to say, society is a Pestalozzian school: all are teachers and pupils in turn. We are equally served by receiving and by imparting. Men who know the same things are not long the best company for each other.

But bring to each an intelligent person of another experience, and it is as if you let off water from a lake, by cutting a lower basin. It seems a mechanical advantage, and great benefit it is to each speaker, as he can now paint out his thought to himself. We pass very fast, in our personal moods, from dignity to dependence. And if any appear never to assume the chair, but always to stand and serve, it is because we do not see the company in a sufficiently long period for the whole rotation of parts to come about. As to what we call the masses, and common men; there are no common men. All men are at last of a size; and true art is only possible, on the conviction that every talent has its apotheosis somewhere. Fair play, and an open field, and freshest laurels to all who have won them! But Heaven reserves an equal scope for every creature. Each is uneasy until he has produced his private ray unto the concave sphere, and beheld his talent also in its last nobility and exaltation.

The heroes of the hour are relatively great: of a faster growth; or they are such, in whom, at the moment of success, a quality is ripe which is then in request. Other days will demand other qualities. Some rays escape the common observer, and want a finely adapted eye. Ask the great man if there be none greater. His companions are; and not the less great, but the more, that society cannot see them. Nature never sends a great man into the planet, without confiding the secret to another soul.

One gracious fact emerges from these studies, — that there is true ascension in our love. The reputations of the nineteenth century will one day be quoted, to prove its barbarism. The genius of humanity is the real subject whose biography is written in our annals. We must infer much, and supply many chasms in the record. The history of the universe is symptomatic, and life is mnemonical. No man, in all the procession of famous men, is reason or illumination, or that essence we were looking for; but is an exhibition, in some quarter, of new possibilities. Could we one day complete the immense figure which these flagrant points compose! The study of many individuals leads us to an elemental region wherein the individual is lost, or wherein all touch by their summits. Thought and feeling, that break out there, cannot be impounded by any fence of personality. This is the key to the power of the greatest men, — their spirit diffuses itself. A new quality of mind travels by night and by day, in concentric circles from its origin, and publishes itself by unknown methods: the union of all minds appears intimate: what gets admission to one, cannot be kept out of any other: the smallest acquisition of truth or of energy, in any quarter, is so much good to the commonwealth of souls. If the disparities of talent and position vanish, when the individuals are seen in the duration which is necessary to complete the career of each; even more swiftly the seeming injustice disappears, when we ascend to the central identity of all the individuals, and know that they are made of the substance which ordaineth and doeth.

The genius of humanity is the right point of view of history. The qualities abide; the men who exhibit them have now more, now less, and pass away; the qualities remain on another brow. No experience is more familiar. Once you saw phœnixes: they are gone; the world is not therefore disenchanted. The vessels on which you read sacred emblems turn out to be common pottery; but the sense of the pictures is sacred, and you may still read them transferred to the walls of the world. For a time, our teachers serve us personally, as metres or milestones of progress. Once they were angels of knowledge, and their figures touched the sky. Then we drew near, saw their means, culture, and limits; and they yielded their place to other geniuses. Happy, if a few names remain so high, that we have not been able to read them nearer, and age and comparison have not robbed them of a ray. But, at last, we shall cease to look in men for completeness, and shall content ourselves with their social and delegated quality. All that respects the individual is temporary and prospective, like the individual himself, who is ascending out of his limits, into a catholic existence. We have never come at the true and best benefit of any genius, so long as we believe him an original force. In the moment when he ceases to help us as a cause, he begins to help us more as an effect. Then he appears as an exponent of a vaster mind and will. The opaque self becomes transparent with the light of the First Cause.

Yet, within the limits of human education and agency, we may say, great men exist that there may be greater men. The destiny of organized nature is amelioration, and who can tell its limits? It is for man to tame the chaos; on every side, whilst he lives, to scatter the seeds of science and of song, that climate, corn, animals, men, may be milder, and the germs of love and benefit may be multiplied.

II.

PLATO; OR, THE PHILOSOPHER.

PLATO; OR, THE PHILOSOPHER.

AMONG books, Plato only is entitled to Omar's fanatical compliment to the Koran, when he said, "Burn the libraries; for, their value is in this book." These sentences contain the culture of nations; these are the corner-stone of schools; these are the fountain-head of literatures. A discipline it is in logic, arithmetic, taste, symmetry, poetry, language, rhetoric, ontology, morals, or practical wisdom. There was never such range of speculation. Out of Plato come all things that are still written and debated among men of thought. Great havoc makes he among our originalities. We have reached the mountain from which all these drift boulders were detached. The Bible of the learned for twenty-two hundred years, every brisk young man, who says in succession fine things to each reluctant generation, — Boethius, Rabelais, Erasmus, Bruno, Locke, Rousseau, Alfieri, Coleridge, — is some reader of Plato, translating into the vernacular, wittily, his good things. Even the men of grander proportion suffer some deduction from the misfortune (shall I say?) of coming after this exhausting generalizer. St. Augustine, Copernicus, Newton, Behmen, Swedenborg, Goethe, are likewise his debtors, and must say after him. For it is fair to credit the broadest generalizer with all the particulars deducible from his thesis.

Plato is philosophy, and philosophy, Plato, — at once the glory and the shame of mankind, since neither Saxon nor Roman have availed to add any idea to his categories. No wife, no children had he, and the thinkers of all civilized nations are his posterity, and are tinged with his mind. How many great men Nature is incessantly sending up out of night, to be *his men*, — Platonists! the Alexandrians, a constellation of genius; the Elizabethans, not less; Sir Thomas More, Henry

More, John Hales, John Smith, Lord Bacon, Jeremy Taylor, Ralph Cudworth, Sydenham, Thomas Taylor; Marcilius Ficinus, and Picus Mirandola. Calvinism is in his Phædo; Christianity is in it. Mahometanism draws all its philosophy, in its hand-book of morals, the Akhlak-y-Jalaly, from him. Mysticism finds in Plato all its texts. This citizen of a town in Greece is no villager nor patriot. An Englishman reads and says, 'how English!' a German, — 'how Teutonic!' an Italian, — 'how Roman and how Greek!' As they say that Helen of Argos had that universal beauty that everybody felt related to her, so Plato seems, to a reader in New England, an American genius. His broad humanity transcends all sectional lines.

This range of Plato instructs us what to think of the vexed question concerning his reputed works, — what are genuine, what spurious. It is singular that wherever we find a man higher, by a whole head, than any of his contemporaries, it is sure to come into doubt, what are his real works. Thus, Homer, Plato, Raffaelle, Shakespeare. For these men magnetize their contemporaries, so that their companions can do for them what they can never do for themselves; and the great man does thus live in several bodies, and write, or paint, or act, by many hands: and, after some time, it is not easy to say what is the authentic work of the master, and what is only of his school.

Plato, too, like every great man, consumed his own times. What is a great man, but one of great affinities, who takes up into himself all arts, sciences, all knowables, as his food? He can spare nothing; he can dispose of everything. What is not good for virtue, is good for knowledge. Hence his contemporaries tax him with plagiarism. But the inventor only knows how to borrow; and society is glad to forget the innumerable laborers who ministered to this architect, and reserves all its gratitude for him. When we are praising Plato, it seems we are praising quotations from Solon, and Sophron, and Philolaus. Be it so. Every book is a quotation; and every house is a quotation out of all forests, and mines, and stone quarries; and every man is a quotation from all his ancestors. And this grasping inventor puts all nations under contribution.

Plato absorbed the learning of his times, — Philolaus, Timæus, Heraclitus, Parmenides, and what else; then his master, Socrates; and, finding himself still capable of a larger synthesis, — beyond all example then or since, — he travelled into Italy, to gain what Pythagoras had for him; then into Egypt, and perhaps still farther east, to import the other element, which Europe wanted, into the European mind. This breadth entitles him to stand as the representative of philosophy. He says, in the Republic, "Such a genius as philosophers must of necessity have, is wont but seldom, in all its parts, to meet in one man; but its different parts generally spring up in different persons." Every man, who would do anything well, must come to it from a higher ground. A philosopher must be more than a philosopher. Plato is clothed with the powers of a poet, stands upon the highest place of the poet, and, (though I doubt he wanted the decisive gift of lyric expression,) mainly is not a poet, because he chose to use the poetic gift to an ulterior purpose.

Great geniuses have the shortest biographies. Their cousins can tell you nothing about them. They lived in their writings, and so their house and street life was trivial and commonplace. If you would know their tastes and complexions, the most admiring of their readers most resembles them. Plato, especially, has no external biography. If he had lover, wife, or children, we hear nothing of them. He ground them all into paint. As a good chimney burns its smoke, so a philosopher converts the value of all his fortunes into his intellectual performances.

He was born 430, A. C., about the time of the death of Pericles; was of patrician connection in his times and city; and is said to have had an early inclination for war; but, in his twentieth year, meeting with Socrates, was easily dissuaded from this pursuit, and remained for ten years his scholar, until the death of Socrates. He then went to Megara; accepted the invitations of Dion and of Dionysius, to the court of Sicily; and went thither three times, though very capriciously treated. He travelled into Italy; then into Egypt, where he stayed a long time; some say three, — some say thirteen years. It is said, he went farther, into Babylonia: this is uncertain. Returning to Athens, he gave lessons, in the Academy, to those whom his fame drew thither; and died, as we have received it, in the act of writing, at eighty-one years.

But the biography of Plato is interior. We are to account for the supreme elevation of this man, in the intellectual history of our race, — how it happens that, in proportion to the culture of men they become his scholars; that, as our Jewish

Bible has implanted itself in the table-talk and household life of every man and woman in the European and American nations, so the writings of Plato have preoccupied every school of learning, every lover of thought, every church, every poet, — making it impossible to think, on certain levels, except through him. He stands between the truth and every man's mind, and has almost impressed language, and the primary forms of thought, with his name and seal. I am struck, in reading him, with the extreme modernness of his style and spirit. Here is the germ of that Europe we know so well, in its long history of arts and arms: here are all its traits, already discernible in the mind of Plato, — and in none before him. It has spread itself since into a hundred histories, but has added no new element. This perpetual modernness is the measure of merit, in every work of art; since the author of it was not misled by anything short-lived or local, but abode by real and abiding traits. How Plato came thus to be Europe, and philosophy, and almost literature, is the problem for us to solve.

This could not have happened, without a sound, sincere, and catholic man, able to honor, at the same time, the ideal, or laws of the mind, and fate, or the order of nature. The first period of a nation, as of an individual, is the period of unconscious strength. Children cry, scream, and stamp with fury, unable to express their desires. As soon as they can speak and tell their want, and the reason of it, they become gentle. In adult life, whilst the perceptions are obtuse, men and women talk vehemently and superlatively, blunder and quarrel; their manners are full of desperation; their speech is full of oaths. As soon as, with culture, things have cleared up a little, and they see them no longer in lumps and masses, but accurately distributed, they desist from that weak vehemence, and explain their meaning in detail. If the tongue had not been framed for articulation, man would still be a beast in the forest. The same weakness and want, on a higher plane, occurs daily in the education of ardent young men and women. 'Ah! you don't understand me; I have never met with any one who comprehends me': and they sigh and weep, write verses, and walk alone, — fault of power to express their precise meaning. In a month or two, through the favor of their good genius, they meet some one so related as to assist their volcanic estate; and, good communication being once established, they are thenceforward good citizens. It is ever thus. The progress is to accuracy, to skill, to truth, from blind force.

There is a moment, in the history of every nation, when, proceeding out of this brute youth, the perceptive powers reach their ripeness, and have not yet become microscopic: so that man, at that instant, extends across the entire scale; and, with his feet still planted on the immense forces of night, converses, by his eyes and brain, with solar and stellar creation. That is the moment of adult health, the culmination of power.

Such is the history of Europe, in all points; and such in philosophy. Its early records, almost perished, are of the immigrations from Asia, bringing with them the dreams of barbarians; a confusion of crude notions of morals, and of natural philosophy, gradually subsiding, through the partial insight of single teachers.

Before Pericles came the Seven Wise Masters; and we have the beginnings of geometry, metaphysics, and ethics: then the partialists, — deducing the origin of things from flux or water, or from air, or from fire, or from mind. All mix with these causes mythologic pictures. At last comes Plato, the distributor, who needs no barbaric paint, or tattoo, or whooping; for he can define. He leaves with Asia the vast and superlative; he is the arrival of accuracy and intelligence. "He shall be as a god to me, who can rightly divide and define."

This defining is philosophy. Philosophy is the account which the human mind gives to itself of the constitution of the world. Two cardinal facts lie forever at the base; the one, and the two. 1. Unity, or Identity; and, 2. Variety. We unite all things, by perceiving the law which pervades them; by perceiving the superficial differences, and the profound resemblances. But every mental act, — this very perception of identity or oneness, recognizes the difference of things. Oneness and otherness. It is impossible to speak or to think, without embracing both.

The mind is urged to ask for one cause of many effects; then for the cause of that; and again the cause, diving still into the profound: self-assured that it shall arrive at an absolute and sufficient one, — a one that shall be all. "In the midst of the sun is the light, in the midst of the light is truth, and in the midst of truth is the imperishable being," say the Vedas. All philosophy, of east and west, has the same centripetence. Urged by an opposite necessity, the mind returns from the one, to that which is not one, but other or many; from cause to effect; and affirms the necessary existence of variety, the self-existence of both, as each is involved in the other. These strictly blended elements it is the problem of thought to separate and to reconcile. Their existence is mutually contradictory and exclusive; and each so fast slides into the other, that we can never say what is one, and what it is not. The Proteus is as nimble in the highest as in the lowest grounds, when we contemplate the one, the true, the good, — as in the surfaces and extremities of matter.

In all nations, there are minds which incline to dwell in the conception of the fundamental Unity. The raptures of prayer and ecstasy of devotion lose all being in one Being. This tendency finds its highest expression in the religious writings of the East, and chiefly, in the Indian Scriptures, in the Vedas, the Bhagavat Geeta, and the Vishnu Purana. Those writings contain little else than this idea, and they rise to pure and sublime strains in celebrating it.

The Same, the Same: friend and foe are of one stuff; the ploughman, the plough, and the furrow, are of one stuff; and the stuff is such, and so much, that the variations of form are unimportant. "You are fit" (says the supreme Krishna to a sage) "to apprehend that you are not distinct from me. That which I am, thou art, and that also is this world, with its gods, and heroes, and mankind. Men contemplate distinctions, because they are stupefied with ignorance." "The words *I* and *mine* constitute ignorance. What is the great end of all, you shall now learn from me. It is soul, — one in all bodies, pervading, uniform, perfect, pre-eminent over nature, exempt from birth, growth, and decay, omnipresent, made up of true knowledge, independent, unconnected with unrealities, with name, species, and the rest, in time past, present, and to come. The knowledge that this spirit, which is essentially one, is in one's own, and in all other bodies, is the wisdom of one who knows the unity of things. As one diffusive air, passing through the perforations of a flute, is distinguished as the notes of a scale, so the nature of the Great Spirit is single, though its forms be manifold, arising from the consequences of acts. When the difference of the investing form, as that of god, or the rest, is destroyed, there is no distinction." "The whole world is but a manifestation of Vishnu, who is identical with all things, and is to be regarded by the wise, as not differing from, but as the same as themselves. I neither am going nor coming; nor is my dwelling in any one place; nor art thou, thou; nor are others, others; nor am I, I." As if he had said, 'All is for the soul, and the soul is Vishnu;

and animals and stars are transient paintings; and light is whitewash; and durations are deceptive; and form is imprisonment; and heaven itself a decoy.' That which the soul seeks is resolution into being, above form, out of Tartarus, and out of heaven, — liberation from nature.

If speculation tends thus to a terrific unity, in which all things are absorbed, action tends directly backwards to diversity. The first is the course or gravitation of mind; the second is the power of nature. Nature is the manifold. The unity absorbs, and melts or reduces. Nature opens and creates. These two principles reappear and interpenetrate all things, all thought; the one, the many. One is being; the other, intellect: one is necessity; the other, freedom: one, rest; the other, motion: one, power; the other, distribution: one, strength; the other, pleasure: one, consciousness; the other, definition: one, genius; the other, talent: one, earnestness; the other, knowledge: one, possession; the other, trade: one, caste; the other, culture: one, king; the other, democracy: and, if we dare carry these generalizations a step higher, and name the last tendency of both, we might say, that the end of the one is escape from organization, — pure science; and the end of the other is the highest instrumentality, or use of means, or executive deity.

Each student adheres, by temperament and by habit, to the first or to the second of these gods of the mind. By religion, he tends to unity; by intellect, or by the senses, to the many. A too rapid unification, and an excessive appliance to parts and particulars, are the twin dangers of speculation.

To this partiality the history of nations corresponded. The country of unity, of immovable institutions, the seat of a philosophy delighting in abstractions, of men faithful in doctrine and in practice to the idea of a deaf, unimplorable, immense fate, is Asia; and it realizes this faith in the social institution of caste. On the other side, the genius of Europe is active and creative: it resists caste by culture; its philosophy was a discipline; it is a land of arts, inventions, trade, freedom. If the East loved infinity, the West delighted in boundaries.

European civility is the triumph of talent, the extension of system, the sharpened understanding, adaptive skill, delight in forms, delight in manifestation, in comprehensible results. Pericles, Athens, Greece, had been working in this element with the joy of genius not yet chilled by any foresight of the detriment of an excess. They saw before them no sinister political economy; no ominous Malthus; no Paris or London; no pitiless subdivision of classes, — the doom of the pin-makers, the doom of the weavers, of dressers, of stockingers, of carders, of spinners, of colliers; no Ireland; no Indian caste, superinduced by the efforts of Europe to throw it off. The understanding was in its health and prime. Art was in its splendid novelty. They cut the Pentelican marble as if it were snow, and their perfect works in architecture and sculpture seemed things of course, not more difficult than the completion of a new ship at the Medford yards, or new mills at Lowell. These things are in course, and may be taken for granted. The Roman legion, Byzantine legislation, English trade, the saloons of Versailles, the cafés of Paris, the steam-mill, steamboat, steam-coach, may all be seen in perspective; the town-meeting, the ballot-box, the newspaper and cheap press.

Meantime, Plato, in Egypt and in Eastern pilgrimages, imbibed the idea of one Deity, in which all things are absorbed. The unity of Asia, and the detail of Europe; the infinitude of the Asiatic soul, and the defining, result-loving, machine-making, surface-seeking, opera-going Europe, — Plato came to join, and by contact, to enhance the energy of each. The excellence of Europe and Asia are in his brain. Metaphysics and natural philosophy expressed the genius of Europe; he substructs the religion of Asia, as the base.

In short, a balanced soul was born, perceptive of the two elements. It is as easy to be great as to be small. The reason why we do not at once believe in admirable souls, is because they are not in our experience. In actual life, they are so rare, as to be incredible; but, primarily, there is not only no presumption against them, but the strongest presumption in favor of their appearance. But whether voices were heard in the sky, or not; whether his mother or his father dreamed that the infant man-child was the son of Apollo; whether a swarm of bees settled on his lips, or not; a man who could see two sides of a thing was born. The wonderful synthesis so familiar in nature; the upper and the under side of the medal of Jove; the union of impossibilities, which reappears in every object; its real and its ideal power, — was now, also, transferred entire to the consciousness of a man.

The balanced soul came. If he loved abstract truth, he saved himself by propounding the most popular of all principles, the absolute good, which rules rulers, and judges the judge. If he made transcendental distinctions, he fortified himself by drawing all his illustrations from sources disdained by orators and polite conversers; from mares and puppies; from pitchers and soup-ladles; from cooks and criers; the shops of potters, horse-doctors, butchers, and fishmongers. He cannot forgive in himself a partiality, but is resolved that the two poles of thought shall appear in his statement. His argument and his sentence are self-poised and spherical. The two poles appear; yes, and become two hands, to grasp and appropriate their own.

Every great artist has been such by synthesis. Our strength is transitional, alternating; or, shall I say, a thread of two strands. The sea-shore, sea seen from shore, shore seen from sea; the taste of two metals in contact; and our enlarged powers at the approach and at the departure of a friend; the experience of poetic creativeness, which is not found in staying at home, nor yet in travelling, but in transitions from one to the other, which must therefore be adroitly managed to present as much transitional surface as possible; this command of two elements must explain the power and the charm of Plato. Art expresses the one, or the same by the different. Thought seeks to know unity in unity; poetry to show it by variety; that is, always by an object or symbol. Plato keeps the two vases, one of æther and one of pigment, at his side, and invariably uses both. Things added to things, as statistics, civil history, are inventories. Things used as language are inexhaustibly attractive. Plato turns incessantly the obverse and the reverse of the medal of Jove.

To take an example: — The physical philosophers had sketched each his theory of the world; the theory of atoms, of fire, of flux, of spirit; theories mechanical and chemical in their genius. Plato, a master of mathematics, studious of all natural laws and causes, feels these, as second causes, to be no theories of the world, but bare inventories and lists. To the study of nature he therefore prefixes the dogma, — "Let us declare the cause which led the Supreme Ordainer to produce and compose the universe. He was good; and he who is good has no kind of envy. Exempt from envy, he wished that all things should be as much as possible like himself. Whosoever, taught by wise men, shall admit this as the prime cause of the origin and foundation of the world, will be in the truth." "All things are for the sake of the good, and it is the cause of everything beautiful." This dogma animates and impersonates his philosophy.

The synthesis which makes the character of his mind appears in all his talents. Where there is great compass of wit, we usually find excellences that combine easily in the living man, but in description appear incompatible. The mind of Plato is not to be exhibited by a Chinese catalogue, but is to be apprehended by an original mind in the exercise of its original power. In him the freest abandonment is united with the precision of a geometer. His daring imagination gives him the more solid grasp of facts; as the birds of highest flight have the strongest alar bones. His patrician polish, his intrinsic elegance, edged by an irony so subtle that it stings and paralyzes, adorn the soundest health and strength of frame. According to the old sentence, "If Jove should descend to the earth, he would speak in the style of Plato."

With this palatial air, there is, for the direct aim of several of his works, and running through the tenor of them all, a certain earnestness, which mounts, in the Republic, and in the Phædo, to piety. He has been charged with feigning sickness at the time of the death of Socrates. But the anecdotes that have come down from the times attest his manly interference before the people in his master's behalf, since even the savage cry of the assembly to Plato is preserved; and the indignation towards popular government, in many of his pieces, expresses a personal exasperation. He has a probity, a native reverence for justice and honor, and a humanity which makes him tender for the superstitions of the people. Add to this, he believes that poetry, prophecy, and the high insight, are from a wisdom of which man is not master; that the gods never philosophize; but, by a celestial mania, these miracles are accomplished. Horsed on these winged steeds, he sweeps the dim regions, visits worlds which flesh cannot enter: he saw the souls in pain; he hears the doom of the judge; he beholds the penal metempsychosis; the Fates, with the rock and shears; and hears the intoxicating hum of their spindle.

But his circumspection never forsook him. One would say, he had read the inscription on the gates of Busyrane, — "Be bold"; and on the second gate, — "Be bold, be bold, and evermore be bold": and then again had paused well at the third gate, — "Be not too bold." His strength is like the momentum of a falling planet; and his discretion, the return of its due and perfect curve, — so excellent is his Greek love of boundary, and his skill in definition. In reading logarithms, one is not more secure, than in following Plato in his flights. Nothing can be colder than his head, when the lightnings of his imagination are playing in the sky. He has finished his thinking, before he brings it to the reader; and he abounds in the surprises of a literary master. He has that opulence which furnishes, at every turn, the precise weapon he needs. As the rich man wears no more garments, drives no more horses, sits in no more chambers, than the poor, — but has that one dress, or equipage, or instrument, which is fit for the hour and the need; so Plato, in his plenty, is never restricted, but has the fit word. There is, indeed, no weapon in all the armory of wit which he did not possess and use, — epic, analysis, mania, intuition, music, satire, and irony, down to the customary and polite. His illustrations are poetry, and his jests illustrations. Socrates' profession of obstetric art is good philosophy; and his finding that word "cookery," and "adulatory art," for rhetoric, in the Gorgias, does us a substantial service still. No orator can measure in effect with him who can give good nicknames.

What moderation, and understatement, and checking his thunder in mid volley! He has good-naturedly furnished the courtier and citizen with all that can be said against the schools. "For philosophy is an elegant thing, if any one modestly meddles with it; but, if he is conversant with it more than is becoming, it corrupts the man." He could well afford to be generous, — he, who from the sunlike centrality and reach of his vision, had a faith without cloud. Such as his perception, was his speech: he plays with the doubt, and makes the most of it: he paints and quibbles; and by and by comes a sentence that moves the sea and land. The admirable earnest comes not only at intervals, in the perfect yes and no of the dialogue, but in bursts of light. "I, therefore, Callicles, am persuaded by these accounts, and consider how I may exhibit my soul before the judge in a healthy condition. Wherefore disregarding the honors that most men value, and looking to the truth, I shall endeavor in reality to live as virtuously as I can; and, when I die, to die so. And I invite all other men, to the utmost of my power; and you, too, I in turn invite to this contest, which, I affirm, surpasses all contests here."

He is a great average man; one who, to the best thinking, adds a proportion and equality in his faculties, so that men see in him their own dreams and glimpses made available, and made to pass for what they are. A great common sense is his warrant and qualification to be the world's interpreter. He has reason, as all the philosophic and poetic class have: but he has, also, what they have not, — this strong solving sense to reconcile his poetry with the appearances of the world, and build a bridge from the streets of cities to the Atlantis. He omits never this graduation, but slopes his thought, however picturesque the precipice on one side, to an access from the plain. He never writes in ecstasy, or catches us up into poetic raptures.

Plato apprehended the cardinal facts. He could prostrate himself on the earth, and cover his eyes, whilst he adored that which cannot be numbered, or gauged, or known, or named: that of which everything can be affirmed and denied: that "which is entity and nonentity." He called it super-essential. He even stood ready, as in the Parmenides, to demonstrate that it was so, — that this Being exceeded the limits of intellect. No man ever more fully acknowledged the Ineffable. Having paid his homage, as for the human race, to the Illimitable, he then stood erect, and for the human race affirmed, 'And yet things are knowable!' — that is, the Asia in his mind was first heartily honored, — the ocean of love and power, before form, before will, before knowledge, the Same, the Good, the One; and now, refreshed and empowered by this worship, the instinct of Europe, namely, culture, returns; and he cries, Yet things are knowable! They are knowable, because, being from one, things correspond. There is a scale: and the correspondence of heaven to earth, of matter to mind, of the part to the whole, is our guide. As there is a science of stars, called astronomy; a science of quantities, called mathematics; a science of qualities, called chemistry; so there is a science of sciences, — I call it Dialectic, — which is the Intellect discriminating the false and the true. It rests on the observation of identity and diversity; for, to judge, is to unite to an object the notion which belongs to it. The sciences, even the best, — mathematics and astronomy, — are like sportsmen, who seize whatever prey offers, even without being able to make any use of it. Dialectic must teach the use of them. "This is of that rank that no intellectual man will enter on any study for its own sake, but only with a view to advance himself in that one sole science which embraces all."

"The essence or peculiarity of man is to comprehend a whole; or that which, in the diversity of sensations, can be comprised under a rational unity." "The soul which has never perceived the truth, cannot pass into the human form." I announce to men the Intellect. I announce the good of being interpenetrated by the mind that made nature; this benefit, namely, that it can understand nature, which it made and maketh. Nature is good, but intellect is better: as the law-giver is before the law-receiver. I give you joy, O sons of men! that truth is altogether wholesome; that we have hope to search out what might be the very self of everything. The misery of man is to be balked of the sight of essence, and to be stuffed with conjectures: but the supreme good is reality; the supreme beauty is reality; and all virtue and all felicity depend on this science of the real: for courage is nothing else than knowledge: the fairest fortune that can befall man, is to be guided by his demon to that which is truly his own. This also is the essence of justice, — to attend every one his own: nay, the notion of virtue is not to be arrived at, except through direct contemplation of the divine essence. Courage, then! for, "the persuasion that we must search that which we do not know, will render us, beyond comparison, better, braver, and more industrious, than if we thought it impossible to discover what we do not know, and useless to search for it." He secures a position not to be commanded, by his passion for reality; valuing philosophy only as it is the pleasure of conversing with real being.

Thus, full of the genius of Europe, he said, *Culture.* He saw the institutions of Sparta, and recognized more genially, one would say, than any since, the hope of education. He delighted in every accomplishment, in every graceful and useful and truthful performance; above all, in the splendors of genius and intellectual achievement. "The whole of life, O Socrates, said Glauco, is, with the wise, the measure of hearing such discourses as these." What a price he sets on the feats of talent, on the powers of Pericles, of Isocrates, of Parmenides! What price, above price, on the talents themselves! He called the several faculties, gods, in his beautiful personation. What value he gives to the art of gymnastic in education; what to geometry; what to music; what to astronomy, whose appeasing and medicinal power he celebrates! In the Timæus, he indicates the highest employment of the eyes. "By us it is asserted, that God invented and bestowed sight on us for this purpose, — that, on surveying the circles of intelligence in the heavens, we might properly employ those of our own minds, which, though disturbed when compared with the others that are uniform, are still allied to their circulations; and that, having thus learned, and being naturally possessed of a correct reasoning faculty, we might, by imitating the uniform revolutions of divinity, set right our own wanderings and blunders." And in the Republic, — "By each of these disciplines, a certain organ of the soul is both purified and reanimated, which is blinded and buried by studies of another kind; an organ better worth saving than ten thousand eyes, since truth is perceived by this alone."

He said, Culture; but he first admitted its basis, and gave immeasurably the first place to advantages of nature. His patrician tastes laid stress on the distinctions of birth. In the doctrine of the organic character and disposition is the origin of caste. "Such as were fit to govern, into their composition the informing Deity mingled gold: into the military, silver; iron and brass for husbandmen and artificers." The East confirms itself, in all ages, in this faith. The Koran is explicit on this point of caste. "Men have their metal, as of gold and silver. Those of you who were the worthy ones in the state of ignorance, will be the worthy ones in the state of faith, as soon as you embrace it." Plato was not less firm. "Of the five orders of things, only four can be taught to the generality of men." In the Republic, he insists on the temperaments of the youth, as first of the first.

A happier example of the stress laid on nature, is in the dialogue with the young Theages, who wishes to receive lessons from Socrates. Socrates declares that, if some have grown wise by associating with him, no thanks are due to him; but, simply, whilst they were with him, they grew wise, not because of him; he pretends not to know the way of it. "It is adverse to many, nor can those be benefited by associating with me, whom the Demon opposes; so that it is not possible for me to live with these. With many, however, he does not prevent me from conversing, who yet are not at all benefited by associating with me. Such, O Theages, is the association with me; for, if it pleases the God, you will make great and rapid proficiency; you will not, if he does not please. Judge whether it is not safer to be instructed by some one of those who have power over the benefit which they impart to men, than by me, who benefit or not, just as it may happen." As if he had said,

'I have no system. I cannot be answerable for you. You will be what you must. If there is love between us, inconceivably delicious and profitable will our intercourse be; if not, your time is lost, and you will only annoy me. I shall seem to you stupid, and the reputation I have, false. Quite above us, beyond the will of you or me, is this secret affinity or repulsion laid. All my good is magnetic, and I educate, not by lessons, but by going about my business.'

He said, Culture; he said, Nature: and he failed not to add, 'There is also the divine.' There is no thought in any mind, but it quickly tends to convert itself into a power, and organizes a huge instrumentality of means. Plato, lover of limits, loved the illimitable, saw the enlargement and nobility which come from truth itself and good itself, and attempted, as if on the part of the human intellect, once for all, to do it adequate homage, — homage fit for the immense soul to receive, and yet homage becoming the intellect to render. He said, then, 'Our faculties run out into infinity, and return to us thence. We can define but a little way; but here is a fact which will not be skipped, and which to shut our eyes upon is suicide. All things are in a scale; and, begin where we will, ascend and ascend. All things are symbolical; and what we call results are beginnings.'

A key to the method and completeness of Plato is his twice bisected line. After he has illustrated the relation between the absolute good and true, and the forms of the intelligible world, he says: "Let there be a line cut in two unequal parts. Cut again each of these two parts, — one representing the visible, the other the intelligible world, — and these two new sections, representing the bright part and the dark part of these worlds, you will have, for one of the sections of the visible world, — images, that is, both shadows and reflections; for the other section, the objects of these images, — that is, plants, animals, and the works of art and nature. Then divide the intelligible world in like manner; the one section will be of opinions and hypotheses, and the other section, of truths." To these four sections, the four operations of the soul correspond, — conjecture, faith, understanding, reason. As every pool reflects the image of the sun, so every thought and thing restores us an image and creature of the supreme Good. The universe is perforated by a million channels for his activity. All things mount and mount.

All his thought has this ascension; in Phædrus, teaching

that beauty is the most lovely of all things, exciting hilarity, and shedding desire and confidence through the universe, wherever it enters; and it enters, in some degree, into all things: but that there is another, which is as much more beautiful than beauty, as beauty is than chaos; namely, wisdom, which our wonderful organ of sight cannot reach unto, but which, could it be seen, would ravish us with its perfect reality. He has the same regard to it as the source of excellence in works of art. "When an artificer, in the fabrication of any work, looks to that which always subsists according *to the same;* and, employing a model of this kind, expresses its idea and power in his work; it must follow, that his production should be beautiful. But when he beholds that which is born and dies, it will be far from beautiful."

Thus ever: the Banquet is a teaching in the same spirit, familiar now to all the poetry, and to all the sermons of the world, that the love of the sexes is initial; and symbolizes, at a distance, the passion of the soul for that immense lake of beauty it exists to seek. This faith in the Divinity is never out of mind, and constitutes the ground of all his dogmas. Body cannot teach wisdom; — God only. In the same mind, he constantly affirms that virtue cannot be taught; that it is not a science, but an inspiration; that the greatest goods are produced to us through mania, and are assigned to us by a divine gift.

This leads me to that central figure, which he has established in his Academy, as the organ through which every considered opinion shall be announced, and whose biography he has likewise so labored, that the historic facts are lost in the light of Plato's mind. Socrates and Plato are the double star, which the most powerful instruments will not entirely separate. Socrates, again, in his traits and genius, is the best example of that synthesis which constitutes Plato's extraordinary power. Socrates, a man of humble stem, but honest enough; of the commonest history; of a personal homeliness so remarkable, as to be a cause of wit in others, — the rather that his broad good-nature and exquisite taste for a joke invited the sally, which was sure to be paid. The players personated him on the stage; the potters copied his ugly face on their stone jugs. He was a cool fellow, adding to his humor a perfect temper, and a knowledge of his man, be he who he might whom he talked with, which laid the companion open to certain defeat in any debate, — and in debate he immoderately delighted. The young men are prodigiously fond of him, and invite him to their feasts, whither he goes for conversation. He can drink, too; has the strongest head in Athens; and, after leaving the whole party under the table, goes away, as if nothing had happened, to begin new dialogues with somebody that is sober. In short, he was what our country-people call *an old one.*

He affected a good many citizen-like tastes, was monstrously fond of Athens, hated trees, never willingly went beyond the walls, knew the old characters, valued the bores and philistines, thought everything in Athens a little better than anything in any other place. He was plain as a Quaker in habit and speech, affected low phrases, and illustrations from cocks and quails, soup-pans and sycamore-spoons, grooms and farriers, and unnameable offices, — especially if he talked with any superfine person. He had a Franklin-like wisdom. Thus, he showed one who was afraid to go on foot to Olympia, that it was no more than his daily walk within doors, if continuously extended, would easily reach.

Plain old uncle as he was, with his great ears, — an immense talker, — the rumor ran, that, on one or two occasions, in the war with Bœotia, he had shown a determination which had covered the retreat of a troop; and there was some story that, under cover of folly, he had, in the city government, when one day he chanced to hold a seat there, evinced a courage in opposing singly the popular voice, which had wellnigh ruined him. He is very poor; but then he is hardy as a soldier, and can live on a few olives; usually, in the strictest sense, on bread and water, except when entertained by his friends. His necessary expenses were exceedingly small, and no one else could live as he did. He wore no under garment; his upper garment was the same for summer and winter; and he went barefooted; and it is said that, to procure the pleasure, which he loves, of talking at his ease all day with the most elegant and cultivated young men, he will now and then return to his shop, and carve statues, good or bad, for sale. However that be, it is certain that he had grown to delight in nothing else than this conversation; and that, under his hypocritical pretence of knowing nothing, he attacks and brings down all the fine speakers, all the fine philosophers of Athens, whether natives, or strangers from Asia Minor and the islands. Nobody can refuse to talk with him, he is so honest, and really curious to know; a man who was willingly confuted, if he did not speak the truth, and who willingly confuted others asserting what was false; and not less pleased when confuted than when confuting; for he thought not any evil happened to men, of such magnitude as false opinion respecting the just and unjust. A pitiless disputant, who knows nothing, but the bounds of whose conquering intelligence no man had ever reached; whose temper was imperturbable; whose dreadful logic was always leisurely and sportive; so careless and ignorant, as to disarm the wariest, and draw them, in the pleasantest manner, into horrible doubts and confusion. But he always knew the way out; knew it, yet would not tell it. No escape; he drives them to terrible choices by his dilemmas, and tosses the Hippiases and Gorgiases, with their grand reputations, as a boy tosses his balls. The tyrannous realist! — Meno has discoursed a thousand times, at length, on virtue, before many companies, and very well, as it appeared to him; but, at this moment, he cannot even tell what it is, — this cramp-fish of a Socrates has so bewitched him.

This hard-headed humorist, whose strange conceits, drollery, and *bonhommie*, diverted the young patricians, whilst the rumor of his sayings and quibbles gets abroad every day, turns out, in the sequel, to have a probity as invincible as his logic, and to be either insane, or, at least, under cover of this play, enthusiastic in his religion. When accused before the judges of subverting the popular creed, he affirms the immortality of the soul, the future reward and punishment; and, refusing to recant, in a caprice of the popular government, was condemned to die, and sent to the prison. Socrates entered the prison, and took away all ignominy from the place, which could not be a prison, whilst he was there. Crito bribed the jailer; but Socrates would not go out by treachery. "Whatever inconvenience ensue, nothing is to be preferred before justice. These things I hear like pipes and drums, whose sound makes me deaf to everything you say." The fame of this prison, the fame of the discourses there, and the drinking of the hemlock, are one of the most precious passages in the history of the world.

The rare coincidence, in one ugly body, of the droll and the martyr, the keen street and market debater with the sweetest saint known to any history at that time, had forcibly struck the mind of Plato, so capacious of these contrasts; and the figure of Socrates, by a necessity, placed itself in the foreground of the scene, as the fittest dispenser of the intellectual treasures he had to communicate. It was a rare fortune, that this Æsop of the mob, and this robed scholar should meet, to make each other immortal in their mutual faculty. The strange synthesis, in the character of Socrates, capped the synthesis in the mind of Plato. Moreover, by this means, he was able, in the direct way, and without envy, to avail himself of the wit and weight of Socrates, to which unquestionably his own debt was great; and these derived again their principal advantage from the perfect art of Plato.

It remains to say, that the defect of Plato in power is only that which results inevitably from his quality. He is intellectual in his aim; and, therefore, in expression, literary. Mounting into heaven, diving into the pit, expounding the laws of the state, the passion of love, the remorse of crime, the hope of the parting soul, — he is literary, and never otherwise. It is almost the sole deduction from the merit of Plato, that his writings have not — what is, no doubt, incident to this regnancy of intellect in his work — the vital authority which the screams of prophets and the sermons of unlettered Arabs and Jews possess. There is an interval; and to cohesion, contact is necessary.

I know not what can be said in reply to this criticism, but that we have come to a fact in the nature of things: an oak is not an orange. The qualities of sugar remain with sugar, and those of salt, with salt.

In the second place, he has not a system. The dearest defenders and disciples are at fault. He attempted a theory of the universe, and his theory is not complete or self-evident. One man thinks he means this; and another, that: he has said one thing in one place, and the reverse of it in another place. He is charged with having failed to make the transition from ideas to matter. Here is the world, sound as a nut, perfect, not the smallest piece of chaos left, never a stitch nor an end, not a mark of haste, or botching, or second thought; but the theory of the world is a thing of shreds and patches.

The longest wave is quickly lost in the sea. Plato would willingly have a Platonism, a known and accurate expression for the world, and it should be accurate. It shall be the world passed through the mind of Plato, — nothing less. Every atom shall have the Platonic tinge; every atom, every relation or quality you knew before, you shall know again, and find here, but now ordered; not nature, but art. And you shall feel that Alexander indeed overran, with men and horses, some countries of the planet; but countries, and things of which countries are made, elements, planet itself, laws of planet and of men, have passed through this man as bread into his body, and become no longer bread, but body: so all this mammoth morsel has become Plato. He has clapped copyright on the world. This is the ambition of individualism. But the mouthful proves too large. *Boa constrictor* has good will to eat it, but he is foiled. He falls abroad in the attempt; and biting, gets strangled: the bitten world holds the biter fast by his own teeth. There he perishes: unconquered nature lives on, and forgets him. So it fares with all: so must it fare with Plato. In view of eternal nature, Plato turns out to be philosophical exercitations. He argues on this side, and on that. The acutest German, the lovingest disciple, could never tell what Platonism was; indeed, admirable texts can be quoted on both sides of every great question from him.

These things we are forced to say, if we must consider the effort of Plato, or of any philosopher, to dispose of Nature, — which will not be disposed of. No power of genius has ever yet had the smallest success in explaining existence. The perfect enigma remains. But there is an injustice in assuming this ambition for Plato. Let us not seem to treat with flippancy his venerable name. Men, in proportion to their intellect, have admitted his transcendent claims. The way to know him, is to compare him, not with nature, but with other men. How many ages have gone by, and he remains unapproached! A chief structure of human wit, like Karnac, or the mediæval cathedrals, or the Etrurian remains, it requires all the breadth of human faculty to know it. I think it is trueliest seen, when seen with the most respect. His sense deepens, his merits multiply, with study. When we say, here is a fine collection of fables; or, when we praise the style; or the common sense; or arithmetic; we speak as boys, and much of our impatient criticism of the dialectic, I suspect, is no better. The criticism is like our impatience of miles, when we are in a hurry; but it is still best that a mile should have seventeen hundred and sixty yards. The great-eyed Plato proportioned the lights and shades after the genius of our life.

PLATO: NEW READINGS.

THE publication, in Mr. Bohn's "Serial Library," of the excellent translations of Plato, which we esteem one of the chief benefits the cheap press has yielded, gives us an occasion to take hastily a few more notes of the elevation and bearings of this fixed star; or, to add a bulletin, like the journals, of *Plato at the latest dates.*

Modern science, by the extent of its generalization, has learned to indemnify the student of man for the defects of individuals, by tracing growth and ascent in races; and, by the simple expedient of lighting up the vast background, generates a feeling of complacency and hope. The human being has the saurian and the plant in his rear. His arts and sciences, the easy issue of his brain, look glorious when prospectively beheld from the distant brain of ox, crocodile, and fish. It seems as if nature, in regarding the geologic night behind her, when, in five or six millenniums, she had turned out five or six men, as Homer, Phidias, Menu, and Columbus, was nowise discontented with the result. These samples attested the virtue of the tree. These were a clear amelioration of trilobite and saurus, and a good basis for further proceeding. With this artist, time and space are cheap, and she is insensible to what you say of tedious preparation. She waited tranquilly the flowing periods of paleontology, for the hour to be struck when man should arrive. Then periods must pass before the motion of the earth can be suspected; then before the map of the instincts and the cultivable powers can be drawn. But as of races, so the succession of individual men is fatal and beautiful, and Plato has the fortune, in the history of mankind, to mark an epoch.

Plato's fame does not stand on a syllogism, or on any masterpieces of the Socratic reasoning, or on any thesis, as, for example, the immortality of the soul. He is more than an expert, or a schoolman, or a geometer, or the prophet of a peculiar message. He represents the privilege of the intellect, the power, namely, of carrying up every fact to successive platforms, and so disclosing, in every fact, a germ of expansion. These expansions are in the essence of thought. The naturalist would never help us to them by any discoveries of the extent of the universe, but is as poor, when cataloguing the resolved nebula of Orion, as when measuring the angles of an acre. But the Republic of Plato, by these expansions, may be said to require, and so to anticipate, the astronomy of Laplace. The expansions are organic. The mind does not create what it perceives, any more than the eye creates the rose. In ascribing to Plato the merit of announcing them, we only say, here was a more complete man, who could apply to nature the whole scale of the senses, the understanding, and the reason. These expansions, or extensions, consist in continuing the spiritual sight where the horizon falls on our natural vision, and, by this second sight, discovering the long lines of law which shoot in every direction. Everywhere he stands on a path which has no end, but runs continuously round the universe. Therefore, every word becomes an exponent of nature. Whatever he looks upon discloses a second sense, and ulterior senses. His perception of the generation of contraries, of death out of life, and life out of death, — that law by which, in nature, decomposition is recomposition, and putrefaction and cholera are only signals of a new creation; his discernment of the little in the large, and the large in the small; studying the state in the citizen, and the citizen in the state; and leaving it doubtful whether he exhibited the Republic as an allegory on the education of the private soul; his beautiful definitions of ideas, of time, of form, of figure, of the line, sometimes hypothetically given, as his defining of virtue, courage, justice, temperance; his love of the apologue, and his apologues themselves; the cave of Trophonius; the ring of Gyges; the charioteer and two horses; the golden, silver, brass, and iron temperaments; Theuth and Thamus; and the visions of Hades and the Fates, — fables which have imprinted themselves in the human memory like the signs of the zodiac; his soliform eye and his boniform soul; his doctrine of assimilation; his doctrine of reminiscence; his clear vision of the laws of return, or reaction, which secure instant justice throughout the universe, instanced everywhere, but specially in the doctrine, "what comes from God to us, returns from us to God," and in Socrates' belief that the laws below are sisters of the laws above.

More striking examples are his moral conclusions. Plato affirms the coincidence of science and virtue; for vice can never know itself and virtue; but virtue knows both itself and vice. The eye attested that justice was best, as long as it was profitable; Plato affirms that it is profitable throughout; that the profit is intrinsic, though the just conceal his justice from gods and men; that it is better to suffer injustice, than to do it; that the sinner ought to covet punishment; that the lie was more hurtful than homicide; and that ignorance, or the involuntary lie, was more calamitous than involuntary homicide; that the soul is unwillingly deprived of true opinions; and that no man sins willingly; that the order or proceeding of nature was from the mind to the body; and, though a sound body cannot restore an unsound mind, yet a good soul can, by its virtue, render the body the best possible. The intelligent have a right over the ignorant, namely, the right of instructing them. The right punishment of one out of tune, is to make him play in tune; the fine which the good, refusing to govern, ought to pay, is, to be governed by a worse man; that his guards shall not handle gold and silver, but shall be instructed that there is gold and silver in their souls, which will make men willing to give them everything which they need.

This second sight explains the stress laid on geometry. He saw that the globe of earth was not more lawful and precise than was the supersensible; that a celestial geometry was in place there, as a logic of lines and angles here below; that the world was throughout mathematical; the proportions are constant of oxygen, azote, and lime; there is just so much water, and slate, and magnesia; not less are the proportions constant of the moral elements.

This eldest Goethe, hating varnish and falsehood, delighted in revealing the real at the base of the accidental: in discovering connection, continuity, and representation everywhere; hating insulation; and appears like the god of wealth among the cabins of vagabonds, opening power and capability in everything he touches. Ethical science was new and vacant, when Plato could write thus: "Of all whose arguments are left to the men of the present time, no one has ever yet condemned injustice, or praised justice, otherwise than as respects the repute, honors, and emoluments arising therefrom; while, as respects either of them in itself, and subsisting by its own power in the soul of the possessor, and concealed both from gods and men, no one has yet sufficiently investigated, either in poetry or prose writings, — how, namely, that the one is the greatest of all the evils that the soul has within it, and justice the greatest good."

His definition of ideas, as what is simple, permanent, uniform, and self-existent, forever discriminating them from the notions of the understanding, marks an era in the world. He was born to behold the self-evolving power of spirit, endless, generator of new ends; a power which is the key at once to the centrality and the evanescence of things. Plato is so centred, that he can well spare all his dogmas. Thus the fact of knowledge and ideas reveals to him the fact of eternity; and the doctrine of reminiscence he offers as the most probable particular explication. Call that fanciful, — it matters not; the connection between our knowledge and the abyss of being is still real, and the explication must be not less magnificent.

He has indicated every eminent point in speculation. He wrote on the scale of the mind itself, so that all things have symmetry in his tablet. He put in all the past, without weariness, and descended into detail with a courage like that he witnessed in nature. One would say, that his forerunners had mapped out each a farm, or a district, or an island, in intellectual geography, but that Plato first drew the sphere. He domesticates the soul in nature; man is the microcosm. All the circles of the visible heaven represent as many circles in the rational soul. There is no lawless particle, and there is nothing casual in the action of the human mind. The names of things, too, are fatal, following the nature of things. All the gods of the Pantheon are, by their names, significant of a profound sense. The gods are the ideas. Pan is speech, or manifestation; Saturn, the contemplative; Jove, the regal soul; and Mars, passion. Venus is proportion; Calliope, the soul of the world; Aglaia, intellectual illustration.

These thoughts, in sparkles of light, had appeared often to pious and to poetic souls; but this well-bred, all-knowing Greek geometer comes with command, gathers them all up into rank and gradation, the Euclid of holiness, and marries the two parts of nature. Before all men, he saw the intellectual values of the moral sentiment. He describes his own ideal, when he paints in Timæus a god leading things from disorder into order. He kindled a fire so truly in the centre, that we see the sphere illuminated, and can distinguish poles, equator, and lines of latitude, every arc and node: a theory so averaged, so modulated that you would say, the winds of ages had swept through this rhythmic structure, and not that it was the brief extempore blotting of one short-lived scribe. Hence it has happened that a very well-marked class of souls, namely, those who delight in giving a spiritual, that is, an ethico-intellectual expression to every truth, by exhibiting an ulterior end which is yet legitimate to it, are said to Platonize. Thus, Michel Angelo is a Platonist, in his sonnets. Shakespeare is a Platonist, when he writes, "Nature is made better by no mean, but nature makes that mean," or,

> "He that can endure
> To follow with allegiance a fallen lord,
> Does conquer him that did his master conquer,
> And earns a place in the story."

Hamlet is a pure Platonist, and 't is the magnitude only of Shakespeare's proper genius that hinders him from being classed as the most eminent of this school. Swedenborg, throughout his prose poem of "Conjugal Love," is a Platonist.

His subtlety commended him to men of thought. The secret of his popular success is the moral aim, which endeared him to mankind. "Intellect," he said, "is king of heaven and of earth"; but, in Plato, intellect is always moral. His writings have also the sempiternal youth of poetry. For their arguments, most of them, might have been couched in sonnets: and poetry has never soared higher than in the Timæus and the Phædrus. As the poet, too, he is only contemplative. He did not, like Pythagoras, break himself with an institution. All his painting in the Republic must be esteemed mythical, with intent to bring out, sometimes in violent colors, his thought. You cannot institute, without peril of charlatanism.

It was a high scheme, his absolute privilege for the best, (which, to make emphatic, he expressed by community of women,) as the premium which he would set on grandeur. There shall be exempts of two kinds: first, those who by demerit have put themselves below protection, — outlaws; and secondly, those who by eminence of nature and desert are out of the reach of your rewards: let such be free of the city, and above the law. We confide them to themselves; let them do with us as they will. Let none presume to measure the irregularities of Michel Angelo and Socrates by village scales.

In his eighth book of the Republic, he throws a little mathematical dust in our eyes. I am sorry to see him, after such noble superiorities, permitting the lie to governors. Plato plays Providence a little with the baser sort, as people allow themselves with their dogs and cats.

III.

SWEDENBORG; OR, THE MYSTIC.

SWEDENBORG; OR, THE MYSTIC.

AMONG eminent persons, those who are most dear to men are not of the class which the economist calls producers: they have nothing in their hands; they have not cultivated corn, nor made bread; they have not led out a colony, nor invented a loom. A higher class, in the estimation and love of this city-building, market-going race of mankind, are the poets who, from the intellectual kingdom, feed the thought and imagination with ideas and pictures which raise men out of the world of corn and money, and console them for the short-comings of the day, and the meanness of labor and traffic. Then, also, the philosopher has his value, who flatters the intellect of this laborer, by engaging him with subtleties which instruct him in new faculties. Others may build cities; he is to understand them, and keep them in awe. But there is a class who lead us into another region, — the world of morals, or of will. What is singular about this region of thought, is its claim. Wherever the sentiment of right comes in, it takes precedence of everything else. For other things, I make poetry of them; but the moral sentiment makes poetry of me.

I have sometimes thought that he would render the greatest service to modern criticism, who shall draw the line of relation that subsists between Shakespeare and Swedenborg. The human mind stands ever in perplexity, demanding intellect, demanding sanctity, impatient equally of each without the other. The reconciler has not yet appeared. If we tire of the saints, Shakespeare is our city of refuge. Yet the instincts presently teach, that the problem of essence must take precedence of all others, — the questions of Whence? What? and Whither? and the solution of these must be in a life, and not in a book. A drama or poem is a proximate or oblique reply;

but Moses, Menu, Jesus, work directly on this problem. The atmosphere of moral sentiment is a region of grandeur which reduces all material magnificence to toys, yet opens to every wretch that has reason the doors of the universe. Almost with a fierce haste it lays its empire on the man. In the language of the Koran, "God said, the heaven and the earth, and all that is between them, think ye that we created them in jest, and that ye shall not return to us?" It is the kingdom of the will, and by inspiring the will, which is the seat of personality, seems to convert the universe into a person;

"The realms of being to no other bow,
Not only all are thine, but all are Thou."

All men are commanded by the saint. The Koran makes a distinct class of those who are by nature good, and whose goodness has an influence on others, and pronounces this class to be the aim of creation: the other classes are admitted to the feast of being, only as following in the train of this. And the Persian poet exclaims to a soul of this kind: —

"Go boldly forth, and feast on being's banquet;
Thou art the called, — the rest admitted with thee."

The privilege of this class is an access to the secrets and structure of nature, by some higher method than by experience. In common parlance, what one man is said to learn by experience, a man of extraordinary sagacity is said, without experience, to divine. The Arabians say that Abul Khain, the mystic, and Abu Ali Seena, the philosopher, conferred together; and, on parting, the philosopher said, "All that he sees, I know"; and the mystic said, "All that he knows, I see." If one should ask the reason of this intuition, the solution would lead us into that property which Plato denoted as Reminiscence, and which is implied by the Bramins in the tenet of Transmigration. The soul having been often born, or, as the Hindoos say, "travelling the path of existence through thousands of births," having beheld the things which are here, those which are in heaven, and those which are beneath, there is nothing of which she has not gained the knowledge: no wonder that she is able to recollect, in regard to any one thing, what formerly she knew. "For, all things in nature being linked and related, and the soul having heretofore known all, nothing hinders but that any man who has recalled to mind, or, according to the common phrase, has learned one thing only, should of himself recover all his ancient knowledge, and find out again all the rest, if he have but courage, and faint not in the midst of his researches. For inquiry and learning is reminiscence all." How much more, if he that inquires be a holy and godlike soul! For, by being assimilated to the original soul, by whom, and after whom, all things subsist, the soul of man does then easily flow into all things, and all things flow into it: they mix; and he is present and sympathetic with their structure and law.

This path is difficult, secret, and beset with terror. The ancients called it *ecstasy* or absence, — a getting out of their bodies to think. All religious history contains traces of the trance of saints, — a beatitude, but without any sign of joy, earnest, solitary, even sad; "the flight," Plotinus called it, "of the alone to the alone"; Μυεσις, the closing of the eyes, — whence our word, *Mystic*. The trances of Socrates, Plotinus, Porphyry, Behmen, Bunyan, Fox, Pascal, Guion, Swedenborg, will readily come to mind. But what as readily comes to mind, is, the accompaniment of disease. This beatitude comes in terror, and with shocks to the mind of the receiver. "It o'er-informs the tenement of clay," and drives the man mad; or, gives a certain violent bias, which taints his judgment. In the chief examples of religious illumination, somewhat morbid has mingled, in spite of the unquestionable increase of mental power. Must the highest good drag after it a quality which neutralizes and discredits it? —

> "Indeed, it takes
> From our achievements, when performed at height,
> The pith and marrow of our attribute."

Shall we say, that the economical mother disburses so much earth and so much fire, by weight and metre, to make a man, and will not add a pennyweight, though a nation is perishing for a leader? Therefore, the men of God purchased their science by folly or pain. If you will have pure carbon, carbuncle, or diamond, to make the brain transparent, the trunk and organs shall be so much the grosser: instead of porcelain, they are potter's earth, clay, or mud.

In modern times, no such remarkable example of this introverted mind has occurred, as in Emanuel Swedenborg, born in Stockholm, in 1688. This man, who appeared to his contemporaries a visionary, and elixir of moonbeams, no doubt led the most real life of any man then in the world: and now, when the royal and ducal Frederics, Cristierns, and Brunswicks, of that day, have slid into oblivion, he begins to spread himself into the minds of thousands. As happens in great men, he seemed, by the variety and amount of his powers, to be a composition of several persons,—like the giant fruits which are matured in gardens by the union of four or five single blossoms. His frame is on a larger scale, and possesses the advantages of size. As it is easier to see the reflection of the great sphere in large globes, though defaced by some crack or blemish, than in drops of water, so men of large calibre, though with some eccentricity or madness, like Pascal or Newton, help us more than balanced mediocre minds.

His youth and training could not fail to be extraordinary. Such a boy could not whistle or dance, but goes grubbing into mines and mountains, prying into chemistry, optics, physiology, mathematics, and astronomy, to find images fit for the measure of his versatile and capacious brain. He was a scholar from a child, and was educated at Upsala. At the age of twenty-eight, he was made Assessor of the Board of Mines, by Charles XII. In 1716, he left home for four years, and visited the universities of England, Holland, France, and Germany. He performed a notable feat of engineering in 1718, at the siege of Fredericshall, by hauling two galleys, five boats, and a sloop, some fourteen English miles overland, for the royal service. In 1721, he journeyed over Europe, to examine mines and smelting-works. He published, in 1716, his Dædalus Hyperboreus, and, from this time, for the next thirty years, was employed in the composition and publication of his scientific works. With the like force, he threw himself into theology. In 1743, when he was fifty-four years old, what is called his illumination began. All his metallurgy, and transportation of ships overland, was absorbed into this ecstasy. He ceased to publish any more scientific books, withdrew from his practical labors, and devoted himself to the writing and publication of his voluminous theological works, which were printed at his own expense, or at that of the Duke of Brunswick, or other prince, at Dresden, Leipsic, London, or Amsterdam. Later, he resigned his office of Assessor: the salary attached to this office continued to be paid to him during his life. His duties had brought him into intimate acquaintance with King Charles XII., by whom he was much consulted and honored. The like favor was continued to him by his successor. At the Diet of 1751, Count Hopken says, the most solid memorials on finance were from his pen. In Sweden, he appears to have attracted a marked regard.

His rare science and practical skill, and the added fame of second sight and extraordinary religious knowledge and gifts, drew to him queens, nobles, clergy, shipmasters, and people about the ports through which he was wont to pass in his many voyages. The clergy interfered a little with the importation and publication of his religious works; but he seems to have kept the friendship of men in power. He was never married. He had great modesty and gentleness of bearing. His habits were simple; he lived on bread, milk, and vegetables; he lived in a house situated in a large garden: he went several times to England, where he does not seem to have attracted any attention whatever from the learned or the eminent; and died at London, March 29, 1772, of apoplexy, in his eighty-fifth year. He is described, when in London, as a man of a quiet, clerical habit, not averse to tea and coffee, and kind to children. He wore a sword when in full velvet dress, and whenever he walked out, carried a gold-headed cane. There is a common portrait of him in antique coat and wig, but the face has a wandering or vacant air.

The genius which was to penetrate the science of the age with a far more subtle science; to pass the bounds of space and time; venture into the dim spirit-realm, and attempt to establish a new religion in the world, — began its lessons in quarries and forges, in the smelting-pot and crucible, in shipyards and dissecting-rooms. No one man is perhaps able to judge of the merits of his works on so many subjects. One is glad to learn that his books on mines and metals are held in the highest esteem by those who understand these matters. It seems that he anticipated much science of the nineteenth century; anticipated, in astronomy, the discovery of the seventh planet, — but, unhappily, not also of the eighth; anticipated the views of modern astronomy in regard to the generation of earths by the sun; in magnetism, some important experiments and conclusions of later students; in chemistry, the atomic theory; in anatomy, the discoveries of Schlichting, Monro, and Wilson; and first demonstrated the office of the lungs. His excellent English editor magnanimously lays no stress on his discoveries, since he was too great to care to be original; and we are to judge, by what he can spare, of what remains.

A colossal soul, he lies vast abroad on his times, uncomprehended by them, and requires a long focal distance to be seen; suggests, as Aristotle, Bacon, Seldon, Humboldt, that a certain vastness of learning, or *quasi* omnipresence of the human soul in nature, is possible. His superb speculation, as from a tower, over nature and arts, without ever losing sight of the texture and sequence of things, almost realizes his own picture, in his "Principia," of the original integrity of man. Over and above the merit of his particular discoveries, is the capital merit of his self-equality. A drop of water has the properties of the sea, but cannot exhibit a storm. There is beauty of a concert, as well as of a flute; strength of a host, as well as of a hero; and, in Swedenborg, those who are best acquainted with modern books will most admire the merit of mass. One of the missouriums and mastodons of literature, he is not to be measured by whole colleges of ordinary scholars. His stalwart presence would flutter the gowns of a university. Our books are false by being fragmentary: their sentences are *bonmots*, and not parts of natural discourse; childish expressions of surprise or pleasure in nature; or, worse, owing a brief notoriety to their petulance, or aversion from the order of nature, — being some curiosity or oddity, designedly not in harmony with nature, and purposely framed to excite surprise, as jugglers do by concealing their means. But Swedenborg is systematic, and respective of the world in every sentence: all the means are orderly given; his faculties work with astronomic punctuality, and this admirable writing is pure from all pertness or egotism.

Swedenborg was born into an atmosphere of great ideas. 'T is hard to say what was his own: yet his life was dignified by noblest pictures of the universe. The robust Aristotelian method, with its breadth and adequateness, shaming our sterile and linear logic by its genial radiation, conversant with series and degree, with effects and ends, skilful to discriminate power from form, essence from accident, and opening, by its terminology and definition, high roads into nature, had trained a race of athletic philosophers. Harvey had shown the circulation of the blood; Gilbert had shown that the earth was a magnet; Descartes, taught by Gilbert's magnet, with its vortex, spiral, and polarity, had filled Europe with the leading thought of vortical motion, as the secret of nature. Newton, in the year in which Swedenborg was born, published the "Principia," and established the universal gravity. Malpighi, following the high doctrines of Hippocrates, Leucippus, and Lucretius, had given emphasis to the dogma that nature works in leasts, — "tota in minimis existit natura." Unrivalled dissectors, Swammerdam, Leeuwenhoek, Winslow, Eustachius, Heister, Vesalius, Boerhaave, had left nothing for scalpel or microscope to reveal in human or comparative anatomy; Linnæus, his contemporary, was affirming, in his beautiful science, that "Nature is always like herself"; and, lastly, the nobility of method, the largest application of principles, had been exhibited by Leibnitz and Christian Wolff, in cosmology; whilst Locke and Grotius had drawn the moral argument. What was left for a genius of the largest calibre, but to go over their ground, and verify and unite? It is easy to see, in these minds, the origin of Swedenborg's studies, and the suggestion of his problems. He had a capacity to entertain and vivify these volumes of thought. Yet the proximity of these geniuses, one or other of whom had introduced all his leading ideas, makes Swedenborg another example of the difficulty, even in a highly fertile genius, of proving originality, the first birth and annunciation of one of the laws of nature.

He named his favorite views, the doctrine of Forms, the doctrine of Series and Degrees, the doctrine of Influx, the doctrine of Correspondence. His statement of these doctrines deserves to be studied in his books. Not every man can read them, but they will reward him who can. His theologic works are valuable to illustrate these. His writings would be a sufficient library to a lonely and athletic student; and the "Economy of the Animal Kingdom" is one of those books which, by the sustained dignity of thinking, is an honor to the human race. He had studied spars and metals to some purpose. His varied and solid knowledge makes his style lustrous with points and shooting spicula of thought, and resembling one of those winter mornings when the air sparkles with crystals. The grandeur of the topics makes the grandeur of the style. He was apt for cosmology, because of that native perception of identity which made mere size of no account to him. In the atom of magnetic iron, he saw the quality which would generate the spiral motion of sun and planet.

The thoughts in which he lived were, the universality of each law in nature; the Platonic doctrine of the scale or degrees; the version or conversion of each into other, and so the correspondence of all the parts; the fine secret that little explains large, and large, little; the centrality of man in nature, and the connection that subsists throughout all things: he saw that the human body was strictly universal, or an instrument through which the soul feeds and is fed by the whole of matter: so that he held, in exact antagonism to the sceptics, that "the wiser a man is, the more will he be a worshipper of the Deity." In short, he was a believer in the Identity-philosophy, which he held not idly, as the dreamers of Berlin or Boston, but which he experimented with and established through years of labor, with the heart and strength of the rudest Viking that his rough Sweden ever sent to battle.

This theory dates from the oldest philosophers, and derives perhaps its best illustration from the newest. It is this: that nature iterates her means perpetually on successive planes. In the old aphorism, *nature is always self-similar*. In the plant, the eye or germinative point opens to a leaf, then to another leaf, with a power of transforming the leaf into radicle, stamen, pistil, petal, bract, sepal, or seed. The whole art of the plant is still to repeat leaf on leaf without end, the more or less of heat, light, moisture, and food determining the form it shall assume. In the animal, nature makes a vertebra, or a spine of vertebræ, and helps herself still by a new spine, with a limited power of modifying its form, — spine on spine, to the end of the world. A poetic anatomist, in our own day, teaches that a snake, being a horizontal line, and man, being an erect line, constitute a right angle; and, between the lines of this mystical quadrant, all animated beings find their place: and he assumes the hair-worm, the span-worm, or the snake, as the type or prediction of the spine. Manifestly, at the end of the spine, nature puts out smaller spines, as arms; at the end of the arms, new spines, as hands; at the other end, she repeats the process, as legs and feet. At the top of the column, she puts out another spine, which doubles or loops itself over, as a span-worm, into a ball, and forms the skull, with extremities again: the hands being now the upper jaw, the feet the lower jaw, the fingers and toes being represented this time by upper and lower teeth. This new spine is destined to high uses. It is a new man on the shoulders of the last. It can almost shed its trunk, and manage to live alone, according to the Platonic idea in the Timæus. Within it, on a higher plane, all that was done in the trunk repeats itself. Nature recites her lesson once more in a higher mood. The mind is a finer body, and resumes its functions of feeding, digesting, absorbing, excluding, and generating, in a new and ethereal element. Here, in the brain, is all the process of alimentation repeated, in the acquiring, comparing, digesting, and assimilating of experience. Here again is the mystery of generation repeated. In the brain are male and female faculties: here is marriage, here is fruit. And there is no limit to this ascending scale, but series on series. Everything, at the end of one use, is taken up into the next, each series punctually repeating every organ and process of the last. We are adapted to infinity. We are hard to please, and love nothing which ends: and in nature is no end; but everything, at the end of one use, is lifted into a superior, and the ascent of these things climbs into demonic and celestial natures. Creative force, like a musical composer, goes on unweariedly repeating a simple air or theme, now high, now low, in solo, in chorus, ten thousand times reverberated, till it fills earth and heaven with the chant.

Gravitation, as explained by Newton, is good; but grander, when we find chemistry only an extension of the law of masses into particles, and that the atomic theory shows the action of chemistry to be mechanical also. Metaphysics shows us a sort of gravitation, operative also in the mental phenomena; and the terrible tabulation of the French statists brings every piece of whim and humor to be reducible also to exact numerical ratios. If one man in twenty thousand, or in thirty thousand, eats shoes, or marries his grandmother, then in every twenty thousand, or thirty thousand, is found one man who eats shoes, or marries his grandmother. What we call gravitation, and fancy ultimate, is one fork of a mightier stream, for which we have yet no name. Astronomy is excellent; but it must come up into life to have its full value, and not remain there in globes and spaces. The globule of blood gyrates around its own axis in the human veins, as the planet in the sky; and the circles of intellect relate to those of the heavens. Each law of nature has the like universality; eating, sleep or hibernation, rotation, generation, metamorphosis, vortical motion, which is seen in eggs as in planets. These grand rhymes or returns in nature, — the dear, best-known face startling us at every turn, under a mask so unexpected that we think it the face of a stranger, and carrying up the semblance into divine forms, — delighted the prophetic eye of Swedenborg; and he must be reckoned a leader in that revolution, which, by giving to science an idea, has given to an aimless accumulation of experiments, guidance and form, and a beating heart.

I own, with some regret, that his printed works amount to about fifty stout octavos, his scientific works being about half of the whole number; and it appears that a mass of manuscript still unedited remains in the royal library at Stockholm.

The scientific works have just now been translated into English, in an excellent edition.

Swedenborg printed these scientific books in the ten years from 1734 to 1744, and they remained from that time neglected: and now, after their century is complete, he has at last found a pupil in Mr. Wilkinson, in London, a philosophic critic, with a coequal vigor of understanding and imagination comparable only to Lord Bacon's, who has produced his master's buried books to the day, and transferred them, with every advantage, from their forgotten Latin into English, to go round the world in our commercial and conquering tongue. This startling reappearance of Swedenborg, after a hundred years, in his pupil, is not the least remarkable fact in his history. Aided, it is said, by the munificence of Mr. Clissold, and also by his literary skill, this piece of poetic justice is done. The admirable preliminary discourses with which Mr. Wilkinson has enriched these volumes, throw all the contemporary philosophy of England into shade, and leave me nothing to say on their proper grounds.

The "Animal Kingdom" is a book of wonderful merits. It was written with the highest end, — to put science and the soul, long estranged from each other, at one again. It was an anatomist's account of the human body, in the highest style of poetry. Nothing can exceed the bold and brilliant treatment of a subject usually so dry and repulsive. He saw nature "wreathing through an everlasting spiral, with wheels that never dry, on axles that never creak," and sometimes sought "to uncover those secret recesses where Nature is sitting at the fires in the depths of her laboratory"; whilst the picture comes recommended by the hard fidelity with which it is based on practical anatomy. It is remarkable that this sublime genius decides, peremptorily for the analytic, against the synthetic method; and, in a book whose genius is a daring poetic synthesis, claims to confine himself to a rigid experience.

He knows, if he only, the flowing of nature, and how wise was that old answer of Amasis to him who bade him drink up the sea, — "Yes, willingly, if you will stop the rivers that flow in." Few knew as much about nature and her subtle manners, or expressed more subtly her goings. He thought as large a demand is made on our faith by nature, as by miracles. "He noted that in her proceeding from first principles through her several subordinations, there was no state through which she did not pass, as if her path lay through all things." "For as often as she betakes herself upward from visible phenomena, or, in other words, withdraws herself inward, she instantly, as it were, disappears, while no one knows what has become of her, or whither she is gone: so that it is necessary to take science as a guide in pursuing her steps."

The pursuing the inquiry under the light of an end or final cause, gives wonderful animation, a sort of personality to the whole writing. This book announces his favorite dogmas. The ancient doctrine of Hippocrates, that the brain is a gland; and of Leucippus, that the atom may be known by the mass; or, in Plato, the macrocosm by the microcosm; and, in the verses of Lucretius, —

> Ossa videlicet e pauxillis atque minutis
> Ossibus sic et de pauxillis atque minutis
> Visceribus viscus gigni, sanguenque creari
> Sanguinis inter se multis coeuntibus guttis;
> Ex aurique putat micis consistere posse
> Aurum, et de terris terram concrescere parvis;
> Ignibus ex igneis, humorem humoribus esse.
>
> LIB. I. 835.

> "The principle of all things, entrails made
> Of smallest entrails; bone, of smallest bone;
> Blood, of small sanguine drops reduced to one;
> Gold, of small grains; earth, of small sands compacted;
> Small drops to water, sparks to fire contracted":

and which Malpighi had summed in his maxim, that "nature exists entire in beasts," — is a favorite thought of Swedenborg. "It is a constant law of the organic body, that large, compound, or visible forms exist and subsist from smaller, simpler, and ultimately from invisible forms, which act similarly to the larger ones, but more perfectly and more universally; and the least forms so perfectly and universally, as to involve an idea representative of their entire universe." The unities of each organ are so many little organs, homogeneous with their compound: the unities of the tongue are little tongues; those of the stomach, little stomachs; those of the heart are little hearts. This fruitful idea furnishes a key to every secret. What was too small for the eye to detect was read by the aggregates; what was too large, by the units. There is no end to his application of the thought. "Hunger is an aggregate of very many little hungers, or losses of blood by the little veins all over the body." It is a key to his theology also. "Man is a kind of very minute heaven, corresponding to the world of spirits and to heaven.

Every particular idea of man, and every affection, yea, every smallest part of his affection, is an image and effigy of him. A spirit may be known from only a single thought. God is the grand man."

The hardihood and thoroughness of his study of nature required a theory of forms, also. "Forms ascend in order from the lowest to the highest. The lowest form is angular, or the terrestrial and corporeal. The second and next higher form is the circular, which is also called the perpetual-angular, because the circumference of a circle is a perpetual angle. The form above this is the spiral, parent and measure of circular forms; its diameters are not rectilinear, but variously circular, and have a spherical surface for centre; therefore it is called the perpetual-circular. The form above this is the vortical, or perpetual-spiral: next, the perpetual-vortical, or celestial: last, the perpetual-celestial, or spiritual."

Was it strange that a genius so bold should take the last step, also, — conceive that he might attain the science of all sciences, to unlock the meaning of the world? In the first volume of the "Animal Kingdom," he broaches the subject, in a remarkable note: —

"In our doctrine of Representations and Correspondences, we shall treat of both these symbolical and typical resemblances, and of the astonishing things which occur, I will not say, in the living body only, but throughout nature, and which correspond so entirely to supreme and spiritual things, that one would swear that the physical world was purely symbolical of the spiritual world; insomuch, that if we choose to express any natural truth in physical and definite vocal terms, and to convert these terms only into the corresponding and spiritual terms, we shall by this means elicit a spiritual truth, or theological dogma, in place of the physical truth or precept: although no mortal would have predicted that anything of the kind could possibly arise by bare literal transposition; inasmuch as the one precept, considered separately from the other, appears to have absolutely no relation to it. I intend, hereafter, to communicate a number of examples of such correspondences, together with a vocabulary containing the terms of spiritual things, as well as of the physical things for which they are to be substituted. This symbolism pervades the living body."

The fact, thus explicitly stated, is implied in all poetry, in allegory, in fable, in the use of emblems, and in the structure of language. Plato knew of it, as is evident from his twice bisected line, in the sixth book of the Republic. Lord Bacon had found that truth and nature differed only as seal and print; and he instanced some physical propositions, with their translation into a moral or political sense. Behmen, and all mystics, imply this law, in their dark riddle-writing. The poets, in as far as they are poets, use it; but it is known to them only, as the magnet was known for ages, as a toy. Swedenborg first put the fact into a detached and scientific statement, because it was habitually present to him, and never not seen. It was involved, as we explained already, in the doctrine of identity and iteration, because the mental series exactly tallies with the material series. It required an insight that could rank things in order and series; or, rather, it required such rightness of position, that the poles of the eye should coincide with the axis of the world. The earth had fed its mankind through five or six millenniums, and they had sciences, religions, philosophies; and yet had failed to see the correspondence of meaning between every part and every other part. And, down to this hour, literature has no book in which the symbolism of things is scientifically opened. One would say, that, as soon as men had the first hint that every sensible object, — animal, rock, river, air, — nay, space and time, subsists not for itself, nor finally to a material end, but as a picture-language to tell another story of beings and duties, other science would be put by, and a science of such grand presage would absorb all faculties: that each man would ask of all objects, what they mean: Why does the horizon hold me fast, with my joy and grief, in this centre? Why hear I the same sense from countless differing voices, and read one never quite expressed fact in endless picture-language? Yet, whether it be, that these things will not be intellectually learned, or, that many centuries must elaborate and compose so rare and opulent a soul, — there is no comet, rock-stratum, fossil, fish, quadruped, spider, or fungus, that, for itself, does not interest more scholars and classifiers, than the meaning and upshot of the frame of things.

But Swedenborg was not content with the culinary use of the world. In his fifty-fourth year, these thoughts held him fast, and his profound mind admitted the perilous opinion, too frequent in religious history, that he was an abnormal person, to whom was granted the privilege of conversing with angels and spirits; and this ecstasy connected itself with just this office of explaining the moral import of the sensible world.

To a right perception, at once broad and minute, of the order of nature, he added the comprehension of the moral laws in their widest social aspects; but whatever he saw, through some excessive determination to form, in his constitution, he saw not abstractedly, but in pictures, heard it in dialogues, constructed it in events. When he attempted to announce the law most sanely, he was forced to couch it in parable.

Modern psychology offers no similar example of a deranged balance. The principal powers continued to maintain a healthy action; and, to a reader who can make due allowance in the report for the reporter's peculiarities, the results are still instructive, and a more striking testimony to the sublime laws he announced, than any that balanced dulness could afford. He attempts to give some account of the *modus* of the new state, affirming that "his presence in the spiritual world is attended with a certain separation, but only as to the intellectual part of his mind, not as to the will part"; and he affirms that "he sees, with the internal sight, the things that are in another life, more clearly than he sees the things which are here in the world."

Having adopted the belief that certain books of the Old and New Testaments were exact allegories, or written in the angelic and ecstatic mode, he employed his remaining years in extricating from the literal, the universal sense. He had borrowed from Plato the fine fable of "a most ancient people, men better than we, and dwelling nigher to the gods"; and Swedenborg added, that they used the earth symbolically; that these, when they saw terrestrial objects, did not think at all about them, but only about those which they signified. The correspondence between thoughts and things henceforward occupied him. "The very organic form resembles the end inscribed on it." A man is in general, and in particular, an organized justice or injustice, selfishness or gratitude. And the cause of this harmony he assigned in the Arcana: "The reason why all and single things, in the heavens and on earth, are representative, is because they exist from an influx of the Lord, through heaven." This design of exhibiting such correspondences, which, if adequately executed, would be the poem of the world, in which all history and science would play an essential part, was narrowed and defeated by the exclusively theologic direction which his inquiries took. His perception of nature is not human and universal, but is mystical and Hebraic. He fastens each natural object to a theologic notion; — a horse signifies carnal understanding; a tree, perception; the moon, faith; a cat means this; an ostrich, that; an artichoke, this other; and poorly tethers every symbol to a several ecclesiastic sense. The slippery Proteus is not so easily caught. In nature, each individual symbol plays innumerable parts, as each particle of matter circulates in turn through every system. The central identity enables any one symbol to express successively all the qualities and shades of real being. In the transmission of the heavenly waters, every hose fits every hydrant. Nature avenges herself speedily on the hard pedantry that would chain her waves. She is no literalist. Everything must be taken genially, and we must be at the top of our condition, to understand anything rightly.

His theological bias thus fatally narrowed his interpretation of nature, and the dictionary of symbols is yet to be written. But the interpreter, whom mankind must still expect, will find no predecessor who has approached so near to the true problem.

Swedenborg styles himself, in the title-page of his books, "Servant of the Lord Jesus Christ"; and by force of intellect, and in effect, he is the last Father in the Church, and is not likely to have a successor. No wonder that his depth of ethical wisdom should give him influence as a teacher. To the withered traditional church yielding dry catechisms, he let in nature again, and the worshipper, escaping from the vestry of verbs and texts, is surprised to find himself a party to the whole of his religion: his religion thinks for him, and is of universal application: he turns it on every side; it fits every part of life, interprets and dignifies every circumstance. Instead of a religion which visited him diplomatically three or four times, — when he was born, when he married, when he fell sick, and when he died, and for the rest never interfered with him, — here was a teaching which accompanied him all day, accompanied him even into sleep and dreams; into his thinking, and showed him through what a long ancestry his thoughts descend; into society, and showed by what affinities he was girt to his equals and his counterparts; into natural objects, and showed their origin and meaning, what are friendly and what are hurtful; and opened the future world by indicating the continuity of the same laws. His disciples allege that their intellect is invigorated by the study of his books.

There is no such problem for criticism as his theological

writings, their merits are so commanding; yet such grave deductions must be made. Their immense and sandy diffuseness is like the prairie, or the desert, and their incongruities are like the last deliration. He is superflously explanatory, and his feeling of the ignorance of men, strangely exaggerated. Men take truths of this nature very fast. Yet he abounds in assertions: he is a rich discoverer, and of things which most import us to know. His thought dwells in essential resemblances, like the resemblance of a house to the man who built it. He saw things in their law, in likeness of function, not of structure. There is an invariable method and order in his delivery of his truth, the habitual proceeding of the mind from inmost to outmost. What earnestness and weightiness, — his eye never roving, without one swell of vanity, or one look to self, in any common form of literary pride! a theoretic or speculative man, but whom no practical man in the universe could affect to scorn. Plato is a gownsman: his garment, though of purple, and almost sky-woven, is an academic robe, and hinders action with its voluminous folds. But this mystic is awful to Cæsar. Lycurgus himself would bow.

The moral insight of Swedenborg, the correction of popular errors, the announcement of ethical laws, take him out of comparison with any other modern writer, and entitle him to a place, vacant for some ages, among the lawgivers of mankind. That slow but commanding influence which he has acquired, like that of other religious geniuses, must be excessive also, and have its tides, before it subsides into a permanent amount. Of course, what is real and universal cannot be confined to the circle of those who sympathize strictly with his genius, but will pass forth into the common stock of wise and just thinking. The world has a sure chemistry, by which it extracts what is excellent in its children, and lets fall the infirmities and limitations of the grandest mind.

That metempsychosis which is familiar in the old mythology of the Greeks, collected in Ovid, and in the Indian Transmigration, and is there *objective*, or really takes place in bodies by alien will, — in Swedenborg's mind, has a more philosophic character. It is subjective, or depends entirely upon the thought of the person. All things in the universe arrange themselves to each person anew, according to his ruling love. Man is such as his affection and thought are. Man is man by virtue of willing, not by virtue of knowing and understanding.

As he is, so he sees. The marriages of the world are broken up. Interiors associate all in the spiritual world. Whatever the angels looked upon was to them celestial. Each Satan appears to himself a man; to those as bad as he, a comely man; to the purified, a heap of carrion. Nothing can resist states: everything gravitates: like will to like: what we call poetic justice takes effect on the spot. We have come into a world which is a living poem. Everything is as I am. Bird and beast is not bird and beast, but emanation and effluvia of the minds and wills of men there present. Every one makes his own house and state. The ghosts are tormented with the fear of death, and cannot remember that they have died. They who are in evil and falsehood are afraid of all others. Such as have deprived themselves of charity, wander and flee: the societies which they approach discover their quality, and drive them away. The covetous seem to themselves to be abiding in cells where their money is deposited, and these to be invested with mice. They who place merit in good works seem to themselves to cut wood. "I asked such, if they were not wearied? They replied, that they have not yet done work enough to merit heaven."

He delivers golden sayings, which express with singular beauty the ethical laws; as when he uttered that famed sentence, that, "in heaven the angels are advancing continually to the springtime of their youth, so that the oldest angel appears the youngest": "The more angels, the more room": "The perfection of man is the love of use": "Man, in his perfect form, is heaven": "What is from Him, is Him": "Ends always ascend as nature descends." And the truly poetic account of the writing in the inmost heaven, which, as it consists of inflexions according to the form of heaven, can be read without instruction. He almost justifies his claim to preternatural vision, by strange insights of the structure of the human body and mind. "It is never permitted to any one, in heaven, to stand behind another and look at the back of his head: for then the influx which is from the Lord is disturbed." The angels, from the sound of the voice, know a man's love; from the articulation of the sound, his wisdom; and from the sense of the words, his science.

In the "Conjugal Love," he has unfolded the science of marriage. Of this book, one would say, that, with the highest elements, it has failed of success. It came near to be the Hymn of Love, which Plato attempted in the "Banquet";

the love, which, Dante says, Casella sang among the angels in Paradise; and which, as rightly celebrated, in its genesis, fruition, and effect, might well entrance the souls, as it would lay open the genesis of all institutions, customs, and manners. The book had been grand, if the Hebraism had been omitted, and the law stated without Gothicism, as ethics, and with that scope for ascension of state which the nature of things requires.

It is a fine platonic development of the science of marriage; teaching that sex is universal, and not local; virility in the male qualifying every organ, act, and thought; and the feminine in woman. Therefore, in the real or spiritual world, the nuptial union is not momentary, but incessant and total; and chastity not a local, but a universal virtue; unchastity being discovered as much in the trading, or planting, or speaking, or philosophizing, as in generation; and that, though the virgins he saw in heaven were beautiful, the wives were incomparably more beautiful, and went on increasing in beauty evermore.

Yet Swedenborg, after his mode, pinned his theory to a temporary form. He exaggerates the circumstance of marriage; and, though he finds false marriages on earth, fancies a wiser choice in heaven. But of progressive souls, all loves and friendships are momentary. *Do you love me?* means, Do you see the same truth? If you do, we are happy with the same happiness: but presently one of us passes into the perception of new truth; we are divorced, and no tension in nature can hold us to each other. I know how delicious is this cup of love, — I existing for you, you existing for me; but it is a child's clinging to his toy; an attempt to eternize the fireside and nuptial chamber; to keep the picture-alphabet through which our first lessons are prettily conveyed. The Eden of God is bare and grand: like the out-door landscape, remembered from the evening fireside, it seems cold and desolate, whilst you cower over the coals; but, once abroad again, we pity those who can forego the magnificence of nature, for candle-light and cards. Perhaps the true subject of the "Conjugal Love" is *Conversation*, whose laws are profoundly eliminated. It is false, if literally applied to marriage. For God is the bride or bridegroom of the soul. Heaven is not the pairing of two, but the communion of all souls. We meet, and dwell an instant under the temple of one thought, and part as though we parted not, to join another thought in other fellowships of joy. So far from there being anything divine in the low and proprietary sense of *Do you love me?* it is only when you leave and lose me, by casting yourself on a sentiment which is higher than both of us, that I draw near, and find myself at your side; and I am repelled, if you fix your eye on me, and demand love. In fact, in the spiritual world, we change sexes every moment. You love the worth in me; then I am your husband: but it is not me, but the worth, that fixes the love; and that worth is a drop of the ocean of worth that is beyond me. Meantime, I adore the greater worth in another, and so become his wife. He aspires to a higher worth in another spirit, and is wife or receiver of that influence.

Whether a self-inquisitorial habit, that he grew into, from jealousy of the sins to which men of thought are liable, he has acquired, in disentangling and demonstrating that particular form of moral disease, an acumen which no conscience can resist. I refer to his feeling of the profanation of thinking to what is good "from scientifics." "To reason about faith, is to doubt and deny." He was painfully alive to the difference between knowing and doing, and this sensibility is incessantly expressed. Philosophers are, therefore, vipers, cockatrices, asps, hemorrhoids, presters, and flying serpents; literary men are conjurers and charlatans.

But this topic suggests a sad afterthought, that here we find the seat of his own pain. Possibly Swedenborg paid the penalty of introverted faculties. Success, or a fortunate genius, seems to depend on a happy adjustment of heart and brain; on a due proportion, hard to hit, of moral and mental power, which, perhaps, obeys the law of those chemical ratios which make a proportion in volumes necessary to combination, as when gases will combine in certain fixed rates, but not at any rate. It is hard to carry a full cup: and this man, profusely endowed in heart and mind, early fell into dangerous discord with himself. In his Animal Kingdom, he surprised us, by declaring that he loved analysis, and not synthesis; and now, after his fiftieth year, he falls into jealousy of his intellect; and, though aware that truth is not solitary, nor is goodness solitary, but both must ever mix and marry, he makes war on his mind, takes the part of the conscience against it, and, on all occasions, traduces and blasphemes it. The violence is instantly avenged. Beauty is disgraced, love is unlovely, when truth, the half part of heaven, is denied, as much as when a bitterness in men of talent leads to satire, and destroys the judgment. He is wise, but wise in his own despite. There is an air of infinite grief, and the sound of wailing, all over and through this lurid universe. A vampire sits in the seat of the prophet, and turns with gloomy appetite to the images of pain. Indeed, a bird does not more readily weave its nest, or a mole bore into the ground, than this seer of souls substructs a new hell and pit, each more abominable than the last, round every new crew of offenders. He was let down through a column that seemed of brass, but it was formed of angelic spirits, that he might descend safely amongst the unhappy, and witness the vastation of souls; and heard there, for a long continuance, their lamentations; he saw their tormentors, who increase and strain pangs to infinity; he saw the hell of jugglers, the hell of assassins, the hell of the lascivious; the hell of robbers, who kill and boil men; the infernal tun of the deceitful; the excrementitious hells; the hell of the revengeful, whose faces resembled a round, broad cake, and their arms rotate like a wheel. Except Rabelais and Dean Swift, nobody ever had such science of filth and corruption.

These books should be used with caution. It is dangerous to sculpture these evanescing images of thought. True in transition, they become false if fixed. It requires, for his just apprehension, almost a genius equal to his own. But when his visions become the stereotyped language of multitudes of persons, of all degrees of age and capacity, they are perverted. The wise people of the Greek race were accustomed to lead the most intelligent and virtuous young men, as part of their education, through the Eleusinian mysteries, wherein, with much pomp and graduation, the highest truths known to ancient wisdom were taught. An ardent and contemplative young man, at eighteen or twenty years, might read once these books of Swedenborg, these mysteries of love and conscience, and then throw them aside forever. Genius is ever haunted by similar dreams, when the hells and the heavens are opened to it. But these pictures are to be held as mystical, that is, as a quite arbitrary and accidental picture of the truth, — not as the truth. Any other symbol would be as good: then this is safely seen.

Swedenborg's system of the world wants central spontaneity; it is dynamic, not vital, and lacks power to generate life. There is no individual in it. The universe is a gigantic crystal, all whose atoms and laminæ lie in uninterrupted order, and with unbroken unity, but cold and still. What seems an individual and a will, is none. There is an immense chain of intermediation, extending from centre to extremes, which bereaves every agency of all freedom and character. The universe, in his poem, suffers under a magnetic sleep, and only reflects the mind of the magnetizer. Every thought comes into each mind by influence from a society of spirits that surround it, and into these from a higher society, and so on. All his types mean the same few things. All his figures speak one speech. All his interlocutors Swedenborgize. Be they who they may, to this complexion must they come at last. This Charon ferries them all over in his boat; kings, counsellors, cavaliers, doctors, Sir Isaac Newton, Sir Hans Sloane, King George II., Mahomet, or whosoever, and all gather one grimness of hue and style. Only when Cicero comes by, our gentle seer sticks a little at saying he talked with Cicero, and, with a touch of human relenting, remarks, "one whom it was given me to believe was Cicero"; and when the *soi disant* Roman opens his mouth, Rome and eloquence have ebbed away, — it is plain theologic Swedenborg, like the rest. His heavens and hells are dull; fault of want of individualism. The thousand-fold relation of men is not there. The interest that attaches in nature to each man, because he is right by his wrong, and wrong by his right, because he defies all dogmatizing and classification, so many allowances, and contingencies, and futurities, are to be taken into account, strong by his vices, often paralyzed by his virtues, — sinks into entire sympathy with his society. This want reacts to the centre of the system. Though the agency of "the Lord" is in every line referred to by name, it never becomes alive. There is no lustre in that eye which gazes from the centre, and which should vivify the immense dependency of beings.

The vice of Swedenborg's mind is its theologic determination. Nothing with him has the liberality of universal wisdom, but we are always in a church. That Hebrew muse, which taught the lore of right and wrong to men, had the same excess of influence for him, it has had for the nations. The mode, as well as the essence, was sacred. Palestine is ever the more valuable as a chapter in universal history, and ever the less an available element in education. The genius of Swedenborg, largest of all modern souls in this department of thought, wasted itself in the endeavor to reanimate and conserve what had already arrived at its natural term, and, in the great secular Providence, was retiring from its prominence, before western modes of thought and expression. Swedenborg and Behmen both failed by attaching themselves to the Christian symbol, instead of to the moral sentiment, which carries innumerable christianities, humanities, divinities, in its bosom.

The excess of influence shows itself in the incongruous importation of a foreign rhetoric. 'What have I to do,' asks the impatient reader, 'with jasper and sardonyx, beryl and chalcedony; what with arks and passovers, ephahs and ephods; what with lepers and emerods: what with heave-offerings and unleavened bread; chariots of fire, dragons crowned and horned, behemoth and unicorn? Good for Orientals, these are nothing to me. The more learning you bring to explain them, the more glaring the impertinence. The more coherent and elaborate the system, the less I like it. I say, with the Spartan, "Why do you speak so much to the purpose, of that which is nothing to the purpose?" My learning is such as God gave me in my birth and habit, in the delight and study of my eyes, and not of another man's. Of all absurdities, this of some foreigner, proposing to take away my rhetoric, and substitute his own, and amuse me with pelican and stork, instead of thrush and robin; palm-trees and shittim-wood, instead of sassafras and hickory, — seems the most needless.'

Locke said, "God, when he makes the prophet, does not unmake the man." Swedenborg's history points the remark. The parish disputes, in the Swedish church, between the friends and foes of Luther and Melancthon, concerning "faith alone," and "works alone," intrude themselves into his speculations upon the economy of the universe, and of the celestial societies. The Lutheran bishop's son, for whom the heavens are opened, so that he sees with eyes, and in the richest symbolic forms, the awful truth of things, and utters again, in his books, as under a heavenly mandate, the indisputable secrets of moral nature, — with all these grandeurs resting upon him, remains the Lutheran bishop's son; his judgments are those of a Swedish polemic, and his vast enlargements are purchased by adamantine limitations. He carries his controversial memory with him in his visits to the souls. He is like Michel Angelo, who, in his frescos, put the cardinal who had offended him to roast under a mountain of devils; or, like Dante, who avenged, in vindictive melodies, all his private wrongs; or, perhaps still more like Montaigne's parish priest, who, if a hail-storm passes over the village, thinks the day of doom is come, and the cannibals already have got the pip. Swedenborg confounds us not less with the pains of Melancthon, and Luther, and Wolfius, and his own books, which he advertises among the angels.

Under the same theologic cramp, many of his dogmas are bound. His cardinal position in morals is, that evils should be shunned as sins. But he does not know what evil is, or what good is, who thinks any ground remains to be occupied, after saying that evil is to be shunned as evil. I doubt not he was led by the desire to insert the element of personality of Deity. But nothing is added. One man, you say, dreads erysipelas, — show him that this dread is evil: or, one dreads hell, — show him that *dread* is evil. He who loves goodness, harbors angels, reveres reverence, and lives with God. The less we have to do with our sins, the better. No man can afford to waste his moments in compunctions. "That is active duty," say the Hindoos, "which is not for our bondage; that is knowledge, which is for our liberation: all other duty is good only unto weariness."

Another dogma, growing out of this pernicious theologic limitation, is this Inferno. Swedenborg has devils. Evil, according to old philosophers, is good in the making. That pure malignity can exist, is the extreme proposition of unbelief. It is not to be entertained by a rational agent; it is atheism; it is the last profanation. Euripides rightly said, —

> "Goodness and being in the gods are one;
> He who imputes ill to them makes them none."

To what a painful perversion had Gothic theology arrived, that Swedenborg admitted no conversion for evil spirits! But the divine effort is never relaxed; the carrion in the sun will convert itself to grass and flowers; and man, though in brothels, or jails, or on gibbets, is on his way to all that is good and true. Burns, with the wild humor of his apostrophe to "poor old Nickie Ben,"

> "O wad ye tak a thought, and mend!"

has the advantage of the vindictive theologian. Everything is superficial, and perishes, but love and truth only. The largest is always the truest sentiment, and we feel the more generous spirit of the Indian Vishnu, — "I am the same to all mankind. There is not one who is worthy of my love or hatred. They who serve me with adoration, — I am in them, and they in me. If one whose ways are altogether evil, serve me alone, he is as respectable as the just man; he is altogether well employed; he soon becometh of a virtuous spirit, and obtaineth eternal happiness."

For the anomalous pretension of Revelations of the other world, — only his probity and genius can entitle it to any serious regard. His revelations destroy their credit by running into detail. If a man say, that the Holy Ghost has informed him that the Last Judgment (or the last of the judgments) took place in 1757; or, that the Dutch, in the other world, live in a heaven by themselves, and the English, in a heaven by themselves; I reply, that the Spirit which is holy, is reserved, taciturn, and deals in laws. The rumors of ghosts and hobgoblins gossip and tell fortunes. The teachings of the High Spirit are abstemious, and, in regard to particulars, negative. Socrates' Genius did not advise him to act or to find, but if he purposed to do somewhat not advantageous, it dissuaded him. "What God is," he said, "I know not; what he is not, I know." The Hindoos have denominated the Supreme Being, the "Internal Check." The illuminated Quakers explained their Light, not as somewhat which leads to any action, but it appears as an obstruction to anything unfit. But the right examples are private experiences, which are absolutely at one on this point. Strictly speaking, Swedenborg's revelation is a confounding of planes, — a capital offence in so learned a categorist. This is to carry the law of surface into the plane of substance, to carry individualism and its fopperies into the realm of essences and generals, which is dislocation and chaos.

The secret of heaven is kept from age to age. No imprudent, no sociable angel, ever dropped an early syllable to answer the longings of saints, the fears of mortals. We should have listened on our knees to any favorite, who, by stricter obedience, had brought his thoughts into parallelism with the celestial currents, and could hint to human ears the scenery and circumstance of the newly parted soul. But it is certain that it must tally with what is best in nature. It must not be inferior in tone to the already known works of the artist who sculptures the globes of the firmament, and writes the moral law. It must be fresher than rainbows, stabler than mountains, agreeing with flowers, with tides, and the rising and setting of autumnal stars. Melodious poets shall be hoarse as street ballads, when once the penetrating key-note of nature and spirit is sounded, — the earth-beat, sea-beat, heart-beat, which makes the tune to which the sun rolls, and the globule of blood, and the sap of trees.

In this mood, we hear the rumor that the seer has arrived, and his tale is told. But there is no beauty, no heaven: for angels, goblins. The sad muse loves night and death, and the pit. His Inferno is mesmeric. His spiritual world bears the same relation to the generosities and joys of truth, of which human souls have already made us cognizant, as a man's bad dreams bear to his ideal life. It is indeed very like, in its endless power of lurid pictures, to the phenomena of dreaming, which nightly turns many an honest gentleman, benevolent, but dyspeptic, into a wretch, skulking like a dog about the outer yards and kennels of creation. When he mounts into the heaven, I do not hear its language. A man should not tell me that he has walked among the angels; his proof is, that his eloquence makes me one. Shall the archangels be less majestic and sweet than the figures that have actually walked the earth? These angels that Swedenborg paints give us no very high idea of their discipline and culture: they are all country parsons: their heaven is a *fête champêtre*, an evangelical picnic, or French distribution of prizes to virtuous peasants. Strange, scholastic, didactic, passionless, bloodless man, who denotes classes of souls as a botanist disposes of a carex, and visits doleful hells as a stratum of chalk or hornblende! He has no sympathy. He goes up and down the world of men, a modern Rhadamanthus in gold-headed cane and peruke, and with nonchalance, and the air of a referee, distributes souls. The warm, many-weathered, passionate-peopled world is to him a grammar of hieroglyphs, or an emblematic freemason's procession. How different is Jacob Behmen! *he* is tremulous with emotion, and listens awe-struck, with the gentlest humanity, to the Teacher whose lessons he conveys; and when he asserts that, "in some sort, love is greater than God," his heart beats so high that the thumping against his leathern coat is audible across the centuries. 'T is a great difference. Behmen is healthily and beautifully wise, notwithstanding the mystical narrowness and incommunicableness. Swedenborg is disagreeably wise, and, with all his accumulated gifts, paralyzes and repels.

It is the best sign of a great nature, that it opens a foreground, and, like the breath of morning landscapes, invites us onward. Swedenborg is retrospective, nor can we divest him of his mattock and shroud. Some minds are forever restrained from descending into nature; others are forever prevented from ascending out of it. With a force of many men, he could never break the umbilical cord which held him to nature, and he did not rise to the platform of pure genius.

It is remarkable that this man, who, by his perception of symbols, saw the poetic construction of things, and the primary relation of mind to matter, remained entirely devoid of the whole apparatus of poetic expression, which that perception creates. He knew the grammar and rudiments of the Mother-Tongue, — how could he not read off one strain into music? Was he like Saadi, who, in his vision, designed to fill his lap with the celestial flowers, as presents for his friends; but the fragrance of the roses so intoxicated him, that the skirt dropped from his hands? or, is reporting a breach of the manners of that heavenly society? or, was it that he saw the vision intellectually, and hence that chiding of the intellectual that pervades his books? Be it as it may, his books have no melody, no emotion, no humor, no relief to the dead prosaic level. In his profuse and accurate imagery is no pleasure, for there is no beauty. We wander forlorn in a lack-lustre landscape. No bird ever sang in all these gardens of the dead. The entire want of poetry in so transcendent a mind betokens the disease, and, like a hoarse voice in a beautiful person, is a kind of warning. I think, sometimes, he will not be read longer. His great name will turn a sentence. His books have become a monument. His laurel so largely mixed with cypress, a charnel-breath so mingles with the temple incense, that boys and maids will shun the spot.

Yet, in this immolation of genius and fame at the shrine of conscience, is a merit sublime beyond praise. He lived to purpose: he gave a verdict. He elected goodness as the clew to which the soul must cling in all this labyrinth of nature. Many opinions conflict as to the true centre. In the shipwreck, some cling to running rigging, some to cask and barrel, some to spars, some to mast; the pilot chooses with science, — I plant myself here; all will sink before this; "he comes to land who sails with me." Do not rely on heavenly favor, or on compassion to folly, or on prudence, on common sense, the old usage and main chance of men: nothing can keep you, — not fate, nor health, nor admirable intellect; none can keep you, but rectitude only, rectitude for ever and ever! — and, with a tenacity that never swerved in all his studies, inventions, dreams, he adheres to this brave choice. I think of him as of some transmigrating votary of Indian legend, who says, 'Though I be dog, or jackal, or pismire, in the last rudiments of nature, under what integument or ferocity, I cleave to right, as the sure ladder that leads up to man and to God.'

Swedenborg has rendered a double service to mankind, which is now only beginning to be known. By the science of experiment and use, he made his first steps: he observed and published the laws of nature; and, ascending by just degrees, from events to their summits and causes, he was fired with piety at the harmonies he felt, and abandoned himself to his joy and worship. This was his first service. If the glory was too bright for his eyes to bear, if he staggered under the trance of delight, the more excellent is the spectacle he saw, the realities of being which beam and blaze through him, and which no infirmities of the prophet are suffered to obscure; and he renders a second passive service to men, not less than the first, — perhaps, in the great circle of being, and in the retributions of spiritual nature, not less glorious or less beautiful to himself.

IV.

MONTAIGNE; OR THE SCEPTIC.

MONTAIGNE; OR, THE SCEPTIC.

EVERY fact is related on one side to sensation, and, on the other, to morals. The game of thought is, on the appearance of one of these two sides, to find the other; given the upper, to find the under side. Nothing so thin, but has these two faces; and, when the observer has seen the obverse, he turns it over to see the reverse. Life is a pitching of this penny, — heads or tails. We never tire of this game, because there is still a slight shudder of astonishment at the exhibition of the other face, at the contrast of the two faces. A man is flushed with success, and bethinks himself what this good luck signifies. He drives his bargain in the street; but it occurs, that he also is bought and sold. He sees the beauty of a human face, and searches the cause of that beauty, which must be more beautiful. He builds his fortunes, maintains the laws, cherishes his children; but he asks himself, why? and whereto? This head and this tail are called, in the language of philosophy, Infinite and Finite; Relative and Absolute; Apparent and Real; and many fine names beside.

Each man is born with a predisposition to one or the other of these sides of nature; and it will easily happen that men will be found devoted to one or the other. One class has the perception of difference, and is conversant with facts and surfaces; cities and persons; and the bringing certain things to pass; — the men of talent and action. Another class have the perception of identity, and are men of faith and philosophy, men of genius.

Each of these riders drives too fast. Plotinus believes only in philosophers; Fenelon, in saints; Pindar and Byron, in poets. Read the haughty language in which Plato and the Platonists speak of all men who are not devoted to their own shining abstractions: other men are rats and mice. The literary class is usually proud and exclusive. The correspondence of Pope and Swift describes mankind around them as monsters; and that of Goethe and Schiller, in our own time, is scarcely more kind.

It is easy to see how this arrogance comes. The genius is a genius by the first look he casts on any object. Is his eye creative? Does he not rest in angles and colors, but beholds the design, — he will presently undervalue the actual object. In powerful moments, his thought has dissolved the works of art and nature into their causes, so that the works appear heavy and faulty. He has a conception of beauty which the sculptor cannot embody. Picture, statue, temple, railroad, steam-engine, existed first in an artist's mind, without flaw, mistake, or friction, which impair the executed models. So did the church, the state, college, court, social circle, and all the institutions. It is not strange that these men, remembering what they have seen and hoped of ideas, should affirm disdainfully the superiority of ideas. Having at some time seen that the happy soul will carry all the arts in power, they say, Why cumber ourselves with superfluous realizations? and, like dreaming beggars, they assume to speak and act as if these values were already substantiated.

On the other part, the men of toil and trade and luxury, — the animal world, including the animal in the philosopher and poet also, — and the practical world, including the painful drudgeries which are never excused to philosopher or poet any more than to the rest, — weigh heavily on the other side. The trade in our streets believes in no metaphysical causes, thinks nothing of the force which necessitated traders and a trading planet to exist; no, but sticks to cotton, sugar, wool, and salt. The ward meetings, on election days, are not softened by any misgiving of the value of these ballotings. Hot life is streaming in a single direction. To the men of this world, to the animal strength and spirits, to the men of practical power, while immersed in it, the man of ideas appears out of his reason. They alone have reason.

Things always bring their own philosophy with them, that is, prudence. No man acquires property without acquiring with it a little arithmetic, also. In England, the richest country that ever existed, property stands for more, compared with personal ability, than in any other. After dinner, a man believes less, denies more: verities have lost some charm. After dinner, arithmetic is the only science: ideas are disturbing, incendiary, follies of young men, repudiated by the solid portion of society: and a man comes to be valued by his athletic and animal qualities. Spence relates, that Mr. Pope was with Sir Godfrey Kneller, one day, when his nephew, a Guinea trader, came in. "Nephew," said Sir Godfrey, "you have the honor of seeing the two greatest men in the world." "I don't know how great men you may be," said the Guinea man, "but I don't like your looks. I have often bought a much better than both of you, all muscles and bones, for ten guineas." Thus, the men of the senses revenge themselves on the professors, and repay scorn for scorn. The first had leaped to conclusions not yet ripe, and say more than is true; the others make themselves merry with the philosopher, and weigh man by the pound. They believe that mustard bites the tongue, and pepper is hot, friction-matches are incendiary, revolvers to be avoided, and suspenders hold up pantaloons; that there is much sentiment in a chest of tea; and a man will be eloquent, if you give him good wine. Are you tender and scrupulous, — you must eat more mince-pie. They hold that Luther had milk in him when he said,

> "Wer nicht liebt Wein, Weib, und Gesang,
> Der bleibt ein Narr sein Leben lang";

and when he advised a young scholar, perplexed with fore-ordination and free-will, to get well drunk. "The nerves," says Cabanis, "they are the man." My neighbor, a jolly farmer, in the tavern bar-room, thinks that the use of money is sure and speedy spending: "for his part," he says, "he puts his down his neck, and gets the good of it."

The inconvenience of this way of thinking is, that it runs into indifferentism, and then into disgust. Life is eating us up. We shall be fables presently. Keep cool: it will be all one a hundred years hence. Life 's well enough; but we shall be glad to get out of it, and they will all be glad to have us. Why should we fret and drudge? Our meat will taste to-morrow as it did yesterday, and we may at last have had enough of it. "Ah," said my languid gentleman at Oxford, "there 's nothing new or true, — and no matter."

With a little more bitterness, the cynic moans: our life is like an ass led to market by a bundle of hay being carried before him: he sees nothing but the bundle of hay. "There is so much trouble in coming into the world," said Lord Bolingbroke, "and so much more, as well as meanness, in going out of it, that 't is hardly worth while to be here at all." I know a philosopher of this kidney, who was accustomed briefly to sum up his experience of human nature in saying, "Mankind is a damned rascal": and the natural corollary is pretty sure to follow, — 'The world lives by humbug, and so will I.'

The abstractionist and the materialist thus mutually exasperating each other, and the scoffer expressing the worst of materialism, there arises a third party to occupy the middle ground between these two, the sceptic, namely. He finds both wrong by being in extremes. He labors to plant his feet, to be the beam of the balance. He will not go beyond his card. He sees the one-sidedness of these men of the street; he will not be a Gibeonite; he stands for the intellectual faculties, a cool head, and whatever serves to keep it cool; no unadvised industry, no unrewarded self-devotion, no loss of the brains in toil. Am I an ox, or a dray? — You are both in extremes, he says. You that will have all solid, and a world of pig-lead, deceive yourselves grossly: you believe yourselves rooted and grounded on adamant; and yet, if we uncover the last facts of our knowledge, you are spinning like bubbles in a river, you know not whither or whence, and you are bottomed and capped and wrapped in delusions.

Neither will he be betrayed to a book, and wrapped in a gown. The studious class are their own victims: they are thin and pale, their feet are cold, their heads are hot, the night is without sleep, the day a fear of interruption, — pallor, squalor, hunger, and egotism. If you come near them, and see what conceits they entertain, — they are abstractionists, and spend their days and nights in dreaming some dream; in expecting the homage of society to some precious scheme built on a truth, but destitute of proportion in its presentment, of justness in its application, and of all energy of will in the schemer to embody and vitalize it.

But I see plainly, he says, that I cannot see. I know that human strength is not in extremes, but in avoiding extremes. I, at least, will shun the weakness of philosophizing beyond my depth. What is the use of pretending to powers we have not? What is the use of pretending to assurances we have not, respecting the other life? Why exaggerate the power of virtue? Why be an angel before your time? These strings, wound up too high, will snap. If there is a wish for immortality, and no evidence, why not say just that? If there are conflicting evidences, why not state them? If there is not ground for a candid thinker to make up his mind, yea or nay,

— why not suspend the judgment? I weary of these dogmatizers. I tire of these hacks of routine, who deny the dogmas. I neither affirm nor deny. I stand here to try the case. I am here to consider, σκεπτειν, to consider how it is. I will try to keep the balance true. Of what use to take the chair, and glibly rattle off theories of society, religion, and nature, when I know that practical objections lie in the way, insurmountable by me and by my mates? Why so talkative in public, when each of my neighbors can pin me to my seat by arguments I cannot refute? Why pretend that life is so simple a game, when we know how subtle and illusive the Proteus is? Why think to shut up all things in your narrow coop, when we know there are not one or two only, but ten, twenty, a thousand things, and unlike? Why fancy that you have all the truth in your keeping? There is much to say on all sides.

Who shall forbid a wise scepticism, seeing that there is no practical question on which anything more than an approximate solution can be had? Is not marriage an open question, when it is alleged, from the beginning of the world, that such as are in the institution wish to get out, and such as are out wish to get in? And the reply of Socrates, to him who asked whether he should choose a wife, still remains reasonable, "that, whether he should choose one or not, he would repent it." Is not the state a question? All society is divided in opinion on the subject of the state. Nobody loves it; great numbers dislike it, and suffer conscientious scruples to allegiance: and the only defence set up, is the fear of doing worse in disorganizing. Is it otherwise with the church? Or, to put any of the questions which touch mankind nearest, — shall the young man aim at a leading part in law, in politics, in trade? It will not be pretended that a success in either of these kinds is quite coincident with what is best and inmost in his mind. Shall he, then, cutting the stays that hold him fast to the social state, put out to sea with no guidance but his genius? There is much to say on both sides. Remember the open question between the present order of "competition," and the friends of "attractive and associated labor." The generous minds embrace the proposition of labor shared by all; it is the only honesty; nothing else is safe. It is from the poor man's hut alone, that strength and virtue come: and yet, on the other side, it is alleged that labor impairs the form, and breaks the spirit of man, and the laborers cry unanimously, 'We have no thoughts.' Culture, how indispensable! I cannot forgive you the want of accomplishments; and yet, culture will instantly impair that chiefest beauty of spontaneousness. Excellent is culture for a savage; but once let him read in the book, and he is no longer able not to think of Plutarch's heroes. In short, since true fortitude of understanding consists "in not letting what we know be embarrassed by what we do not know," we ought to secure those advantages which we can command, and not risk them by clutching after the airy and unattainable. Come, no chimeras! Let us go abroad; let us mix in affairs; let us learn, and get, and have, and climb. "Men are a sort of moving plants, and, like trees, receive a great part of their nourishment from the air. If they keep too much at home, they pine." Let us have a robust, manly life; let us know what we know, for certain; what we have, let it be solid, and seasonable, and our own. A world in the hand is worth two in the bush. Let us have to do with real men and women, and not with skipping ghosts.

This, then, is the right ground of the sceptic, — this of consideration, of self-containing; not at all of unbelief; not at all of universal denying, nor of universal doubting, — doubting even that he doubts; least of all, of scoffing and profligate jeering at all that is stable and good. These are no more his moods than are those of religion and philosophy. He is the considerer, the prudent, taking in sail, counting stock, husbanding his means, believing that a man has too many enemies, than that he can afford to be his own; that we cannot give ourselves too many advantages, in this unequal conflict, with powers so vast and unweariable ranged on one side, and this little, conceited, vulnerable popinjay that a man is, bobbing up and down into every danger, on the other. It is a position taken up for better defence, as of more safety, and one that can be maintained; and it is one of more opportunity and range: as, when we build a house, the rule is to set it not too high nor too low, under the wind, but out of the dirt.

The philosophy we want is one of fluxions and mobility. The Spartan and Stoic schemes are too stark and stiff for our occasion. A theory of Saint John, and of nonresistance, seems, on the other hand, too thin and aerial. We want some coat woven of elastic steel, stout as the first, and limber as the second. We want a ship in these billows we inhabit. An angular, dogmatic house would be rent to chips and splinters, in this storm of many elements. No, it must be tight, and fit to the form of man, to live at all; as a shell must dictate the architecture of a house founded on the sea. The soul of man must be the type of our scheme, just as the body of man is the type after which a dwelling-house is built. Adaptiveness is the peculiarity of human nature. We are golden averages, volitant stabilities, compensated or periodic errors, houses founded on the sea. The wise sceptic wishes to have a near view of the best game, and the chief players; what is best in the planet; art, and nature, places and events, but mainly men. Everything that is excellent in mankind, — a form of grace, an arm of iron, lips of persuasion, a brain of resources, every one skilful to play and win, — he will see and judge.

The terms of admission to this spectacle, are, that he have a certain solid and intelligible way of living of his own; some method of answering the inevitable needs of human life; proof that he has played with skill and success; that he has evinced the temper, stoutness, and the range of qualities which, among his contemporaries and countrymen, entitle him to fellowship and trust. For, the secrets of life are not shown except to sympathy and likeness. Men do not confide themselves to boys, or coxcombs, or pedants, but to their peers. Some wise limitation, as the modern phrase is; some condition between the extremes, and having itself a positive quality; some stark and sufficient man, who is not salt or sugar, but sufficiently related to the world to do justice to Paris or London, and, at the same time, a vigorous and original thinker, whom cities cannot overawe, but who uses them, — is the fit person to occupy this ground of speculation.

These qualities meet in the character of Montaigne. And yet, since the personal regard which I entertain for Montaigne may be unduly great, I will, under the shield of this prince of egotists, offer, as an apology for electing him as the representative of scepticism, a word or two to explain how my love began and grew for this admirable gossip.

A single odd volume of Cotton's translation of the Essays remained to me from my father's library, when a boy. It lay long neglected, until, after many years, when I was newly escaped from college, I read the book, and procured the remaining volumes. I remember the delight and wonder in which I lived with it. It seemed to me as if I had myself written the book, in some former life, so sincerely it spoke to my thought and experience. It happened, when in Paris, in 1833, that, in the cemetery of Père la Chaise, I came to a tomb of Auguste Collignon, who died in 1830, aged sixty-eight years, and who, said the monument, "lived to do right, and had formed himself to virtue on the Essays of Montaigne." Some years later, I became acquainted with an accomplished English poet, John Sterling; and, in prosecuting my correspondence, I found that, from a love of Montaigne, he had made a pilgrimage to his chateau, still standing near Castellan, in Perigord, and, after two hundred and fifty years, had copied from the walls of his library the inscriptions which Montaigne had written there. That Journal of Mr. Sterling's, published in the Westminster Review, Mr. Hazlitt has reprinted in the *Prolegomena* to his edition of the Essays. I heard with pleasure that one of the newly discovered autographs of William Shakespeare was in a copy of Florio's translation of Montaigne. It is the only book which we certainly know to have been in the poet's library. And, oddly enough, the duplicate copy of Florio, which the British Museum purchased, with a view of protecting the Shakespeare autograph, (as I was informed in the Museum,) turned out to have the autograph of Ben Jonson in the fly-leaf. Leigh Hunt relates of Lord Byron, that Montaigne was the only great writer of past times whom he read with avowed satisfaction. Other coincidences, not needful to be mentioned here, concurred to make this old Gascon still new and immortal for me.

In 1571, on the death of his father, Montaigne, then thirty-eight years old, retired from the practice of law, at Bordeaux, and settled himself on his estate. Though he had been a man of pleasure, and sometimes a courtier, his studious habits now grew on him, and he loved the compass, staidness, and independence of the country gentleman's life. He took up his economy in good earnest, and made his farms yield the most. Downright and plain dealing, and abhorring to be deceived or to deceive, he was esteemed in the country for his sense and probity. In the civil wars of the League, which converted every house into a fort, Montaigne kept his gates open, and his house without defence. All parties freely came and went, his courage and honor being universally esteemed. The neighboring lords and gentry brought jewels and papers to him for safe-keeping. Gibbon reckons, in these bigoted times, but two men of liberality in France, — Henry IV. and Montaigne.

Montaigne is the frankest and honestest of all writers. His French freedom runs into grossness; but he has anticipated all censure by the bounty of his own confessions. In his times, books were written to one sex only, and almost all were written in Latin; so that, in a humorist, a certain nakedness of statement was permitted, which our manners, of a literature addressed equally to both sexes, do not allow. But, though a Biblical plainness, coupled with a most uncanonical levity, may shut his pages to many sensitive readers, yet the offence is superficial. He parades it: he makes the most of it: nobody can think or say worse of him than he does. He pretends to most of the vices; and, if there be any virtue in him, he says, it got in by stealth. There is no man, in his opinion, who has not deserved hanging five or six times; and he pretends no exception in his own behalf. "Five or six as ridiculous stories," too, he says, "can be told of me, as of any man living." But, with all this really superfluous frankness, the opinion of an invincible probity grows into every reader's mind.

"When I the most strictly and religiously confess myself, I find that the best virtue I have has in it some tincture of vice; and I am afraid that Plato, in his purest virtue, (I, who am as sincere and perfect a lover of virtue of that stamp as any other whatever,) if he had listened, and laid his ear close to himself, would have heard some jarring sound of human mixture; but faint and remote, and only to be perceived by himself."

Here is an impatience and fastidiousness at color or pretence of any kind. He has been in courts so long as to have conceived a furious disgust at appearances; he will indulge himself with a little cursing and swearing; he will talk with sailors and gypsies, use flash and street ballads: he has stayed in-doors till he is deadly sick; he will to the open air, though it rain bullets. He has seen too much of gentlemen of the long robe, until he wishes for cannibals; and is so nervous, by factitious life, that he thinks, the more barbarous man is, the better he is. He likes his saddle. You may read theology, and grammar, and metaphysics elsewhere. Whatever you get here, shall smack of the earth and of real life, sweet, or smart, or stinging. He makes no hesitation to entertain you with the records of his disease; and his journey to Italy is quite full of that matter. He took and kept this position of equilibrium. Over his name, he drew an emblematic pair of scales, and wrote *Que sçais je?* under it. As I look at his effigy opposite the title-page, I seem to hear him say, 'You may play old Poz, if you will; you may rail and exaggerate, — I stand here for truth, and will not, for all the states, and churches, and revenues, and personal reputations of Europe, overstate the dry fact, as I see it; I will rather mumble and prose about what I certainly know, — my house and barns; my father, my wife, and my tenants; my old lean bald pate; my knives and forks; what meats I eat, and what drinks I prefer; and a hundred straws just as ridiculous, — than I will write, with a fine crow-quill, a fine romance. I like gray days, and autumn and winter weather. I am gray and autumnal myself, and think an undress, and old shoes that do not pinch my feet, and old friends who do not constrain me, and plain topics where I do not need to strain myself and pump my brains, the most suitable. Our condition as men is risky and ticklish enough. One cannot be sure of himself and his fortune an hour, but he may be whisked off into some pitiable or ridiculous plight. Why should I vapor and play the philosopher, instead of ballasting, the best I can, this dancing balloon? So, at least, I live within compass, keep myself ready for action, and can shoot the gulf, at last, with decency. If there be anything farcical in such a life, the blame is not mine: let it lie at fate's and nature's door.'

The Essays, therefore, are an entertaining soliloquy on every random topic that comes into his head; treating everything without ceremony, yet with masculine sense. There have been men with deeper insight; but, one would say, never a man with such abundance of thoughts: he is never dull, never insincere, and has the genius to make the reader care for all that he cares for.

The sincerity and marrow of the man reaches to his sentences. I know not anywhere the book that seems less written. It is the language of conversation transferred to a book. Cut these words and they would bleed; they are vascular and alive. One has the same pleasure in it that we have in listening to the necessary speech of men about their work, when any unusual circumstance gives momentary importance to the dialogue. For blacksmiths and teamsters do not trip in their speech; it is a shower of bullets. It is Cambridge men who correct themselves, and begin again at every half-sentence, and, moreover, will pun, and refine too much, and swerve from the matter to the expression. Montaigne talks with shrewdness, knows the world, and books, and himself, and uses the positive degree: never shrieks, or protests, or prays: no weakness, no convulsion, no superlative: does not wish to jump out of his skin, or play any antics, or annihilate space or time; but is stout and solid; tastes every moment of the day; likes pain, because it makes him feel himself, and realize things, as we pinch ourselves to know that we are awake. He keeps the plain; he rarely mounts or sinks; likes to feel solid ground, and the stones underneath. His writing has no enthusiasms, no aspiration; contented, self-respecting, and keeping the middle of the road. There is but one exception, — in his love for Socrates. In speaking of him, for once his cheek flushes, and his style rises to passion.

Montaigne died of a quinsy, at the age of sixty, in 1592. When he came to die, he caused the mass to be celebrated in his chamber. At the age of thirty-three, he had been married. "But," he says, "might I have had my own will, I would not have married Wisdom herself, if she would have had me: but 't is to much purpose to evade it, the common custom and use of life will have it so. Most of my actions are guided by example, not choice." In the hour of death, he gave the same weight to custom. *Que sçais je?* What do I know?

This book of Montaigne the world has indorsed, by translating it into all tongues, and printing seventy-five editions of it in Europe: and that, too, a circulation somewhat chosen, namely, among courtiers, soldiers, princes, men of the world, and men of wit and generosity.

Shall we say that Montaigne has spoken wisely, and given the right and permanent expression of the human mind, on the conduct of life?

We are natural believers. Truth, or the connection between cause and effect, alone interests us. We are persuaded that a thread runs through all things: all worlds are strung on it, as beads: and men, and events, and life, come to us, only because of that thread: they pass and repass, only that we may know the direction and continuity of that line. A book or statement which goes to show that there is no line, but random and chaos, a calamity out of nothing, a prosperity and no account of it, a hero born from a fool, a fool from a hero, — dispirits us. Seen or unseen, we believe the tie exists. Talent makes counterfeit ties; genius finds the real ones. We hearken to the man of science, because we anticipate the sequence in natural phenomena which he uncovers. We love whatever affirms, connects, preserves; and dislike what scatters or pulls down. One man appears whose nature is to all men's eyes conserving and constructive: his presence supposes a well-ordered society, agriculture, trade, large institutions, and empire. If these did not exist, they would begin to exist through his endeavors. Therefore, he cheers and comforts men, who feel all this in him very readily. The nonconformist and the rebel say all manner of unanswerable things against the existing republic, but discover to our sense no plan of house or state of their own. Therefore, though the town, and state, and way of living, which our counsellor contemplated, might be a very modest or musty prosperity, yet men rightly go for him, and reject the reformer, so long as he comes only with axe and crowbar.

But though we are natural conservers and causationists, and reject a sour, dumpish unbelief, the sceptical class, which Montaigne represents, have reason, and every man, at some time, belongs to it. Every superior mind will pass through this domain of equilibration, — I should rather say, will know how to avail himself of the checks and balances in nature, as a natural weapon against the exaggeration and formalism of bigots and blockheads.

Scepticism is the attitude assumed by the student in relation to the particulars which society adores, but which he sees to be reverend only in their tendency and spirit. The ground occupied by the sceptic is the vestibule of the temple. Society does not like to have any breath of question blown on the existing order. But the interrogation of custom at all points is an inevitable stage in the growth of every superior mind, and is the evidence of its perception of the flowing power which remains itself in all changes.

The superior mind will find itself equally at odds with the evils of society, and with the projects that are offered to relieve them. The wise sceptic is a bad citizen; no conservative; he sees the selfishness of property, and the drowsiness of institutions. But neither is he fit to work with any democratic party that ever was constituted; for parties wish every one committed, and he penetrates the popular patriotism. His politics are those of the "Soul's Errand" of Sir Walter Raleigh; or of Krishna, in the Bhagavat, "There is none who is worthy of my love or hatred"; whilst he sentences law, physic, divinity, commerce, and custom. He is a reformer: yet he is no better member of the philanthropic association. It turns out that he is not the champion of the operative, the pauper, the prisoner, the slave. It stands in his mind, that our life in this world is not of quite so easy interpretation as churches and school-books say. He does not wish to take ground against these benevolences, to play the part of devil's attorney, and blazon every doubt and sneer that darkens the sun for him. But he says, There are doubts.

I mean to use the occasion, and celebrate the calendar-day of our Saint Michel de Montaigne, by counting and describing these doubts or negations. I wish to ferret them out of their holes, and sun them a little. We must do with them as the police do with old rogues, who are shown up to the public at the marshal's office. They will never be so formidable, when once they have been identified and registered. But I mean honestly by them, — that justice shall be done to their terrors. I shall not take Sunday objections, made up on purpose to be put down. I shall take the worst I can find, whether I can dispose of them, or they of me.

I do not press the scepticism of the materialist. I know, the quadruped opinion will not prevail. 'T is of no importance what bats and oxen think. The first dangerous symptom I report, is, the levity of intellect; as if it were fatal to earnestness to know much. Knowledge is the knowing that we cannot know. The dull pray; the geniuses are light mockers. How respectable is earnestness on every platform! but intellect kills it. Nay, San Carlo, my subtle and admirable friend, one of the most penetrating of men, finds that all direct ascension, even of lofty piety, leads to this ghastly insight, and sends back the votary orphaned. My astonishing San Carlo thought the lawgivers and saints infected. They found the ark empty; saw, and would not tell; and tried to choke off their approaching followers, by saying, 'Action, action, my dear fellows, is for you!' Bad as was to me this detection by San Carlo, this frost in July, this blow from a bride, there was still a worse, namely, the cloy or satiety of the saints. In the mount of vision, ere they have yet risen from their knees, they say, 'We discover that this our homage and beatitude is partial and deformed: we must fly for relief to the suspected and reviled Intellect, to the Understanding, the Mephistopheles, to the gymnastics of talent.'

This is hobgoblin the first; and, though it has been the subject of much elegy, in our nineteenth century, from Byron, Goethe, and other poets of less fame, not to mention many distinguished private observers, — I confess it is not very affecting to my imagination; for it seems to concern the shattering of baby-houses and crockery-shops. What flutters the church of Rome, or of England, or of Geneva, or of Boston, may yet be very far from touching any principle of faith. I think that the intellect and moral sentiment are unanimous; and that, though philosophy extirpates bugbears, yet it supplies the natural checks of vice, and polarity to the soul. I think that the wiser a man is, the more stupendous he finds the natural and moral economy, and lifts himself to a more absolute reliance.

There is the power of moods, each setting at naught all but its own tissue of facts and beliefs. There is the power of complexions, obviously modifying the dispositions and sentiments. The beliefs and unbeliefs appear to be structural; and, as soon as each man attains the poise and vivacity which allow the whole machinery to play, he will not need extreme examples, but will rapidly alternate all opinions in his own life. Our life is March weather, savage and serene in one hour. We go forth austere, dedicated, believing in the iron links of Destiny, and will not turn on our heel to save our life: but a book or a bust, or only the sound of a name, shoots a spark through the nerves, and we suddenly believe in will: my finger-ring shall be the seal of Solomon: fate is for imbeciles: all is possible to the resolved mind. Presently, a new experience gives a new turn to our thoughts: common sense resumes its tyranny: we say, 'Well, the army, after all, is the gate to fame, manners, and poetry: and, look you, — on the whole, selfishness plants best, prunes best, makes the best commerce, and the best citizen.' Are the opinions of a man on right and wrong, on fate and causation, at the mercy of a broken sleep or an indigestion? Is his belief in God and Duty no deeper than a stomach evidence? And what guaranty for the permanence of his opinions? I like not the French celerity, — a new church and state once a week. This is the second negation; and I shall let it pass for what it will. As far as it asserts rotation of states of mind, I suppose it suggests its own remedy, namely, in the record of larger periods. What is the mean of many states; of all the states? Does the general voice of ages affirm any principle, or is no community of sentiment discoverable in distant times and places? And when it shows the power of self-interest, I accept that as part of the divine law, and must reconcile it with aspiration the best I can.

The word Fate, or Destiny, expresses the sense of mankind, in all ages, — that the laws of the world do not always befriend, but often hurt and crush us. Fate, in the shape of *Kinde* or nature, grows over us like grass. We paint Time with a scythe; Love and Fortune, blind; and Destiny, deaf. We have too little power of resistance against this ferocity which champs us up. What front can we make against these unavoidable, victorious, maleficent forces? What can I do against the influence of Race, in my history? What can I do against hereditary and constitutional habits, against scrofula, lymph, impotence; against climate, against barbarism, in my country? I can reason down or deny everything, except this perpetual Belly: feed he must and will, and I cannot make him respectable.

But the main resistance which the affirmative impulse finds, and one including all others, is in the doctrine of the Illusionists. There is a painful rumor in circulation, that we have been practised upon in all the principal performances of life, and free agency is the emptiest name. We have been sopped and drugged with the air, with food, with woman, with children, with sciences, with events, which leave us exactly where they found us. The mathematics, 't is complained, leave the mind where they find it: so do all sciences; and so do all events and actions. I find a man who has passed through all the sciences, the churl he was; and through all the offices, learned, civil, and social, can detect the child. We are not the less necessitated to dedicate life to them. In fact, we may come to accept it as the fixed rule and theory of our state of education, that God is a substance, and his method is illusion. The Eastern sages owned the goddess Yoganidra, the great illusory energy of Vishnu, by whom, as utter ignorance, the whole world is beguiled.

Or, shall I state it thus? — The astonishment of life, is, the absence of any appearance of reconciliation between the theory and practice of life. Reason, the prized reality, the Law, is apprehended, now and then, for a serene and profound moment, amidst the hubbub of cares and works which have no direct bearing on it; — is then lost, for months or years, and again found, for an interval, to be lost again. If we compute it in time, we may, in fifty years, have half a dozen reasonable hours. But what are these cares and works the better? A method in the world we do not see, but this parallelism of great and little, which never react on each other, nor discover the smallest tendency to converge. Experiences, fortunes, governings, readings, writings, are nothing to the purpose; as when a man comes into the room, it does not appear whether he has been fed on yams or buffalo, — he has contrived to get so much bone and fibre as he wants, out of rice or out of snow. So vast is the disproportion between the sky of law and the pismire of performance under it, that, whether he is a man of worth or a sot, is not so great a matter as we say. Shall I add, as one juggle of this enchantment, the stunning non-intercourse law which makes co-operation impossible? The young spirit pants to enter society. But all the ways of culture and greatness lead to solitary imprisonment. He has been often balked. He did not expect a sympathy with his thought from the village, but he went with it to the chosen and intelligent, and found no entertainment for it, but mere misapprehension, distaste, and scoffing. Men are strangely mistimed and misapplied; and the excellence of each is an inflamed individualism which separates him more.

There are these, and more than these, diseases of thought, which our ordinary teachers do not attempt to remove. Now shall we, because a good nature inclines us to virtue's side, say, There are no doubts, — and lie for the right? Is life to be led in a brave or in a cowardly manner? and is not the satisfaction of the doubts essential to all manliness? Is the name of virtue to be a barrier to that which is virtue? Can you not believe that a man of earnest and burly habit may find small good in tea, essays, and catechism, and want a rougher instruction, want men, labor, trade, farming, war, hunger, plenty, love, hatred, doubt, and terror, to make things plain to him; and has he not a right to insist on being convinced in his own way? When he is convinced, he will be worth the pains.

Belief consists in accepting the affirmations of the soul; unbelief, in denying them. Some minds are incapable of scepticism. The doubts they profess to entertain are rather a civility or accommodation to the common discourse of their company. They may well give themselves leave to speculate, for they are secure of a return. Once admitted to the heaven of thought, they see no relapse into night, but infinite invitation on the other side. Heaven is within heaven, and sky over sky, and they are encompassed with divinities. Others there are, to whom the heaven is brass, and it shuts down to the surface of the earth. It is a question of temperament, or of more or less immersion in nature. The last class must needs have a reflex or parasite faith; not a sight of realities, but an instinctive reliance on the seers and believers of realities. The manners and thoughts of believers astonish them, and convince them that these have seen something which is hid from themselves. But their sensual habit would fix the believer to his last position, whilst he as inevitably advances; and presently the unbeliever, for love of belief, burns the believer.

Great believers are always reckoned infidels, impracticable, fantastic, atheistic, and really men of no account. The spiritualist finds himself driven to express his faith by a series of scepticisms. Charitable souls comes with their projects, and ask his co-operation. How can he hesitate? It is the rule of mere comity and courtesy to agree where you can, and to turn your sentence with something auspicious, and not freezing and sinister. But he is forced to say: 'O, these things will be as they must be: what can you do? These particular griefs and crimes are the foliage and fruit of such trees as we see growing. It is vain to complain of the leaf or the berry: cut it off; it will bear another just as bad. You must begin your cure lower down.' The generosities of the day prove an intractable element for him. The people's questions are not his; their methods are not his; and, against all the dictates of good-nature, he is driven to say, he has no pleasure in them.

Even the doctrines dear to the hope of man, of the divine Providence, and of the immortality of the soul, his neighbors cannot put the statement so that he shall affirm it. But he denies out of more faith, and not less. He denies out of honesty. He had rather stand charged with the imbecility of scepticism, than with untruth. I believe, he says, in the moral design of the universe; it exists hospitably for the weal of souls; but your dogmas seem to me caricatures: why should I make believe them? Will any say, this is cold and infidel? The wise and magnanimous will not say so. They will exult in his far-sighted good-will, that can abandon to the adversary all the ground of tradition and common belief, without losing a jot of strength. It sees to the end of all transgression. George Fox saw "that there was an ocean of darkness and death; but withal, an infinite ocean of light and love which flowed over that of darkness."

The final solution in which scepticism is lost, is, in the moral sentiment, which never forfeits its supremacy. All moods may be safely tried, and their weight allowed to all objections: the moral sentiment as easily outweighs them all, as any one. This is the drop which balances the sea. I play with the miscellany of facts, and take those superficial views which we call scepticism; but I know that they will presently appear to me in that order which makes scepticism impossible. A man of thought must feel the thought that is parent of the universe: that the masses of nature do undulate and flow. This faith avails to the whole emergency of life and objects. The world is saturated with deity and with law. He is content with just and unjust, with sots and fools, with the triumph of folly and fraud. He can behold with serenity the yawning gulf between the ambition of man and his power of performance, between the demand and supply of power, which makes the tragedy of all souls.

Charles Fourier announced that "the attractions of man are proportioned to his destinies"; in other words, that every desire predicts its own satisfaction. Yet, all experience exhibits the reverse of this; the incompetency of power is the universal grief of young and ardent minds. They accuse the divine providence of a certain parsimony. It has shown the heaven and earth to every child, and filled him with a desire for the whole; a desire raging, infinite; a hunger, as of space to be filled with planets; a cry of famine, as of devils for souls. Then for the satisfaction, — to each man is administered a single drop, a bead of dew of vital power, *per day*, — a cup as large as space, and one drop of the water of life in it. Each man woke in the morning, with an appetite that could eat the solar system like a cake; a spirit for action and passion without bounds; he could lay his hand on the morning star: he could try conclusions with gravitation or chemistry; but, on the first motion to prove his strength, — hands, feet, senses, gave way, and would not serve him. He was an emperor deserted by his states, and left to whistle by himself, or thrust into a mob of emperors, all whistling: and still the sirens sang, "The attractions are proportioned to the destinies." In every house, in the heart of each maiden, and of each boy, in the soul of the soaring saint, this chasm is found,

— between the largest promise of ideal power, and the shabby experience.

The expansive nature of truth comes to our succor, elastic, not to be surrounded. Man helps himself by larger generalizations. The lesson of life is practically to generalize; to believe what the years and the centuries say against the hours; to resist the usurpation of particulars; to penetrate to their catholic sense. Things seem to say one thing, and say the reverse. The appearance is immoral; the result is moral. Things seem to tend downward, to justify despondency, to promote rogues, to defeat the just; and, by knaves, as by martyrs, the just cause is carried forward. Although knaves win in every political struggle, although society seems to be delivered over from the hands of one set of criminals into the hands of another set of criminals, as fast as the government is changed, and the march of civilization is a train of felonies, yet, general ends are somehow answered. We see, now, events forced on, which seem to retard or retrograde the civility of ages. But the world-spirit is a good swimmer, and storms and waves cannot drown him He snaps his finger at laws: and so, throughout history, heaven seems to affect low and poor means. Through the years and the centuries, through evil agents, through toys and atoms, a great and beneficent tendency irresistibly streams.

Let a man learn to look for the permanent in the mutable and fleeting; let him learn to bear the disappearance of things he was wont to reverence, without losing his reverence; let him learn that he is here, not to work, but to be worked upon; and that, though abyss open under abyss, and opinion displace opinion, all are at last contained in the Eternal Cause.

"If my bark sink, 't is to another sea."

V.

SHAKESPEARE; OR, THE POET.

SHAKESPEARE; OR, THE POET.

GREAT men are more distinguished by range and extent, than by originality. If we require the originality, which consists in weaving, like a spider, their web from their own bowels; in finding clay, and making bricks, and building the house; no great men are original. Nor does valuable originality consist in unlikeness to other men. The hero is in the press of knights, and the thick of events; and, seeing what men want, and sharing their desire, he adds the needful length of sight and of arm, to come at the desired point. The greatest genius is the most indebted man. A poet is no rattle-brain, saying what comes uppermost, and, because he says everything, saying, at last, something good; but a heart in unison with his time and country. There is nothing whimsical and fantastic in his production, but sweet and sad earnest, freighted with the weightiest convictions, and pointed with the most determined aim which any man or class knows of in his times.

The Genius of our life is jealous of individuals, and will not have any individual great, except through the general. There is no choice to genius. A great man does not wake up on some fine morning, and say, 'I am full of life, I will go to sea, and find an Antarctic continent: to-day I will square the circle: I will ransack botany, and find a new food for man: I have a new architecture in my mind: I foresee a new mechanic power': no, but he finds himself in the river of the thoughts and events, forced onward by the ideas and necessities of his contemporaries. He stands where all the eyes of men look one way, and their hands all point in the direction in which he should go. The church has reared him amidst rites and pomps, and he carries out the advice which her music gave him, and builds a cathedral needed by her chants and processions. He finds a war raging: it educates him, by trumpet, in barracks, and he betters the instruction. He finds two counties groping to bring coal, or flour, or fish, from the place of production to the place of consumption, and he hits on a railroad. Every master has found his materials collected, and his power lay in his sympathy with his people, and in his love of the materials he wrought in. What an economy of power! and what a compensation for the shortness of life! All is done to his hand. The world has brought him thus far on his way. The human race has gone out before him, sunk the hills, filled the hollows, and bridged the rivers. Men, nations, poets, artisans, women, all have worked for him, and he enters into their labors. Choose any other thing, out of the line of tendency, out of the national feeling and history, and he would have all to do for himself: his powers would be expended in the first preparations. Great genial power, one would almost say, consists in not being original at all; in being altogether receptive; in letting the world do all, and suffering the spirit of the hour to pass unobstructed through the mind.

Shakespeare's youth fell in a time when the English people were importunate for dramatic entertainments. The court took offence easily at political allusions, and attempted to suppress them. The Puritans, a growing and energetic party, and the religious among the Anglican church, would suppress them. But the people wanted them. Inn-yards, houses without roofs, and extemporaneous enclosures at country fairs, were the ready theatres of strolling players. The people had tasted this new joy; and, as we could not hope to suppress newspapers now, — no, not by the strongest party, — neither then could king, prelate, or puritan, alone or united, suppress an organ, which was ballad, epic, newspaper, caucus, lecture, Punch, and library, at the same time. Probably king, prelate, and puritan, all found their own account in it. It had become, by all causes, a national interest, — by no means conspicuous, so that some great scholar would have thought of treating it in an English history, — but not a whit less considerable, because it was cheap, and of no account, like a baker's shop. The best proof of its vitality is the crowd of writers which suddenly broke into this field; Kyd, Marlow, Greene, Jonson, Chapman, Dekker, Webster, Heywood, Middleton, Peele, Ford, Massinger, Beaumont and Fletcher.

The secure possession, by the stage, of the public mind, is

of the first importance to the poet who works for it. He loses no time in idle experiments. Here is audience and expectation prepared. In the case of Shakespeare there is much more. At the time when he left Stratford, and went up to London, a great body of stage-plays, of all dates and writers, existed in manuscript, and were in turn produced on the boards. Here is the Tale of Troy, which the audience will bear hearing some part of, every week; the Death of Julius Cæsar, and other stories out of Plutarch, which they never tire of; a shelf full of English history, from the chronicles of Brut and Arthur, down to the royal Henries, which men hear eagerly; and a string of doleful tragedies, merry Italian tales, and Spanish voyages, which all the London prentices know. All the mass has been treated, with more or less skill, by every playwright, and the prompter has the soiled and tattered manuscripts. It is now no longer possible to say who wrote them first. They have been the property of the Theatre so long, and so many rising geniuses have enlarged or altered them, inserting a speech, or a whole scene, or adding a song, that no man can any longer claim copyright in this work of numbers. Happily, no man wishes to. They are not yet desired in that way. We have few readers, many spectators and hearers. They had best lie where they are.

Shakespeare, in common with his comrades, esteemed the mass of old plays, waste stock, in which any experiment could be freely tried. Had the *prestige* which hedges about a modern tragedy existed, nothing could have been done. The rude warm blood of the living England circulated in the play, as in street-ballads, and gave body which he wanted to his airy and majestic fancy. The poet needs a ground in popular tradition on which he may work, and which, again, may restrain his art within the due temperance. It holds him to the people, supplies a foundation for his edifice; and, in furnishing so much work done to his hand, leaves him at leisure, and in full strength for the audacities of his imagination. In short, the poet owes to his legend what sculpture owed to the temple. Sculpture in Egypt, and in Greece, grew up in subordination to architecture. It was the ornament of the temple wall: at first, a rude relief carved on pediments, then the relief became bolder, and a head or arm was projected from the wall, the groups being still arranged with reference to the building, which serves also as a frame to hold the figures; and when, at last, the greatest freedom of style and treatment was reached, the prevailing genius of architecture still enforced a certain calmness and continence in the statue. As soon as the statue was begun for itself, and with no reference to the temple or palace, the art began to decline; freak, extravagance, and exhibition took the place of the old temperance. This balance-wheel, which the sculptor found in architecture, the perilous irritability of poetic talent found in the accumulated dramatic materials to which the people were already wonted, and which had a certain excellence which no single genius, however extraordinary, could hope to create.

In point of fact, it appears that Shakespeare did owe debts in all directions, and was able to use whatever he found; and the amount of indebtedness may be inferred from Malone's laborious computations in regard to the First, Second, and Third Parts of Henry VI., in which "out of 6043 lines, 1771 were written by some author preceding Shakespeare; 2373 by him, on the foundation laid by his predecessors; and 1899 were entirely his own." And the proceeding investigation hardly leaves a single drama of his absolute invention. Malone's sentence is an important piece of external history. In Henry VIII., I think I see plainly the cropping out of the original rock on which his own finer stratum was laid. The first play was written by a superior, thoughtful man, with a vicious ear. I can mark his lines, and know well their cadence. See Wolsey's soliloquy, and the following scene with Cromwell, where, — instead of the metre of Shakespeare, whose secret is, that the thought constructs the tune, so that reading for the sense will best bring out the rhythm, — here the lines are constructed on a given tune, and the verse has even a trace of pulpit eloquence. But the play contains, through all its length, unmistakable traits of Shakespeare's hand, and some passages, as the account of the coronation, are like autographs. What is odd, the compliment to Queen Elizabeth is in the bad rhythm.

Shakespeare knew that tradition supplies a better fable than any invention can. If he lost any credit of design, he augmented his resources; and, at that day, our petulant demand for originality was not so much pressed. There was no literature for the million. The universal reading, the cheap press, were unknown. A great poet, who appears in illiterate times, absorbs into his sphere all the light which is anywhere radiating. Every intellectual jewel, every flower of sentiment, it is his fine office to bring to his people; and he comes to value his memory equally with his invention. He is therefore little solicitous whence his thoughts have been derived; whether through translation, whether through tradition, whether by travel in distant countries, whether by inspiration; from whatever source, they are equally welcome to his uncritical audience. Nay, he borrows very near home. Other men say wise things as well as he; only they say a good many foolish things, and do not know when they have spoken wisely. He knows the sparkle of the true stone, and puts it in high place, wherever he finds it. Such is the happy position of Homer, perhaps; of Chaucer, of Saadi. They felt that all wit was their wit. And they are librarians and historiographers, as well as poets. Each romancer was heir and dispenser of all the hundred tales of the world, —

"Presenting Thebes' and Pelops' line
And the tale of Troy divine."

The influence of Chaucer is conspicuous in all our early literature; and, more recently, not only Pope and Dryden have been beholden to him, but, in the whole society of English writers, a large unacknowledged debt is easily traced. One is charmed with the opulence which feeds so many pensioners. But Chaucer is a huge borrower. Chaucer, it seems, drew continually, through Lydgate and Caxton, from Guido di Colonna, whose Latin romance of the Trojan war was in turn a compilation from Dares Phrygius, Ovid, and Statius. Then Petrarch, Boccaccio, and the Provençal poets, are his benefactors: the Romaunt of the Rose is only judicious translation from William of Lorris and John of Meun: Troilus and Creseide, from Lollius of Urbino: the Cock and the Fox, from the *Lais* of Marie: The House of Fame, from the French or Italian: and poor Gower he uses as if he were only a brick-kiln or stone-quarry, out of which to build his house. He steals by this apology, — that what he takes has no worth where he finds it, and the greatest where he leaves it. It has come to be practically a sort of rule in literature, that a man, having once shown himself capable of original writing, is entitled thenceforth to steal from the writings of others at discretion. Thought is the property of him who can entertain it; and of him who can adequately place it. A certain awkwardness marks the use of borrowed thoughts; but, as soon as we have learned what to do with them, they become our own.

Thus, all originality is relative. Every thinker is retrospective. The learned member of the Legislature, at Westminster, or at Washington, speaks and votes for thousands. Show us the constituency, and the now invisible channels by which the senator is made aware of their wishes, the crowd of practical and knowing men, who, by correspondence or conversation, are feeding him with evidence, anecdotes, and estimates, and it will bereave his fine attitude and resistance of something of their impressiveness. As Sir Robert Peel and Mr. Webster vote, so Locke and Rousseau think for thousands; and so there were fountains all around Homer, Menu, Saadi, or Milton, from which they drew; friends, lovers, books, traditions, proverbs, — all perished, — which, if seen, would go to reduce the wonder. Did the bard speak with authority? Did he feel himself overmatched by any companion? The appeal is to the consciousness of the writer. Is there at least in his breast a Delphi whereof to ask concerning any thought or thing, whether it be verily so, yea or nay? and to have answer, and to rely on that? All the debts which such a man could contract to other wit, would never disturb his consciousness of originality: for the ministrations of books, and of other minds, are a whiff of smoke to that most private reality with which he has conversed.

It is easy to see that what is best written or done by genius, in the world, was no man's work, but came by wide social labor, when a thousand wrought like one, sharing the same impulse. Our English Bible is a wonderful specimen of the strength and music of the English language. But it was not made by one man, or at one time; but centuries and churches brought it to perfection. There never was a time when there was not some translation existing. The Liturgy, admired for its energy and pathos, is an anthology of the piety of ages and nations, a translation of the prayers and forms of the Catholic church, — these collected, too, in long periods, from the prayers and meditations of every saint and sacred writer, all over the world. Grotius makes the like remark in respect to the Lord's Prayer, that the single clauses of which it is composed were already in use, in the time of Christ, in the rabbinical forms. He picked out the grains of gold. The nervous language of the Common Law, the impressive forms of our courts, and the precision and substantial truth of the legal distinctions, are the contribution of all the sharp-sighted, strong-minded men who have lived in the countries where these laws govern. The translation of Plutarch gets its excellence by being translation on translation. There never was a time when there was none. All the truly idiomatic and national phrases are kept, and all others successively picked out, and thrown away. Something like the same process had gone on, long before, with the originals of these books. The world takes liberties with world-books. Vedas, Æsop's Fables, Pilpay, Arabian Nights, Cid, Iliad, Robin Hood, Scottish Minstrelsy, are not the work of single men. In the composition of such works, the time thinks, the market thinks, the mason, the carpenter, the merchant, the farmer, the fop, all think for us. Every book supplies its time with one good word; every municipal law, every trade, every folly of the day, and the generic catholic genius who is not afraid or ashamed to owe his originality to the originality of all, stands with the next age as the recorder and embodiment of his own.

We have to thank the researches of antiquaries, and the Shakespeare Society, for ascertaining the steps of the English drama, from the Mysteries celebrated in churches and by churchmen, and the final detachment from the church, and the completion of secular plays, from Ferrex and Porrex, and Gammer Gurton's Needle, down to the possession of the stage by the very pieces which Shakespeare altered, remodelled, and finally made his own. Elated with success, and piqued by the growing interest of the problem, they have left no book-stall unsearched, no chest in a garret unopened, no file of old yellow accounts to decompose in damp and worms, so keen was the hope to discover whether the boy Shakespeare poached or not, whether he held horses at the theatre door, whether he kept school, and why he left in his will only his second-best bed to Ann Hathaway, his wife.

There is somewhat touching in the madness with which the passing age mischooses the object on which all candles shine, and all eyes are turned; the care with which it registers every trifle touching Queen Elizabeth, and King James, and the Essexes, Leicesters, Burleighs, and Buckinghams; and lets pass without a single valuable note the founder of another dynasty, which alone will cause the Tudor dynasty to be remembered, — the man who carries the Saxon race in him by the inspiration which feeds him, and on whose thoughts the foremost people of the world are now for some ages to be nourished, and minds to receive this and not another bias. A popular player, — nobody suspected he was the poet of the human race; and the secret was kept as faithfully from poets and intellectual men, as from courtiers and frivolous people.

Bacon, who took the inventory of the human understanding for his times, never mentioned his name. Ben Jonson, though we have strained his few words of regard and panegyric, had no suspicion of the elastic fame whose first vibrations he was attempting. He no doubt thought the praise he has conceded to him generous, and esteemed himself, out of all question, the better poet of the two.

If it need wit to know wit, according to the proverb, Shakespeare's time should be capable of recognizing it. Sir Henry Wotton was born four years after Shakespeare, and died twenty-three years after him; and I find, among his correspondents and acquaintances, the following persons: Theodore Beza, Isaac Casaubon, Sir Philip Sidney, Earl of Essex, Lord Bacon, Sir Walter Raleigh, John Milton, Sir Henry Vane, Isaac Walton, Dr. Donne, Abraham Cowley, Bellarmine, Charles Cotton, John Pym, John Hales, Kepler, Vieta, Albericus Gentilis, Paul Sarpi, Arminius; with all of whom exists some token of his having communicated, without enumerating many others, whom doubtless he saw, — Shakespeare, Spenser, Jonson, Beaumont, Massinger, two Herberts, Marlow, Chapman, and the rest. Since the constellation of great men who appeared in Greece in the time of Pericles, there was never any such society; yet their genius failed them to find out the best head in the universe. Our poet's mask was impenetrable. You cannot see the mountain near. It took a century to make it suspected; and not until two centuries had passed, after his death, did any criticism which we think adequate begin to appear. It was not possible to write the history of Shakespeare till now; for he is the father of German literature: it was on the introduction of Shakespeare into German, by Lessing, and the translation of his works by Wieland and Schlegel, that the rapid burst of German literature was most intimately connected. It was not until the nineteenth century, whose speculative genius is a sort of living Hamlet, that the tragedy of Hamlet could find such wondering readers. Now, literature, philosophy, and thought are Shakespearized. His mind is the horizon beyond which, at present, we do not see. Our ears are educated to music by his rhythm. Coleridge and Goethe are the only critics who have expressed our convictions with any adequate fidelity; but there is in all cultivated minds a silent appreciation of his superlative power and beauty, which, like Christianity, qualifies the period.

The Shakespeare Society have inquired in all directions, advertised the missing facts, offered money for any information that will lead to proof; and with what result? Beside some important illustration of the history of the English stage, to which I have adverted, they have gleaned a few facts touching the property, and dealings in regard to property, of the poet. It appears that, from year to year, he owned a larger share in the Blackfriars' Theatre: its wardrobe and other appurtenances were his: that he bought an estate in his native village, with his earnings, as writer and shareholder; that he lived in the best house in Stratford; was intrusted by his neighbors with their commissions in London, as of borrowing money, and the like; that he was a veritable farmer. About the time when he was writing Macbeth, he sues Philip Rogers, in the borough-court of Stratford, for thirty-five shillings, ten pence, for corn delivered to him at different times; and, in all respects, appears as a good husband, with no reputation for eccentricity or excess. He was a good-natured sort of man, an actor and shareholder in the theatre, not in any striking manner distinguished from other actors and managers. I admit the importance of this information. It was well worth the pains that have been taken to procure it.

But whatever scraps of information concerning his condition these researches may have rescued, they can shed no light upon that infinite invention which is the concealed magnet of his attraction for us. We are very clumsy writers of history. We tell the chronicle of parentage, birth, birthplace, schooling, schoolmates, earning of money, marriage, publication of books, celebrity, death; and when we have come to an end of this gossip, no ray of relation appears between it and the goddess-born; and it seems as if, had we dipped at random into the "Modern Plutarch," and read any other life there, it would have fitted the poems as well. It is the essence of poetry to spring, like the rainbow daughter of Wonder, from the invisible, to abolish the past, and refuse all history. Malone, Warburton, Dyce, and Collier have wasted their oil. The famed theatres, Covent Garden, Drury Lane, the Park, and Tremont, have vainly assisted. Betterton, Garrick, Kemble, Kean, and Macready dedicate their lives to this genius; him they crown, eludicate, obey, and express. The genius knows them not. The recitation begins; one golden word leaps out immortal from all this painted pedantry, and sweetly torments us with invitations to its own inaccessible homes. I remember, I went once to see the Hamlet of a famed performer, the pride of the English stage; and all I then heard, and all I now remember, of the tragedian, was that in which the tragedian had no part; simply, Hamlet's question to the ghost, —

> "What may this mean,
> That thou, dead corse, again in complete steel
> Revisit'st thus the glimpses of the moon?"

That imagination which dilates the closet he writes in to the world's dimension, crowds it with agents in rank and order, as quickly reduces the big reality to be the glimpses of the moon. These tricks of his magic spoil for us the illusions of the green-room. Can any biography shed light on the localities into which the Midsummer Night's Dream admits me? Did Shakespeare confide to any notary or parish recorder, sacristan, or surrogate, in Stratford, the genesis of that delicate creation? The forest of Arden, the nimble air of Scone Castle, the moonlight of Portia's villa, "the antres vast and desarts idle," of Othello's captivity, — where is the third cousin, or grand-nephew, the chancellor's file of accounts, or private letter, that has kept one word of those transcendent secrets? In fine, in this drama, as in all great works of art, — in the Cyclopæan architecture of Egypt and India; in the Phidian sculpture; the Gothic minsters; the Italian painting; the Ballads of Spain and Scotland, — the Genius draws up the ladder after him, when the creative age goes up to heaven, and gives way to a new age, which sees the works and asks in vain for a history.

Shakespeare is the only biographer of Shakespeare; and even he can tell nothing, except to the Shakespeare in us; that is, to our most apprehensive and sympathetic hour. He cannot step from off his tripod, and give us anecdotes of his inspirations. Read the antique documents extricated, analyzed, and compared by the assiduous Dyce and Collier; and now read one of those skyey sentences, — aerolites, — which seem to have fallen out of heaven, and which, not your experience, but the man within the breast, has accepted as words of fate; and tell me if they match; if the former account in any manner for the latter; or which gives the most historical insight into the man.

Hence, though our external history is so meagre, yet, with Shakespeare for biographer, instead of Aubrey and Rowe, we have really the information which is material, that which describes character and fortune, that which, if we were about to meet the man and deal with him, would most import us to know. We have his recorded convictions on those questions which knock for answer at every heart, — on life and death, on love, on wealth and poverty, on the prizes of life, and the ways whereby we come at them; on the characters of men, and the influences, occult and open, which affect their fortunes; and on those mysterious and demoniacal powers which defy our science, and which yet interweave their malice and their gift in our brightest hours. Who ever read the volume of the Sonnets, without finding that the poet had there revealed, under masks that are no masks to the intelligent, the lore of friendship and of love; the confusion of sentiments in the most susceptible, and, at the same time, the most intellectual of men? What trait of his private mind has he hidden in his dramas? One can discern, in his ample pictures of the gentleman and the king, what forms and humanities pleased him; his delight in troops of friends, in large hospitality, in cheerful giving. Let Timon, let Warwick, let Antonio the merchant, answer for his great heart. So far from Shakespeare's being the least known, he is the one person, in all modern history, known to us. What point of morals, of manners, of economy, of philosophy, of religion, of taste, of the conduct of life, has he not settled? What mystery has he not signified his knowledge of? What office, or function, or district of man's work, has he not remembered? What king has he not taught state, as Talma taught Napoleon? What maiden has not found him finer than her delicacy? What lover has he not outloved? What sage has he not outseen? What gentleman has he not instructed in the rudeness of his behavior?

Some able and appreciating critics think no criticism on Shakespeare valuable, that does not rest purely on the dramatic merit; that he is falsely judged as poet and philosopher. I think as highly as these critics of his dramatic merit, but still think it secondary. He was a full man, who liked to talk; a brain exhaling thoughts and images, which, seeking vent, found the drama next at hand. Had he been less, we should have had to consider how well he filled his place, how good a dramatist he was, — and he is the best in the world. But it turns out, that what he has to say is of that weight as to withdraw some attention from the vehicle; and he is like some saint whose history is to be rendered into all languages, into verse and prose, into songs and pictures, and cut up into proverbs; so that the occasion which gave the saint's meaning the form of a conversation, or of a prayer, or of a code of laws, is immaterial, compared with the universality of its application. So it fares with the wise Shakespeare and his book of life. He wrote the airs for all our modern music: he wrote the text of modern life; the text of manners: he drew the man of England and Europe; the father of the man in America: he drew the man, and described the day, and what is done in it; he read the hearts of men and women, their probity, and their second thought, and wiles; the wiles of innocence, and the transitions by which virtues and vices slide into their contraries: he could divide the mother's part from the father's part in the face of the child, or draw the fine demarcations of freedom and of fate: he knew the laws of repression which make the police of nature: and all the sweets and all the terrors of human lot lay in his mind as truly but as softly as the landscape lies on the eye. And the importance of this wisdom of life sinks the form, as of Drama or Epic, out of notice. 'T is like making a question concerning the paper on which a king's message is written.

Shakespeare is as much out of the category of eminent authors, as he is out of the crowd. He is inconceivably wise; the others, conceivably. A good reader can, in a sort, nestle into Plato's brain, and think from thence; but not into Shakespeare's. We are still out of doors. For executive faculty, for creation, Shakespeare is unique. No man can imagine it better. He was the furthest reach of subtlety compatible with an individual self, — the subtilest of authors, and only just within the possibility of authorship. With this wisdom of life, is the equal endowment of imaginative and of lyric power. He clothed the creatures of his legend with form and sentiments, as if they were people who had lived under his roof; and few real men have left such distinct characters as these fictions. And they spoke in language as sweet as it was fit. Yet his talents never seduced him into an ostentation, nor did he harp on one string. An omnipresent humanity co-ordinates all his faculties. Give a man of talents a story to tell, and his partiality will presently appear. He has certain observations, opinions, topics, which have some accidental prominence, and which he disposes all to exhibit. He crams this part, and starves that other part, consulting not the fitness of the thing, but his fitness and strength. But Shakespeare has no peculiarity, no importunate topic; but all is duly given; no veins, no curiosities: no cow-painter, no bird-fancier, no mannerist is he; he has no discoverable egotism: the great he tells greatly; the small, subordinately. He is wise without emphasis or assertion; he is strong, as nature is strong, who lifts the land into mountain slopes without effort, and by the same rule as she floats a bubble in the air, and likes as well to do the one as the other. This makes that equality of power in farce, tragedy, narrative, and love-songs; a merit so incessant, that each reader is incredulous of the perception of other readers.

This power of expression, or of transferring the inmost truth of things into music and verse, makes him the type of the poet, and has added a new problem to metaphysics. This is that which throws him into natural history, as a main production of the globe, and as announcing new eras and ameliorations. Things were mirrored in his poetry without loss or blur; he could paint the fine with precision, the great with compass; the tragic and the comic indifferently, and without any distortion or favor. He carried his powerful execution into minute details, to a hair point; finishes an eyelash or a dimple as firmly as he draws a mountain; and yet these, like nature's, will bear the scrutiny of the solar microscope.

In short, he is the chief example to prove that more or less of production, more or fewer pictures, is a thing indifferent. He had the power to make one picture. Daguerre learned how to let one flower etch its image on his plate of iodine; and then proceeds at leisure to etch a million. There are always objects; but there was never representation. Here is perfect representation, at last; and now let the world of figures sit for their portraits. No recipe can be given for the making of a Shakespeare; but the possibility of the translation of things into song is demonstrated.

His lyric power lies in the genius of the piece. The sonnets, though their excellence is lost in the splendor of the dramas, are as inimitable as they: and it is not a merit of lines, but a total merit of the piece; like the tone of voice of some incomparable person, so is this a speech of poetic beings, and any clause as unproducible now as a whole poem.

Though the speeches in the plays, and single lines, have a beauty which tempts the ear to pause on them for their euphuism, yet the sentence is so loaded with meaning, and so linked with its foregoers and followers, that the logician is satisfied. His means are as admirable as his ends; every subordinate invention, by which he helps himself to connect some irreconcilable opposites, is a poem too. He is not reduced to dismount and walk, because his horses are running off with him in some distant direction : he always rides.

The finest poetry was first experience : but the thought has suffered a transformation since it was an experience. Cultivated men often attain a good degree of skill in writing verses ; but it is easy to read, through their poems, their personal history : any one acquainted with parties can name every figure : this is Andrew, and that is Rachel. The sense thus remains prosaic. It is a caterpillar with wings, and not yet a butterfly. In the poet's mind, the fact has gone quite over into the new element of thought, and has lost all that is exuvial. This generosity abides with Shakespeare. We say, from the truth and closeness of his pictures, that he knows the lesson by heart. Yet there is not a trace of egotism.

One more royal trait properly belongs to the poet. I mean his cheerfulness, without which no man can be a poet, — for beauty is his aim. He loves virtue, not for its obligation, but for its grace : he delights in the world, in man, in woman, for the lovely light that sparkles from them. Beauty, the spirit of joy and hilarity, he sheds over the universe. Epicurus relates, that poetry hath such charms that a lover might forsake his mistress to partake of them. And the true bards have been noted for their firm and cheerful temper. Homer lies in sunshine ; Chaucer is glad and erect ; and Saadi says, "It was rumored abroad that I was penitent ; but what had I to do with repentance ?" Not less sovereign and cheerful, — much more sovereign and cheerful, is the tone of Shakespeare. His name suggests joy and emancipation to the heart of men. If he should appear in any company of human souls, who would not march in his troop ? He touches nothing that does not borrow health and longevity from his festal style.

And now, how stands the account of man with this bard and benefactor, when in solitude, shutting our ears to the reverberations of his fame, we seek to strike the balance ? Solitude has austere lessons ; it can teach us to spare both heroes and poets ; and it weighs Shakespeare also, and finds him to share the halfness and imperfection of humanity.

Shakespeare, Homer, Dante, Chaucer, saw the splendor of meaning that plays over the visible world ; knew that a tree had another use than for apples, and corn another than for meal, and the ball of the earth, than for tillage and roads : that these things bore a second and finer harvest to the mind, being emblems of its thoughts, and conveying in all their natural history a certain mute commentary on human life. Shakespeare employed them as colors to compose his picture. He rested in their beauty; and never took the step which seemed inevitable to such genius, namely, to explore the virtue which resides in these symbols, and imparts this power, — what is that which they themselves say? He converted the elements, which waited on his command, into entertainments. He was master of the revels to mankind. Is it not as if one should have, through majestic powers of science, the comets given into his hand, or the planets and their moons, and should draw them from their orbits to glare with the municipal fireworks on a holiday night, and advertise in all towns, "very superior pyrotechny this evening!" Are the agents of nature, and the power to understand them, worth no more than a street serenade, or the breath of a cigar? One remembers again the trumpet-text in the Koran, — "The heavens and the earth, and all that is between them, think ye we have created them in jest?" As long as the question is of talent and mental power, the world of men has not his equal to show. But when the question is to life, and its materials, and its auxiliaries, how does he profit me? What does it signify? It is but a Twelfth Night, or Midsummer Night's Dream, or a Winter Evening's Tale: what signifies another picture more or less? The Egyptian verdict of the Shakespeare Societies comes to mind, that he was a jovial actor and manager. I cannot marry this fact to his verse. Other admirable men have led lives in some sort of keeping with their thought; but this man, in wide contrast. Had he been less, had he reached only the common measure of great authors, of Bacon, Milton, Tasso, Cervantes, we might leave the fact in the twilight of human fate: but, that this man of men, he who gave to the science of mind a new and larger subject than had ever existed, and planted the standard of humanity some furlongs forward into Chaos, — that he should not be wise for himself, — it must even go into the world's history, that the best poet led an obscure and profane life, using his genius for the public amusement.

Well, other men, priest and prophet, Israelite, German, and Swede, beheld the same objects: they also saw through them that which was contained. And to what purpose? The beauty straightway vanished; they read commandments, all-excluding mountainous duty; an obligation, a sadness, as of piled mountains, fell on them, and life became ghastly, joyless, a pilgrim's progress, a probation, beleaguered round with doleful histories of Adam's fall and curse, behind us; with doomsdays and purgatorial and penal fires before us; and the heart of the seer and the heart of the listener sank in them.

It must be conceded that these are half-views of half-men. The world still wants its poet-priest, a reconciler, who shall not trifle with Shakespeare the player, nor shall grope in graves with Swedenborg the mourner; but who shall see, speak, and act, with equal inspiration. For knowledge will brighten the sunshine; right is more beautiful than private affection; and love is compatible with universal wisdom.

VI.

NAPOLEON; OR, THE MAN OF THE WORLD.

NAPOLEON; OR, THE MAN OF THE WORLD.

AMONG the eminent persons of the nineteenth century, Bonaparte is far the best known, and the most powerful; and owes his predominance to the fidelity with which he expresses the tone of thought and belief, the aims of the masses of active and cultivated men. It is Swedenborg's theory, that every organ is made up of homogeneous particles; or, as it is sometimes expressed, every whole is made of similars; that is, the lungs are composed of infinitely small lungs; the liver, of infinitely small livers; the kidney, of little kidneys, &c. Following this analogy, if any man is found to carry with him the power and affections of vast numbers, if Napoleon is France, if Napoleon is Europe, it is because the people whom he sways are little Napoleons.

In our society, there is a standing antagonism between the conservative and the democratic classes; between those who have made their fortunes, and the young and the poor who have fortunes to make; between the interests of dead labor, — that is, the labor of hands long ago still in the grave, which labor is now entombed in money stocks, or in land and buildings owned by idle capitalists, — and the interests of living labor, which seeks to possess itself of land, and buildings, and money stocks. The first class is timid, selfish, illiberal, hating innovation, and continually losing numbers by death. The second class is selfish also, encroaching, bold, self-relying, always outnumbering the other, and recruiting its numbers every hour by births. It desires to keep open every avenue to the competition of all, and to multiply avenues; — the class of business men in America, in England, in France, and throughout Europe; the class of industry and skill. Napoleon is its representative. The instinct of active, brave, able men, throughout the middle class everywhere, has pointed out Napoleon as the incarnate Democrat. He had their virtues and their vices; above all, he had their spirit or aim. That tendency is material, pointing at a sensual success, and employing the richest and most various means to that end; conversant with mechanical powers, highly intellectual, widely and accurately learned and skilful, but subordinating all intellectual and spiritual forces into means to a material success. To be the rich man, is the end. "God has granted," says the Koran, "to every people a prophet in its own tongue." Paris, and London, and New York, the spirit of commerce, of money, and material power, were also to have their prophet; and Bonaparte was qualified and sent.

Every one of the million readers of anecdotes, or memoirs, or lives of Napoleon, delights in the page, because he studies in it his own history. Napoleon is thoroughly modern, and, at the highest point of his fortunes, has the very spirit of the newspapers. He is no saint, — to use his own word, "no capuchin," and he is no hero, in the high sense. The man in the street finds in him the qualities and powers of other men in the street. He finds him, like himself, by birth a citizen, who, by very intelligible merits, arrived at such a commanding position, that he could indulge all those tastes which the common man possesses, but is obliged to conceal and deny: good society, good books, fast travelling, dress, dinners, servants without number, personal weight, the execution of his ideas, the standing in the attitude of a benefactor to all persons about him, the refined enjoyments of pictures, statues, music, palaces, and conventional honors, — precisely what is agreeable to the heart of every man in the nineteenth century, — this powerful man possessed.

It is true that a man of Napoleon's truth of adaptation to the mind of the masses around him, becomes not merely representative, but actually a monopolizer and usurper of other minds. Thus Mirabeau plagiarized every good thought, every good word, that was spoken in France. Dumont relates, that he sat in the gallery of the Convention, and heard Mirabeau make a speech. It struck Dumont that he could fit it with a peroration, which he wrote in pencil immediately, and showed it to Lord Elgin, who sat by him. Lord Elgin approved it, and Dumont, in the evening, showed it to Mirabeau. Mirabeau read it, pronounced it admirable, and declared he would incorporate it into his harangue to-morrow, to the Assembly. "It is impossible," said Dumont, "as, unfortunately, I have shown it to Lord Elgin." "If you have shown it to Lord Elgin, and to fifty persons beside, I shall still speak it to-morrow": and he did speak it, with much effect, at the next day's session. For Mirabeau, with his overpowering personality, felt that these things, which his presence inspired, were as much his own as if he had said them, and that his adoption of them gave them their weight. Much more absolute and centralizing was the successor to Mirabeau's popularity, and to much more than his predominance in France. Indeed, a man of Napoleon's stamp almost ceases to have a private speech and opinion. He is so largely receptive, and is so placed, that he comes to be a bureau for all the intelligence, wit, and power, of the age and country. He gains the battle; he makes the code; he makes the system of weights and measures; he levels the Alps; he builds the road. All distinguished engineers, savans, statists, report to him: so, likewise, do all good heads in every kind: he adopts the best measures, sets his stamp on them, and not these alone, but on every happy and memorable expression. Every sentence spoken by Napoleon, and every line of his writing, deserves reading, as it is the sense of France.

Bonaparte was the idol of common men, because he had in transcendent degree the qualities and powers of common men. There is a certain satisfaction in coming down to the lowest ground of politics, for we get rid of cant and hypocrisy. Bonaparte wrought, in common with that great class he represented, for power and wealth, — but Bonaparte, specially, without any scruple as to the means. All the sentiments which embarrass men's pursuit of these objects, he set aside. The sentiments were for women and children. Fontanes, in 1804, expressed Napoleon's own sense, when, in behalf of the Senate, he addressed him, — "Sire, the desire of perfection is the worst disease that ever afflicted the human mind." The advocates of liberty, and of progress, are "ideologists"; — a word of contempt often in his mouth; — "Necker is an ideologist": "Lafayette is an ideologist."

An Italian proverb, too well known, declares that, "if you would succeed, you must not be too good." It is an advantage, within certain limits, to have renounced the dominion of the sentiments of piety, gratitude, and generosity; since, what was an impassable bar to us, and still is to others, becomes a convenient weapon for our purposes; just as the river which was a formidable barrier, winter transforms into the smoothest of roads.

Napoleon renounced, once for all, sentiments and affections, and would help himself with his hands and his head. With him is no miracle, and no magic. He is a worker in brass, in iron, in wood, in earth, in roads, in buildings, in money, and in troops, and a very consistent and wise master-workman. He is never weak and literary, but acts with the solidity and the precision of natural agents. He has not lost his native sense and sympathy with things. Men give way before such a man, as before natural events. To be sure, there are men enough who are immersed in things, as farmers, smiths, sailors, and mechanics generally; and we know how real and solid such men appear in the presence of scholars and grammarians: but these men ordinarily lack the power of arrangement, and are like hands without a head. But Bonaparte superadded to this mineral and animal force, insight and generalization, so that men saw in him combined the natural and the intellectual power, as if the sea and land had taken flesh and begun to cipher. Therefore the land and sea seem to presuppose him. He came unto his own and they received him. This ciphering operative knows what he is working with, and what is the product. He knew the properties of gold and iron, of wheels and ships, of troops and diplomatists, and required that each should do after its kind.

The art of war was the game in which he exerted his arithmetic. It consisted, according to him, in having always more forces than the enemy, on the point where the enemy is attacked, or where he attacks; and his whole talent is strained by endless manœuvre and evolution, to march always on the enemy at an angle, and destroy his forces in detail. It is obvious that a very small force, skilfully and rapidly manœuvring, so as always to bring two men against one at the point of engagement, will be an overmatch for a much larger body of men.

The times, his constitution, and his early circumstances, combined to develop this pattern democrat. He had the virtues of his class, and the conditions for their activity. That common sense, which no sooner respects any end, than it finds the means to effect it; the delight in the use of means; in the choice, simplification, and combining of means; the directness and thoroughness of his work; the prudence with which all was seen, and the energy with which all was done, make him the natural organ and head of what I may almost call, from its extent, the *modern* party.

Nature must have far the greatest share in every success, and so in his. Such a man was wanted, and such a man was born; a man of stone and iron, capable of sitting on horseback sixteen or seventeen hours, of going many days together without rest or food, except by snatches, and with the speed and spring of a tiger in action; a man not embarrassed by any scruples; compact, instant, selfish, prudent, and of a perception which did not suffer itself to be balked or misled by any pretences of others, or any superstition, or any heat or haste of his own. "My hand of iron," he said, "was not at the extremity of my arm; it was immediately connected with my head." He respected the power of nature and fortune, and ascribed it to his superiority, instead of valuing himself, like inferior men, on his opinionativeness, and waging war with nature. His favorite rhetoric lay in allusion to his star; and he pleased himself, as well as the people, when he styled himself the "Child of Destiny." "They charge me," he said, "with the commission of great crimes: men of my stamp do not commit crimes. Nothing has been more simple than my elevation: 't is in vain to ascribe it to intrigue or crime: it was owing to the peculiarity of the times, and to my reputation of having fought well against the enemies of my country. I have always marched with the opinion of great masses, and with events. Of what use, then, would crimes be to me?" Again he said, speaking of his son: "My son cannot replace me: I could not replace myself. I am the creature of circumstances."

He had a directness of action never before combined with so much comprehension. He is a realist terrific to all talkers, and confused truth-obscuring persons. He sees where the matter hinges, throws himself on the precise point of resistance, and slights all other considerations. He is strong in the right manner, namely, by insight. He never blundered into victory, but won his battles in his head, before he won them on the field. His principal means are in himself. He asks counsel of no other. In 1796, he writes to the Directory: "I have conducted the campaign without consulting any one. I should have done no good, if I had been under the necessity of conforming to the notions of another person. I have gained some advantages over superior forces, and when totally destitute of everything, because, in the persuasion that your confidence was reposed in me, my actions were as prompt as my thoughts."

History is full, down to this day, of the imbecility of kings and governors. They are a class of persons much to be pitied, for they know not what they should do. The weavers strike for bread; and the king and his ministers, not knowing what to do, meet them with bayonets. But Napoleon understood his business. Here was a man who, in each moment and emergency, knew what to do next. It is an immense comfort and refreshment to the spirits, not only of kings, but of citizens. Few men have any next; they live from hand to mouth, without plan, and are ever at the end of their line, and, after each action, wait for an impulse from abroad. Napoleon had been the first man of the world, if his ends had been purely public. As he is, he inspires confidence and vigor by the extraordinary unity of his action. He is firm, sure, self-denying, self-postponing, sacrificing everything to his aim, — money, troops, generals, and his own safety also, to his aim; not misled, like common adventurers, by the splendor of his own means. "Incidents ought not to govern policy," he said, "but policy, incidents." "To be hurried away by every event, is to have no political system at all." His victories were only so many doors, and he never for a moment lost sight of his way onward, in the dazzle and uproar of the present circumstance. He knew what to do, and he flew to his mark. He would shorten a straight line to come at his object. Horrible anecdotes may, no doubt, be collected from his history, of the price at which he bought his successes; but he must not therefore be set down as cruel; but only as one who knew no impediment to his will; not bloodthirsty, not cruel, — but woe to what thing or person stood in his way! Not bloodthirsty, but not sparing of blood, — and pitiless. He saw only the object: the obstacle must give way. "Sire, General Clarke cannot combine with General Junot, for the dreadful fire of the Austrian battery." — "Let him carry the battery." — "Sire, every regiment that approaches the heavy artillery is sacrificed: Sire, what orders?" — "Forward, forward!" Seruzier, a colonel of artillery, gives, in his *Military Memoirs*, the following sketch of a scene after the battle of Austerlitz: "At the moment in which the Russian army was making its retreat, painfully, but in good order, on the ice of the lake, the Emperor Napoleon came riding at full speed toward the artillery. 'You are losing time,' he cried;

'fire upon those masses; they must be ingulfed: fire upon the ice!' The order remained unexecuted for ten minutes. In vain several officers and myself were placed on the slope of a hill to produce the effect: their balls and mine rolled upon the ice, without breaking it up. Seeing that, I tried a simple method of elevating light howitzers. The almost perpendicular fall of the heavy projectiles produced the desired effect. My method was immediately followed by the adjoining batteries, and in less than no time we buried" some* "thousands of Russians and Austrians under the waters of the lake."

In the plenitude of his resources, every obstacle seemed to vanish. "There shall be no Alps," he said; and he built his perfect roads, climbing by graded galleries their steepest precipices, until Italy was as open to Paris as any town in France. He laid his bones to, and wrought for his crown. Having decided what was to be done, he did that with might and main. He put out all his strength. He risked everything, and spared nothing, neither ammunition, nor money, nor troops, nor generals, nor himself.

We like to see everything do its office after its kind, whether it be a milch-cow or a rattle-snake; and, if fighting be the best mode of adjusting national differences (as large majorities of men seem to agree), certainly Bonaparte was right in making it thorough. "The grand principle of war," he said, "was, that an army ought always to be ready, by day and by night, and at all hours, to make all the resistance it is capable of making." He never economized his ammunition, but, on a hostile position, rained a torrent of iron, — shells, balls, grapeshot, — to annihilate all defence. On any point of resistance, he concentrated squadron on squadron in overwhelming numbers, until it was swept out of existence. To a regiment of horse-chasseurs at Lobenstein, two days before the battle of Jena, Napoleon said: "My lads, you must not fear death; when soldiers brave death, they drive him into the enemy's ranks." In the fury of assault, he no more spared himself. He went to the edge of his possibility. It is plain that in Italy he did what he could, and all that he could. He came, several times, within an inch of ruin; and his own person was all but lost. He was flung into the marsh at Arcola. The Austrians were between him and his troops, in the *mêlée*, and he

* As I quote at second-hand, and cannot procure Seruzier, I dare not adopt the high figure I find.

was brought off with desperate efforts. At Lonato, and at other places, he was on the point of being taken prisoner. He fought sixty battles. He had never enough. Each victory was a new weapon. "My power would fall, were I not to support it by new achievements. Conquest has made me what I am, and conquest must maintain me." He felt, with every wise man, that as much life is needed for conservation, as for creation. We are always in peril, always in a bad plight, just on the edge of destruction, and only to be saved by invention and courage.

This vigor was guarded and tempered by the coldest prudence and punctuality. A thunderbolt in the attack, he was found invulnerable in his intrenchments. His very attack was never the inspiration of courage, but the result of calculation. His idea of the best defence consists in being still the attacking party. "My ambition," he says, "was great, but was of a cold nature." In one of his conversations with Las Casas, he remarked, "As to moral courage, I have rarely met with the two-o'clock-in-the-morning kind: I mean unprepared courage, that which is necessary on an unexpected occasion; and which, in spite of the most unforeseen events, leaves full freedom of judgment and decision": and he did not hesitate to declare that he was himself eminently endowed with this "two-o'clock-in-the-morning courage, and that he had met with few persons equal to himself in this respect."

Everything depended on the nicety of his combinations, and the stars were not more punctual than his arithmetic. His personal attention descended to the smallest particulars. "At Montebello, I ordered Kellermann to attack with eight hundred horse, and with these he separated the six thousand Hungarian grenadiers, before the very eyes of the Austrian cavalry. This cavalry was half a league off, and required a quarter of an hour to arrive on the field of action; and I have observed, that it is always these quarters of an hour that decide the fate of a battle." "Before he fought a battle, Bonaparte thought little about what he should do in case of success, but a great deal about what he should do in case of a reverse of fortune." The same prudence and good sense mark all his behavior. His instructions to his secretary at the Tuileries are worth remembering. "During the night, enter my chamber as seldom as possible. Do not awake me when you have any good news to communicate; with that there is no hurry. But when you bring bad news, rouse me instantly, for then there is not a moment to be lost." It was a whimsical economy of the same kind which dictated his practice, when general in Italy, in regard to his burdensome correspondence. He directed Bourrienne to leave all letters unopened for three weeks, and then observed with satisfaction how large a part of the correspondence had thus disposed of itself, and no longer required an answer. His achievement of business was immense, and enlarges the known powers of man. There have been many working kings, from Ulysses to William of Orange, but none who accomplished a tithe of this man's performance.

To these gifts of nature, Napoleon added the advantage of having been born to a private and humble fortune. In his later days, he had the weakness of wishing to add to his crowns and badges the prescription of aristocracy; but he knew his debt to his austere education, and made no secret of his contempt for the born kings, and for "the hereditary asses," as he coarsely styled the Bourbons. He said that, "in their exile, they have learned nothing and forgot nothing." Bonaparte had passed through all the degrees of military service, but also was citizen before he was emperor, and so has the key to citizenship. His remarks and estimates discover the information and justness of measurement of the middle class. Those who had to deal with him, found that he was not to be imposed upon, but could cipher as well as another man. This appears in all parts of his Memoirs, dictated at St. Helena. When the expenses of the empress, of his household, of his palaces, had accumulated great debts, Napoleon examined the bills of the creditors himself, detected overcharges and errors, and reduced the claims by considerable sums.

His grand weapon, namely, the millions whom he directed, he owed to the representative character which clothed him. He interests us as he stands for France and for Europe; and he exists as captain and king, only as far as the revolution, or the interest of the industrious masses, found an organ and a leader in him. In the social interests, he knew the meaning and value of labor, and threw himself naturally on that side. I like an incident mentioned by one of his biographers at St. Helena. "When walking with Mrs. Balcombe, some servants, carrying heavy boxes, passed by on the road, and Mrs. Balcombe desired them, in rather an angry tone, to keep back. Napoleon interfered, saying, 'Respect the burden, Madam.'" In the time of the empire, he directed attention to the improvement and embellishment of the markets of the capital. "The market-place," he said, "is the Louvre of the common people." The principal works that have survived him are his magnificent roads. He filled the troops with his spirit, and a sort of freedom and companionship grew up between him and them, which the forms of his court never permitted between the officers and himself. They performed, under his eye, that which no others could do. The best document of his relation to his troops is the order of the day on the morning of the battle of Austerlitz, in which Napoleon promises the troops that he will keep his person out of reach of fire. This declaration, which is the reverse of that ordinarily made by generals and sovereigns on the eve of a battle, sufficiently explains the devotion of the army to their leader.

But though there is in particulars this identity between Napoleon and the mass of the people, his real strength lay in their conviction that he was their representative in his genius and aims, not only when he courted, but when he controlled, and even when he decimated them by his conscriptions. He knew, as well as any Jacobin in France, how to philosophize on liberty and equality; and, when allusion was made to the precious blood of centuries, which was spilled by the killing of the Duc d'Enghien, he suggested, "Neither is my blood ditch-water." The people felt that no longer the throne was occupied, and the land sucked of its nourishment, by a small class of legitimates, secluded from all community with the children of the soil, and holding the ideas and superstitions of a long-forgotten state of society. Instead of that vampire, a man of themselves held, in the Tuileries, knowledge and ideas like their own, opening, of course, to them and their children, all places of power and trust. The day of sleepy, selfish policy, ever narrowing the means and opportunities of young men, was ended, and a day of expansion and demand was come. A market for all the powers and productions of man was opened; brilliant prizes glittered in the eyes of youth and talent. The old, iron-bound, feudal France was changed into a young Ohio or New York; and those who smarted under the immediate rigors of the new monarch, pardoned them, as the necessary severities of the military system which had driven out the oppressor. And even when the majority of the people had begun to ask, whether they had really gained anything under the exhausting levies of men and money of the new master, — the whole talent of the county, in every rank and kindred, took his part, and defended him as its natural patron. In 1814, when advised to rely on the higher classes, Napoleon said to those around him: "Gentlemen, in the situation in which I stand, my only nobility is the rabble of the Faubourgs."

Napoleon met this natural expectation. The necessity of his position required a hospitality to every sort of talent, and its appointment to trusts; and his feeling went along with this policy. Like every superior person, he undoubtedly felt a desire for men and compeers, and a wish to measure his power with other masters, and an impatience of fools and underlings. In Italy, he sought for men, and found none. "Good God!" he said, "how rare men are! There are eighteen millions in Italy, and I have with difficulty found two, — Dandolo and Melzi." In later years, with larger experience, his respect for mankind was not increased. In a moment of bitterness, he said, to one of his oldest friends: "Men deserve the contempt with which they inspire me. I have only to put some gold lace on the coat of my virtuous republicans, and they immediately become just what I wish them." This impatience at levity was, however, an oblique tribute of respect to those able persons who commanded his regard, not only when he found them friends and coadjutors, but also when they resisted his will. He could not confound Fox and Pitt, Carnot, Lafayette, and Bernadotte, with the danglers of his court; and, in spite of the detraction which his systematic egotism dictated toward the great captains who conquered with and for him, ample acknowledgments are made by him to Lannes, Duroc, Kleber, Dessaix, Massena, Murat, Ney, and Augereau. If he felt himself their patron, and the founder of their fortunes, as when he said, "I made my generals out of mud," he could not hide his satisfaction in receiving from them a seconding and support commensurate with the grandeur of his enterprise. In the Russian campaign, he was so much impressed by the courage and resources of Marshal Ney, that he said, "I have two hundred millions in my coffers, and I would give them all for Ney." The characters which he has drawn of several of his marshals are discriminating, and, though they did not content the insatiable vanity of French officers, are, no doubt, substantially just. And, in fact, every species of merit was sought and advanced under his government. "I know," he said, "the depth and draught of water of every one of my generals." Natural power was sure to be well received at his court. Seventeen men, in his time, were raised from common soldiers to the rank of king, marshal, duke, or general; and the crosses of his Legion of Honor were given to personal valor, and not to family connection. "When soldiers have been baptized in the fire of a battle-field, they have all one rank in my eyes."

When a natural king becomes a titular king, everybody is pleased and satisfied. The Revolution entitled the strong populace of the Faubourg St. Antoine, and every horse-boy and powder-monkey in the army, to look on Napoleon, as flesh of his flesh, and the creature of *his* party; but there is something in the success of grand talent which enlists a universal sympathy. For, in the prevalence of sense and spirit over stupidity and malversation, all reasonable men have an interest; and, as intellectual beings, we feel the air purified by the electric shock, when material force is overthrown by intellectual energies. As soon as we are removed out of the reach of local and accidental partialities, man feels that Napoleon fights for him; these are honest victories; this strong steam-engine does our work. Whatever appeals to the imagination, by transcending the ordinary limits of human ability, wonderfully encourages and liberates us. This capacious head, revolving and disposing sovereignly trains of affairs, and animating such multitudes of agents; this eye, which looked through Europe; this prompt invention; this inexhaustible resource; — what events! what romantic pictures! what strange situations! — when spying the Alps, by a sunset in the Sicilian sea; drawing up his army for battle, in sight of the Pyramids, and saying to his troops, "From the tops of those pyramids, forty centuries look down on you"; fording the Red Sea; wading in the gulf of the Isthmus of Suez. On the shore of Ptolemais, gigantic projects agitated him. "Had Acre fallen, I should have changed the face of the world." His army, on the night of the battle of Austerlitz, which was the anniversary of his inauguration as Emperor, presented him with a bouquet of forty standards taken in the fight. Perhaps it is a little puerile, the pleasure he took in making these contrasts glaring; as, when he pleased himself with making kings wait in his antechambers, at Tilsit, at Paris, and at Erfurt.

We cannot, in the universal imbecility, indecision, and indolence of men, sufficiently congratulate ourselves on this strong and ready actor, who took occasion by the beard, and showed us how much may be accomplished by the mere force of such virtues as all men possess in less degrees; namely, by punctuality, by personal attention, by courage, and thoroughness. "The Austrians," he said, "do not know the value of time." I should cite him, in his earlier years, as a model of prudence. His power does not consist in any wild or extravagant force; in any enthusiasm, like Mahomet's; or singular power of persuasion; but in the exercise of common sense on each emergency, instead of abiding by rules and customs. The lesson he teaches is that which vigor always teaches, — that there is always room for it. To what heaps of cowardly doubts is not that man's life an answer. When he appeared, it was the belief of all military men that there could be nothing new in war; as it is the belief of men to-day, that nothing new can be undertaken in politics, or in church, or in letters, or in trade, or in farming, or in our social manners and customs; and as it is, at all times, the belief of society that the world is used up. But Bonaparte knew better than society; and, moreover, knew that he knew better. I think all men know better than they do; know that the institutions we so volubly commend are go-carts and bawbles; but they dare not trust their presentiments. Bonaparte relied on his own sense, and did not care a bean for other people's. The world treated his novelties just as it treats everybody's novelties, — made infinite objection; mustered all the impediments: but he snapped his finger at their objections. "What creates great difficulty," he remarks, "in the profession of the land-commander, is the necessity of feeding so many men and animals. If he allows himself to be guided by the commissaries, he will never stir, and all his expeditions will fail." An example of his common sense is what he says of the passage of the Alps in winter, which all writers, one repeating after the other, had described as impracticable. "The winter," says Napoleon, "is not the most unfavorable season for the passage of lofty mountains. The snow is then firm, the weather settled, and there is nothing to fear from avalanches, the real and only danger to be apprehended in the Alps. On those high mountains, there are often very fine days in December, of a dry cold, with extreme calmness in the air." Read his account, too, of the way in which battles are gained. "In all battles, a moment occurs, when the bravest troops, after having made the greatest efforts, feel inclined to run. That terror proceeds from a want of confidence in their own courage; and it only requires a slight opportunity, a pretence, to restore confidence to them. The art is to give rise to the opportunity, and to invent the pretence. At Arcola, I won the battle with twenty-five horsemen. I seized that moment of lassitude, gave every man a trumpet, and gained the day with this handful. You see that two armies are two bodies which meet, and endeavor to frighten each other: a moment of panic occurs, and that moment must be turned to advantage. When a man has been present in many actions, he distinguishes that moment without difficulty: it is as easy as casting up an addition."

This deputy of the nineteenth century added to his gifts a capacity for speculation on general topics. He delighted in running through the range of practical, of literary, and of abstract questions. His opinion is always original, and to the purpose. On the voyage to Egypt, he liked, after dinner, to fix on three or four persons to support a proposition, and as many to oppose it. He gave a subject, and the discussions turned on questions of religion, the different kinds of government, and the art of war. One day, he asked, whether the planets were inhabited? On another, what was the age of the world? Then he proposed to consider the probability of the destruction of the globe, either by water or by fire: at another time, the truth or fallacy of presentiments, and the interpretation of dreams. He was very fond of talking of religion. In 1806, he conversed with Fournier, Bishop of Montpellier, on matters of theology. There were two points on which they could not agree, viz., that of hell, and that of salvation out of the pale of the church. The Emperor told Josephine, that he disputed like a devil on these two points, on which the Bishop was inexorable. To the philosophers he readily yielded all that was proved against religion as the work of men and time; but he would not hear of materialism. One fine night, on deck, amid a clatter of materialism, Bonaparte pointed to the stars, and said, "You may talk as long as you please, gentlemen, but who made all that?" He delighted in the conversation of men of science, particularly of Monge and Berthollet; but the men of letters he slighted; "they were manufacturers of phrases." Of medicine, too, he was fond of talking, and with those of its practitioners whom he most esteemed, — with Corvisart at Paris, and with Antonomarchi at St. Helena. "Believe me," he said to the last, "we had better leave off all these remedies: life is a fortress which neither you nor I know anything about. Why throw obstacles in the way of its defence? Its own means are superior to all the apparatus of your laboratories. Corvisart candidly agreed with me, that all your filthy mixtures are good for nothing. Medicine is a collection of uncertain prescriptions, the results of which, taken collectively, are more fatal than useful to mankind. Water, air, and cleanliness are the chief articles in my pharmacopeia."

His memoirs, dictated to Count Montholon and General Gourgaud, at St. Helena, have great value, after all the deduction that, it seems, is to be made from them, on account of his known disingenuousness. He has the good-nature of strength and conscious superiority. I admire his simple, clear narrative of his battles; good as Cæsar's; his good-natured and sufficiently respectful account of Marshal Wurmser and his other antagonists, and his own equality as a writer to his varying subject. The most agreeable portion is the Campaign in Egypt.

He had hours of thought and wisdom. In intervals of leisure, either in the camp or the palace, Napoleon appears as a man of genius, directing on abstract questions the native appetite for truth, and the impatience of words, he was wont to show in war. He could enjoy every play of invention, a romance, a *bon mot*, as well as a stratagem in a campaign. He delighted to fascinate Josephine and her ladies, in a dim-lighted apartment, by the terrors of a fiction, to which his voice and dramatic power lent every addition.

I call Napoleon the agent or attorney of the middle class of modern society; of the throng who fill the markets, shops, counting-houses, manufactories, ships, of the modern world, aiming to be rich. He was the agitator, the destroyer of prescription, the internal improver, the liberal, the radical, the inventor of means, the opener of doors and markets, the subverter of monopoly and abuse. Of course, the rich and aristocratic did not like him. England, the centre of capital, and Rome and Austria, centres of tradition and genealogy, opposed him. The consternation of the dull and conservative classes, the terror of the foolish old men and old women of the Roman conclave, — who in their despair took hold of anything, and would cling to red-hot iron, — the vain attempts of statists to amuse and deceive him, of the Emperor of Austria to bribe him; and the instinct of the young, ardent, and active men, everywhere, which pointed him out as the giant of the middle class, make his history bright and commanding. He had the virtues of the masses of his constituents: he had also their vices. I am sorry that the brilliant picture has its reverse.

But that is the fatal quality which we discover in our pursuit of wealth, that it is treacherous, and is bought by the breaking or weakening of the sentiments; and it is inevitable that we should find the same fact in the history of this champion, who proposed to himself simply a brilliant career, without any stipulation or scruple concerning the means.

Bonaparte was singularly destitute of generous sentiments The highest-placed individual in the most cultivated age and population of the world, — he has not the merit of common truth and honesty. He is unjust to his generals; egotistic, and monopolizing; meanly stealing the credit of their great actions from Kellermann, from Bernadotte; intriguing to involve his faithful Junot in hopeless bankruptcy, in order to drive him to a distance from Paris, because the familiarity of his manners offends the new pride of his throne. He is a boundless liar. The official paper, his *Moniteurs*, and all his bulletins, are proverbs for saying what he wished to be believed; and worse, — he sat, in his premature old age, in his lonely island, coldly falsifying facts, and dates, and characters, and giving to history a theatrical *éclat*. Like all Frenchmen, he has a passion for stage effect. Every action that breathes of generosity is poisoned by this calculation. His star, his love of glory, his doctrine of the immortality of the soul, are all French. "I must dazzle and astonish. If I were to give the liberty of the press, my power could not last three days." To make a great noise is his favorite design. "A great reputation is a great noise: the more there is made, the farther off it is heard. Laws, institutions, monuments, nations, all fall; but the noise continues, and resounds in after ages." His doctrine of immortality is simply fame. His theory of influence is not flattering. "There are two levers for moving men, — interest and fear. Love is a silly infatuation, depend upon it. Friendship is but a name. I love nobody. I do not even love my brothers: perhaps Joseph, a little, from habit, and because he is my elder; and Duroc, I love him too; but why? — because his character pleases me: he is stern and resolute, and, I believe, the fellow never shed a tear. For my part, I know very well that I have no true friends. As long as I continue to be what I am, I may have as many pretended friends as I please. Leave sensibility to women: but men should be firm in heart and purpose, or they should have nothing to do with war and government." He was thoroughly unscrupulous. He would steal, slander, assassinate, drown, and poison, as his interest dictated.

He had no generosity; but mere vulgar hatred: he was intensely selfish: he was perfidious: he cheated at cards: he was a prodigious gossip; and opened letters; and delighted in his infamous police; and rubbed his hands with joy when he had intercepted some morsel of intelligence concerning the men and women about him, boasting that "he knew everything"; and interfered with the cutting the dresses of the women; and listened after the hurrahs and the compliments of the street, incognito. His manners were coarse. He treated women with low familiarity. He had the habit of pulling their ears, and pinching their cheeks, when he was in good-humor, and of pulling the ears and whiskers of men, and of striking and horse-play with them, to his last days. It does not appear that he listened at keyholes, or, at least, that he was caught at it. In short, when you have penetrated through all the circles of power and splendor, you were not dealing with a gentleman, at last; but with an impostor and a rogue and he fully deserves the epithet of *Jupiter Scapin,* or a sort of Scamp Jupiter.

In describing the two parties into which modern society divides itself, — the democrat and the conservative, — I said, Bonaparte represents the Democrat, or the party of men of business, against the stationary or conservative party. I omitted then to say, what is material to the statement, namely, that these two parties differ only as young and old. The democrat is a young conservative; the conservative is an old democrat. The aristocrat is the democrat ripe, and gone to seed, — because both parties stand on the one ground of the supreme value of property, which one endeavors to get, and the other to keep. Bonaparte may be said to represent the whole history of this party, its youth and its age; yes, and with poetic justice, its fate, in his own. The counter-revolution, the counter-party, still waits for its organ and representative, in a lover and a man of truly public and universal aims.

Here was an experiment, under the most favorable conditions, of the powers of intellect without conscience. Never was such a leader so endowed, and so weaponed; never leader found such aids and followers. And what was the result of this vast talent and power, of these immense armies, burned cities, squandered treasures, immolated millions of men, of this demoralized Europe? It came to no result. All passed away, like the smoke of his artillery, and left no trace.

He left France smaller, poorer, feebler, than he found it; and the whole contest for freedom was to be begun again. The attempt was, in principle, suicidal. France served him with life, and limb, and estate, as long as it could identify its interest with him; but when men saw that after victory was another war; after the destruction of armies, new conscriptions; and they who had toiled so desperately were never nearer to the reward, — they could not spend what they had earned, nor repose on their down-beds, nor strut in their chateaux, — they deserted him. Men found that his absorbing egotism was deadly to all other men. It resembled the torpedo, which inflicts a succession of shocks on any one who takes hold of it, producing spasms which contract the muscles of the hand, so that the man cannot open his fingers; and the animal inflicts new and more violent shocks, until he paralyzes and kills his victim. So, this exorbitant egotist narrowed, impoverished, and absorbed the power and existence of those who served him; and the universal cry of France, and of Europe, in 1814, was, "enough of him": "assez de Bonaparte."

It was not Bonaparte's fault. He did all that in him lay, to live and thrive without moral principle. It was the nature of things, the eternal law of the man and the world, which balked and ruined him; and the result, in a million experiments would be the same. Every experiment, by multitudes or by individuals, that has a sensual and selfish aim, will fail. The pacific Fourier will be as inefficient as the pernicious Napoleon. As long as our civilization is essentially one of property, of fences, of exclusiveness, it will be mocked by delusions. Our riches will leave us sick; there will be bitterness in our laughter; and our wine will burn our mouth. Only that good profits, which we can taste with all doors open, and which serves all men.

VII.

GOETHE; OR, THE WRITER.

GOETHE; OR, THE WRITER.

I FIND a provision, in the constitution of the world, for the writer or secretary, who is to report the doings of the miraculous spirit of life that everywhere throbs and works. His office is a reception of the facts into the mind, and then a selection of the eminent and characteristic experiences.

Nature will be reported. All things are engaged in writing their history. The planet, the pebble, goes attended by its shadow. The rolling rock leaves its scratches on the mountain; the river, its channel in the soil; the animal, its bones in the stratum; the fern and leaf, their modest epitaph in the coal. The falling drop makes its sculpture in the sand or the stone. Not a foot steps into the snow, or along the ground, but prints, in characters more or less lasting, a map of its march. Every act of the man inscribes itself in the memories of his fellows, and in his own manners and face. The air is full of sounds; the sky, of tokens; the ground is all memoranda and signatures; and every object covered over with hints, which speak to the intelligent.

In nature, this self-registration is incessant, and the narrative is the print of the seal. It neither exceeds nor comes short of the fact. But nature strives upward; and, in man, the report is something more than print of the seal. It is a new and finer form of the original. The record is alive, as that which it recorded is alive. In man, the memory is a kind of looking-glass, which, having received the images of surrounding objects, is touched with life, and disposes them in a new order. The facts which transpired do not lie in it inert; but some subside, and others shine; so that soon we have a new picture, composed of the eminent experiences. The man co-operates. He loves to communicate; and that which is for him to say lies as a load on his heart until it is delivered. But, besides the universal joy of conversation, some men are born with exalted powers for this second creation. Men are born to write. The gardener saves every slip, and seed, and peach-stone: his vocation is to be a planter of plants. Not less does the writer attend his affair. Whatever he beholds or experiences, comes to him as a model, and sits for its picture. He counts it all nonsense that they say, that some things are undescribable. He believes that all that can be thought can be written, first or last; and he would report the Holy Ghost, or attempt it. Nothing so broad, so subtle, or so dear, but comes therefore commended to his pen, — and he will write. In his eyes, a man is the faculty of reporting, and the universe is the possibility of being reported. In conversation, in calamity, he finds new materials; as our German poet said, "Some God gave me the power to paint what I suffer." He draws his rents from rage and pain. By acting rashly, he buys the power of talking wisely. Vexations, and a tempest of passion, only fill his sail; as the good Luther writes, "When I am angry, I can pray well, and preach well": and if we knew the genesis of fine strokes of eloquence, they might recall the complaisance of Sultan Amurath, who struck off some Persian heads, that his physician, Vesalius, might see the spasms in the muscles of the neck. His failures are the preparation of his victories. A new thought, or a crisis of passion, apprises him that all that he has yet learned and written is exoteric, — is not the fact, but some rumor of the fact. What then? Does he throw away the pen? No; he begins again to describe in the new light which has shined on him, — if, by some means, he may yet save some true word. Nature conspires. Whatever can be thought can be spoken, and still rises for utterance, though to rude and stammering organs. If they cannot compass it, it waits and works, until, at last, it moulds them to its perfect will, and is articulated.

This striving after imitative expression, which one meets everywhere, is significant of the aim of nature, but is mere stenography. There are higher degrees, and Nature has more splendid endowments for those whom she elects to a superior office; for the class of scholars or writers, who see connection where the multitude see fragments, and who are impelled to exhibit the facts in ideal order, and so to supply the axis on which the frame of things turns. Nature has dearly at heart the formation of the speculative man, or scholar. It is an end never lost sight of, and is prepared in the original casting of things. He is no permissive or accidental appearance, but an organic agent, one of the estates of the realm, provided and prepared, from of old and from everlasting, in the knitting and contexture of things. Presentiments, impulses, cheer him. There is a certain heat in the breast, which attends the perception of a primary truth, which is the shining of the spiritual sun down into the shaft of the mine. Every thought which dawns on the mind, in the moment of its emergence announces its own rank, whether it is some whimsy, or whether it is a power.

If he have his incitements, there is, on the other side, invitation and need enough of his gift. Society has, at all times, the same want, namely, of one sane man with adequate powers of expression to hold up each object of monomania in its right relations. The ambitious and mercenary bring their last new mumbo-jumbo, whether tariff, Texas railroad, Romanism, mesmerism, or California; and, by detaching the object from its relations, easily succeed in making it seen in a glare; and a multitude go mad about it, and they are not to be reproved or cured by the opposite multitude, who are kept from this particular insanity by an equal frenzy on another crotchet. But let one man have the comprehensive eye that can replace this isolated prodigy in its right neighborhood and bearings, — the illusion vanishes, and the returning reason of the community thanks the reason of the monitor.

The scholar is the man of the ages, but he must also wish with other men to stand well with his contemporaries. But there is a certain ridicule, among superficial people, thrown on the scholars or clerisy, which is of no import, unless the scholar heed it. In this country, the emphasis of conversation, and of public opinion, commends the practical man; and the solid portion of the community is named with significant respect in every circle. Our people are of Bonaparte's opinion concerning ideologists. Ideas are subversive of social order and comfort, and at last make a fool of the possessor. It is believed, the ordering a cargo of goods from New York to Smyrna; or, the running up and down to procure a company of subscribers to set agoing five or ten thousand spindles; or, the negotiations of a caucus, and the practising on the prejudices and facility of country-people, to secure their votes in November, — is practical and commendable.

If I were to compare action of a much higher strain with a life of contemplation, I should not venture to pronounce with much confidence in favor of the former. Mankind have such a deep stake in inward illumination, that there is much to be said by the hermit or monk in defence of his life of thought and prayer. A certain partiality, a headiness, and loss of balance, is the tax which all action must pay. Act, if you like, — but you do it at your peril. Men's actions are too strong for them. Show me a man who has acted, and who has not been the victim and slave of his action. What they have done commits and enforces them to do the same again. The first act, which was to be an experiment, becomes a sacrament. The fiery reformer embodies his aspiration in some rite or covenant, and he and his friends cleave to the form, and lose the aspiration. The Quaker has established Quakerism, the Shaker has established his monastery and his dance; and, although each prates of spirit, there is no spirit, but repetition, which is anti-spiritual. But where are his new things of today? In actions of enthusiasm, this drawback appears: but in those lower activities, which have no higher aim than to make us more comfortable and more cowardly, in actions of cunning, actions that steal and lie, actions that divorce the speculative from the practical faculty, and put a ban on reason and sentiment, there is nothing else but drawback and negation. The Hindoos write in their sacred books, "Children only, and not the learned, speak of the speculative and the practical faculties as two. They are but one, for both obtain the selfsame end, and the place which is gained by the followers of the one is gained by the followers of the other. That man seeth, who seeth that the speculative and the practical doctrines are one." For great action must draw on the spiritual nature. The measure of action is the sentiment from which it proceeds. The greatest action may easily be one of the most private circumstance.

This disparagement will not come from the leaders, but from inferior persons. The robust gentlemen who stand at the head of the practical class, share the ideas of the time, and have too much sympathy with the speculative class. It is not from men excellent in any kind, that disparagement of any other is to be looked for. With such, Talleyrand's question is ever the main one; not, is he rich? is he committed? is he well-meaning? has he this or that faculty? is he of the movement? is he of the establishment? — but, *Is he anybody?* does he stand for something? He must be good of his kind. That is all that Talleyrand, all that State Street, all that the common sense of mankind asks. Be real and admirable, not as we know, but as you know. Able men do not care in what kind a man is able, so only that he is able. A master likes a master, and does not stipulate whether it be orator, artist, craftsman, or king.

Society has really no graver interest than the well-being of the literary class. And it is not to be denied that men are cordial in their recognition and welcome of intellectual accomplishments. Still the writer does not stand with us on any commanding ground. I think this to be his own fault. A pound passes for a pound. There have been times when he was a sacred person; he wrote Bibles; the first hymns; the codes; the epics; tragic songs; Sibylline verses; Chaldean oracles; Laconian sentences, inscribed on temple walls. Every word was true, and woke the nations to new life. He wrote without levity, and without choice. Every word was carved before his eyes, into the earth and the sky; and the sun and stars were only letters of the same purport, and of no more necessity. But how can he be honored, when he does not honor himself; when he loses himself in the crowd; when he is no longer the lawgiver, but the sycophant, ducking to the giddy opinion of a reckless public; when he must sustain with shameless advocacy some bad government, or must bark all the year round, in opposition; or write conventional criticism, or profligate novels; or, at any rate, write without thought, and without recurrence, by day and by night, to the sources of inspiration?

Some reply to these questions may be furnished by looking over the list of men of literary genius in our age. Among these, no more instructive name occurs than that of Goethe, to represent the powers and duties of the scholar or writer.

I described Bonaparte as a representative of the popular external life and aims of the nineteenth century. Its other half, its poet, is Goethe, a man quite domesticated in the century, breathing its air, enjoying its fruits, impossible at any earlier time, and taking away, by his colossal parts, the reproach of weakness, which, but for him, would lie on the intellectual works of the period. He appears at a time when a general culture has spread itself, and has smoothed down all sharp individual traits; when, in the absence of heroic characters, a social comfort and co-operation have come in. There is no poet, but scores of poetic writers; no Columbus, but hundreds of post-captains, with transit-telescope, barometer, and concentrated soup and pemmican; no Demosthenes, no Chatham, but any number of clever parliamentary and forensic debaters; no prophet or saint, but colleges of divinity; no learned man, but learned societies, a cheap press, reading-rooms, and book-clubs, without number. There was never such a miscellany of facts. The world extends itself like American trade. We conceive Greek or Roman life — life in the Middle Ages — to be a simple and comprehensible affair; but modern life to respect a multitude of things, which is distracting.

Goethe was the philosopher of this multiplicity; hundred-handed, Argus-eyed, able and happy to cope with this rolling miscellany of facts and sciences, and, by his own versatility, to dispose of them with ease; a manly mind, unembarrassed by the variety of coats of convention, with which life had got incrusted, easily able by his subtlety to pierce these, and to draw his strength from nature, with which he lived in full communion. What is strange, too, he lived in a small town, in a petty state, in a defeated state, and in a time when Germany played no such leading part in the world's affairs as to swell the bosoms of her sons with any metropolitan pride, such as might have cheered a French, or English, or once, a Roman or Attic genius. Yet there is no trace of provincial limitation in his muse. He is not a debtor to his position, but was born with a free and controlling genius.

The Helena, or the second part of Faust, is a philosophy of literature set in poetry; the work of one who found himself the master of histories, mythologies, philosophies, sciences, and national literatures, in the encyclopædical manner in which modern erudition, with its international intercourse of the whole earth's population, researches into Indian, Etruscan, and all Cyclopæan arts, geology, chemistry, astronomy; and every one of these kingdoms assuming a certain aerial and poetic character, by reason of the multitude. One looks at a king with reverence; but if one should chance to be at a congress of kings, the eye would take liberties with the peculiarities of each. These are not wild miraculous songs, but elaborate forms, to which the poet has confided the results of eighty years of observation. This reflective and critical wisdom makes the poem more truly the flower of this time. It dates itself. Still he is a poet, — poet of a prouder laurel than any contemporary, and, under this plague of microscopes, (for he seems to see out of every pore of his skin,) strikes the harp with a hero's strength and grace.

The wonder of the book is its superior intelligence. In the menstruum of this man's wit, the past and the present ages, and their religions, politics, and modes of thinking, are dissolved into archetypes and ideas. What new mythologies sail through his head! The Greeks said, that Alexander went as far as Chaos; Goethe went, only the other day, as far; and one step farther he hazarded, and brought himself safe back.

There is a heart-cheering freedom in his speculation. The immense horizon which journeys with us lends its majesty to trifles, and to matters of convenience and necessity, as to solemn and festal performances. He was the soul of his century. If that was learned, and had become, by population, compact organization, and drill of parts, one great Exploring Expedition, accumulating a glut of facts and fruits too fast for any hitherto-existing savans to classify, this man's mind had ample chambers for the distribution of all. He had a power to unite the detached atoms again by their own law. He has clothed our modern existence with poetry. Amid littleness and detail, he detected the Genius of life, the old cunning Proteus, nestling close beside us, and showed that the dulness and prose we ascribe to the age was only another of his masks: —

"His very flight is presence in disguise":

that he had put off a gay uniform for a fatigue dress, and was not a whit less vivacious or rich in Liverpool, or the Hague, than once in Rome or Antioch. He sought him in public squares and main streets, in boulevards and hotels; and, in the solidest kingdom of routine and the senses, he showed the lurking demonic power; that, in actions of routine, a thread of mythology and fable spins itself: and this, by tracing the pedigree of every usage and practice, every institution, utensil, and means, home to its origin in the structure of man. He had an extreme impatience of conjecture and of rhetoric. "I have guesses enough of my own; if a man write a book, let him set down only what he knows." He writes in the plainest and lowest tone, omitting a great deal more than he writes, and putting ever a thing for a word. He has explained the distinction between the antique and the modern spirit and art. He has defined art, its scope and laws. He has said the best things about nature that ever were said. He treats nature as the old philosophers, as the seven wise masters did, — and, with whatever loss of French tabulation and dissection, poetry and humanity remain to us; and they have some doctoral skill. Eyes are better, on the whole, than telescopes or microscopes. He has contributed a key to many parts of nature, through the rare turn for unity and simplicity in his mind. Thus Goethe suggested the leading idea of modern botany, that a leaf, or the eye of a leaf, is the unit of botany, and that every part of the plant is only a transformed leaf to meet a new condition; and, by varying the conditions, a leaf may be converted into any other organ; and any other organ into a leaf. In like manner, in osteology, he assumed that one vertebra of the spine might be considered the unit of the skeleton: the head was only the uppermost vertebra transformed. "The plant goes from knot to knot, closing, at last, with the flower and the seed. So the tape-worm, the caterpillar, goes from knot to knot, and closes with the head. Man and the higher animals are built up through the vertebræ, the powers being concentrated in the head." In optics, again, he rejected the artificial theory of seven colors, and considered that every color was the mixture of light and darkness in new proportions. It is really of very little consequence what topic he writes upon. He sees at every pore, and has a certain gravitation towards truth. He will realize what you say. He hates to be trifled with, and to be made to say over again some old wife's fable, that has had possession of men's faith these thousand years. He may as well see if it is true as another. He sifts it. I am here, he would say, to be the measure and judge of these things. Why should I take them on trust? And, therefore, what he says of religion, of passion, of marriage, of manners, of property, of paper money, of periods of belief, of omens, of luck, or whatever else, refuses to be forgotten.

Take the most remarkable example that could occur of this tendency to verify every term in popular use. The Devil had played an important part in mythology in all times. Goethe would have no word that does not cover a thing. The same measure will still serve: "I have never heard of any crime which I might not have committed." So he flies at the throat of this imp. He shall be real; he shall be modern; he shall be European; he shall dress like a gentleman, and accept the manners, and walk in the streets, and be well initiated in the life of Vienna, and of Heidelberg, in 1820, — or he shall not exist. Accordingly, he stripped him of mythologic gear, of horns, cloven foot, harpoon tail, brimstone, and blue-fire, and, instead of looking in books and pictures, looked for him in his own mind, in every shade of coldness, selfishness, and unbelief that, in crowds, or in solitude, darkens over the human thought, — and found that the portrait gained reality and terror by everything he added, and by everything he took away. He found that the essence of this hobgoblin, which had hovered in shadow about the habitations of men, ever since there were men, was pure intellect, applied — as always there is a tendency— to the service of the senses: and he flung into literature, in his Mephistopheles, the first organic figure that has been added for some ages, and which will remain as long as the Prometheus.

I have no design to enter into any analysis of his numerous works. They consist of translations, criticisms, dramas, lyric and every other description of poems, literary journals, and portraits of distinguished men. Yet I cannot omit to specify Wilhelm Meister.

Wilhelm Meister is a novel in every sense, the first of its kind, called by its admirers the only delineation of modern society, — as if other novels, those of Scott, for example, dealt with costume and condition, this with the spirit of life. It is a book over which some veil is still drawn. It is read by very intelligent persons with wonder and delight. It is preferred by some such to Hamlet, as a work of genius. I suppose, no book of this century can compare with it in its delicious sweetness, so new, so provoking to the mind, gratifying it with so many and so solid thoughts, just insights into life, and manners, and characters; so many good hints for the conduct of life, so many unexpected glimpses into a higher sphere, and never a trace of rhetoric or dulness. A very provoking book to the curiosity of young men of genius, but a very unsatisfactory one. Lovers of light reading, those who look in it for the entertainment they find in a romance, are disappointed. On the other hand, those who begin it with the higher hope to read in it a worthy history of genius, and the just award of the laurel to its toils and denials, have also reason to complain. We had an English romance here, not long ago, professing to embody the hope of a new age, and to unfold the political hope of the party called 'Young England,' in which the only reward of virtue is a seat in parliament, and a peerage. Goethe's romance has a conclusion as lame and immoral. George Sand, in Consuelo and its continuation, has sketched a truer and more dignified picture. In the progress of the story, the characters of the hero and heroine expand at a rate that shivers the porcelain chess-table of aristocratic convention: they quit the society and habits of their rank; they lose their wealth; they become the servants of great ideas, and of the most generous social ends; until, at last, the hero, who is the centre and fountain of an association for the rendering of the noblest benefits to the human race, no longer answers to his own titled name: it sounds foreign and remote in his ear. "I am only man," he says; "I breathe and work for man," and this in poverty and extreme sacrifices. Goethe's hero, on the contrary, has so many weaknesses and impurities, and keeps such bad company, that the sober English public, when the book was translated, were disgusted. And yet it is so crammed with wisdom, with knowledge of the world, and with knowledge of laws; the persons so truly and subtly drawn, and with such few strokes, and not a word too much, the book remains ever so new and unexhausted, that we must even let it go its way, and be willing to get what good from it we can, assured that it has only begun its office, and has millions of readers yet to serve.

The argument is the passage of a democrat to the aristocracy, using both words in their best sense. And this passage is not made in any mean or creeping way, but through the hall door. Nature and character assist, and the rank is made real by sense and probity in the nobles. No generous youth can escape this charm of reality in the book, so that it is highly stimulating to intellect and courage.

The ardent and holy Novalis characterized the book as "thoroughly modern and prosaic; the romantic is completely levelled in it; so is the poetry of nature; the wonderful. The book treats only of the ordinary affairs of men: it is a poeticized civic and domestic story. The wonderful in it is expressly treated as fiction and enthusiastic dreaming": — and yet, what is also characteristic, Novalis soon returned to this book, and it remained his favorite reading to the end of his life.

What distinguishes Goethe for French and English readers, is, a property which he shares with his nation, — an habitual reference to interior truth. In England and in America, there is a respect for talent; and, if it is exerted in support of any ascertained or intelligible interest or party, or in regular opposition to any, the public is satisfied. In France, there is even a greater delight in intellectual brilliancy, for its own sake. And, in all these countries, men of talent write from talent. It is enough if the understanding is occupied, the taste propitiated, — so many columns, so many hours, filled in a lively and creditable way. The German intellect wants the French sprightliness, the fine practical understanding of the English, and the American adventure; but it has a certain probity, which never rests in a superficial performance, but asks steadily, *To what end?* A German public asks for a controlling sincerity. Here is activity of thought; but what is it for? What does the man mean? Whence, whence all these thoughts?

Talent alone cannot make a writer. There must be a man behind the book; a personality which, by birth and quality, is pledged to the doctrines there set forth, and which exists to see and state things so, and not otherwise; holding things because they are things. If he cannot rightly express himself to-day, the same things subsist, and will open themselves to-morrow. There lies the burden on his mind, — the burden of truth to be declared, — more or less understood; and it constitutes his business and calling in the world, to see those facts through, and to make them known. What signifies that he trips and stammers; that his voice is harsh or hissing; that his method or his tropes are inadequate? That message will find method and imagery, articulation and melody. Though he were dumb, it would speak. If not, — if there be no such God's word in the man, — what care we how adroit, how fluent, how brilliant he is?

It makes a great difference to the force of any sentence, whether there be a man behind it, or no. In the learned journal, in the influential newspaper, I discern no form: only some irresponsible shadow; oftener some moneyed corporation, or some dangler, who hopes, in the mask and robes of his paragraph, to pass for somebody. But, through every clause and part of speech of a right book, I meet the eyes of the most determined of men; his force and terror inundate every word: the commas and dashes are alive; so that the writing is athletic and nimble, — can go far and live long.

In England and America, one may be an adept in the writings of a Greek or Latin poet, without any poetic taste or fire. That a man has spent years on Plato and Proclus, does not afford a presumption that he holds heroic opinions, or undervalues the fashions of his town. But the German nation have the most ridiculous good faith on these subjects; the student out of the lecture-room, still broods on the lessons; and the professor cannot divest himself of the fancy, that the truths of philosophy have some application to Berlin and Munich.

This earnestness enables them to outsee men of much more talent. Hence, almost all the valuable distinctions which are current in higher conversation, have been derived to us from Germany. But, whilst men distinguished for wit and learning, in England and France, adopt their study and their side with a certain levity, and are not understood to be very deeply engaged, from grounds of character, to the topic or the part they espouse, — Goethe, the head and body of the German nation, does not speak from talent, but the truth shines through : he is very wise, though his talent often veils his wisdom. However excellent his sentence is, he has somewhat better in view. It awakens my curiosity. He has the formidable independence which converse with truth gives ; hear you, or forbear, his fact abides ; and your interest in the writer is not confined to his story, and he dismissed from memory, when he has performed his task creditably, as a baker when he has left his loaf ; but his work is the least part of him. The old Eternal Genius who built the world has confided himself more to this man than to any other. I dare not say that Goethe ascended to the highest grounds from which genius has spoken. He has not worshipped the highest unity ; he is incapable of a self-surrender to the moral sentiment. There are nobler strains in poetry than any he has sounded. There are writers poorer in talent, whose tone is purer, and more touches the heart. Goethe can never be dear to men. His is not even the devotion to pure truth ; but to truth for the sake of culture. He has no aims less large than the conquest of universal nature, of universal truth, to be his portion : a man not to be bribed, nor deceived, nor overawed ; of a stoical self-command and self-denial, and having one test for all men, — *What can you teach me?* All possessions are valued by him for that only ; rank, privileges, health, time, being itself.

He is the type of culture, the amateur of all arts, and sciences, and events ; artistic, but not artist ; spiritual, but not spiritualist. There is nothing he had not right to know : there is no weapon in the armory of universal genius he did not take into his hand, but with peremptory heed that he should not be for a moment prejudiced by his instruments. He lays a ray of light under every fact, and between himself and his dearest property. From him nothing was hid, nothing withholden. The lurking demons sat to him, and the saint who saw the demons ; and the metaphysical elements took form. "Piety itself is no aim, but only a means, whereby, through purest inward peace, we may attain to highest culture." And his penetration of every secret of the fine arts will make Goethe still more statuesque. His affections help him, like women employed by Cicero to worm out the secret of conspirators. Enmities he has none. Enemy of him you may be, — if so you shall teach him aught which your good-will cannot, — were it only what experience will accrue from your ruin. Enemy and welcome, but enemy on high terms. He cannot hate anybody; his time is worth too much. Temperamental antagonisms may be suffered, but like feuds of emperors, who fight dignifiedly across kingdoms.

His autobiography, under the title of "Poetry and Truth out of my Life," is the expression of the idea, — now familiar to the world through the German mind, but a novelty to England, Old and New, when that book appeared, — that a man exists for culture; not for what he can accomplish, but for what can be accomplished in him. The reaction of things on the man is the only noteworthy result. An intellectual man can see himself as a third person; therefore his faults and delusions interest him equally with his successes. Though he wishes to prosper in affairs, he wishes more to know the history and destiny of man; whilst the clouds of egotists drifting about him are only interested in a low success.

This idea reigns in the *Dichtung und Wahrheit*, and directs the selection of the incidents; and nowise the external importance of events, the rank of the personages, or the bulk of incomes. Of course, the book affords slender materials for what would be reckoned with us a "Life of Goethe"; — few dates; no correspondence; no details of offices or employments; no light on his marriage; and, a period of ten years, that should be the most active in his life, after his settlement at Weimar, is sunk in silence. Meantime, certain love-affairs, that came to nothing, as people say, have the strangest importance: he crowds us with details: — certain whimsical opinions, cosmogonies, and religions of his own invention, and, especially his relations to remarkable minds, and to critical epochs of thought: — these he magnifies. His "Daily and Yearly Journal," his "Italian Travels," his "Campaign in France," and the historical part of his "Theory of Colors," have the same interest. In the last, he rapidly notices Kepler, Roger Bacon, Galileo, Newton, Voltaire, &c.; and the charm of this portion of the book consists in the simplest statement of the relation betwixt these grandees of European scientific history and himself; the mere drawing of the lines from Goethe to Kepler, from Goethe to Bacon, from Goethe to Newton. The drawing of the line is for the time and person, a solution of the formidable problem, and gives pleasure when Iphigenia and Faust do not, without any cost of invention comparable to that of Iphigenia and Faust.

This lawgiver of art is not an artist. Was it that he knew too much, that his sight was microscopic, and interfered with the just perspective, the seeing of the whole? He is fragmentary; a writer of occasional poems, and of an encyclopædia of sentences. When he sits down to write a drama or a tale, he collects and sorts his observations from a hundred sides, and combines them into the body as fitly as he can. A great deal refuses to incorporate: this he adds loosely, as letters of the parties, leaves from their journals, or the like. A great deal still is left that will not find any place. This the bookbinder alone can give any cohesion to: and hence, notwithstanding the looseness of many of his works, we have volumes of detached paragraphs, aphorisms, *xenien*, &c.

I suppose the worldly tone of his tales grew out of the calculations of self-culture. It was the infirmity of an admirable scholar, who loved the world out of gratitude; who knew where libraries, galleries, architecture, laboratories, savans, and leisure were to be had, and who did not quite trust the compensations of poverty and nakedness. Socrates loved Athens; Montaigne, Paris; and Madame de Staël said she was only vulnerable on that side (namely, of Paris). It has its favorable aspect. All the geniuses are usually so ill-assorted and sickly, that one is ever wishing them somewhere else. We seldom see anybody who is not uneasy or afraid to live. There is a slight blush of shame on the cheek of good men and aspiring men, and a spice of caricature. But this man was entirely at home and happy in his century and the world. None was so fit to live, or more heartily enjoyed the game. In this aim of culture, which is the genius of his works, is their power. The idea of absolute, eternal truth, without reference to my own enlargement by it, is higher. The surrender to the torrent of poetic inspiration is higher; but, compared with any motives on which books are written in England and America, this is very truth, and has the power to inspire which belongs to truth. Thus has he brought back to a book some of its ancient might and dignity.

Goethe, coming into an over-civilized time and country,

when original talent was oppressed under the load of books and mechanical auxiliaries, and the distracting variety of claims, taught men how to dispose of this mountainous miscellany, and make it subservient. I join Napoleon with him, as being both representatives of the impatience and reaction of nature against the *morgue* of conventions, — two stern realists, who, with their scholars, have severally set the axe at the root of the tree of cant and seeming, for this time, and for all time. This cheerful laborer, with no external popularity or provocation, drawing his motive and his plan from his own breast, tasked himself with stints for a giant, and, without relaxation or rest, except by alternating his pursuits, worked on for eighty years with the steadiness of his first zeal.

It is the last lesson of modern science, that the highest simplicity of structure is produced, not by few elements, but by the highest complexity. Man is the most composite of all creatures: the wheel-insect, *volvox globator*, is at the other extreme. We shall learn to draw rents and revenues from the immense patrimony of the old and the recent ages. Goethe teaches courage, and the equivalence of all times; that the disadvantages of any epoch exist only to the faint-hearted. Genius hovers with his sunshine and music close by the darkest and deafest eras. No mortgage, no attainder, will hold on men or hours. The world is young: the former great men call to us affectionately. We too must write Bibles, to unite again the heavens and the earthly world. The secret of genius is to suffer no fiction to exist for us; to realize all that we know; in the high refinement of modern life, in arts, in sciences, in books, in men, to exact good faith, reality, and a purpose; and first, last, midst, and without end, to honor every truth by use.

ENGLISH TRAITS.

ENGLISH TRAITS.

CHAPTER I.

FIRST VISIT TO ENGLAND.

I HAVE been twice in England. In 1833, on my return from a short tour in Sicily, Italy, and France, I crossed from Boulogne, and landed in London at the Tower stairs. It was a dark Sunday morning; there were few people in the streets; and I remember the pleasure of that first walk on English ground, with my companion, an American artist, from the Tower up through Cheapside and the Strand, to a house in Russell Square, whither we had been recommended to good chambers. For the first time for many months we were forced to check the saucy habit of travellers' criticism, as we could no longer speak aloud in the streets without being understood. The shop-signs spoke our language; our country names were on the door-plates; and the public and private buildings wore a more native and wonted front.

Like most young men at that time, I was much indebted to the men of Edinburgh, and of the Edinburgh Review, — to Jeffrey, Mackintosh, Hallam, and to Scott, Playfair, and De Quincey; and my narrow and desultory reading had inspired the wish to see the faces of three or four writers, — Coleridge, Wordsworth, Landor, De Quincey, and the latest and strongest contributor to the critical journals, Carlyle; and I suppose if I had sifted the reasons that led me to Europe, when I was ill and was advised to travel, it was mainly the attraction of these persons. If Goethe had been still living, I might have wandered into Germany also. Besides those I have named (for Scott was dead), there was not in Britain the man living whom I cared to behold, unless it were the Duke of Wellington, whom I afterwards saw at Westminster Abbey, at the funeral of Wilberforce. The young scholar fancies it happiness enough to live with people who can give an inside to the world; without reflecting that they are prisoners, too, of their own thought, and cannot apply themselves to yours. The conditions of literary success are almost destructive of the best social power, as they do not leave that frolic liberty which only can encounter a companion on the best terms. It is probable you left some obscure comrade at a tavern, or in the farms, with right mother-wit, and equality to life, when you crossed sea and land to play bo-peep with celebrated scribes. I have, however, found writers superior to their books, and I cling to my first belief, that a strong head will dispose fast enough of these impediments, and give one the satisfaction of reality, the sense of having been met, and a larger horizon.

On looking over the diary of my journey in 1833, I find nothing to publish in my memoranda of visits to places. But I have copied the few notes I made of visits to persons, as they respect parties quite too good and too transparent to the whole world to make it needful to affect any prudery of suppression about a few hints of those bright personalities.

At Florence, chief among artists, I found Horatio Greenough, the American sculptor. His face was so handsome, and his person so well formed, that he might be pardoned, if, as was alleged, the face of his Medora, and the figure of a colossal Achilles in clay, were idealizations of his own. Greenough was a superior man, ardent and eloquent, and all his opinions had elevation and magnanimity. He believed that the Greeks had wrought in schools or fraternities, — the genius of the master imparting his design to his friends, and inflaming them with it, and when his strength was spent, a new hand, with equal heat, continued the work; and so by relays, until it was finished in every part with equal fire. This was necessary in so refractory a material as stone; and he thought art would never prosper until we left our shy jealous ways, and worked in society as they. All his thoughts breathed the same generosity. He was an accurate and a deep man. He was a votary of the Greeks, and impatient of Gothic art. His paper on Architecture, published in 1843, announced in advance the leading thoughts of Mr. Ruskin on the *morality* in architecture, notwithstanding the antagonism in their views of the history of art. I have a private letter from him, — later, but respecting the same period, — in which he roughly sketches his own theory. "Here is my theory of structure: A scientific arrangement of spaces and forms to functions and to site; an emphasis of features proportioned to their *gradated* importance in function; color and ornament to be decided and arranged and varied by strictly organic laws, having a distinct reason for each decision; the entire and immediate banishment of all make-shift and make-believe."

Greenough brought me, through a common friend, an invitation from Mr. Landor, who lived at San Domenica di Fiesole. On the 15th May I dined with Mr. Landor. I found him noble and courteous, living in a cloud of pictures at his Villa Gherardesca, a fine house commanding a beautiful landscape. I had inferred from his books, or magnified from some anecdotes, an impression of Achillean wrath, — an untamable petulance. I do not know whether the imputation were just or not, but certainly on this May day his courtesy veiled that haughty mind, and he was the most patient and gentle of hosts. He praised the beautiful cyclamen which grows all about Florence; he admired Washington; talked of Wordsworth, Byron, Massinger, Beaumont and Fletcher. To be sure, he is decided in his opinions, likes to surprise, and is well content to impress, if possible, his English whim upon the immutable past. No great man ever had a great son, if Philip and Alexander be not an exception; and Philip he calls the greater man. In art, he loves the Greeks, and in sculpture, them only. He prefers the Venus to everything else, and, after that, the head of Alexander, in the gallery here. He prefers John of Bologna to Michel Angelo; in painting, Raffaelle; and shares the growing taste for Perugino and the early masters. The Greek histories he thought the only good; and after them, Voltaire's. I could not make him praise Mackintosh, nor my more recent friends; Montaigne very cordially, — and Charron also, which seemed undiscriminating. He thought Degerando indebted to "Lucas on Happiness" and "Lucas on Holiness"! He pestered me with Southey; but who is Southey?

He invited me to breakfast on Friday. On Friday I did not fail to go, and this time with Greenough. He entertained us at once with reciting half a dozen hexameter lines of Julius Cæsar's! — from Donatus, he said. He glorified Lord Chesterfield more than was necessary, and undervalued Burke, and undervalued Socrates; designated as three of the greatest of men, Washington, Phocion, and Timoleon; much as our pomologists, in their lists, select the three or the six best pears "for a small orchard"; and did not even omit to remark the similar termination of their names. "A great man," he said, "should make great sacrifices, and kill his hundred oxen, without knowing whether they would be consumed by gods and heroes, or whether the flies would eat them." I had visited Professor Amici, who had shown me his microscopes, magnifying (it was said) two thousand diameters; and I spoke of the uses to which they were applied. Landor despised entomology, yet, in the same breath, said, "the sublime was in a grain of dust." I suppose I teased him about recent writers, but he professed never to have heard of Herschel, *not even by name.* One room was full of pictures, which he likes to show, especially one piece, standing before which, he said "he would give fifty guineas to the man that would swear it was a Domenichino." I was more curious to see his library, but Mr. H——, one of the guests, told me that Mr. Landor gives away his books, and has never more than a dozen at a time in his house.

Mr. Landor carries to its height the love of freak which the English delight to indulge, as if to signalize their commanding freedom. He has a wonderful brain, despotic, violent, and inexhaustible, meant for a soldier, by what chance converted to letters, in which there is not a style nor a tint not known to him, yet with an English appetite for action and heroes. The thing done avails, and not what is said about it. An original sentence, a step forward, is worth more than all the censures. Landor is strangely undervalued in England; usually ignored; and sometimes savagely attacked in the Reviews. The criticism may be right or wrong, and is quickly forgotten; but year after year the scholar must still go back to Landor for a multitude of elegant sentences,—for wisdom, wit, and indignation that are unforgetable.

From London, on the 5th August, I went to Highgate, and wrote a note to Mr. Coleridge, requesting leave to pay my respects to him. It was near noon. Mr. Coleridge sent a verbal message, that he was in bed, but if I would call after one o'clock, he would see me. I returned at one, and he appeared, a short, thick old man, with bright blue eyes and fine clear complexion, leaning on his cane. He took snuff freely, which presently soiled his cravat and neat black suit. He asked whether I knew Allston, and spoke warmly of his merits and doings when he knew him in Rome; what a master of the

Titianesque he was, &c., &c. He spoke of Dr. Channing. It was an unspeakable misfortune that he should have turned out a Unitarian after all. On this, he burst into a declamation on the folly and ignorance of Unitarianism, — its high unreasonableness; and taking up Bishop Waterland's book, which lay on the table, he read with vehemence two or three pages written by himself in the fly-leaves, — passages, too, which, I believe, are printed in the "Aids to Reflection." When he stopped to take breath, I interposed, that, "whilst I highly valued all his explanations, I was bound to tell him that I was born and bred a Unitarian." "Yes," he said, "I supposed so"; and continued as before. 'It was a wonder, that after so many ages of unquestioning acquiescence in the doctrine of St. Paul, — the doctrine of the Trinity, which was also, according to Philo Judæus, the doctrine of the Jews before Christ, — this handful of Priestleians should take on themselves to deny it, &c., &c. He was very sorry that Dr. Channing, — a man to whom he looked up, — no, to say that he looked *up* to him would be to speak falsely; but a man whom he looked *at* with so much interest, — should embrace such views. When he saw Dr. Channing, he had hinted to him that he was afraid he loved Christianity for what was lovely and excellent, — he loved the good in it, and not the true; and I tell you, sir, that I have known ten persons who loved the good, for one person who loved the true; but it is a far greater virtue to love the true for itself alone, than to love the good for itself alone. He (Coleridge) knew all about Unitarianism perfectly well, because he had once been a Unitarian, and knew what quackery it was. He had been called "the rising star of Unitarianism."' He went on defining, or rather refining: 'The Trinitarian doctrine was realism; the idea of God was not essential, but super-essential'; talked of *trinism* and *tetrakism*, and much more, of which I only caught this: "that the will was that by which a person is a person; because, if one should push me in the street, and so I should force the man next me into the kennel, I should at once exclaim, "I did not do it, sir," meaning it was not my will.' And this also: 'that if you should insist on your faith here in England, and I on mine, mine would be the hotter side of the fagot.'

I took advantage of a pause to say, that he had many readers of all religious opinions in America, and I proceeded to inquire if the "extract" from the Independent's pamphlet, in the third volume of the Friend, were a veritable quotation.

He replied that it was really taken from a pamphlet in his possession, entitled "A Protest of one of the Independents," or something to that effect. I told him how excellent I thought it, and how much I wished to see the entire work. "Yes," he said, "the man was a chaos of truths, but lacked the knowledge that God was a god of order. Yet the passage would no doubt strike you more in the quotation than in the original, for I have filtered it."

When I rose to go, he said, "I do not know whether you care about poetry, but I will repeat some verses I lately made on my baptismal anniversary"; and he recited with strong emphasis, standing, ten or twelve lines, beginning, —

"Born unto God in Christ — "

He inquired where I had been travelling; and on learning that I had been in Malta and Sicily, he compared one island with the other, 'repeating what he had said to the Bishop of London when he returned from that country, that Sicily was an excellent school of political economy; for, in any town there, it only needed to ask what the government enacted, and reverse *that* to know what ought to be done; it was the most felicitously opposite legislation to anything good and wise. There were only three things which the government had brought into that garden of delights, namely, itch, pox, and famine; whereas, in Malta, the force of law and mind was seen, in making that barren rock of semi-Saracen inhabitants the seat of population and plenty.' Going out, he showed me in the next apartment a picture of Allston's, and told me 'that Montague, a picture-dealer, once came to see him, and, glancing towards this, said, "Well, you have got a picture!" thinking it the work of an old master; afterwards, Montague, still talking with his back to the canvas, put up his hand and touched it, and exclaimed, "By Heaven! this picture is not ten years old": — so delicate and skilful was that man's touch.'

I was in his company for about an hour, but find it impossible to recall the largest part of his discourse, which was often like so many printed paragraphs in his book, — perhaps the same, — so readily did he fall into certain commonplaces. As I might have foreseen, the visit was rather a spectacle than a conversation, of no use beyond the satisfaction of my curiosity. He was old and preoccupied, and could not bend to a new companion and think with him.

From Edinburgh I went to the Highlands. On my return, I came from Glasgow to Dumfries, and being intent on delivering a letter which I had brought from Rome, inquired for Craigenputtock. It was a farm in Nithsdale, in the parish of Dunscore, sixteen miles distant. No public coach passed near it, so I took a private carriage from the inn. I found the house amid desolate heathery hills, where the lonely scholar nourished his mighty heart. Carlyle was a man from his youth, an author who did not need to hide from his readers, and as absolute a man of the world, unknown and exiled on that hill-farm, as if holding on his own terms what is best in London. He was tall and gaunt, with a cliff-like brow, self-possessed, and holding his extraordinary powers of conversation in easy command; clinging to his northern accent with evident relish; full of lively anecdote, and with a streaming humor, which floated everything he looked upon. His talk playfully exalting the familiar objects, put the companion at once into an acquaintance with his Lars and Lemurs, and it was very pleasant to learn what was predestined to be a pretty mythology. Few were the objects and lonely the man, "not a person to speak to within sixteen miles except the minister of Dunscore"; so that books inevitably made his topics.

He had names of his own for all the matters familiar to his discourse. "Blackwood's" was the "sand magazine"; "Fraser's" nearer approach to possibility of life was the "mud magazine"; a piece of road near by that marked some failed enterprise was the "grave of the last sixpence." When too much praise of any genius annoyed him, he professed hugely to admire the talent shown by his pig. He had spent much time and contrivance in confining the poor beast to one enclosure in his pen, but pig, by great strokes of judgment, had found out how to let a board down, and had foiled him. For all that, he still thought man the most plastic little fellow in the planet, and he liked Nero's death, "*Qualis artifex pereo!*" better than most history. He worships a man that will manifest any truth to him. At one time he had inquired and read a good deal about America. Landor's principle was mere rebellion, and *that* he feared was the American principle. The best thing he knew of that country was, that in it a man can have meat for his labor. He had read in Stewart's book, that when he inquired in a New York hotel for the Boots, he had been shown across the street and had found Mungo in his own house dining on roast turkey.

We talked of books. Plato he does not read, and he disparaged Socrates; and, when pressed, persisted in making Mirabeau a hero. Gibbon he called the splendid bridge from the old world to the new. His own reading had been multifarious. Tristram Shandy was one of his first books after Robinson Crusoe, and Robertson's America an early favorite. Rousseau's Confessions had discovered to him that he was not a dunce; and it was now ten years since he had learned German, by the advice of a man who told him he would find in that language what he wanted.

He took despairing or satirical views of literature at this moment; recounted the incredible sums paid in one year by the great booksellers for puffing. Hence it comes that no newspaper is trusted now, no books are bought, and the booksellers are on the eve of bankruptcy.

He still returned to English pauperism, the crowded country, the selfish abdication by public men of all that public persons should perform. 'Government should direct poor men what to do. Poor Irish folk come wandering over these moors. My dame makes it a rule to give to every son of Adam bread to eat, and supplies his wants to the next house. But here are thousands of acres which might give them all meat, and nobody to bid these poor Irish go to the moor and till it. They burned the stacks, and so found a way to force the rich people to attend to them.'

We went out to walk over long hills, and looked at Criffel, then without his cap, and down into Wordsworth's country. There we sat down, and talked of the immortality of the soul. It was not Carlyle's fault that we talked on that topic, for he had the natural disinclination of every nimble spirit to bruise itself against walls, and did not like to place himself where no step can be taken. But he was honest and true, and cognizant of the subtile links that bind ages together, and saw how every event affects all the future. 'Christ died on the tree: that built Dunscore kirk yonder: that brought you and me together. Time has only a relative existence.'

He was already turning his eyes towards London with a scholar's appreciation. London is the heart of the world, he said, wonderful only from the mass of human beings. He liked the huge machine. Each keeps its own round. The baker's boy brings muffins to the window at a fixed hour every day, and that is all the Londoner knows or wishes to know on the subject. But it turned out good men. He named certain individuals, especially one man of letters, his friend, the best mind he knew, whom London had well served.

On the 28th August, I went to Rydal Mount, to pay my respects to Mr. Wordsworth. His daughters called in their father, a plain, elderly, white-haired man, not prepossessing, and disfigured by green goggles. He sat down, and talked with great simplicity. He had just returned from a journey. His health was good, but he had broken a tooth by a fall, when walking with two lawyers, and had said, that he was glad it did not happen forty years ago; whereupon they had praised his philosophy.

He had much to say of America, the more that it gave occasion for his favorite topic,—that society is being enlightened by a superficial tuition, out of all proportion to its being restrained by moral culture. Schools do no good. Tuition is not education. He thinks more of the education of circumstances than of tuition. 'T is not a question whether there are offences of which the law takes cognizance, but whether there are offences of which the law does not take cognizance. Sin is what he fears, and how society is to escape without gravest mischiefs from this source—? He has even said, what seemed a paradox, that they needed a civil war in America, to teach the necessity of knitting the social ties stronger. 'There may be,' he said, 'in America some vulgarity in manner, but that 's not important. That comes of the pioneer state of things. But I fear they are too much given to the making of money; and secondly, to politics; that they make political distinction the end, and not the means. And I fear they lack a class of men of leisure,— in short, of gentlemen,— to give a tone of honor to the community. I am told that things are boasted of in the second class of society there, which, in England,— God knows, are done in England every day,— but would never be spoken of. In America I wish to know not how many churches or schools, but what newspapers? My friend, Colonel Hamilton, at the foot of the hill, who was a year in America, assures me that the newspapers are atrocious, and accuse members of Congress of stealing spoons!' He was against taking off the tax on newspapers in England, which the reformers represent as a tax upon knowledge, for this reason, that they would be inundated with base prints. He said, he talked on political aspects, for he wished to impress on me and all good Americans to cultivate the moral, the conservative, &c., &c., and never to call into action the physical strength of the people, as had just now been done in England in the Reform Bill, — a thing prophesied by Delolme. He alluded once or twice to his conversation with Dr. Channing, who had recently visited him (laying his hand on a particular chair in which the Doctor had sat).

The conversation turned on books. Lucretius he esteems a far higher poet than Virgil: not in his system, which is nothing, but in his power of illustration. Faith is necessary to explain anything, and to reconcile the foreknowledge of God with human evil. Of Cousin (whose lectures we had all been reading in Boston) he knew only the name.

I inquired if he had read Carlyle's critical articles and translations. He said, he thought him sometimes insane. He proceeded to abuse Goethe's Wilhelm Meister heartily. It was full of all manner of fornication. It was like the crossing of flies in the air. He had never gone further than the first part; so disgusted was he that he threw the book across the room. I deprecated this wrath, and said what I could for the better parts of the book; and he courteously promised to look at it again. Carlyle, he said, wrote most obscurely. He was clever and deep, but he defied the sympathies of everybody. Even Mr. Coleridge wrote more clearly, though he had always wished Coleridge would write more to be understood. He led me out into his garden, and showed me the gravel walk in which thousands of his lines were composed. His eyes are much inflamed. This is no loss, except for reading, because he never writes prose, and of poetry he carries even hundreds of lines in his head before writing them. He had just returned from a visit to Staffa, and within three days had made three sonnets on Fingal's Cave, and was composing a fourth, when he was called in to see me. He said, "If you are interested in my verses, perhaps you will like to hear these lines." I gladly assented; and he recollected himself for a few moments, and then stood forth and repeated, one after the other, the three entire sonnets with great animation. I fancied the second and third more beautiful than his poems are wont to be. The third is addressed to the flowers, which, he said, especially the ox-eye daisy, are very abundant on the top of the rock. The second alludes to the name of the cave, which is "Cave of Music"; the first to the circumstance of its being visited by the promiscuous company of the steamboat.

This recitation was so unlooked for and surprising, — he, the old Wordsworth, standing apart, and reciting to me in a garden-walk, like a school-boy declaiming, — that I at first was near to laugh; but recollecting myself, that I had come thus far to see a poet, and he was chanting poems to me, I saw that he was right and I was wrong, and gladly gave myself up to hear. I told him how much the few printed extracts had quickened the desire to possess his unpublished poems. He replied, he never was in haste to publish; partly, because he corrected a good deal, and every alteration is ungraciously received after printing; but what he had written would be printed, whether he lived or died. I said, "Tintern Abbey" appeared to be the favorite poem with the public, but more contemplative readers preferred the first books of the "Excursion," and the Sonnets. He said, "Yes, they are better." He preferred such of his poems as touched the affections, to any others; for whatever is didactic — what theories of society, and so on — might perish quickly; but whatever combined a truth with an affection was κτημα ες αει, good to-day and good forever. He cited the sonnet "On the feelings of a high-minded Spaniard," which he preferred to any other (I so understood him), and the "Two Voices"; and quoted, with evident pleasure, the verses addressed "To the Skylark." In this connection, he said of the Newtonian theory, that it might yet be superseded and forgotten; and Dalton's atomic theory.

When I prepared to depart, he said he wished to show me what a common person in England could do, and he led me into the enclosure of his clerk, a young man, to whom he had given this slip of ground, which was laid out, or its natural capabilities shown, with much taste. He then said he would show me a better way towards the inn; and he walked a good part of a mile, talking, and ever and anon stopping short to impress the word or the verse, and finally parted from me with great kindness, and returned across the fields.

Wordsworth honored himself by his simple adherence to truth, and was very willing not to shine; but he surprised by the hard limits of his thought. To judge from a single conversation, he made the impression of a narrow and very English mind; of one who paid for his rare elevation by general tameness and conformity. Off his own beat, his opinions were of no value. It is not very rare to find persons loving sympathy and ease, who expiate their departure from the common in one direction, by their conformity in every other.

CHAPTER II.

VOYAGE TO ENGLAND.

THE occasion of my second visit to England was an invitation from some Mechanics' Institutes in Lancashire and Yorkshire, which separately are organized much in the same way as our New England Lyceums, but, in 1847, had been linked into a "Union," which embraced twenty or thirty towns and cities, and presently extended into the middle counties, and northward into Scotland. I was invited, on liberal terms, to read a series of lectures in them all. The request was urged with every kind suggestion, and every assurance of aid and comfort, by friendliest parties in Manchester, who, in the sequel, amply redeemed their word. The remuneration was equivalent to the fees at that time paid in this country for the like services. At all events, it was sufficient to cover any travelling expenses, and the proposal offered an excellent opportunity of seeing the interior of England and Scotland, by means of a home, and a committee of intelligent friends, awaiting me in every town.

I did not go very willingly. I am not a good traveller, nor have I found that long journeys yield a fair share of reasonable hours. But the invitation was repeated and pressed at a moment of more leisure, and when I was a little spent by some unusual studies. I wanted a change and a tonic, and England was proposed to me. Besides, there were, at least, the dread attraction and salutary influences of the sea. So I took my berth in the packet-ship Washington Irving, and sailed from Boston on Tuesday, 5th October, 1847.

On Friday, at noon, we had only made one hundred and thirty-four miles. A nimble Indian would have swum as far; but the captain affirmed that the ship would show us in time all her paces, and we crept along through the floating drift of boards, logs, and chips, which the rivers of Maine and New Brunswick pour into the sea after a freshet.

At last, on Sunday night, after doing one day's work in four, the storm came, the winds blew, and we flew before a northwester, which strained every rope and sail. The good ship darts through the water all day, all night, like a fish, quivering with speed, gliding through liquid leagues, sliding from horizon to horizon. She has passed Cape Sable; she has reached the Banks; the land-birds are left; gulls, haglets, ducks, petrels, swim, dive, and hover around; no fishermen; she has passed the Banks; left five sail behind her, far on the edge of the west at sundown, which were far east of us at morn, — though they say at sea a stern chase is a long race, — and still we fly for our lives. The shortest sea-line from Boston to Liverpool is 2850 miles. This a steamer keeps, and saves 150 miles. A sailing ship can never go in a shorter line than 3000, and usually it is much longer. Our good master keeps his kites up to the last moment, studding-sails alow and aloft, and, by incessant straight steering, never loses a rod of way. Watchfulness is the law of the ship, — watch on watch, for advantage and for life. Since the ship was built, it seems, the master never slept but in his day-clothes whilst on board. "There are many advantages," says Saadi, "in sea-voyaging, but security is not one of them." Yet in hurrying over these abysses, whatever dangers we are running into, we are certainly running out of the risks of hundreds of miles every day, which have their own chances of squall, collision, sea-stroke, piracy, cold, and thunder. Hour for hour, the risk on a steamboat is greater; but the speed is safety, or twelve days of danger, instead of twenty-four.

Our ship was registered 750 tons, and weighed perhaps, with all her freight, 1500 tons. The mainmast, from the deck to the top-button, measured 115 feet; the length of the deck, from stem to stern, 155. It is impossible not to personify a ship; everybody does, in everything they say: — she behaves well; she minds her rudder; she swims like a duck; she runs her nose into the water; she looks into a port. Then that wonderful *esprit du corps*, by which we adopt into our self-love everything we touch, makes us all champions of her sailing-qualities.

The conscious ship hears all the praise. In one week she has made 1467 miles, and now, at night, seems to hear the steamer behind her, which left Boston to-day at two, has mended her speed, and is flying before the gray south wind eleven and a half knots the hour. The sea-fire shines in her wake, and far around wherever a wave breaks. I read the hour, 9h. 45′, on my watch by this light. Near the equator, you can read small print by it; and the mate describes the phosphoric insects, when taken up in a pail, as shaped like a Carolina potato.

I find the sea-life an acquired taste, like that for tomatoes and olives. The confinement, cold, motion, noise, and odor are not to be dispensed with. The floor of your room is sloped at an angle of twenty or thirty degrees, and I waked every morning with the belief that some one was tipping up my berth. Nobody likes to be treated ignominiously, upset, shoved against the side of the house, rolled over, suffocated with bilge, mephitis, and stewing oil. We get used to these annoyances at last, but the dread of the sea remains longer. The sea is masculine, the type of active strength. Look, what egg-shells are drifting all over it, each one, like ours, filled with men in ecstasies of terror, alternating with cockney conceit, as the sea is rough or smooth. Is this sad-colored circle an eternal cemetery? In our graveyards we scoop a pit, but this aggressive water opens mile-wide pits and chasms, and makes a mouthful of a fleet. To the geologist, the sea is the only firmament; the land is in perpetual flux and change, now blown up like a tumor, now sunk in a chasm, and the registered observations of a few hundred years find it in a perpetual tilt, rising and falling. The sea keeps its old level; and 't is no wonder that the history of our race is so recent, if the roar of the ocean is silencing our traditions. A rising of the sea, such as has been observed, say an inch in a century, from east to west on the land, will bury all the towns, monuments, bones, and knowledge of mankind, steadily and insensibly. If it is capable of these great and secular mischiefs, it is quite as ready at private and local damage; and of this no landsman seems so fearful as the seaman. Such discomfort and such danger as the narratives of the captain and mate disclose are bad enough as the costly fee we pay for entrance to Europe; but the wonder is always new that any sane man can be a sailor. And here, on the second day of our voyage, stepped out a little boy in his shirt-sleeves, who had hid himself, whilst the ship was in port, in the bread-closet, having no money, and wishing to go to England. The sailors have dressed him in Guernsey frock, with a knife in his belt, and he is climbing nimbly about after them, "likes the work first-rate, and, if the captain will take him, means now to come back again in the ship." The mate avers that this is the history of all sailors; nine out of ten are runaway boys; and adds, that all of them are sick of the sea, but stay in it out of pride. Jack has a life of risks, incessant abuse, and the worst pay. It is a little better with the mate, and not very much better with the captain. A hundred dollars a month is reckoned high pay. If sailors were contented, if they had not resolved again and again not to go to sea any more, I should respect them.

Of course, the inconveniences and terrors of the sea are not of any account to those whose minds are preoccupied. The water-laws, arctic frost, the mountain, the mine, only shatter cockneyism; every noble activity makes room for itself. A great mind is a good sailor, as a great heart is. And the sea is not slow in disclosing inestimable secrets to a good naturalist.

'T is a good rule in every journey to provide some piece of liberal study to rescue the hours which bad weather, bad company, and taverns steal from the best economist. Classics which at home are drowsily read have a strange charm in a country inn, or in the transom of a merchant brig. I remember that some of the happiest and most valuable hours I have owed to books, passed, many years ago, on shipboard. The worst impediment I have found at sea is the want of light in the cabin.

We found on board the usual cabin library; Basil Hall, Dumas, Dickens, Bulwer, Balzac, and Sand were our sea-gods. Among the passengers, there was some variety of talent and profession; we exchanged our experiences, and all learned something. The busiest talk with leisure and convenience at sea, and sometimes a memorable fact turns up, which you have long had a vacant niche for, and seize with the joy of a collector. But, under the best conditions, a voyage is one of the severest tests to try a man. A college examination is nothing to it. Sea-days are long, — these lack-lustre, joyless days which whistled over us; but they were few, — only fifteen, as the captain counted, sixteen according to me. Reckoned from the time when we left soundings, our speed was such that the captain drew the line of his course in red ink on his chart, for the encouragement or envy of future navigators.

It has been said that the King of England would consult his dignity by giving audience to foreign ambassadors in the cabin of a man-of-war. And I think the white path of an Atlantic ship the right avenue to the palace front of this seafaring people, who for hundreds of years claimed the strict sovereignty of the sea, and exacted toll and the striking sail from the ships of all other peoples. When their privilege was disputed by the Dutch and other junior marines, on the plea that you could never anchor on the same wave, or hold property in what was always flowing, the English did not stick to claim the channel, or bottom of all the main. "As if," said they, "we contended for the drops of the sea, and not for its situation, or the bed of those waters. The sea is bounded by his Majesty's empire."

As we neared the land, its genius was felt. This was inevitably the British side. In every man's thought arises now a new system, English sentiments, English loves and fears, English history and social modes. Yesterday, every passenger had measured the speed of the ship by watching the bubbles over the ship's bulwarks. To-day, instead of bubbles, we measure by Kinsale, Cork, Waterford, and Ardmore. There lay the green shore of Ireland, like some coast of plenty. We could see towns, towers, churches, harvests; but the curse of eight hundred years we could not discern.

CHAPTER III.

LAND.

ALFIERI thought Italy and England the only countries worth living in; the former, because there nature vindicates her rights, and triumphs over the evils inflicted by the governments; the latter, because art conquers nature, and transforms a rude, ungenial land into a paradise of comfort and plenty. England is a garden. Under an ash-colored sky, the fields have been combed and rolled till they appear to have been finished with a pencil instead of a plough. The solidity of the structures that compose the towns speaks the industry of ages. Nothing is left as it was made. Rivers, hills, valleys, the sea itself, feel the hand of a master. The long habitation of a powerful and ingenious race has turned every rood of land to its best use, has found all the capabilities, the arable soil, the quarriable rock, the highways, the byways, the fords, the navigable waters; and the new arts of intercourse meet you everywhere; so that England is a huge phalanstery, where all that man wants is provided within the precinct. Cushioned and comforted in every manner, the traveller rides as on a cannon-ball, high and low, over rivers and towns, through mountains, in tunnels of three or four miles, at near twice the speed of our trains; and reads quietly the *Times* newspaper, which, by its immense correspondence and reporting, seems to have machinized the rest of the world for his occasion.

The problem of the traveller landing at Liverpool is, Why England is England. What are the elements of that power which the English hold over other nations? If there be one test of national genius universally accepted, it is success; and if there be one successful country in the universe for the last millennium, that country is England.

A wise traveller will naturally choose to visit the best of actual nations; and an American has more reasons than another to draw him to Britain. In all that is done or begun by the Americans towards right thinking or practice, we are met by a civilization already settled and overpowering. The culture of the day, the thoughts and aims of men, are English thoughts and aims. A nation considerable for a thousand years since Egbert, it has, in the last centuries, obtained the ascendant, and stamped the knowledge, activity, and power of mankind with its impress. Those who resist it do not feel it or obey it less. The Russian in his snows is aiming to be English. The Turk and Chinese also are making awkward efforts to be English. The practical common-sense of modern society, the utilitarian direction which labor, laws, opinion, religion take, is the natural genius of the British mind. The influence of France is a constituent of modern civility, but not enough opposed to the English for the most wholesome effect. The American is only the continuation of the English genius into new conditions, more or less propitious.

See what books fill our libraries. Every book we read, every biography, play, romance, in whatever form, is still English history and manners. So that a sensible Englishman once said to me, "As long as you do not grant us copyright, we shall have the teaching of you."

But we have the same difficulty in making a social or moral estimate of England, as the sheriff finds in drawing a jury to try some cause which has agitated the whole community, and on which everybody finds himself an interested party. Officers, jurors, judges, have all taken sides. England has inoculated all nations with her civilization, intelligence, and tastes; and, to resist the tyranny and prepossession of the British element, a serious man must aid himself, by comparing with it the civilizations of the farthest east and west, the old Greek, the Oriental, and, much more, the ideal standard, if only by means of the very impatience which English forms are sure to awaken in independent minds.

Besides, if we will visit London, the present time is the best time, as some signs portend that it has reached its highest point. It is observed that the English interest us a little less within a few years; and hence the impression that the British power has culminated, is in solstice, or already declining.

As soon as you enter England, which, with Wales, is no larger than the State of Georgia,* this little land stretches by an illusion to the dimensions of an empire. The innumerable details, the crowded succession of towns, cities, cathedrals, castles, and great and decorated estates, the number and power of the trades and guilds, the military strength and splendor, the multitudes of rich and of remarkable people, the servants and equipages, — all these catching the eye, and never allowing it to pause, hide all boundaries, by the impression of magnificence and endless wealth.

I reply to all the urgencies that refer me to this and that object indispensably to be seen, — Yes, to see England well needs a hundred years; for, what they told me was the merit of Sir John Soane's Museum, in London, — that it was well packed and well saved, — is the merit of England; — it is stuffed full, in all corners and crevices, with towns, towers, churches, villas, palaces, hospitals, and charity-houses. In the history of art, it is a long way from a cromlech to York minster; yet all the intermediate steps may still be traced in this all-preserving island.

The territory has a singular perfection. The climate is warmer by many degrees than it is entitled to by latitude. Neither hot nor cold, there is no hour in the whole year when one cannot work. Here is no winter, but such days as we have in Massachusetts in November, a temperature which makes no exhausting demand on human strength, but allows the attainment of the largest stature. Charles the Second said, "It invited men abroad more days in the year and more hours in the day than another country." Then England has all the materials of a working country except wood. The constant rain, — a rain with every tide, in some parts of the island, — keeps its multitude of rivers full, and brings agricultural production up to the highest point. It has plenty of water, of stone, of potter's clay, of coal, of salt, and of iron. The land naturally abounds with game, immense heaths and downs are paved with quails, grouse, and woodcock, and the shores are animated

* Add South Carolina, and you have more than an equivalent for the area of Scotland.

by water-birds. The rivers and the surrounding sea spawn with fish ; there are salmon for the rich, and sprats and herrings for the poor. In the northern lochs, the herring are in innumerable shoals ; at one season, the country people say, the lakes contain one part water and two parts fish.

The only drawback on this industrial conveniency is the darkness of its sky. The night and day are too nearly of a color. It strains the eyes to read and to write. Add the coal-smoke. In the manufacturing towns, the fine soot or *blacks* darken the day, give white sheep the color of black sheep, discolor the human saliva, contaminate the air, poison many plants, and corrode the monuments and buildings.

The London fog aggravates the distempers of the sky, and sometimes justifies the epigram on the climate by an English wit, "in a fine day, looking up a chimney; in a foul day, looking down one." A gentleman in Liverpool told me that he found he could do without a fire in his parlor about one day in the year. It is however pretended, that the enormous consumption of coal in the island is also felt in modifying the general climate.

Factitious climate, factitious position. England resembles a ship in its shape, and, if it were one, its best admiral could not have worked it, or anchored it in a more judicious or effective position. Sir John Herschel said, "London was the centre of the terrene globe." The shopkeeping nation, to use a shop word, has a *good stand.* The old Venetians pleased themselves with the flattery, that Venice was in 45°, midway between the poles and the line ; as if that were an imperial centrality. Long of old, the Greeks fancied Delphi the navel of the earth, in their favorite mode of fabling the earth to be an animal. The Jews belived Jerusalem to be the centre. I have seen a kratometric chart designed to show that the city of Philadelphia was in the same thermic belt, and, by inference, in the same belt of empire, as the cities of Athens, Rome, and London. It was drawn by a patriotic Philadelphian, and was examined with pleasure, under his showing, by the inhabitants of Chestnut Street. But, when carried to Charleston, to New Orleans, and to Boston, it somehow failed to convince the ingenious scholars of all those capitals.

But England is anchored at the side of Europe, and right in the heart of the modern world. The sea, which, according to Virgil's famous line, divided the poor Britons utterly from the world, proved to be the ring of marriage with all nations.

It is not down in the books, — it is written only in the geologic strata, — that fortunate day when a wave of the German Ocean burst the old isthmus which joined Kent and Cornwall to France, and gave to this fragment of Europe its impregnable sea-wall, cutting off an island of eight hundred miles in length, with an irregular breadth reaching to three hundred miles; a territory large enough for independence enriched with every seed of national power, so near, that it can see the harvests of the continent; and so far, that who would cross the strait must be an expert mariner, ready for tempests. As America, Europe, and Asia lie, these Britons have precisely the best commercial position in the whole planet, and are sure of a market for all the goods they can manufacture. And to make these advantages avail, the river Thames must dig its spacious outlet to the sea from the heart of the kingdom, giving road and landing to innumerable ships, and all the conveniency to trade, that a people so skilful and sufficient in economizing water-front by docks, warehouses, and lighters required. When James the First declared his purpose of punishing London by removing his Court, the Lord Mayor replied, "that, in removing his royal presence from his lieges, they hoped he would leave them the Thames."

In the variety of surface, Britain is a miniature of Europe, having plain, forest, marsh, river, sea-shore; mines in Cornwall; caves in Matlock and Derbyshire; delicious landscape in Dovedale, delicious sea-view at Tor Bay, Highlands in Scotland, Snowdon in Wales; and, in Westmoreland and Cumberland, a pocket Switzerland, in which the lakes and mountains are on a sufficient scale to fill the eye and touch the imagination. It is a nation conveniently small. Fontenelle thought, that nature had sometimes a little affectation; and there is such an artificial completeness in this nation of artificers, as if there were a design from the beginning to elaborate a bigger Birmingham. Nature held counsel with herself, and said, 'My Romans are gone. To build my new empire, I will choose a rude race, all masculine, with brutish strength. I will not grudge a competition of the roughest males. Let buffalo gore buffalo, and the pasture to the strongest! For I have work that requires the best will and sinew. Sharp and temperate northern breezes shall blow, to keep that will alive and alert. The sea shall disjoin the people from others, and knit them to a fierce nationality. It shall give them markets on every side. Long time I will keep them on their feet, by poverty, border-wars, seafaring, sea-risks, and the stimulus of gain. An island, — but not so large, the people not so many as to glut the great markets and depress one another, but proportioned to the size of Europe and the continents.'

With its fruits, and wares, and money, must its civil influence radiate. It is a singular coincidence to this geographic centrality, the spiritual centrality, which Emanuel Swedenborg ascribes to the people. "For the English nation, the best of them are in the centre of all Christians, because they have interior intellectual light. This appears conspicuously in the spiritual world. This light they derive from the liberty of speaking and writing, and thereby of thinking."

CHAPTER IV.

RACE.

AN ingenious anatomist has written a book * to prove that races are imperishable, but nations are pliant political constructions, easily changed or destroyed. But this writer did not found his assumed races on any necessary law, disclosing their ideal or metaphysical necessity; nor did he, on the other hand, count with precision the existing races, and settle the true bounds; a point of nicety, and the popular test of the theory. The individuals at the extremes of divergence in one race of men are as unlike as the wolf to the lapdog. Yet each variety shades down imperceptibly into the next, and you cannot draw the line where a race begins or ends. Hence every writer makes a different count. Blumenbach reckons five races; Humboldt, three; and Mr. Pickering, who lately, in our Exploring Expedition, thinks he saw all the kinds of men that can be on the planet, makes eleven.

The British Empire is reckoned to contain 222,000,000 souls, — perhaps a fifth of the population of the globe; and to comprise a territory of 5,000,000 square miles. So far have British people predominated. Perhaps forty of these millions are of British stock. Add the United States of America, which reckon, exclusive of slaves, 20,000,000 of people, on a territory of 3,000,000 square miles, and in which the

* The Races, a Fragment. By Robert Knox. London: 1850.

foreign element, however considerable, is rapidly assimilated, and you have a population of English descent and language, of 60,000,000, and governing a population of 245,000,000 souls.

The British census proper reckons twenty-seven and a half millions in the home countries. What makes this census important is the quality of the units that compose it. They are free forcible men, in a country where life is safe, and has reached the greatest value. They give the bias to the current age; and that, not by chance or by mass, but by their character, and by the number of individuals among them of personal ability. It has been denied that the English have genius. Be it as it may, men of vast intellect have been born on their soil, and they have made or applied the principal inventions. They have sound bodies, and supreme endurance in war and in labor. The spawning force of the race has sufficed to the colonization of great parts of the world; yet it remains to be seen whether they can make good the exodus of millions from Great Britain, amounting, in 1852, to more than a thousand a day. They have assimilating force, since they are imitated by their foreign subjects; and they are still aggressive and propagandist, enlarging the dominion of their arts and liberty. Their laws are hospitable, and slavery does not exist under them. What oppression exists is incidental and temporary; their success is not sudden or fortunate, but they have maintained constancy and self-equality for many ages.

Is this power due to their race, or to some other cause? Men hear gladly of the power of blood or race. Everybody likes to know that his advantages cannot be attributed to air, soil, sea, or to local wealth, as mines and quarries, nor to laws and traditions, nor to fortune, but to superior brain, as it makes the praise more personal to him.

We anticipate in the doctrine of race something like that law of physiology, that, whatever bone, muscle, or essential organ is found in one healthy individual, the same part or organ may be found in or near the same place in its congener; and we look to find in the son every mental and moral property that existed in the ancestor. In race, it is not the broad shoulders, or litheness, or stature that give advantage, but a symmetry that reaches as far as to the wit. Then the miracle and renown begin. Then first we care to examine the pedigree, and copy heedfully the training, — what food they ate, what nursing, school, and exercises they had, which resulted in this mother-wit, delicacy of thought, and robust wisdom.

How came such men as King Alfred, and Roger Bacon, William of Wykeham, Walter Raleigh, Philip Sidney, Isaac Newton, William Shakespeare, George Chapman, Francis Bacon, George Herbert, Henry Vane, to exist here? What made these delicate natures? was it the air? was it the sea? was it the parentage? For it is certain that these men are samples of their contemporaries. The hearing ear is always found close to the speaking tongue; and no genius can long or often utter anything which is not invited and gladly entertained by men around him.

It is race, is it not? that puts the hundred millions of India under the dominion of a remote island in the north of Europe. Race avails much, if that be true, which is alleged, that all Celts are Catholics, and all Saxons are Protestants; that Celts love unity of power, and Saxons the representative principle. Race is a controlling influence in the Jew, who, for two millenniums, under every climate, has preserved the same character and employments. Race in the negro is of appalling importance. The French in Canada, cut off from all intercourse with the parent people, have held their national traits. I chanced to read Tacitus "on the Manners of the Germans," not long since, in Missouri, and the heart of Illinois, and I found abundant points of resemblance between the Germans of the Hercynian forest, and our *Hoosiers*, *Suckers*, and *Badgers* of the American woods.

But whilst race works immortally to keep its own, it is resisted by other forces. Civilization is a re-agent, and eats away the old traits. The Arabs of to-day are the Arabs of Pharaoh; but the Briton of to-day is a very different person from Cassibelaunus or Ossian. Each religious sect has its physiognomy. The Methodists have acquired a face; the Quakers, a face; the nuns, a face. An Englishman will pick out a dissenter by his manners. Trades and professions carve their own lines on face and form. Certain circumstances of English life are not less effective: as, personal liberty; plenty of food; good ale and mutton; open market, or good wages for every kind of labor; high bribes to talent and skill; the island life, or the million opportunities and outlets for expanding and misplaced talent; readiness of combination among themselves for politics or for business; strikes; and sense of superiority founded on habit of victory in labor and in war; and the appetite for superiority grows by feeding.

It is easy to add to the counteracting forces to race. Credence is a main element. 'T is said, that the views of nature held by any people determine all their institutions. Whatever influences add to mental or moral faculty, take men out of nationality, as out of other conditions, and make the national life a culpable compromise.

These limitations of the formidable doctrine of race suggest others which threaten to undermine it, as not sufficiently based. The fixity or inconvertibleness of races as we see them, is a weak argument for the eternity of these frail boundaries, since all our historical period is a point to the duration in which nature has wrought. Any the least and solitariest fact in our natural history, such as the melioration of fruits and of animal stocks, has the worth of a *power* in the opportunity of geologic periods. Moreover, though we flatter the self-love of men and nations by the legend of pure races, all our experience is of the gradation and resolution of races, and strange resemblances meet us everywhere. It need not puzzle us that Malay and Papuan, Celt and Roman, Saxon and Tartar, should mix, when we see the rudiments of tiger and baboon in our human form, and know that the barriers of races are not so firm, but that some spray sprinkles us from the antediluvian seas.

The low organizations are simplest; a mere mouth, a jelly, or a straight worm. As the scale mounts, the organizations become complex. We are piqued with pure descent, but nature loves inoculation. A child blends in his face the faces of both parents, and some feature from every ancestor whose face hangs on the wall. The best nations are those most widely related; and navigation, as effecting a world-wide mixture, is the most potent advancer of nations.

The English composite character betrays a mixed origin. Everything English is a fusion of distant and antagonistic elements. The language is mixed; the names of men are of different nations, — three languages, three or four nations; — the currents of thought are counter: contemplation and practical skill; active intellect and dead conservatism; world-wide enterprise, and devoted use and wont; aggressive freedom and hospitable law, with bitter class-legislation; a people scattered by their wars and affairs over the face of the whole earth, and homesick to a man; a country of extremes, — dukes and chartists, Bishops of Durham and naked heathen colliers; — nothing can be praised in it without damning exceptions, and nothing denounced without salvos of cordial praise.

Neither do this people appear to be of one stem; but collectively a better race than any from which they are derived. Nor is it easy to trace it home to its original seats. Who can call by right names what races are in Britain? Who can trace them historically? Who can discriminate them anatomically, or metaphysically?

In the impossibility of arriving at satisfaction on the historical question of race, and — come of whatever disputable ancestry — the indisputable Englishman before me, himself very well marked, and nowhere else to be found, — I fancied I could leave quite aside the choice of a tribe as his lineal progenitors. Defoe said in his wrath, "the Englishman was the mud of all races." I incline to the belief, that, as water, lime, and sand make mortar, so certain temperaments marry well, and, by well-managed contrarieties, develop as drastic a character as the English. On the whole, it is not so much a history of one or of certain tribes of Saxons, Jutes, or Frisians, coming from one place, and genetically identical, as it is an anthology of temperaments out of them all. Certain temperaments suit the sky and soil of England, say eight or ten or twenty varieties, as, out of a hundred pear-trees, eight or ten suit the soil of an orchard, and thrive, whilst all the unadapted temperaments die out.

The English derive their pedigree from such a range of nationalities, that there needs sea-room and land-room to unfold the varieties of talent and character. Perhaps the ocean serves as a galvanic battery to distribute acids at one pole, and alkalies at the other. So England tends to accumulate her liberals in America, and her conservatives at London. The Scandinavians in her race still hear in every age the murmurs of their mother, the ocean; the Briton in the blood hugs the homestead still.

Again, as if to intensate the influences that are not of race, what we think of when we talk of English traits really narrows itself to a small district. It excludes Ireland, and Scotland, and Wales, and reduces itself at last to London, that is, to those who come and go thither. The portraits that hang on the walls in the Academy Exhibition at London, the figures in Punch's drawings of the public men, or of the club-houses, the prints in the shop-windows, are distinctive English, and not American, no, nor Scotch, nor Irish: but 't is a very restricted nationality. As you go north into the manufacturing and agricultural districts, and to the population that never travels, as you go into Yorkshire, as you enter Scotland, the world's Englishman is no longer found. In Scotland, there is a rapid loss of all grandeur of mien and manners; a provincial eagerness and acuteness appear; the poverty of the country makes itself remarked, and a coarseness of manners; and, among the intellectual, is the insanity of dialectics. In Ireland, are the same climate and soil as in England, but less food, no right relation to the land, political dependence, small tenantry, and an inferior or misplaced race.

These queries concerning ancestry and blood may be well allowed, for there is no prosperity that seems more to depend on the kind of man than British prosperity. Only a hardy and wise people could have made this small territory great. We say, in a regatta or yacht-race, that if the boats are anywhere nearly matched, it is the man that wins. Put the best sailing-master into either boat, and he will win.

Yet it is fine for us to speculate in face of unbroken traditions, though vague, and losing themselves in fable. The traditions have got footing, and refuse to be disturbed. The kitchen-clock is more convenient than sidereal time. We must use the popular category, as we do by the Linnæan classification, for convenience, and not as exact and final. Otherwise, we are presently confounded, when the best-settled traits of one race are claimed by some new ethnologist as precisely characteristic of the rival tribe.

I found plenty of well-marked English types, the ruddy complexion fair and plump, robust men, with faces cut like a die, and a strong island speech and accent; a Norman type, with the complacency that belongs to that constitution. Others, who might be Americans, for anything that appeared in their complexion or form: and their speech was much less marked, and their thought much less bound. We will call them Saxons. Then the Roman has implanted his dark complexion in the trinity or quaternity of bloods.

1. The sources from which tradition derives their stock are mainly three. And, first, they are of the oldest blood of the world, — the Celtic. Some peoples are deciduous or transitory. Where are the Greeks? where the Etrurians? where the Romans? But the Celts or Sidonides are an old family, of whose beginning there is no memory, and their end is likely to be still more remote in the future; for they have endurance and productiveness. They planted Britain, and gave to the

seas and mountains names which are poems, and imitate the pure voices of nature. They are favorably remembered in the oldest records of Europe. They had no violent feudal tenure, but the husbandman owned the land. They had an alphabet, astronomy, priestly culture, and a sublime creed. They have a hidden and precarious genius. They made the best popular literature of the Middle Ages in the songs of Merlin, and the tender and delicious mythology of Arthur.

2. The English come mainly from the Germans, whom the Romans found hard to conquer in two hundred and ten years, — say, impossible to conquer, — when one remembers the long sequel; a people about whom, in the old empire, the rumor ran, there was never any that meddled with them that repented it not.

3. Charlemagne, halting one day in a town of Narbonnese Gaul, looked out of a window, and saw a fleet of Northmen cruising in the Mediterranean. They even entered the port of the town where he was, causing no small alarm and sudden manning and arming of his galleys. As they put out to sea again, the emperor gazed long after them, his eyes bathed in tears. "I am tormented with sorrow," he said, "when I foresee the evils they will bring on my posterity." There was reason for these Xerxes' tears. The men who have built a ship and invented the rig, — cordage, sail, compass, and pump, — the working in and out of port, have acquired much more than a ship. Now arm them, and every shore is at their mercy. For, if they have not numerical superiority where they anchor, they have only to sail a mile or two to find it. Bonaparte's art of war, namely, of concentrating force on the point of attack, must always be theirs who have the choice of the battle-ground. Of course they come into the fight from a higher ground of power than the land-nations; and can engage them on shore with a victorious advantage in the retreat. As soon as the shores are sufficiently peopled to make piracy a losing business, the same skill and courage are ready for the service of trade.

The *Heimskringla*,* or Sagas of the Kings of Norway, collected by Snorro Sturleson, is the Iliad and Odyssey of English history. Its portraits, like Homer's, are strongly individualized. The Sagas describe a monarchical republic like Sparta. The government disappears before the importance of

* Heimskringla. Translated by Samuel Laing, Esq. London: 1844.

citizens. In Norway, no Persian masses fight and perish to aggrandize a king, but the actors are bonders or land-holders, every one of whom is named and personally and patronymically described, as the king's friend and companion. A sparse population gives this high worth to every man. Individuals are often noticed as very handsome persons, which trait only brings the story nearer to the English race. Then the solid material interest predominates, so dear to English understanding, wherein the association is logical, between merit and land. The heroes of the Sagas are not the knights of South Europe. No vaporing of France and Spain has corrupted them. They are substantial farmers, whom the rough times have forced to defend their properties. They have weapons which they use in a determined manner, by no means for chivalry, but for their acres. They are people considerably advanced in rural arts, living amphibiously on a rough coast, and drawing half their food from the sea, and half from the land. They have herds of cows, and malt, wheat, bacon, butter, and cheese. They fish in the fiord, and hunt the deer. A king among these farmers has a varying power, sometimes not exceeding the authority of a sheriff. A king was maintained much as, in some of our country districts, a winter-schoolmaster is quartered, a week here, a week there, and a fortnight on the next farm, — on all the farmers in rotation. This the king calls going into guest-quarters; and it was the only way in which, in a poor country, a poor king, with many retainers, could be kept alive, when he leaves his own farm to collect his dues through the kingdom.

These Norsemen are excellent persons in the main, with good sense, steadiness, wise speech, and prompt action. But they have a singular turn for homicide; their chief end of man is to murder or to be murdered; oars, scythes, harpoons, crowbars, peat-knives, and hayforks are tools valued by them all the more for their charming aptitude for assassinations. A pair of kings, after dinner, will divert themselves by thrusting each his sword through the other's body, as did Yngve and Alf. Another pair ride out on a morning for a frolic, and, finding no weapon near, will take the bits out of their horses' mouths, and crush each other's heads with them, as did Alric and Eric. The sight of a tent-cord or a cloak-string puts them on hanging somebody, a wife, or a husband, or, best of all, a king. If a farmer has so much as a hayfork, he sticks it into a King Dag. King Ingiald finds it vastly amusing to burn up half a dozen kings in a hall, after getting them drunk. Never was poor gentleman so surfeited with life, so furious to be rid of it, as the Northman. If he cannot pick any other quarrel, he will get himself comfortably gored by a bull's horns, like Egil, or slain by a land-slide, like the agricultural King Onund. Odin died in his bed, in Sweden; but it was a proverb of ill condition, to die the death of old age. King Hake of Sweden cuts and slashes in battle, as long as he can stand, then orders his war-ship, loaded with his dead men and their weapons, to be taken out to sea, the tiller shipped, and the sails spread; being left alone, he sets fire to some tar-wood, and lies down contented on deck. The wind blew off the land, the ship flew burning in clear flame, out between the islets into the ocean, and there was the right end of King Hake.

The early Sagas are sanguinary and piratical; the later are of a noble strain. History rarely yields us better passages than the conversation between King Sigurd the Crusader, and King Eystein, his brother, on their respective merits, — one, the soldier, and the other, a lover of the arts of peace.

But the reader of the Norman history must steel himself by holding fast the remote compensations which result from animal vigor. As the old fossil world shows that the first steps of reducing the chaos were confided to saurians and other huge and horrible animals, so the foundations of the new civility were to be laid by the most savage men.

The Normans came out of France into England worse men than they went into it, one hundred and sixty years before. They had lost their own language, and learned the Romance or barbarous Latin of the Gauls; and had acquired, with the language, all the vices it had names for. The conquest has obtained in the chronicles, the name of the "memory of sorrow." Twenty thousand thieves landed at Hastings. These founders of the House of Lords were greedy and ferocious dragoons, sons of greedy and ferocious pirates. They were all alike, they took everything they could carry, they burned, harried, violated, tortured, and killed, until everything English was brought to the verge of ruin. Such, however, is the illusion of antiquity and wealth, that decent and dignified men now existing boast their descent from these filthy thieves, who showed a far juster conviction of their own merits, by assuming for their types the swine, goat, jackal, leopard, wolf, and snake, which they severally resembled.

England yielded to the Danes and Northmen in the tenth and eleventh centuries, and was the receptacle into which all the mettle of that strenuous population was poured. The continued draught of the best men in Norway, Sweden, and Denmark, to these piratical expeditions, exhausted those countries, like a tree which bears much fruit when young, and these have been second-rate powers ever since. The power of the race migrated, and left Norway void. King Olaf said: "When King Harold, my father, went westward to England, the chosen men in Norway followed him; but Norway was so emptied then, that such men have not since been to find in the country, nor especially such a leader as King Harold was for wisdom and bravery."

It was a tardy recoil of these invasions, when, in 1801, the British government sent Nelson to bombard the Danish forts in the Sound; and, in 1807, Lord Cathcart, at Copenhagen, took the entire Danish fleet, as it lay in the basins, and all the equipments from the Arsenal, and carried them to England. Konghelle, the town where the kings of Norway, Sweden, and Denmark were wont to meet, is now rented to a private English gentleman for a hunting-ground.

It took many generations to trim, and comb, and perfume the first boat-load of Norse pirates into royal highnesses and most noble Knights of the Garter: but every sparkle of ornament dates back to the Norse boat. There will be time enough to mellow this strength into civility and religion. It is a medical fact, that the children of the blind see; the children of felons have a healthy conscience. Many a mean, dastardly boy is, at the age of puberty, transformed into a serious and generous youth.

The mildness of the following ages has not quite effaced these traits of Odin; as the rudiment of a structure matured in the tiger is said to be still found unabsorbed in the Caucasian man. The nation has a tough, acrid, animal nature, which centuries of churching and civilizing have not been able to sweeten. Alfieri said, "the crimes of Italy were the proof of the superiority of the stock"; and one may say of England, that this watch moves on a splinter of adamant. The English uncultured are a brutal nation. The crimes recorded in their calendars leave nothing to be desired in the way of cold malignity. Dear to the English heart is a fair stand-up fight. The brutality of the manners in the lower class appears in the boxing, bear-baiting, cock-fighting, love of executions, and in the readiness for a set-to in the streets, delightful to the English of all classes. The costermongers of London streets hold cowardice in loathing: — "we must work our fists well; we are all handy with our fists." The public schools are charged with being bear-gardens of brutal strength, and are liked by the people for that cause. The fagging is a trait of the same quality. Medwin, in the Life of Shelley, relates, that, at a military school, they rolled up a young man in a snowball, and left him so in his room, while the other cadets went to church; — and crippled him for life. They have retained impressment, deck-flogging, army-flogging, and school-flogging. Such is the ferocity of the army discipline, that a soldier sentenced to flogging, sometimes prays that his sentence may be commuted to death. Flogging banished from the armies of Western Europe, remains here by the sanction of the Duke of Wellington. The right of the husband to sell the wife has been retained down to our times. The Jews have been the favorite victims of royal and popular persecution. Henry III. mortgaged all the Jews in the kingdom to his brother, the Earl of Cornwall, as security for money which he borrowed. The torture of criminals, and the rack for extorting evidence, were slowly disused. Of the criminal statutes, Sir Samuel Romilly said, "I have examined the codes of all nations, and ours is the worst, and worthy of the Anthropophagi." In the last session, the House of Commons was listening to details of flogging and torture practised in the jails.

As soon as this land, thus geographically posted, got a hardy people into it, they could not help becoming the sailors and factors of the globe. From childhood, they dabbled in water, they swum like fishes, their playthings were boats. In the case of the ship-money, the judges delivered it for law, that "England being an island, the very midland shires therein are all to be accounted maritime": and Fuller adds, "the genius even of land-locked countries driving the natives with a maritime dexterity." As early as the conquest, it is remarked in explanation of the wealth of England, that its merchants trade to all countries.

The English, at the present day, have great vigor of body and endurance. Other countrymen look slight and undersized beside them, and invalids. They are bigger men than the Americans. I suppose a hundred English taken at random out of the street would weigh a fourth more than so many Americans. Yet, I am told, the skeleton is not larger. They are round, ruddy, and handsome; at least, the whole bust is well formed; and there is a tendency to stout and powerful frames. I remarked the stoutness, on my first landing at Liverpool; porter, drayman, coachman, guard, — what substantial, respectable, grandfatherly figures, with costume and manners to suit. The American has arrived at the old mansion-house, and finds himself among uncles, aunts, and grandsires. The pictures on the chimney-tiles of his nursery were pictures of these people. Here they are in the identical costumes and air, which so took him.

It is the fault of their forms that they grow stocky, and the women have that disadvantage, — few tall, slender figures of flowing shape, but stunted and thickset persons. The French say, that the Englishwomen have two left hands. But, in all ages, they are a handsome race. The bronze monuments of crusaders lying cross-legged, in the Temple Church at London, and those in Worcester and in Salisbury Cathedrals, which are seven hundred years old, are of the same type as the best youthful heads of men now in England; — please by beauty of the same character, an expression blending good-nature, valor, and refinement, and, mainly, by that uncorrupt youth in the face of manhood, which is daily seen in the streets of London.

Both branches of the Scandinavian race are distinguished for beauty. The anecdote of the handsome captives which Saint Gregory found at Rome, A. D. 600, is matched by the testimony of the Norman chroniclers, five centuries later, who wondered at the beauty and long flowing hair of the young English captives. Meantime, the Heimskringla has frequent occasion to speak of the personal beauty of its heroes. When it is considered what humanity, what resources of mental and moral power, the traits of the blond race betoken, — its accession to empire marks a new and finer epoch, wherein the old mineral force shall be subjugated at last by humanity, and shall plough in its furrow henceforward. It is not a final race, once a crab always crab, but a race with a future.

On the English face are combined decision and nerve, with the fair complexion, blue eyes, and open and florid aspect. Hence the love of truth, hence the sensibility, the fine perception, and poetic construction. The fair Saxon man, with open front, and honest meaning, domestic, affectionate, is not the wood out of which cannibal, or inquisitor, or assassin is made. But he is moulded for law, lawful trade, civility, marriage, the nurture of children, for colleges, churches, charities, and colonies.

They are rather manly than warlike. When the war is over, the mask falls from the affectionate and domestic tastes, which make them women in kindness. This union of qualities is fabled in their national legend of *Beauty and the Beast*, or long before, in the Greek legend of *Hermaphrodite*. The two sexes are co-present in the English mind. I apply to Britannia, queen of seas and colonies, the words in which her latest novelist portrays his heroine : " she is as mild as she is game, and as game as she is mild." The English delight in the antagonism which combines in one person the extremes of courage and tenderness. Nelson, dying at Trafalgar, sends his love to Lord Collingwood, and, like an innocent school-boy that goes to bed, says, " Kiss me, Hardy," and turns to sleep. Lord Collingwood, his comrade, was of a nature the most affectionate and domestic. Admiral Rodney's figure approached to delicacy and effeminacy, and he declared himself very sensible to fear, which he surmounted only by considerations of honor and public duty. Clarendon says, the Duke of Buckingham was so modest and gentle, that some courtiers attempted to put affronts on him, until they found that this modesty and effeminacy was only a mask for the most terrible determination. And Sir Edward Parry said, the other day, of Sir John Franklin, that, " if he found Wellington Sound open, he explored it ; for he was a man who never turned his back on a danger, yet of that tenderness, that he would not brush away a mosquito." Even for their highwaymen the same virtue is claimed, and Robin Hood comes described to us as *mitissimus prædonum*, the gentlest thief. But they know where their war-dogs lie. Cromwell, Blake, Marlborough, Chatham, Nelson, and Wellington are not to be trifled with, and the brutal strength which lies at the bottom of society, the animal ferocity of the quays and cockpits, the bullies of the costermongers of Shoreditch, Seven Dials, and Spitalfields, they know how to wake up.

They have a vigorous health, and last well into middle and old age. The old men are as red as roses, and still handsome. A clear skin, a peach-bloom complexion, and good teeth, are found all over the island. They use a plentiful and nutritious diet. The operative cannot subsist on water-cresses. Beef, mutton, wheat-bread, and malt-liquors are universal among the first-class laborers. Good feeding is a chief point of national pride among the vulgar, and, in their caricatures, they represent the Frenchman as a poor, starved body. It is curious that Tacitus found the English beer already in use among the Germans : " they make from barley or wheat a drink corrupted into some resemblance to wine." Lord Chief Justice Fortescue in Henry VI.'s time, says : " The inhabitants of England drink no water, unless at certain times, on a religious score, and by way of penance." The extremes of poverty and ascetic penance, it would seem, never reach cold water in England. Wood, the antiquary, in describing the poverty and maceration of Father Lacey, an English Jesuit, does not deny him beer. He says, " his bed was under a thatching, and the way to it up a ladder; his fare was coarse; his drink, of a penny a gawn, or gallon."

They have more constitutional energy than any other people. They think, with Henri Quatre, that manly exercises are the foundation of that elevation of mind which gives one nature ascendant over another; or, with the Arabs, that the days spent in the chase are not counted in the length of life. They box, run, shoot, ride, row, and sail from pole to pole. They eat and drink, and live jolly in the open air, putting a bar of solid sleep between day and day. They walk and ride as fast as they can, their heads bent forward, as if urged on some pressing affair. The French say, that Englishmen in the street always walk straight before them like mad dogs. Men and women walk with infatuation. As soon as he can handle a gun, hunting is the fine art of every Englishman of condition. They are the most voracious people of prey that ever existed. Every season turns out the aristocracy into the country, to shoot and fish. The more vigorous run out of the island to Europe, to America, to Asia, to Africa, and Australia, to hunt with fury by gun, by trap, by harpoon, by lasso, with dog, with horse, with elephant, or with dromedary, all the game that is in nature. These men have written the game-books of all countries, as Hawker, Scrope, Murray, Herbert, Maxwell, Cumming, and a host of travellers. The people at home are addicted to boxing, running, leaping, and rowing matches.

I suppose, the dogs and horses must be thanked for the fact, that the men have muscles almost as tough and supple as their own. If in every efficient man, there is first a fine animal, in the English race it is of the best breed, a wealthy, juicy, broad-chested creature, steeped in ale and good cheer, and a little overloaded by his flesh. Men of animal nature rely, like animals, on their instincts. The Englishman associates well with dogs and horses. His attachment to the horse arises from the courage and address required to manage it. The horse finds out who is afraid of it, and does not disguise its opinion. Their young boiling clerks and lusty collegians like the company of horses better than the company of professors. I suppose, the horses are better company for them. The horse has more uses than Buffon noted. If you go into the streets, every driver in bus or dray is a bully, and, if I wanted a good troop of soldiers, I should recruit among the stables. Add a certain degree of refinement to the vivacity of these riders, and you obtain the precise quality which makes the men and women of polite society formidable.

They come honestly by their horsemanship, with *Hengst* and *Horsa* for their Saxon founders. The other branch of their race had been Tartar nomads. The horse was all their wealth. The children were fed on mares' milk. The pastures of Tartary were still remembered by the tenacious practice of the Norsemen to eat horse-flesh at religious feasts. In the Danish invasions, the marauders seized upon horses where they landed, and were at once converted into a body of expert cavalry.

At one time, this skill seems to have declined. Two centuries ago, the English horse never performed any eminent service beyond the seas; and the reason assigned, was, that the genius of the English hath always more inclined them to foot-service, as pure and proper manhood, without any mixture; whilst, in a victory on horseback, the credit ought to be divided betwixt the man and his horse. But in two hundred years, a change has taken place. Now, they boast that they understand horses better than any other people in the world, and that their horses are become their second selves.

"William the Conqueror being," says Camden, "better affected to beasts than to men, imposed heavy fines and punishments on those that should meddle with his game." The Saxon Chronicle says, "he loved the tall deer as if he were their father." And rich Englishmen have followed his example, according to their ability, ever since, in encroaching on the tillage and commons with their game-preserves. It is a proverb in England, that it is safer to shoot a man than a hare. The severity of the game-laws certainly indicates an extravagant sympathy of the nation with horses and hunters. The gentlemen are always on horseback, and have brought horses to an ideal perfection, — the English racer is a factitious breed. A score or two of mounted gentlemen may frequently be seen running like centaurs down a hill nearly as steep as the roof of a house. Every inn-room is lined with pictures of races; telegraphs communicate, every hour, tidings of the heats from Newmarket and Ascot: and the House of Commons adjourns over the 'Derby Day.'

CHAPTER V.

ABILITY.

THE Saxon and the Northman are both Scandinavians. History does not allow us to fix the limits of the application of these names with any accuracy; but from the residence of a portion of these people in France, and from some effect of that powerful soil on their blood and manners, the Norman has come popularly to represent in England the aristocratic, and the Saxon the democratic principle. And though, I doubt not, the nobles are of both tribes, and the workers of both, yet we are forced to use the names a little mythically, one to represent the worker, and the other the enjoyer.

The island was a prize for the best race. Each of the dominant races tried its fortune in turn. The Phœnician, the Celt, and the Goth, had already got in. The Roman came, but in the very day when his fortune culminated. He looked in the eyes of a new people that was to supplant his own. He disembarked his legions, erected his camps and towers, — presently he heard bad news from Italy, and worse and worse, every year: at last, he made a handsome compliment of roads and walls, and departed. But the Saxon seriously settled in the land, builded, tilled, fished, and traded, with German truth and adhesiveness. The Dane came, and divided with him. Last of all, the Norman, or French-Dane, arrived, and formally conquered, harried, and ruled the kingdom. A century later, it came out, that the Saxon had the most bottom and longevity, had managed to make the victor speak the language and accept the law and usage of the victim; forced the baron to dictate Saxon terms to Norman kings; and, step by step, got all the essential securities of civil liberty invented and confirmed. The genius of the race and the genius of the place conspired to this effect. The island is lucrative to free labor, but not worth possession on other terms. The race was so intellectual, that a feudal or military tenure could not last longer than the war. The power of the Saxon-Danes, so thoroughly beaten in the war, that the name of English and villein were synonymous, yet so vivacious as to extort charters from the kings, stood on the strong personality of these people. Sense and economy must rule in a world which is made of sense and economy, and the banker, with his seven per cent, drives the earl out of his castle. A nobility of soldiers cannot keep down a commonalty of shrewd scientific persons. What signifies a pedigree of a hundred links, against a cotton-spinner with steam in his mill; or, against a company of broad-shouldered Liverpool merchants, for whom Stephenson and Brunel are contriving locomotives and a tubular bridge?

These Saxons are the hands of mankind. They have the taste for toil, a distaste for pleasure or repose, and the telescopic appreciation of distant gain. They are the wealth-makers, — and by dint of mental faculty which has its own conditions. The Saxon works after liking, or, only for himself; and to set him at work, and to begin to draw his monstrous values out of barren Britain, all dishonor, fret, and barrier must be removed, and then his energies begin to play.

The Scandinavian fancied himself surrounded by Trolls, — a kind of goblin men, with vast power of work and skilful production, — divine stevedores, carpenters, reapers, smiths, and masons, swift to reward every kindness done them, with gifts of gold and silver. In all English history, this dream comes to pass. Certain Trolls or working brains, under the names of Alfred, Bede, Caxton, Bracton, Camden, Drake, Selden, Dugdale, Newton, Gibbon, Brindley, Watt, Wedgwood, dwell in the troll-mounts of Britain, and turn the sweat of their face to power and renown.

If the race is good, so is the place. Nobody landed on this spell-bound island with impunity. The enchantments of barren shingle and rough weather transformed every adventurer into a laborer. Each vagabond that arrived bent his neck to the yoke of gain, or found the air too tense for him. The strong survived, the weaker went to the ground. Even the pleasure-hunters and sots of England are of a tougher texture. A hard temperament had been formed by Saxon and Saxon-Dane, and such of these French or Normans as could reach it, were naturalized in every sense.

All the admirable expedients or means hit upon in England, must be looked at as growths or irresistible offshoots of the expanding mind of the race. A man of that brain thinks and acts thus; and his neighbor, being afflicted with the same kind of brain, though he is rich, and called a baron, or a duke, thinks the same thing, and is ready to allow the justice of the thought and act in his retainer or tenant, though sorely against his baronial or ducal will.

The island was renowned in antiquity for its breed of mastiffs, so fierce, that when their teeth were set, you must cut their heads off to part them. The man was like his dog. The people have that nervous bilious temperament, which is known by medical men to resist every means employed to make its possessor subservient to the will of others. The English game is main force to main force, the planting of foot to foot, fair play and open field, — a rough tug without trick or dodging, till one or both come to pieces. King Ethelwald spoke the language of his race, when he planted himself at Wimborne, and said, 'he would do one of two things, or there live, or there lie.' They hate craft and subtlety. They neither poison, nor waylay, nor assassinate; and, when they have pounded each other to a poultice, they will shake hands and be friends for the remainder of their lives.

You shall trace these Gothic touches at school, at country fairs, at the hustings, and in parliament. No artifice, no breach of truth and plain dealing, — not so much as secret ballot, is suffered in the island. In parliament, the tactics of the opposition is to resist every step of the government, by a pitiless attack; and in a bargain, no prospect of advantage is so dear to the merchant, as the thought of being tricked is mortifying.

Sir Kenelm Digby, a courtier of Charles and James, who won the sea-fight of Scanderoon, was a model Englishman in his day. "His person was handsome and gigantic, he had so graceful elocution and noble address, that, had he been dropt out of the clouds in any part of the world, he would have made himself respected: he was skilled in six tongues, and master of arts and arms." * Sir Kenelm wrote a book, "Of Bodies and of Souls," in which he propounds, that "syllogisms do breed or rather are all the variety of man's life. They are the steps by which we walk in all our businesses. Man, as he is man, doth nothing else but weave such chains. Whatsoever he

* Antony Wood.

doth, swarving from this work, he doth as deficient from the nature of man : and, if he do aught beyond this, by breaking out into divers sorts of exterior actions, he findeth, nevertheless, in this linked sequel of simple discourses, the art, the cause, the rule, the bounds, and the model of it." *

There spoke the genius of the English people. There is a necessity on them to be logical. They would hardly greet the good that did not logically fall, — as if it excluded their own merit, or shook their understandings. They are jealous of minds that have much facility of association, from an instinctive fear that the seeing many relations to their thought might impair this serial continuity and lucrative concentration. They are impatient of genius, or of minds addicted to contemplation, and cannot conceal their contempt for sallies of thought, however lawful, whose steps they cannot count by their wonted rule. Neither do they reckon better a syllogism that ends in syllogism. For they have a supreme eye to facts, and theirs is a logic that brings salt to soup, hammer to nail, oar to boat, the logic of cooks, carpenters, and chemists, following the sequence of nature, and one on which words make no impression. Their mind is not dazzled by its own means, but locked and bolted to results. They love men, who, like Samuel Johnson, a doctor in the schools, would jump out of his syllogism the instant his major proposition was in danger, to save that, at all hazards. Their practical vision is spacious, and they can hold many threads without entangling them. All the steps they orderly take; but with the high logic of never confounding the minor and major proposition; keeping their eye on their aim, in all the complicity and delay incident to the several series of means they employ. There is room in their minds for this and that, — a science of degrees. In the courts, the independence of the judges and the loyalty of the suitors are equally excellent. In Parliament, they have hit on that capital invention of freedom, a constitutional opposition. And when courts and parliament are both deaf, the plaintiff is not silenced. Calm, patient, his weapon of defence from year to year is the obstinate reproduction of the grievance, with calculations and estimates. But, meantime, he is drawing numbers and money to his opinion, resolved that if all remedy fails, right of revolution is at the bottom of his charter-box. They are bound to see their measure carried, and stick to it through ages of defeat.

* Man's Soule, p. 29.

Into this English logic, however, an infusion of justice enters, not so apparent in other races, — a belief in the existence of two sides, and the resolution to see fair play. There is on every question, an appeal from the assertion of the parties, to the proof of what is asserted. They are impious in their scepticism of a theory, but kiss the dust before a fact. Is it a machine, is it a charter, is it a boxer in the ring, is it a candidate on the hustings, — the universe of Englishmen will suspend their judgment, until the trial can be had. They are not to be led by a phrase, they want a working plan, a working machine, a working constitution, and will sit out the trial, and abide by the issue, and reject all preconceived theories. In politics they put blunt questions, which must be answered; who is to pay the taxes? what will you do for trade? what for corn? what for the spinner?

This singular fairness and its results strike the French with surprise. Philip de Commines says: "Now, in my opinion, among all the sovereignties I know in the world, that in which the public good is best attended to, and the least violence exercised on the people, is that of England." Life is safe, and personal rights; and what is freedom, without security? whilst, in France, 'fraternity,' 'equality,' and 'indivisible unity,' are names for assassination. Montesquieu said: "England is the freest country in the world. If a man in England had as many enemies as hairs on his head, no harm would happen to him."

Their self-respect, their faith in causation, and their realistic logic or coupling of means to ends, have given them the leadership of the modern world. Montesquieu said, "No people have true common sense but those who are born in England." This common sense is a perception of all the conditions of our earthly existence, of laws that can be stated, and of laws that cannot be stated, or that are learned only by practice, in which allowance for friction is made. They are impious in their scepticism of theory, and in high departments they are cramped and sterile. But the unconditional surrender to facts, and the choice of means to reach their ends, are as admirable as with ants and bees.

The bias of the nation is a passion for utility. They love the lever, the screw, and pulley, the Flanders draught-horse, the waterfall, wind-mills, tide-mills; the sea and the wind to bear their freight ships. More than the diamond Koh-i-noor, which glitters among their crown jewels, they prize that dull pebble which is wiser than a man, whose poles turn themselves to the poles of the world, and whose axis is parallel to the axis of the world. Now, their toys are steam and galvanism. They are heavy at the fine arts, but adroit at the coarse; not good in jewelry or mosaics, but the best iron-masters, colliers, wool-combers, and tanners, in Europe. They apply themselves to agriculture, to draining, to resisting encroachments of sea, wind, travelling sands, cold and wet subsoil; to fishery, to manufacture of indispensable staples, — salt, plumbago, leather, wool, glass, pottery, and brick, — to bees and silkworms; and by their steady combinations they succeed. A manufacturer sits down to dinner in a suit of clothes which was wool on a sheep's back at sunrise. You dine with a gentleman on venison, pheasant, quail, pigeons, poultry, mushrooms, and pine-apples, all the growth of his estate. They are neat husbands for ordering all their tools pertaining to house and field. All are well kept. There is no want and no waste. They study use and fitness in their building, in the order of their dwellings, and in their dress. The Frenchman invented the ruffle, the Englishman added the shirt. The Englishman wears a sensible coat buttoned to the chin, of rough but solid and lasting texture. If he is a lord, he dresses a little worse than a commoner. They have diffused the taste for plain substantial hats, shoes, and coats through Europe. They think him the best dressed man, whose dress is so fit for his use that you cannot notice or remember to describe it.

They secure the essentials in their diet, in their arts, and manufactures. Every article of cutlery shows, in its shape, thought and long experience of workmen. They put the expense in the right place, as, in their sea-steamers, in the solidity of the machinery and the strength of the boat. The admirable equipment of their arctic ships carries London to the pole. They build roads, aqueducts, warm and ventilate houses. And they have impressed their directness and practical habit on modern civilization.

In trade, the Englishman believes that nobody breaks who ought not to break; and, that, if he do not make trade everything, it will make him nothing; and acts on this belief. The spirit of system, attention to details, and the subordination of details, or, the not driving things too finely, (which is charged on the Germans,) constitute that despatch of business, which makes the mercantile power of England.

In war, the Englishman looks to his means. He is of the

opinion of Civilis, his German ancestor, whom Tacitus reports as holding "that the gods are on the side of the strongest"; — a sentence which Bonaparte unconsciously translated, when he said, "that he had noticed, that Providence always favored the heaviest battalion." Their military science propounds that if the weight of the advancing column is greater than that of the resisting, the latter is destroyed. Therefore Wellington, when he came to the army in Spain, had every man weighed, first with accoutrements, and then without; believing that the force of an army depended on the weight and power of the individual soldiers, in spite of cannon. Lord Palmerston told the House of Commons, that more care is taken of the health and comfort of English troops than of any other troops in the world; and that hence the English can put more men into the rank, on the day of action, on the field of battle, than any other army. Before the bombardment of the Danish forts in the Baltic, Nelson spent day after day, himself in the boats, on the exhausting service of sounding the channel. Clerk of Eldin's celebrated manœuvre of breaking the line of sea-battle, and Nelson's feat of *doubling*, or stationing his ships one on the outer bow, and another on the outer quarter of each of the enemy's were only translations into naval tactics of Bonaparte's rule of concentration. Lord Collingwood was accustomed to tell his men, that, if they could fire three well-directed broadsides in five minutes, no vessel could resist them; and, from constant practice, they came to do it in three minutes and a half.

But conscious that no race of better men exists, they rely most on the simplest means; and do not like ponderous and difficult tactics, but delight to bring the affair hand to hand, where the victory lies with the strength, courage, and endurance of the individual combatants. They adopt every improvement in rig, in motor, in weapons, but they fundamentally believe that the best stratagem in naval war is to lay your ship close alongside of the enemy's ship, and bring all your guns to bear on him, until you or he go to the bottom. This is the old fashion, which never goes out of fashion, neither in nor out of England.

It is not usually a point of honor, nor a religious sentiment, and never any whim that they will shed their blood for; but usually property, and right measured by property, that breeds revolution. They have no Indian taste for a tomahawk-dance, no French taste for a badge or a proclamation.

The Englishman is peaceably minding his business and earning his day's wages. But if you offer to lay hand on his day's wages, on his cow, or his right in common, or his shop, he will fight to the Judgment. Magna-charta, jury-trial, *habeas-corpus*, star-chamber, ship-money, Popery, Plymouth-colony, American Revolution, are all questions involving a yeoman's right to his dinner, and, except as touching that, would not have lashed the British nation to rage and revolt.

Whilst they are thus instinct with a spirit of order, and of calculation, it must be owned they are capable of larger views; but the indulgence is expensive to them, costs great crises, or accumulations of mental power. In common, the horse works best with blinders. Nothing is more in the line of English thought, than our unvarnished Connecticut question, "Pray, sir, how do you get your living when you are at home?" The questions of freedom, of taxation, of privilege, are money questions. Heavy fellows, steeped in beer and flesh-pots, they are hard of hearing and dim of sight. Their drowsy minds need to be flagellated by war and trade and politics and persecution. They cannot well read a principle, except by the light of fagots and of burning towns.

Tacitus says of the Germans, "powerful only in sudden efforts, they are impatient of toil and labor." This highly destined race, if it had not somewhere added the chamber of patience to its brain, would not have built London. I know not from which of the tribes and temperaments that went to the composition of the people this tenacity was supplied, but they clinch every nail they drive. They have no running for luck, and no immoderate speed. They spend largely on their fabric, and await the slow return. Their leather lies tanning seven years in the vat. At Rogers's mills, in Sheffield, where I was shown the process of making a razor and a penknife, I was told there is no luck in making good steel; that they make no mistakes, every blade in the hundred and in the thousand is good. And that is characteristic of all their work, — no more is attempted than is done.

When Thor and his companions arrive at Utgard, he is told that "nobody is permitted to remain here, unless he understand some art, and excel in it all other men." The same question is still put to the posterity of Thor. A nation of laborers, every man is trained to some one art or detail, and aims at perfection in that: not content unless he has something in which he thinks he surpasses all other men. He would rather not do anything at all, than not do it well. I suppose no people have such thoroughness: from the highest to the lowest, every man meaning to be master of his art.

"To show capacity," a Frenchman described as the end of a speech in debate: "no," said an Englishman, "but to set your shoulder at the wheel, — to advance the business." Sir Samuel Romilly refused to speak in popular assemblies, confining himself to the House of Commons, where a measure can be carried by a speech. The business of the House of Commons is conducted by a few persons, but these are hard-worked. Sir Robert Peel "knew the Blue Books by heart." His colleagues and rivals carry Hansard in their heads. The high civil and legal offices are not beds of ease, but posts which exact frightful amounts of mental labor. Many of the great leaders, like Pitt, Canning, Castlereagh, Romilly, are soon worked to death. They are excellent judges in England of a good worker, and when they find one, like Clarendon, Sir Philip Warwick, Sir William Coventry, Ashley, Burke, Thurlow, Mansfield, Pitt, Eldon, Peel, or Russell, there is nothing too good or too high for him.

They have a wonderful heat in the pursuit of a public aim. Private persons exhibit, in scientific and antiquarian researches, the same pertinacity as the nation showed in the coalitions in which it yoked Europe against the Empire of Bonaparte, one after the other defeated, and still renewed, until the sixth hurled him from his seat.

Sir John Herschel, in completion of the work of his father, who had made the catalogue of the stars of the northern hemisphere, expatriated himself for years at the Cape of Good Hope, finished his inventory of the southern heaven, came home, and redacted it in eight years more; — a work whose value does not begin until thirty years have elapsed, and thenceforward a record to all ages of the highest import. The Admiralty sent out the Arctic expeditions year after year, in search of Sir John Franklin, until, at last, they have threaded their way through polar pack and Behring's Straits, and solved the geographical problem. Lord Elgin, at Athens, saw the imminent ruin of the Greek remains, set up his scaffoldings, in spite of epigrams, and, after five years' labor to collect them, got his marbles on shipboard. The ship struck a rock, and went to the bottom. He had them all fished up, by divers, at a vast expense, and brought to London; not knowing that Haydon, Fuseli, and Canova, and all good heads in all the world, were to be his applauders. In the same spirit, were the excavation and research by Sir Charles Fellowes, for the Xanthian monument; and of Layard, for his Nineveh sculptures.

The nation sits in the immense city they have builded, a London extended into every man's mind, though he live in Van Dieman's Land or Capetown. Faithful performance of what is undertaken to be performed, they honor in themselves, and exact in others, as certificate of equality with themselves. The modern world is theirs. They have made and make it day by day. The commercial relations of the world are so intimately drawn to London, that every dollar on earth contributes to the strength of the English government. And if all the wealth in the planet should perish by war or deluge, they know themselves competent to replace it.

They have approved their Saxon blood, by their sea-going qualities; their descent from Odin's smiths, by their hereditary skill in working in iron; their British birth, by husbandry and immense wheat harvests; and justified their occupancy of the centre of habitable land, by their supreme ability and cosmopolitan spirit. They have tilled, builded, forged, spun, and woven. They have made the island a thoroughfare; and London a shop, a law-court, a record-office, and scientific bureau, inviting to strangers; a sanctuary to refugees of every political and religious opinion; and such a city, that almost every active man, in any nation, finds himself, at one time or other, forced to visit it.

In every path of practical activity, they have gone even with the best. There is no secret of war, in which they have not shown mastery. The steam-chamber of Watt, the locomotive of Stephenson, the cotton-mule of Roberts, perform the labor of the world. There is no department of literature, of science, or of useful art, in which they have not produced a first-rate book. It is England, whose opinion is waited for on the merit of a new invention, an improved science. And in the complications of the trade and politics of their vast empire, they have been equal to every exigency, with counsel and with conduct. Is it their luck, or is it in the chambers of their brain, — it is their commercial advantage, that whatever light appears in better method or happy invention, breaks out *in their race.* They are a family to which a destiny attaches, and the Banshee has sworn that a male heir shall never be wanting. They have a wealth of men to fill important posts, and the vigilance of party criticism insures the selection of a competent person.

A proof of the energy of the British people is the highly artificial construction of the whole fabric. The climate and geography, I said, were factitious, as if the hands of man had arranged the conditions. The same character pervades the whole kingdom. Bacon said, "Rome was a state not subject to paradoxes"; but England subsists by antagonisms and contradictions. The foundations of its greatness are the rolling waves; and, from first to last, it is a museum of anomalies. This foggy and rainy country furnishes the world with astronomical observations. Its short rivers do not afford water-power, but the land shakes under the thunder of the mills. There is no gold-mine of any importance, but there is more gold in England than in all other countries. It is too far north for the culture of the vine, but the wines of all countries are in its docks. The French Comte de Lauraguais said, "no fruit ripens in England but a baked apple"; but oranges and pine-apples are as cheap in London as in the Mediterranean. The Mark-Lane Express, or the Custom-House Returns bear out to the letter the vaunt of Pope, —

> "Let India boast her palms, nor envy we
> The weeping amber, nor the spicy tree,
> While, by our oaks, those precious loads are borne,
> And realms commanded which those trees adorn."

The native cattle are extinct, but the island is full of artificial breeds. The agriculturist Bakewell created sheep and cows and horses to order, and breeds in which everything was omitted but what is economical. The cow is sacrificed to her bag, the ox to his surloin. Stall-feeding makes sperm-mills of the cattle, and converts the stable to a chemical factory. The rivers, lakes, and ponds, too much fished, or obstructed by factories, are artificially filled with the eggs of salmon, turbot, and herring.

Chat Moss and the fens of Lincolnshire and Cambridgeshire are unhealthy and too barren to pay rent. By cylindrical tiles, and gutta-percha tubes, five millions of acres of bad land have been drained and put on equality with the best, for rape-culture and grass. The climate too, which was already believed to have become milder and drier by the enormous consumption of coal, is so far reached by this new action, that fogs and storms are said to disappear. In due course, all England will be drained, and rise a second time out of the waters. The latest step was to call in the aid of steam to agriculture. Steam is almost an Englishman. I do not know but they will send him to Parliament, next, to make laws. He weaves, forges, saws, pounds, fans, and now he must pump, grind, dig, and plough for the farmer. The markets created by the manufacturing population have erected agriculture into a great thriving and spending industry. The value of the houses in Britain is equal to the value of the soil. Artificial aids of all kinds are cheaper than the natural resources. No man can afford to walk, when the parliamentary train carries him for a penny a mile. Gas-burners are cheaper than daylight in numberless floors in the cities. All the houses in London buy their water. The English trade does not exist for the exportation of native products, but on its manufactures, or the making well everything which is ill made elsewhere. They make ponchos for the Mexican, bandannas for the Hindoo, ginseng for the Chinese, beads for the Indian, laces for the Flemings, telescopes for astronomers, cannons for kings.

The Board of Trade caused the best models of Greece and Italy to be placed within the reach of every manufacturing population. They caused to be translated from foreign languages and illustrated by elaborate drawings, the most approved works of Munich, Berlin, and Paris. They have ransacked Italy to find new forms, to add a grace to the products of their looms, their potteries, and their foundries.*

The nearer we look, the more artificial is their social system. Their law is a network of fictions. Their property, a scrip or certificate of right to interest on money that no man ever saw. Their social classes are made by statute. Their ratios of power and representation are historical and legal. The last reform-bill took away political power from a mound, a ruin, and a stone-wall, whilst Birmingham and Manchester, whose mills paid for the wars of Europe, had no representative. Purity in the elective Parliament is secured by the purchase of seats.† Foreign power is kept by armed colonies; power at home, by a standing army of police. The pauper lives better than the free laborer; the thief better than the pauper; and the transported felon better than the one under imprisonment. The crimes are factitious, as smuggling, poaching, non-conformity,

* See Memorial of H. Greenough, p. 66, New York, 1853.

† Sir S. Romilly, purest of English patriots, decided that the only independent mode of entering Parliament was to buy a seat, and he bought Horsham.

heresy, and treason. Better, they say in England, kill a man than a hare. The sovereignty of the seas is maintained by the impressment of seamen. "The impressment of seamen," said Lord Eldon, "is the life of our navy." Solvency is maintained by means of a national debt, on the principle, "if you will not lend me the money, how can I pay you?" For the administration of justice, Sir Samuel Romilly's expedient for clearing the arrears of business in Chancery, was, the Chancellor's staying away entirely from his court. Their system of education is factitious. The Universities galvanize dead languages into a semblance of life. Their church is artificial. The manners and customs of society are artificial; — made-up men with made-up manners; — and thus the whole is Birminghamized, and we have a nation whose existence is a work of art; — a cold, barren, almost arctic isle, being made the most fruitful, luxurious, and imperial land in the whole earth.

Man in England submits to be a product of political economy. On a bleak moor, a mill is built, a banking-house is opened, and men come in, as water in a sluice-way, and towns and cities rise. Man is made as a Birmingham button. The rapid doubling of the population dates from Watt's steam-engine. A landlord, who owns a province, says, "the tenantry are unprofitable; let me have sheep." He unroofs the houses, and ships the population to America. The nation is accustomed to the instantaneous creation of wealth. It is the maxim of their economists, "that the greater part in value of the wealth now existing in England, has been produced by human hands within the last twelve months." Meantime, three or four days' rain will reduce hundreds to starving in London.

One secret of their power is their mutual good understanding. Not only good minds are born among them, but all the people have good minds. Every nation has yielded some good wit, if, as has chanced to many tribes, only one. But the intellectual organization of the English admits a communicableness of knowledge and ideas among them all. An electric touch by any of their national ideas, melts them into one family, and brings the hoards of power which their individuality is always hiving, into use and play for all. Is it the smallness of the country, or is it the pride and affection of race, — they have solidarity, or responsibleness, and trust in each other.

Their minds, like wool, admit of a dye which is more lasting than the cloth. They embrace their cause with more tenacity than their life. Though not military, yet every common subject by the poll is fit to make a soldier of. These private reserved mute family-men can adopt a public end with all their heat, and this strength of affection makes the romance of their heroes. The difference of rank does not divide the national heart. The Danish poet Oehlenschläger complains, that who writes in Danish writes to two hundred readers. In Germany, there is one speech for the learned, and another for the masses, to that extent, that, it is said, no sentiment or phrase from the works of any great German writer is ever heard among the lower classes. But in England, the language of the noble is the language of the poor. In Parliament, in pulpits, in theatres, when the speakers rise to thought and passion, the language becomes idiomatic; the people in the street best understand the best words. And their language seems drawn from the Bible, the common law, and the works of Shakespeare, Bacon, Milton, Pope, Young, Cowper, Burns, and Scott. The island has produced two or three of the greatest men that ever existed, but they were not solitary in their own time. Men quickly embodied what Newton found out, in Greenwich observatories, and practical navigation. The boys knew all that Hutton knew of strata, or Dalton of atoms, or Harvey of blood-vessels; and these studies, once dangerous, are in fashion. So what is invented or known in agriculture, or in trade, or in war, or in art, or in literature, and antiquities. A great ability, not amassed on a few giants, but poured into the general mind, so that each of them could at a pinch stand in the shoes of the other; and they are more bound in character than differenced in ability or in rank. The laborer is a possible lord. The lord is a possible basket-maker. Every man carries the English system in his brain, knows what is confided to him, and does therein the best he can. The chancellor carries England on his mace, the midshipman at the point of his dirk, the smith on his hammer, the cook in the bowl of his spoon; the postilion cracks his whip for England, and the sailor times his oars to "God save the King!" The very felons have their pride in each other's English stanchness. In politics and in war, they hold together as by hooks of steel. The charm in Nelson's history, is, the unselfish greatness; the assurance of being supported to the uttermost by those whom he supports to the uttermost. Whilst they are some ages ahead of the rest of the world in the art of living; whilst in some directions they do not represent the modern spirit, but constitute it, — this vanguard of civility and power they coldly hold, marching in phalanx, lockstep, foot after foot, file after file of heroes, ten thousand deep.

CHAPTER VI.

MANNERS.

I FIND the Englishman to be him of all men who stands firmest in his shoes. They have in themselves what they value in their horses, mettle and bottom. On the day of my arrival at Liverpool, a gentleman, in describing to me the Lord Lieutenant of Ireland, happened to say, " Lord Clarendon has pluck like a cock, and will fight till he dies " ; and, what I heard first I heard last, and the one thing the English value, is *pluck*. The word is not beautiful, but on the quality they signify by it the nation is unanimous. The cabmen have it ; the merchants have it ; the bishops have it ; the women have it ; the journals have it ; the Times newspaper, they say, is the pluckiest thing in England, and Sidney Smith had made it a proverb, that little Lord John Russell, the minister, would take the command of the Channel fleet to-morrow.

They require you to dare to be of your own opinion, and they hate the practical cowards who cannot in affairs answer directly yes or no. They dare to displease, nay, they will let you break all the commandments, if you do it natively, and with spirit. You must be somebody ; then you may do this or that, as you will.

Machinery has been applied to all work, and carried to such perfection, that little is left for the men but to mind the engines and feed the furnaces. But the machines require punctual service, and as they never tire, they prove too much for their tenders. Mines, forges, mills, breweries, railroads, steam-pump, steam-plough, drill of regiments, drill of police, rule of court, and shop-rule, have operated to give a mechanical regularity to all the habit and action of men. A terrible machine has possessed itself of the ground, the air, the men and women, and hardly even thought is free.

The mechanical might and organization require in the people constitution and answering spirits ; and he who goes among them must have some weight of metal. At last, you take your hint from the fury of life you find, and say, one thing is plain, this is no country for faint-hearted people : don't creep about diffidently ; make up your mind ; take your own course, and you shall find respect and furtherance.

It requires, men say, a good constitution to travel in Spain. I say as much of England, for other cause, simply on account of the vigor and brawn of the people. Nothing but the most serious business, could give one any counterweight to these Baresarks, though they were only to order eggs and muffins for their breakfast. The Englishman speaks with all his body. His elocution is stomachic, — as the American's is labial. The Englishman is very petulant and precise about his accommodation at inns, and on the roads; a quiddle about his toast and his chop, and every species of convenience, and loud and pungent in his expressions of impatience at any neglect. His vivacity betrays itself, at all points, in his manners, in his respiration, and the inarticulate noises he makes in clearing the throat, — all significant of burly strength. He has stamina; he can take the initiative in emergencies. He has that *aplomb*, which results from a good adjustment of the moral and physical nature, and the obedience of all the powers to the will; as if the axes of his eyes were united to his backbone, and only moved with the trunk.

This vigor appears in the incuriosity, and stony neglect, each of every other. Each man walks, eats, drinks, shaves, dresses, gesticulates, and, in every manner, acts, and suffers without reference to the bystanders, in his own fashion, only careful not to interfere with them, or annoy them; not that he is trained to neglect the eyes of his neighbors, — he is really occupied with his own affair, and does not think of them. Every man in this polished country consults only his convenience, as much as a solitary pioneer in Wisconsin. I know not where any personal eccentricity is so freely allowed, and no man gives himself any concern with it. An Englishman walks in a pouring rain, swinging his closed umbrella like a walking-stick; wears a wig, or a shawl, or a saddle, or stands on his head, and no remark is made. And as he has been doing this for several generations, it is now in the blood.

In short, every one of these islanders is an island himself, safe, tranquil, incommunicable. In a company of strangers, you would think him deaf; his eyes never wander from his table and newspaper. He is never betrayed into any curiosity or unbecoming emotion. They have all been trained in one severe school of manners, and never put off the harness.

He does not give his hand. He does not let you meet his eye. It is almost an affront to look a man in the face, without being introduced. In mixed or in select companies they do not introduce persons; so that a presentation is a circumstance as valid as a contract. Introductions are sacraments. He withholds his name. At the hotel, he is hardly willing to whisper it to the clerk at the book-office. If he give you his private address on a card, it is like an avowal of friendship; and his bearing on being introduced is cold, even though he is seeking your acquaintance, and is studying how he shall serve you.

It was an odd proof of this impressive energy, that, in my lectures, I hesitated to read and threw out for its impertinence many a disparaging phrase, which I had been accustomed to spin, about poor, thin, unable mortals; so much had the fine physique and the personal vigor of this robust race worked on my imagination.

I happened to arrive in England at the moment of a commercial crisis. But it was evident that, let who will fail, England will not. These people have sat here a thousand years, and here will continue to sit. They will not break up, or arrive at any desperate revolution, like their neighbors; for they have as much energy, as much continence of character, as they ever had. The power and possession which surround them are their own creation, and they exert the same commanding industry at this moment.

They are positive, methodical, cleanly, and formal, loving routine, and conventional ways; loving truth and religion, to be sure, but inexorable on points of form. All the world praises the comfort and private appointments of an English inn, and of English households. You are sure of neatness and of personal decorum. A Frenchman may possibly be clean: an Englishman is conscientiously clean. A certain order and complete propriety is found in his dress and in his belongings.

Born in a harsh and wet climate, which keeps him in doors whenever he is at rest, and being of an affectionate and loyal temper, he dearly loves his house. If he is rich, he buys a demesne, and builds a hall; if he is in middle condition, he spares no expense on his house. Without, it is all planted: within, it is wainscoted, carved, curtained, hung with pictures, and filled with good furniture. 'T is a passion which survives all others, to deck and improve it. Hither he brings all that is rare and costly, and with the national tendency to sit fast in the same spot for many generations, it comes to be, in the course of time, a museum of heirlooms, gifts, and trophies of the adventures and exploits of the family. He is very fond of silver plate, and, though he have no gallery of portraits of his ancestors, he has of their punch-bowls and porringers. Incredible amounts of plate are found in good houses, and the poorest have some spoon or saucepan, gift of a godmother, saved out of better times.

An English family consists of a few persons, who, from youth to age, are found revolving within a few feet of each other, as if tied by some invisible ligature, tense as that cartilage which we have seen attaching the two Siamese. England produces under favorable conditions of ease and culture the finest women in the world. And, as the men are affectionate and true-hearted, the women inspire and refine them. Nothing can be more delicate without being fantastical, nothing more firm and based in nature and sentiment, than the courtship and mutual carriage of the sexes. The song of 1596 says, "The wife of every Englishman is counted blest." The sentiment of Imogen in Cymbeline is copied from English nature; and not less the Portia of Brutus, the Kate Percy, and the Desdemona. The romance does not exceed the height of noble passion in Mrs. Lucy Hutchinson, or in Lady Russell, or even as one discerns through the plain prose of Pepys's Diary, the sacred habit of an English wife. Sir Samuel Romilly could not bear the death of his wife. Every class has its noble and tender examples.

Domesticity is the taproot which enables the nation to branch wide and high. The motive and end of their trade and empire is to guard the independence and privacy of their homes. Nothing so much marks their manners as the concentration on their household ties. This domesticity is carried into court and camp. Wellington governed India and Spain and his own troops, and fought battles like a good family-man, paid his debts, and, though general of an army in Spain, could not stir abroad for fear of public creditors. This taste for house and parish merits has of course its doting and foolish side. Mr. Cobbett attributes the huge popularity of Perceval, prime minister in 1810, to the fact that he was wont to go to church every Sunday, with a large quarto gilt prayer-book under one arm, his wife hanging on the other, and followed by a long brood of children.

They keep their old customs, costumes, and pomps, their wig and mace, sceptre and crown. The Middle Ages still lurk in the streets of London. The Knights of the Bath take oath to defend injured ladies; the gold-stick-in-waiting survives. They repeated the ceremonies of the eleventh century in the coronation of the present Queen. A hereditary tenure is natural to them. Offices, farms, trades, and traditions descend so. Their leases run for a hundred and a thousand years. Terms of service and partnership are lifelong, or are inherited. "Holdship has been with me," said Lord Eldon, "eight-and-twenty years, knows all my business and books." Antiquity of usage is sanction enough. Wordsworth says of the small freeholders of Westmoreland, "Many of these humble sons of the hills had a consciousness that the land which they tilled had for more than five hundred years been possessed by men of the same name and blood." The ship-carpenter in the public yards, my lord's gardener and porter, have been there for more than a hundred years, grandfather, father, and son.

The English power resides also in their dislike of change. They have difficulty in bringing their reason to act, and on all occasions use their memory first. As soon as they have rid themselves of some grievance, and settled the better practice, they make haste to fix it as a finality, and never wish to hear of alteration more.

Every Englishman is an embryonic chancellor: his instinct is to search for a precedent. The favorite phrase of their law is, "a custom whereof the memory of man runneth not back to the contrary." The barons say, "*Nolumus mutari*"; and the cockneys stifle the curiosity of the foreigner on the reason of any practice, with, "Lord, sir, it was always so." They hate innovation. Bacon told them, Time was the right reformer; Chatham, that "confidence was a plant of slow growth"; Canning, to "advance with the times"; and Wellington, that "habit was ten times nature." All their statesmen learn the irresistibility of the tide of custom, and have invented many fine phrases to cover this slowness of perception, and prehensility of tail.

A sea-shell should be the crest of England, not only because it represents a power built on the waves, but also the hard finish of the men. The Englishman is finished like a cowry or a murex. After the spire and the spines are formed, or, with the formation, a juice exudes, and a hard enamel varnishes every part. The keeping of the proprieties is as indispensable as clean linen. No merit quite countervails the want of this, whilst this sometimes stands in lieu of all. "'T is in bad taste," is the most formidable word an Englishman can pronounce. But this japan costs them dear. There is a prose in certain Englishmen, which exceeds in wooden deadness all rivalry with other countrymen. There is a knell in the conceit and externality of their voice, which seems to say, *Leave all hope behind.* In this Gibraltar of propriety, mediocrity gets intrenched, and consolidated, and founded in adamant. An Englishman of fashion is like one of those souvenirs, bound in gold vellum, enriched with delicate engravings, on thick hot-pressed paper, fit for the hands of ladies and princes, but with nothing in it worth reading or remembering.

A severe decorum rules the court and the cottage. When Thalberg, the pianist, was one evening performing before the Queen, at Windsor, in a private party, the Queen accompanied him with her voice. The circumstance took air, and all England shuddered from sea to sea. The indecorum was never repeated. Cold, repressive manners prevail. No enthusiasm is permitted except at the opera. They avoid everything marked. They require a tone of voice that excites no attention in the room. Sir Philip Sidney is one of the patron saints of England, of whom Wotton said, "His wit was the measure of congruity."

Pretension and vaporing are once for all distasteful. They keep to the other extreme of low tone in dress and manners. They avoid pretension and go right to the heart of the thing. They hate nonsense, sentimentalism, and highflown expression; they use a studied plainness. Even Brummell their fop was marked by the severest simplicity in dress. They value themselves on the absence of everything theatrical in the public business, and on conciseness and going to the point, in private affairs.

In an aristocratical country, like England, not the Trial by Jury, but the dinner is the capital institution. It is the mode of doing honor to a stranger, to invite him to eat, — and has been for many hundred years. "And they think," says the Venetian traveller of 1500, "no greater honor can be conferred or received, than to invite others to eat with them, or to be invited themselves, and they would sooner give five or six ducats to provide an entertainment for a person, than, a groat to assist him in any distress." * It is reserved to the end

* "Relation of England." Printed by the Camden Society.

of the day, the family-hour being generally six, in London, and, if any company is expected, one or two hours later. Every one dresses for dinner, in his own house, or in another man's. The guests are expected to arrive within half an hour of the time fixed by card of invitation, and nothing but death or mutilation is permitted to detain them. The English dinner is precisely the model on which our own are constructed in the Atlantic cities. The company sit one or two hours, before the ladies leave the table. The gentlemen remain over their wine an hour longer, and rejoin the ladies in the drawing-room, and take coffee. The dress-dinner generates a talent of table-talk, which reaches great perfection : the stories are so good, that one is sure they must have been often told before, to have got such happy turns. Hither come all manner of clever projects, bits of popular science, of practical invention, of miscellaneous humor ; political, literary, and personal news ; railroads, horses, diamonds, agriculture, horticulture, pisciculture, and wine.

English stories, bon-mots, and the recorded table-talk of their wits, are as good as the best of the French. In America, we are apt scholars, but have not yet attained the same perfection : for the range of nations from which London draws, and the steep contrasts of condition create the picturesque in society, as broken country makes picturesque landscape, whilst our prevailing equality makes a prairie tameness : and secondly, because the usage of a dress-dinner every day at dark has a tendency to hive and produce to advantage everything good. Much attrition has worn every sentence into a bullet. Also one meets now and then with polished men, who know everything, have tried everything, can do everything, and are quite superior to letters and science. What could they not, if only they would?

CHAPTER VII.

TRUTH.

THE Teutonic tribes have a national singleness of heart, which contrasts with the Latin races. The German name has a proverbial significance of sincerity and honest meaning. The arts bear testimony to it. The faces of clergy and laity in old sculptures and illuminated missals are charged with earnest belief. Add to this hereditary rectitude, the punctuality and precise dealing which commerce creates, and you have the English truth and credit. The government strictly performs its engagements. The subjects do not understand trifling on its part. When any breach of promise occurred, in the old days of prerogative, it was resented by the people as an intolerable grievance. And, in modern times, any slipperiness in the government in political faith, or any repudiation or crookedness in matters of finance, would bring the whole nation to a committee of inquiry and reform. Private men keep their promises, never so trivial. Down goes the flying word on the tablets, and is indelible as Domesday Book.

Their practical power rests on their national sincerity. Veracity derives from instinct, and marks superiority in organization. Nature has endowed some animals with cunning, as a compensation for strength withheld; but it has provoked the malice of all others, as if avengers of public wrong. In the nobler kinds, where strength could be afforded, her races are loyal to truth, as truth is the foundation of the social state. Beasts that make no truce with man, do not break faith with each other. 'T is said, that the wolf, who makes a *cache* of his prey, and brings his fellows with him to the spot, if, on digging it is not found, is instantly and unresistingly torn in pieces. English veracity seems to result on a sounder animal structure, as if they could afford it. They are blunt in saying what they think, sparing of promises, and they require plain dealing of others. We will not have to do with a man in a mask. Let us know the truth. Draw a straight line, hit whom and where it will. Alfred, whom the affection of the nation makes the type of their race, is called by a writer at the Norman Conquest, the *truth-speaker; Alueredus veridicus.* Geoffrey of

Monmouth says of King Aurelius, uncle of Arthur, that "above all things he hated a lie." The Northman Guttorm said to King Olaf, "It is royal work to fulfil royal words." The mottoes of their families are monitory proverbs, as, *Fare fac,* — Say, do, — of the Fairfaxes; *Say and seal,* of the house of Fiennes; *Vero nil verius,* of the De Veres. To be king of their word, is their pride. When they unmask cant, they say, "The English of this is," &c.; and to give the lie is the extreme insult. The phrase of the lowest of the people is "honor-bright," and their vulgar praise, "his word is as good as his bond." They hate shuffling and equivocation, and the cause is damaged in the public opinion, on which any paltering can be fixed. Even Lord Chesterfield, with his French breeding, when he came to define a gentleman, declared that truth made his distinction; and nothing ever spoken by him would find so hearty a suffrage from his nation. The Duke of Wellington, who had the best right to say so, advises the French General Kellermann, that he may rely on the parole of an English officer. The English, of all classes, value themselves on this trait, as distinguishing them from the French, who, in the popular belief, are more polite than true. An Englishman understates, avoids the superlative, checks himself in compliments, alleging, that in the French language, one cannot speak without lying.

They love reality in wealth, power, hospitality, and do not easily learn to make a show, and take the world as it goes. They are not fond of ornaments, and if they wear them, they must be gems. They read gladly in old Fuller, that a lady, in the reign of Elizabeth, "would have as patiently digested a lie, as the wearing of false stones or pendants of counterfeit pearl." They have the earth-hunger, or preference for property in land, which is said to mark the Teutonic nations. They build of stone; public and private buildings are massive and durable. In comparing their ships' houses, and public offices with the American, it is commonly said, that they spend a pound, where we spend a dollar. Plain rich clothes, plain rich equipage, plain rich finish throughout their house and belongings, mark the English truth.

They confide in each other, — English believes in English. The French feel the superiority of this probity. The Englishman is not springing a trap for his admiration, but is honestly minding his business. The Frenchman is vain. Madame de Staël says, that the English irritated Napoleon, mainly, because they have found out how to unite success with honesty.

She was not aware how wide an application her foreign readers would give to the remark. Wellington discovered the ruin of Bonaparte's affairs, by his own probity. He augured ill of the empire, as soon as he saw that it was mendacious, and lived by war. If war do not bring in its sequel new trade, better agriculture and manufactures, but only games, fireworks, and spectacles, — no prosperity could support it; much less, a nation decimated for conscripts, and out of pocket, like France. So he drudged for years on his military works at Lisbon, and from this base at last extended his gigantic lines to Waterloo, believing in his countrymen and their syllogisms above all the rhodomontade of Europe.

At a St. George's festival, in Montreal, where I happened to be a guest, since my return home, I observed that the chairman complimented his compatriots, by saying, "they confided that wherever they met an Englishman, they found a man who would speak the truth." And one cannot think this festival fruitless, if, all over the world, on the 23d of April, wherever two or three English are found, they meet to encourage each other in the nationality of veracity.

In the power of saying rude truth, sometimes in the lion's mouth, no men surpass them. On the king's birthday, when each bishop was expected to offer the king a purse of gold, Latimer gave Henry VIII. a copy of the Vulgate, with a mark at the passage, "Whoremongers and adulterers God will judge"; and they so honor stoutness in each other, that the king passed it over. They are tenacious of their belief, and cannot easily change their opinions to suit the hour. They are like ships with too much head on to come quickly about, nor will prosperity or even adversity be allowed to shake their habitual view of conduct. Whilst I was in London, M. Guizot arrived there on his escape from Paris, in February, 1848. Many private friends called on him. His name was immediately proposed as an honorary member to the Athenæum. M. Guizot was blackballed. Certainly, they knew the distinction of his name. But the Englishman is not fickle. He had really made up his mind, now for years as he read his newspaper, to hate and despise M. Guizot; and the altered position of the man as an illustrious exile, and a guest in the country, makes no difference to him, as it would instantly, to an American.

They require the same adherence, thorough conviction and reality in public men. It is the want of character which makes the low reputation of the Irish members. "See them," they said, "one hundred and twenty-seven all voting like sheep, never proposing anything, and all but four voting the income tax," — which was an ill-judged concession of the government, relieving Irish property from the burdens charged on English.

They have a horror of adventurers in or out of Parliament. The ruling passion of Englishmen, in these days, is a terror of humbug. In the same proportion, they value honesty, stoutness, and adherence to your own. They like a man committed to his objects. They hate the French, as frivolous; they hate the Irish, as aimless; they hate the Germans, as professors. In February, 1848, they said, Look, the French king and his party fell for want of a shot; they had not conscience to shoot, so entirely was the pith and heart of monarchy eaten out.

They attack their own politicians every day, on the same grounds, as adventurers. They love stoutness in standing for your right, in declining money or promotion that costs any concession. The barrister refuses the silk gown of Queen's Counsel, if his junior have it one day earlier. Lord Collingwood would not accept his medal for victory on 14th February, 1797, if he did not receive one for victory on 1st June, 1794; and the long-withholden medal was accorded. When Castlereagh dissuaded Lord Wellington from going to the king's levee, until the unpopular Cintra business had been explained, he replied: "You furnish me a reason for going. I will go to this, or I will never go to a king's levee." The radical mob at Oxford cried after the tory Lord Eldon, "There 's old Eldon; cheer him; he never ratted." They have given the parliamentary nickname of *Trimmers* to the time-servers, whom English character does not love.*

They are very liable in their politics to extraordinary delusions, thus, to believe what stands recorded in the gravest books, that the movement of 10 April, 1848, was urged or assisted by foreigners: which, to be sure, is paralleled by the democratic whimsy in this country, which I have noticed to be shared by men sane on other points, that the English are

* It is an unlucky moment to remember these sparkles of solitary virtue in the face of the honors lately paid in England to the Emperor Louis Napoleon. I am sure that no Englishman whom I had the happiness to know, consented, when the aristocracy and the commons of London cringed like a Neapolitan rabble, before a successful thief. But — how to resist one step, though odious, in a linked series of state necessities? — Governments must always learn too late, that the use of dishonest agents is as runious for nations as for single men.

at the bottom of the agitation of slavery, in American politics: and then again to the French popular legends on the subject of *perfidious Albion.* But suspicion will make fools of nations as of citizens.

A slow temperament makes them less rapid and ready than other countrymen, and has given occasion to the observation that English wit comes afterwards, — which the French denote as *esprit d'escalier.* This dulness makes their attachment to home, and their adherence in all foreign countries to home habits. The Englishman who visits Mount Etna will carry his tea-kettle to the top. The old Italian author of the "Relation of England" (in 1500) says: "I have it on the best information, that, when the war is actually raging most furiously, they will seek for good eating, and all their other comforts, without thinking what harm might befall them." Then their eyes seem to be set at the bottom of a tunnel, and they affirm the one small fact they know, with the best faith in the world that nothing else exists. And, as their own belief in guineas is perfect, they readily, on all occasions, apply the pecuniary argument as final. Thus when the Rochester rappings began to be heard of in England, a man deposited £ 100 in a sealed box in the Dublin Bank, and then advertised in the newspapers to all somnambulists, mesmerizers, and others, that whoever could tell him the number of his note should have the money. He let it lie there six months, the newspapers now and then, at his instance, stimulating the attention of the adepts; but none could ever tell him; and he said, "Now let me never be bothered more with this proven lie." It is told of a good Sir John, that he heard a case stated by counsel, and made up his mind; then the counsel for the other side taking their turn to speak, he found himself so unsettled and perplexed, that he exclaimed, "So help me God! I will never listen to evidence again." Any number of delightful examples of this English stolidity are the anecdotes of Europe. I knew a very worthy man, — a magistrate, I believe he was, in the town of Derby, — who went to the opera, to see Malibran. In one scene, the heroine was to rush across a ruined bridge. Mr. B. arose, and mildly yet firmly called the attention of the audience and the performers to the fact that, in his judgment, the bridge was unsafe! This English stolidity contrasts with French wit and tact. The French, it is commonly said, have greatly more influence in Europe than the English. What influence the English have is by brute force of wealth and pow-

or; that of the French by affinity and talent. The Italian is subtle, the Spaniard treacherons: tortures, it was said, could never wrest from an Egyptian the confession of a secret. None of these traits belong to the Englishman. His choler and conceit force everything out. Defoe, who knew his countrymen well, says of them: —

"In close intrigue, their faculty 's but weak,
For generally whate'er they know, they speak,
And often their own counsels undermine
By mere infirmity without design;
From whence, the learned say, it doth proceed,
That English treasons never can succeed;
For they 're so open-hearted, you may know
Their own most secret thoughts, and others' too."

CHAPTER VIII.

CHARACTER.

THE English race are reputed morose. I do not know that they have sadder brows than their neighbors of northern climates. They are sad by comparison with the singing and dancing nations: not sadder, but slow and staid, as finding their joys at home. They, too, believe that where there is no enjoyment of life, there can be no vigor and art in speech or thought; that your merry heart goes all the way, your sad one tires in a mile. This trait of gloom has been fixed on them by French travellers, who, from Froissart, Voltaire, Le Sage, Mirabeau, down to the lively journalists of the *feuilletons,* have spent their wit on the solemnity of their neighbors. The French say, gay conversation is unknown in their island: the Englishman finds no relief from reflection except in reflection: when he wishes for amusement, he goes to work: his hilarity is like an attack of fever. Religion, the theatre, and the reading the books of his country, all feed and increase his natural melancholy. The police does not interfere with public diversions. It thinks itself bound in duty to respect the pleasures and rare gayety of this inconsolable nation; and their well-known courage is entirely attributable to their disgust of life.

I suppose their gravity of demeanor and their few words have obtained this reputation. As compared with the Americans, I think them cheerful and contented. Young people, in this country, are much more prone to melancholy. The English have a mild aspect, and a ringing cheerful voice. They are large-natured, and not so easily amused as the southerners, and are among them as grown people among children, requiring war, or trade, or engineering, or science, instead of frivolous games. They are proud and private, and, even if disposed to recreation, will avoid an open garden. They sported sadly; *ils s'amusaient tristement, selon la coutume de leur pays*, said Froissart; and, I suppose, never nation built their party walls so thick, or their garden fences so high. Meat and wine produce no effect on them: they are just as cold, quiet, and composed, at the end, as at the beginning of dinner.

The reputation of taciturnity they have enjoyed for six or seven hundred years; and a kind of pride in bad public speaking is noted in the House of Commons, as if they were willing to show that they did not live by their tongues, or thought they spoke well enough if they had the tone of gentlemen. In mixed company, they shut their mouths. A Yorkshire mill-owner told me, he had ridden more than once all the way from London to Leeds, in the first-class carriage, with the same persons, and no word exchanged. The club-houses were established to cultivate social habits, and it is rare that more than two eat together, and oftenest one eats alone. Was it then a stroke of humor in the serious Swedenborg, or was it only his pitiless logic, that made him shut up the English souls in a heaven by themselves?

They are contradictorily described as sour, splenetic, and stubborn, — and as mild, sweet, and sensible. The truth is, they have great range and variety of character. Commerce sends abroad multitudes of different classes. The choleric Welshman, the fervid Scot, the bilious resident in the East or West Indies, are wide of the perfect behavior of the educated and dignified man of family. So is the burly farmer; so is the country 'squire, with his narrow and violent life. In every inn, is the Commercial-Room, in which 'travellers,' or bagmen who carry patterns, and solicit orders, for the manufacturers, are wont to be entertained. It easily happens that this class should characterize England to the foreigner, who meets them on the road, and at every public house, whilst the gentry avoid the taverns, or seclude themselves whilst in them.

But these classes are the right English stock, and may

fairly show the national qualities, before yet art and education have dealt with them. They are good lovers, good haters, slow but obstinate admirers, and, in all things, very much steeped in their temperament, like men hardly awaked from deep sleep, which they enjoy. Their habits and instincts cleave to nature. They are of the earth, earthy; and of the sea, as the sea-kinds, attached to it for what it yields them, and not from any sentiment. They are full of coarse strength, rude exercise, butcher's meat, and sound sleep; and suspect any poetic insinuation or any hint for the conduct of life which reflects on this animal existence, as if somebody were fumbling at the umbilical cord and might stop their supplies. They doubt a man's sound judgment, if he does not eat with appetite, and shake their heads if he is particularly chaste. Take them as they come, you shall find in the common people a surly indifference, sometimes gruffness and ill temper; and, in minds of more power, magazines of inexhaustible war, challenging

> " The ruggedest hour that time and spite dare bring
> To frown upon the enraged Northumberland."

They are headstrong believers and defenders of their opinion, and not less resolute in maintaining their whim and perversity. Hezekiah Woodward wrote a book against the Lord's Prayer. And one can believe that Burton the Anatomist of Melancholy, having predicted from the stars the hour of his death, slipped the knot himself round his own neck, not to falsify his horoscope.

Their looks bespeak an invincible stoutness; they have extreme difficulty to run away, and will die game. Wellington said of the young coxcombs of the Life-Guards delicately brought up, "But the puppies fight well"; and Nelson said of his sailors, "They really mind shot no more than peas." Of absolute stoutness no nation has more or better examples. They are good at storming redoubts, at boarding frigates, at dying in the last ditch, or any desperate service which has daylight and honor in it; but not, I think, at enduring the rack, or any passive obedience, like jumping off a castle-roof at the word of a czar. Being both vascular and highly organized, so as to be very sensible of pain; and intellectual, so as to see reason and glory in a matter.

Of that constitutional force, which yields the supplies of the day, they have the more than enough, the excess which creates courage on fortitude, genius in poetry, invention in mechanics, enterprise in trade, magnificence in wealth, splendor in ceremonies, petulance and projects in youth. The young men have a rude health which runs into peccant humors. They drink brandy like water, cannot expend their quantities of waste strength on riding, hunting, swimming, and fencing, and run into absurd frolics with the gravity of the Eumenides. They stoutly carry into every nook and corner of the earth their turbulent sense : leaving no lie uncontradicted ; no pretension unexamined. They chew hasheesh ; cut themselves with poisoned creases ; swing their hammock in the boughs of the Bohon Upas ; taste every poison ; buy every secret ; at Naples, they put St. Januarius's blood in an alembic ; they saw a hole into the head of the " winking Virgin," to know why she winks ; measure with an English foot-rule every cell of the Inquisition, every Turkish caaba, every Holy of holies ; translate and send to Bentley the arcanum bribed and bullied away from shuddering Bramins ; and measure their own strength by the terror they cause. These travellers are of every class, the best and the worst ; and it may easily happen that those of rudest behavior are taken notice of and remembered. The Saxon melancholy in the vulgar rich and poor appears as gushes of ill-humor, which every check exasperates into sarcasm and vituperation. There are multitudes of rude young English who have the self-sufficiency and bluntness of their nation, and who, with their disdain of the rest of mankind, and with this indigestion and choler, have made the English traveller a proverb for uncomfortable and offensive manners. It was no bad description of the Briton generically, what was said two hundred years ago, of one particular Oxford scholar : " He was a very bold man, uttered anything that came into his mind, not only among his companions, but in public coffee-houses, and would often speak his mind of particular persons then accidentally present, without examining the company he was in ; for which he was often reprimanded, and several times threatened to be kicked and beaten."

The common Englishman is prone to forget a cardinal article in the bill of social rights, that every man has a right to his own ears. No man can claim to usurp more than a few cubic feet of the audibilities of a public room, or to put upon the company with the loud statements of his crotchets or personalities.

But it is in the deep traits of race that the fortunes of nations are written, and however derived, whether a happier tribe or mixture of tribes, the air, or what circumstance, that mixed for them the golden mean of temperament, — here exists the best stock in the world, broad-fronted, broad-bottomed, best for depth, range, and equability, men of aplomb and reserves, great range and many moods, strong instincts, yet apt for culture; war-class as well as clerks; earls and tradesmen; wise minority, as well as foolish majority; abysmal temperament, hiding wells of wrath, and glooms on which no sunshine settles; alternated with a common sense and humanity which hold them fast to every piece of cheerful duty; making this temperament a sea to which all storms are superficial; a race to which their fortunes flow, as if they alone had the elastic organization at once fine and robust enough for dominion; as if the burly inexpressive, now mute and contumacious, now fierce and sharp-tongued dragon, which once made the island light with his fiery breath, had bequeathed his ferocity to his conqueror. They hide virtues under vices, or the semblance of them. It is the misshapen hairy Scandinavian troll again, who lifts the cart out of the mire, or "threshes the corn that ten day-laborers could not end," but it is done in the dark, and with muttered maledictions. He is a churl with a soft place in his heart, whose speech is a brash of bitter waters, but who loves to help you at a pinch. He says no, and serves you, and your thanks disgust him. Here was lately a cross-grained miser, odd and ugly, resembling in countenance the portrait of Punch, with the laugh left out; rich by his own industry; sulking in a lonely house; who never gave a dinner to any man, and disdained all courtesies; yet as true a worshipper of beauty in form and color as ever existed, and profusely pouring over the cold mind of his countrymen creations of grace and truth, removing the reproach of sterility from English art, catching from their savage climate every fine hint, and importing into their galleries every tint and trait of sunnier cities and skies; making an era in painting; and, when he saw that the splendor of one of his pictures in the Exhibition dimmed his rival's that hung next it, secretly took a brush and blackened his own.

They do not wear their heart in their sleeve for daws to peck at. They have that phlegm or staidness, which it is a compliment to disturb. "Great men," said Aristotle, "are always of a nature originally melancholy." 'T is the habit of a mind which attaches to abstractions with a passion which gives vast results. They dare to displease, they do not speak to expectation. They like the sayers of No, better than the sayers of

Yes. Each of them has an opinion which he feels it becomes him to express all the more that it differs from yours. They are meditating opposition. This gravity is inseparable from minds of great resources.

There is an English hero superior to the French, the German, the Italian, or the Greek. When he is brought to the strife with fate, he sacrifices a richer material possession, and on more purely metaphysical grounds. He is there with his own consent, face to face with fortune, which he defies. On deliberate choice, and from grounds of character, he has elected his part to live and die for, and dies with grandeur. This race has added new elements to humanity, and has a deeper root in the world.

They have great range of scale, from ferocity to exquisite refinement. With larger scale, they have great retrieving power. After running each tendency to an extreme, they try another tack with equal heat. More intellectual than other races, when they live with other races, they do not take their language, but bestow their own. They subsidize other nations, and are not subsidized. They proselyte, and are not proselyted. They assimilate other races to themselves, and are not assimilated. The English did not calculate the conquest of the Indies. It fell to their character. So they administer in different parts of the world, the codes of every empire and race; in Canada, old French law; in the Mauritius, the Code Napoleon; in the West Indies, the edicts of the Spanish Cortes; in the East Indies, the Laws of Menu; in the Isle of Man, of the Scandinavian Thing; at the Cape of Good Hope, of the old Netherlands; and in the Ionian Islands, the Pandects of Justinian.

They are very conscious of their advantageous position in history. England is the lawgiver, the patron, the instructor, the ally. Compare the tone of the French and of the English press: the first querulous, captious, sensitive, about English opinion; the English press is never timorous about French opinion, but arrogant and contemptuous.

They are testy and headstrong through an excess of will and bias; churlish as men sometimes please to be who do not forget a debt, who ask no favors, and who will do what they like with their own. With education and intercourse these asperities wear off, and leave the good-will pure. If anatomy is reformed according to national tendencies, I suppose, the spleen will hereafter be found in the Englishman, not found in the American, and differencing the one from the other. I anticipate another anatomical discovery, that this organ will be found to be cortical and caducous, that they are superficially morose, but at last tender-hearted, herein differing from Rome and the Latin nations. Nothing savage, nothing mean resides in the English heart. They are subject to panics of credulity and of rage, but the temper of the nation, however disturbed, settles itself soon and easily, as, in this temperate zone, the sky after whatever storms clears again, and serenity is its normal condition.

A saving stupidity masks and protects their perception as the curtain of the eagle's eye. Our swifter American's, when they first deal with English, pronounce them stupid; but, later, do them justice as people who wear well, or hide their strength. To understand the power of performance that is in their finest wits, in the patient Newton, or in the versatile transcendent poets, or in the Dugdales, Gibbons, Hallams, Eldons, and Peels, one should see how English day-laborers hold out. High and low, they are of an unctuous texture. There is an adipocere in their constitution, as if they had oil also for their mental wheels, and could perform vast amounts of work without damaging themselves.

Even the scale of expense on which people live, and to which scholars and professional men conform, proves the tension of their muscle, when vast numbers are found who can each lift this enormous load. I might even add, their daily feasts argue a savage vigor of body.

No nation was ever so rich in able men: "Gentlemen," as Charles I. said of Strafford, "whose abilities might make a prince rather afraid than ashamed in the greatest affairs of state": men of such temper, that, like Baron Vere, "had one seen him returning from a victory, he would by his silence have suspected that he had lost the day; and, had he beheld him in a retreat, he would have collected him a conqueror by the cheerfulness of his spirit." *

The following passage from the Heimskringla might almost stand as a portrait of the modern Englishman:— "Haldor was very stout and strong, and remarkably handsome in appearances. King Harold gave him this testimony, that he, among all his men, cared least about doubtful circumstances, whether they betokened danger or pleasure; for, whatever turned up, he was never in higher nor in lower spir-

* Fuller. Worthies of England.

its, never slept less nor more on account of them, nor ate nor drank but according to his custom. Haldor was not a man of many words, but short in conversation, told his opinion bluntly, and was obstinate and hard; and this could not please the king, who had many clever people about him, zealous in his service. Haldor remained a short time with the king, and then came to Iceland, where he took up his abode in Hiardaholt, and dwelt in that farm to a very advanced age." *

The national temper, in the civil history, is not flashy or whiffling. The slow, deep English mass smoulders with fire, which at last sets all its borders in flame. The wrath of London is not French wrath, but has a long memory, and, in its hottest heat, a register and rule.

Half their strength they put not forth. They are capable of a sublime resolution, and if hereafter the war of races, often predicted, and making itself a war of opinions also (a question of despotism and liberty coming from Eastern Europe), should menace the English civilization, these sea-kings may take once again to their floating castles, and find a new home and a second millennium of power in their colonies.

The stability of England is the security of the modern world. If the English race were as mutable as the French, what reliance? But the English stand for liberty. The conservative, money-loving, lord-loving English are yet liberty-loving; and so freedom is safe: for they have more personal force than other people. The nation always resist the immoral action of their government. They think humanely on the affairs of France, of Turkey, of Poland, of Hungary, of Schleswig Holstein, though overborne by the statecraft of the rulers at last.

Does the early history of each tribe show the permanent bias, which, though not less potent, is masked, as the tribe spreads its activity into colonies, commerce, codes, arts, letters? The early history shows it, as the musician plays the air which he proceeds to conceal in a tempest of variations. In Alfred, in the Northmen, one may read the genius of the English society, namely, that private life is the place of honor. Glory, a career, and ambition, words familiar to the longitude of Paris, are seldom heard in English speech. Nelson wrote from their hearts his homely telegraph, "England expects every man to do his duty."

* Heimskringla, Laing's translation, Vol. III. p. 37.

For actual service, for the dignity of a profession, or to appease diseased or inflamed talent, the army and navy may be entered (the worst boys doing well in the navy); and the civil service, in departments where serious official work is done; and they hold in esteem the barrister engaged in the severer studies of the law. But the calm, sound, and most British Briton shrinks from public life, as charlatanism, and respects an economy founded on agriculture, coal-mines, manufactures, or trade, which secures an independence through the creation of real values.

They wish neither to command or obey, but to be kings in their own houses. They are intellectual and deeply enjoy literature; they like well to have the world served up to them in books, maps, models, and every mode of exact information, and, though not creators in the art, they value its refinement. They are ready for leisure, can direct and fill their own day, nor need so much as others the constraint of a necessity. But the history of the nation discloses, at every turn, this original predilection for private independence, and, however this inclination may have been disturbed by the bribes with which their vast colonial power has warped men out of orbit, the inclination endures, and forms and reforms the laws, letters, manners, and occupations. They choose that welfare which is compatible with the commonwealth, knowing that such alone is stable; as wise merchants prefer investments in three per cents.

CHAPTER IX.

COCKAYNE.

THE English are a nation of humorists. Individual right is pushed to the uttermost bound compatible with public order. Property is so perfect, that it seems the craft of that race, and not to exist elsewhere. The king cannot step on an acre which the peasant refuses to sell. A testator endows a dog or a rookery, and Europe cannot interfere with his absurdity. Every individual has his particular way of living, which he pushes to folly, and the decided sympathy of his compatriots is engaged to back up Mr. Crump's whim by statutes, and chancellors, and horse-guards. There is no freak so ridiculous but some Englishman has attempted to immortalize by money and law. British citizenship is as omnipotent as Roman was. Mr. Cockayne is very sensible of this. The pursy man means by freedom the right to do as he pleases, and does wrong in order to feel his freedom, and makes a conscience of persisting in it.

He is intensely patriotic, for his country is so small. His confidence in the power and performance of his nation makes him provokingly incurious about other nations. He dislikes foreigners. Swedenborg, who lived much in England, notes "the similitude of minds among the English, in consequence of which they contract familiarity with friends who are of that nation, and seldom with others; and they regard foreigners, as one looking through a telescope from the top of a palace regards those who dwell or wander about out of the city." A much older traveller, the Venetian who wrote the "Relation of England,"* in 1500, says: "The English are great lovers of themselves, and of everything belonging to them. They think that there are no other men than themselves, and no other world but England; and, whenever they see a handsome foreigner, they say that he looks like an Englishman, and it is a great pity he should not be an Englishman; and whenever they partake of any delicacy with a foreigner, they ask him whether such a thing is made in his country." When he adds epithets of praise, his climax is "so English"; and when he wishes to pay you the highest compliment, he says, I should not know you from an Englishman. France is, by its natural contrast, a kind of blackboard on which English character draws its own traits in chalk. This arrogance habitually exhibits itself in allusions to the French. I suppose that all men of English blood in America, Europe, or Asia, have a secret feeling of joy that they are not French natives. Mr. Coleridge is said to have given public thanks to God, at the close of a lecture, that he had defended him from being able to utter a single sentence in the French language. I have found that Englishmen have such a good opinion of England, that the ordinary phrases, in all good society, of postponing or disparaging one's own things in talking with a stranger, are seriously mistaken by them for an insuppressible homage to the merits of their nation; and the New-Yorker or Pennsylvanian who modestly laments the disadvantage of a new country, log-huts, and savages, is surprised

* Printed by the Camden Society.

by the instant and unfeigned commiseration of the whole company, who plainly account all the world out of England a heap of rubbish.

The same insular limitation pinches his foreign politics. He sticks to his traditions and usages, and, so help him God! he will force his island by-laws down the throat of great countries, like India, China, Canada, Australia, and not only so, but impose Wapping on the Congress of Vienna, and trample down all nationalities with his taxed boots. Lord Chatham goes for liberty, and no taxation without representation; — for that is British law; but not a hobnail shall they dare make in America, but buy their nails in England, — for that also is British law; and the fact that British commerce was to be re-created by the independence of America, took them all by surprise.

In short, I am afraid that English nature is so rank and aggressive as to be a little incompatible with every other. The world is not wide enough for two.

But, beyond this nationality, it must be admitted, the island offers a daily worship to the old Norse god Brage, celebrated among our Scandinavian forefathers, for his eloquence and majestic air. The English have a steady courage, that fits them for great attempts and endurance: they have also a petty courage, through which every man delights in showing himself for what he is, and in doing what he can; so that, in all companies, each of them has too good an opinion of himself to imitate anybody. He hides no defect of his form, features, dress, connection, or birthplace, for he thinks every circumstance belonging to him comes recommended to you. If one of them have a bald, or a red, or a green head, or bow legs, or a scar, or mark, or a paunch, or a squeaking or a raven voice, he has persuaded himself that there is something modish and becoming in it, and that it sits well on him.

But nature makes nothing in vain, and this little superfluity of self-regard in the English brain is one of the secrets of their power and history. For, it sets every man on being and doing what he really is and can. It takes away a dodging, skulking, secondary air, and encourages a frank and manly bearing, so that each man makes the most of himself, and loses no opportunity for want of pushing. A man's personal defects will commonly have with the rest of the world precisely that importance which they have to himself. If he makes light of them, so will other men. We all find in these a convenient meter of character, since a little man would be ruined by the vexation. I remember a shrewd politician, in one of our Western cities, told me, "that he had known several successful statesmen made by their foible." And another, an ex-governor of Illinois, said to me: "If a man knew anything, he would sit in a corner and be modest; but he is such an ignorant peacock, that he goes bustling up and down, and hits on extraordinary discoveries."

There is also this benefit in brag, that the speaker is unconsciously expressing his own ideal. Humor him by all means, draw it all out, and hold him to it. Their culture generally enables the travelled English to avoid any ridiculous extremes of this self-pleasing, and to give it an agreeable air. Then the natural disposition is fostered by the respect which they find entertained in the world for English ability. It was said of Louis XIV., that his gait and air were becoming enough in so great a monarch, yet would have been ridiculous in another man; so the prestige of the English name warrants a certain confident bearing, which a Frenchman or Belgian could not carry. At all events, they feel themselves at liberty to assume the most extraordinary tone on the subject of English merits.

An English lady on the Rhine hearing a German speaking of her party as foreigners, exclaimed, "No, we are not foreigners; we are English; it is you that are foreigners." They tell you daily, in London, the story of the Frenchman and Englishman who quarrelled. Both were unwilling to fight, but their companions put them up to it; at last, it was agreed, that they should fight alone, in the dark, and with pistols: the candles were put out, and the Englishman, to make sure not to hit anybody, fired up the chimney, and brought down the Frenchman. They have no curiosity about foreigners, and answer any information you may volunteer with, "Oh, Oh!" until the informant makes up his mind, that they shall die in their ignorance, for any help he will offer. There are really no limits to this conceit, though brighter men among them make painful efforts to be candid.

The habit of brag runs through all classes, from the *Times* newspaper through politicians and poets, through Wordsworth, Carlyle, Mill, and Sydney Smith, down to the boys of Eton. In the gravest treatise on political economy, in a philosophical essay, in books of science, one is surprised by the most innocent exhibition of unflinching nationality. In a tract on Corn, a most amiable and accomplished gentleman writes thus: "Though Britain, according to Bishop Berkeley's idea, were surrounded by a wall of brass ten thousand cubits in height, still, she would as far excel the rest of the globe in riches, as she now does, both in this secondary quality, and in the more important ones of freedom, virtue, and science." *

The English dislike the American structure of society, whilst yet trade, mills, public education, and chartism are doing what they can to create in England the same social condition. America is the paradise of the economists; is the favorable exception invariably quoted to the rules of ruin; but when he speaks directly of the Americans, the islander forgets his philosophy, and remembers his disparaging anecdotes.

But this childish patriotism costs something, like all narrowness. The English sway of their colonies has no root of kindness. They govern by their arts and ability; they are more just than kind; and, whenever an abatement of their power is felt, they have not conciliated the affection on which to rely.

Coarse local distinctions, as those of nation, province, or town, are useful in the absence of real ones; but we must not insist on these accidental lines. Individual traits are always triumphing over national ones. There is no fence in metaphysics discriminating Greek, or English, or Spanish science. Æsop, and Montaigne, Cervantes and Saadi, are men of the world; and to wave our own flag at the dinner-table or in the University, is to carry the boisterous dulness of a fire-club into a polite circle. Nature and destiny are always on the watch for our follies. Nature trips us up when we strut; and there are curious examples in history on this very point of national pride.

George of Cappadocia, born at Epiphania in Cilicia, was a low parasite, who got a lucrative contract to supply the army with bacon. A rogue and informer, he got rich, and was forced to run from justice. He saved his money, embraced Arianism, collected a library, and got promoted by a faction to the episcopal throne of Alexandria. When Julian came, A. D. 361, George was dragged to prison; the prison was burst open by the mob, and George was lynched, as he deserved. And this precious knave became, in good time, Saint George of England, patron of chivalry, emblem of victory and civility, and the pride of the best blood of the modern world.

Strange, that the solid truth-speaking Briton should derive from an impostor. Strange, that the New World should have no better luck, — that broad America must wear the name of a thief. Amerigo Vespucci, the pickle-dealer at Seville, who

* William Spence.

went out, in 1499, a subaltern with Hojeda, and whose highest naval rank was boatswain's mate in an expedition that never sailed, managed in this lying world to supplant Columbus, and baptize half the earth with his own dishonest name. Thus nobody can throw stones. We are equally badly off in our founders; and the false pickle-dealer is an offset to the false bacon-seller.

CHAPTER X.

WEALTH.

THERE is no country in which so absolute a homage is paid to wealth. In America, there is a touch of shame when a man exhibits the evidences of large property, as if, after all, it needed apology. But the Englishman has pure pride in his wealth, and esteems it a final certificate. A coarse logic rules throughout all English souls; — if you have merit, can you not show it by your good clothes, and coach, and horses? How can a man be a gentleman without a pipe of wine? Haydon says, "There is a fierce resolution to make every man live according to the means he possesses." There is a mixture of religion in it. They are under the Jewish law, and read with sonorous emphasis that their days shall be long in the land, they shall have sons and daughters, flocks and herds, wine and oil. In exact proportion is the reproach of poverty. They do not wish to be represented except by opulent men. An Englishman who has lost his fortune is said to have died of a broken heart. The last term of insult is, "a beggar." Nelson said, "The want of fortune is a crime which I can never get over." Sydney Smith said, "Poverty is infamous in England." And one of their recent writers speaks, in reference to a private and scholastic life, of "the grave moral deterioration which follows an empty exchequer." You shall find this sentiment, if not so frankly put, yet deeply implied, in the novels and romances of the present century, and not only in these, but in biography, and in the votes of public assemblies, in the tone of the preaching, and in the table-talk.

I was lately turning over Wood's *Athenæ Oxonienses*, and looking naturally for another standard in a chronicle of the scholars of Oxford for two hundred years. But I found the two disgraces in that, as in most English books, are, first, disloyalty to Church and State, and, second, to be born poor, or to come to poverty. A natural fruit of England is the brutal political economy. Malthus finds no cover laid at nature's table for the laborer's son. In 1809, the majority in Parliament expressed itself by the language of Mr. Fuller in the House of Commons, "If you do not like the country, damn you, you can leave it." When Sir S. Romilly proposed his bill forbidding parish officers to bind children apprentices at a greater distance than forty miles from their home, Peel opposed, and Mr. Wortley said, "though, in the higher ranks, to cultivate family affections was a good thing, 't was not so among the lower orders. Better take them away from those who might deprave them. And it was highly injurious to trade to stop binding to manufacturers, as it must raise the price of labor, and of manufactured goods."

The respect for truth of facts in England is equalled only by the respect for wealth. It is at once the pride of art of the Saxon, as he is a wealth-maker, and his passion for independence. The Englishman believes that every man must take care of himself, and has himself to thank, if he do not mend his condition. To pay their debts is their national point of honor. From the Exchequer and the East India House to the huckster's shop, everything prospers, because it is solvent. The British armies are solvent, and pay for what they take. The British empire is solvent; for, in spite of the huge national debt, the valuation mounts. During the war from 1789 to 1815, whilst they complained that they were taxed within an inch of their lives, and, by dint of enormous taxes, were subsidizing all the continent against France, the English were growing rich every year faster than any people ever grew before. It is their maxim, that the weight of taxes must be calculated, not by what is taken, but by what is left. Solvency is in the ideas and mechanism of an Englishman. The Crystal Palace is not considered honest until it pays; no matter how much convenience, beauty, or *éclat* it must be self-supporting. They are contented with slower steamers, as long as they know that swifter boats lose money. They proceed logically by the double method of labor and thrift. Every household exhibits an exact economy, and nothing of that uncalculated headlong expenditure which families use in America. If they cannot pay, they do not buy; for they have no presumption of better fortunes next year, as our people have;

and they say without shame, I cannot afford it. Gentlemen do not hesitate to ride in the second-class cars, or in the second cabin. An economist, or a man who can proportion his means and his ambition, or bring the year round with expenditure which expresses his character, without embarrassing one day of his future, is already a master of life, and a freeman. Lord Burleigh writes to his son, "that one ought never to devote more than two thirds of his income to the ordinary expenses of life, since the extraordinary will be certain to absorb the other third."

The ambition to create value evokes every kind of ability, government becomes a manufacturing corporation, and every house a mill. The headlong bias to utility will let no talent lie in a napkin, — if possible, will teach spiders to weave silk stockings. An Englishman, while he eats and drinks no more, or not much more than another man, labors three times as many hours in the course of a year, as any other European; or, his life as a workman is three lives. He works fast. Everything in England is at a quick pace. They have reinforced their own productivity, by the creation of that marvellous machinery which differences this age from any other age.

'T is a curious chapter in modern history, the growth of the machine-shop. Six hundred years ago, Roger Bacon explained the precession of the equinoxes, the consequent necessity of the reform of the calendar; measured the length of the year, invented gunpowder; and announced (as if looking from his lofty cell, over five centuries, into ours) "that machines can be constructed to drive ships more rapidly than a whole galley of rowers could do; nor would they need anything but a pilot to steer them. Carriages also might be constructed to move with an incredible speed, without the aid of any animal. Finally, it would not be impossible to make machines, which, by means of a suit of wings, should fly in the air in the manner of birds." But the secret slept with Bacon. The six hundred years have not yet fulfilled his words. Two centuries ago, the sawing of timber was done by hand; the carriage wheels ran on wooden axles; the land was tilled by wooden ploughs. And it was to little purpose that they had pit-coal or that looms were improved, unless Watt and Stephenson had taught them to work force-pumps and power-looms by steam. The great strides were all taken within the last hundred years. The life of Sir Robert Peel, who died, the other day, the model Englishman, very properly has, for a frontispiece, a drawing of the spinning-jenny, which wove the web of his fortunes. Hargreaves invented the spinning-jenny, and died in a workhouse. Arkwright improved the invention; and the machine dispensed with the work of ninety-nine men: that is, one spinner could do as much work as one hundred had done before. The loom was improved further. But the men would sometimes strike for wages, and combine against the masters, and, about 1829 – 30, much fear was felt, lest the trade would be drawn away by these interruptions, and the emigration of the spinners, to Belgium and the United States. Iron and steel are very obedient. Whether it were not possible to make a spinner that would not rebel, nor mutter, nor scowl, nor strike for wages, nor emigrate? At the solicitation of the masters, after a mob and riot at Staley Bridge, Mr. Roberts of Manchester undertook to create this peaceful fellow, instead of the quarrelsome fellow God had made. After a few trials, he succeeded, and, in 1830, procured a patent for his self-acting mule; a creation, the delight of mill-owners, and "destined," they said, "to restore order among the industrious classes"; a machine requiring only a child's hand to piece the broken yarns. As Arkwright had destroyed domestic spinning, so Roberts destroyed the factory spinner. The power of machiney in Great Britain, in mills, has been computed to be equal to 600,000,000 men, one man being able by the aid of steam to do the work which required two hundred and fifty men to accomplish fifty years ago. The production has been commensurate. England already had this laborious race, rich soil, water, wood, coal, iron, and favorable climate. Eight hundred years ago, commerce had made it rich, and it was recorded, "England is the richest of all the northern nations." The Norman historians recite, that "in 1067, William carried with him into Normandy, from England, more gold and silver than had ever before been seen in Gaul. But when, to this labor and trade, and these native resources was added this goblin of steam, with his myriad arms, never tired, working night and day everlastingly, the amassing of property has run out of all figures. It makes the motor of the last ninety years. The steam-pipe has added to her population and wealth the equivalent of four or five Englands. Forty thousand ships are entered in Lloyd's lists. The yield of wheat has gone on from 2,000,000 quarters in the time of the Stuarts, to 13,000,000 in 1854. A thousand million of pounds sterling are said to compose the floating money of commerce. In 1848, Lord John Russell stated that the people of this country had laid out £ 300,000,000 of capital in railways, in the last four years. But a better measure than these sounding figures is the estimate, that there is wealth enough in England to support the entire population in idleness for one year.

The wise, versatile, all-giving machinery makes chisels, roads, locomotives, telegraphs. Whitworth divides a bar to a millionth of an inch. Steam twines huge cannon into wreaths, as easily as it braids straw, and vies with the volcanic forces which twisted the strata. It can clothe shingle mountains with ship-oaks, make sword-blades that will cut gun-barrels in two. In Egypt, it can plant forests, and bring rain after three thousand years. Already it is ruddering the balloon, and the next war will be fought in the air. But another machine more potent in England than steam, is the Bank. It votes an issue of bills, population is stimulated, and cities rise; it refuses loans, and emigration empties the country; trade sinks; revolutions break out; kings are dethroned. By these new agents our social system is moulded. By dint of steam and of money, war and commerce are changed. Nations have lost their old omnipotence; the patriotic tie does not hold. Nations are getting obsolete, we go and live where we will. Steam has enabled men to choose what law they will live under. Money makes place for them. The telegraph is a limp-band that will hold the Fenris-wolf of war. For now, that a telegraph line runs through France and Europe, from London, every message it transmits makes stronger by one thread the band which war will have to cut.

The introduction of these elements gives new resources to existing proprietors. A sporting duke may fancy that the state depends on the House of Lords, but the engineer sees, that every stroke of the steam-piston gives value to the duke's land, fills it with tenants; doubles, quadruples, centuples the duke's capital, and creates new measures and new necessities for the culture of his children. Of course, it draws the nobility into the competition as stockholders in the mine, the canal, the railway, in the application of steam to agriculture, and sometimes into trade. But it also introduces large classes into the same competition; the old energy of the Norse race arms itself with these magnificent powers; new men prove an overmatch for the land-owner, and the mill buys out the castle. Scandinavian Thor, who once forged his bolts in icy Hecla, and built galleys by lonely fiords; in England, has advanced with the times, has shorn his beard, enters Parliament, sits down at a desk in the India House, and lends Miollnir to Birmingham for a steam-hammer.

The creation of wealth in England in the last ninety years is a main fact in modern history. The wealth of London determines prices all over the globe. All things precious, or useful, or amusing, or intoxicating, are sucked into this commerce and floated to London. Some English private fortunes reach, and some exceed, a million of dollars a year. A hundred thousand palaces adorn the island. All that can feed the senses and passions, all that can succor the talent, or arm the hands of the intelligent middle class who never spare in what they buy for their own consumption; all that can aid science, gratify taste, or soothe comfort, is in open market. Whatever is excellent and beautiful in civil, rural, or ecclesiastic architecture; in fountain, garden, or grounds; the English noble crosses sea and land to see and to copy at home. The taste and science of thirty peaceful generations; the gardens which Evelyn planted; the temples and pleasure-houses which Inigo Jones and Christopher Wren built; the wood that Gibbons carved; the taste of foreign and domestic artists, Shenstone, Pope, Brown, Loudŏn, Paxton, are in the vast auction, and the hereditary principle heaps on the owner of to-day the benefit of ages of owners. The present possessors are to the full as absolute as any of their fathers, in choosing and procuring what they like. This comfort and splendor, the breadth of lake and mountain, tillage, pasture, and park, sumptuous castle and modern villa, — all consist with perfect order. They have no revolutions; no horse-guards dictating to the crown; no Parisian *poissardes* and barricades; no mob: but drowsy habitude, daily dress-dinners, wine, and ale, and beer, and gin, and sleep.

With this power of creation, and this passion for independence, property has reached an ideal perfection. It is felt and treated as the national life-blood. The laws are framed to give property the securest possible basis, and the provisions to lock and transmit it have exercised the cunningest heads in a profession which never admits a fool. The rights of property nothing but felony and treason can override. The house is a castle which the king cannot enter. The Bank is a strong box to which the king has no key. Whatever surly sweetness possession can give, is tasted in England to the dregs. Vested rights are awful things, and absolute possession gives the smallest freeholder identity of interest with the duke. High stone fences, and padlocked garden-gates announce the absolute will of the owner to be alone. Every whim of exaggerated egotism is put into stone and iron, into silver and gold, with costly deliberation and detail.

An Englishman hears that the Queen Dowager wishes to establish some claim to put her park paling a rod forward into his grounds, so as to get a coachway, and save her a mile to the avenue. Instantly he transforms his paling into stone masonry, solid as the walls of Cuma, and all Europe cannot prevail on him to sell or compound for an inch of the land. They delight in a freak as the proof of their sovereign freedom. Sir Edward Boynton, at Spic Park, at Cadenham, on a precipice of incomparable prospect, built a house like a long barn, which had not a window on the prospect side. Strawberry Hill of Horace Walpole, Fonthill Abbey of Mr. Beckford, were freaks; and Newstead Abbey became one in the hands of Lord Byron.

But the proudest result of this creation has been the great and refined forces it has put at the disposal of the private citizen. In the social world, an Englishman to-day has the best lot. He is a king in a plain coat. He goes with the most powerful protection, keeps the best company, is armed by the best education, is seconded by wealth; and his English name and accidents are like a flourish of trumpets announcing him. This, with his quiet style of manners, gives him the power of a sovereign, without the inconveniences which belong to that rank. I much prefer the condition of an English gentleman of the better class, to that of any potentate in Europe, — whether for travel, or for opportunity of society, or for access to means of science or study, or for mere comfort and easy healthy relation to people at home.

Such as we have seen is the wealth of England, a mighty mass, and made good in whatever details we care to explore. The cause and spring of it is the wealth of temperament in the people. The wonder of Britain is this plenteous nature. Her worthies are ever surrounded by as good men as themselves; each is a captain a hundred strong, and that wealth of men is represented again in the faculty of each individual, — that he has waste strength, power to spare. The English are so rich, and seem to have established a taproot in the bowels of the planet, because they are constitutionally fertile and creative.

But a man must keep an eye on his servants, if he would not have them rule him. Man is a shrewd inventor, and is ever taking the hint of a new machine from his own structure, adapting some secret of his own anatomy in iron, wood, and leather, to some required function in the work of the world. But it is found that the machine unmans the user. What he gains in making cloth, he loses in general power. There should be temperance in making cloth, as well as in eating. A man should not be a silkworm; nor a nation a tent of caterpillars. The robust rural Saxon degenerates in the mills to the Leicester stockinger, to the imbecile Manchester spinner, — far on the way to be spiders and needles. The incessant repetition of the same hand-work dwarfs the man, robs him of his strength, wit, and versatility, to make a pin-polisher, a buckle-maker, or any other specialty; and presently, in a change of industry, whole towns are sacrificed like ant-hills, when the fashion of shoe-strings supersedes buckles, when cotton takes the place of linen, or railways of turnpikes, or when commons are enclosed by landlords. Then society is admonished of the mischief of the division of labor, and that the best political economy is care and culture of men; for, in these crises, all are ruined except such as are proper individuals, capable of thought, and of new choice and the application of their talent to new labor. Then again come in new calamities. England is aghast at the disclosure of her fraud in the adulteration of food, of drugs, and of almost every fabric in her mills and shops; finding that milk will not nourish, nor sugar sweeten, nor bread satisfy, nor pepper bite the tongue, nor glue stick. In true England all is false and forged. This too is the reaction of machinery, but of the larger machinery of commerce. 'T is not, I suppose, want of probity, so much as the tyranny of trade, which necessitates a perpetual competition of underselling, and that again a perpetual deterioration of the fabric.

The machinery has proved, like the balloon, unmanageable, and flies away with the aeronaut. Steam from the first hissed and screamed to warn him; it was dreadful with its explosion, and crushed the engineer. The machinist has wrought and watched, engineers and firemen without number have been sacrificed in learning to tame and guide the monster. But harder still it has proved to resist and rule the dragon Money, with his paper wings. Chancellors and Boards of Trade, Pitt, Peel, and Robinson, and their Parliaments, and their whole generation, adopted false principles, and went to their graves in the belief that they were enriching the country which they were impoverishing. They congratulated each other on ruinous expedients. It is rare to find a merchant who knows why a crisis occurs in trade, why prices rise or fall, or who knows the mischief of paper money. In the culmination of national prosperity, in the annexation of countries; building of ships, depots, towns; in the influx of tons of gold and silver; amid the chuckle of chancellors and financiers, it was found that bread rose to famine prices, that the yeoman was forced to sell his cow and pig, his tools, and his acre of land; and the dreadful barometer of the poor-rates was touching the point of ruin. The poor-rate was sucking in the solvent classes, and forcing an exodus of farmers and mechanics. What befalls from the violence of financial crises, befalls daily in the violence of artificial legislation.

Such a wealth has England earned, ever new, bounteous, and augmenting. But the question recurs, does she take the step beyond, namely, to the wise use, in view of the supreme wealth of nations? We estimate the wisdom of nations by seeing what they did with their surplus capital. And, in view of these injuries, some compensation has been attempted in England. A part of the money earned returns to the brain to buy schools, libraries, bishops, astronomers, chemists, and artists with; and a part to repair the wrongs of this intemperate weaving, by hospitals, savings-banks, Mechanics' Institutes, public grounds, and other charities and amenities. But the antidotes are frightfully inadequate, and the evil requires a deeper cure, which time and a simpler social organization must supply. At present, she does not rule her wealth. She is simply a good England, but no divinity, or wise and instructed soul. She too is in the stream of fate, one victim more in a common catastrophe.

But being in the fault, she has the misfortune of greatness to be held as the chief offender. England must be held responsible for the despotism of expense. Her prosperity, the splendor which so much manhood and talent and perseverance has thrown upon vulgar aims, is the very argument of materialism. Her success strengthens the hands of base wealth. Who can propose to youth poverty and wisdom, when mean gain has arrived at the conquest of letters and arts; when English success has grown out of the very renunciation of principles, and the dedication to outsides. A civility of trifles, of money and expense, an erudition of sensation takes place, and the putting as many impediments as we can, between the man and his objects. Hardly the bravest among them have the manliness to resist it successfully. Hence, it has come, that not the aims of a manly life, but the means of meeting a certain ponderous expense, is that which is to be considered by a youth in England, emerging from his minority. A large family is reckoned a misfortune. And it is a consolation in the death of the young, that a source of expense is closed.

CHAPTER XI.

ARISTOCRACY.

THE feudal character of the English state, now that it is getting obsolete, glares a little, in contrast with the democratic tendencies. The inequality of power and property shocks republican nerves. Palaces, halls, villas, walled parks, all over England, rival the splendor of royal seats. Many of the halls, like Haddon, or Kedleston, are beautiful desolations. The proprietor never saw them, or never lived in them. Primogeniture built these sumptuous piles, and, I suppose, it is the sentiment of every traveller, as it was mine, 'T was well to come ere these were gone. Primogeniture is a cardinal rule of English property and institutions. Laws, customs, manners, the very persons and faces, affirm it.

The frame of society is aristocratic, the taste of the people is loyal. The estates, names, and manners of the nobles flatter the fancy of the people, and conciliate the necessary support. In spite of broken faith, stolen charters, and the devastation of society by the profligacy of the court, we take sides as we read for the loyal England and King Charles's "return to his right" with his Cavaliers, — knowing what a heartless trifler he is, and what a crew of God-forsaken robbers they are. The people of England knew as much. But the fair idea of a settled government connecting itself with heraldic names, with the written and oral history of Europe, and, at last, with the Hebrew religion, and the oldest traditions of the world, was too pleasing a vision to be shattered by a few offensive realities, and the politics of shoemakers and costermongers. The hopes of the commoners take the same direction with the interest of the patricians. Every man who becomes rich buys land, and does what he can to fortify the nobility, into which he hopes to rise. The Anglican clergy are identified with the aristocracy. Time and law have made the joining and moulding perfect in every part. The Cathedrals, the Universities, the national music, the popular romances, conspire to uphold the heraldry, which the current politics of the day are sapping. The taste of the people is conservative. They are proud of the castles, and of the language and symbol of chivalry. Even the word "lord" is the luckiest style that is used in any language to designate a patrician. The superior education and manners of the nobles recommend them to the country.

The Norwegian pirate got what he could, and held it for his eldest son. The Norman noble, who was the Norwegian pirate baptized, did likewise. There was this advantage of Western over Oriental nobility, that this was recruited from below. English history is aristocracy with the doors open. Who has courage and faculty, let him come in. Of course, the terms of admission to this club are hard and high. The selfishness of the nobles comes in aid of the interest of the nation to require signal merit. Piracy and war gave place to trade, politics, and letters; the war-lord to the law-lord; the law-lord to the merchant and the mill-owner; but the privilege was kept, whilst the means of obtaining it were changed.

The foundations of these families lie deep in Norwegian exploits by sea, and Saxon sturdiness on land. All nobility in its beginnings was somebody's natural superiority. The things these English have done were not done without peril of life, nor without wisdom and conduct; and the first hands, it may be presumed, were often challenged to show their right to their honors, or yield them to better men. "He that will be a head, let him be a bridge," said the Welsh chief Benegridran, when he carried all his men over the river on his back. "He shall have the book," said the mother of Alfred, "who can read it"; and Alfred won it by that title: and I make no doubt that feudal tenure was no sinecure, but baron, knight, and tenant often had their memories refreshed, in regard to the service by which they held their lands. The De Veres,

Bohuns, Mowbrays, and Plantagenets were not addicted to contemplation. The Middle Age adorned itself with proofs of manhood and devotion. Of Richard Beauchamp, Earl of Warwick, the Emperor told Henry V. that no Christian king had such another knight for wisdom, nurture, and manhood, and caused him to be named, "Father of curtesie." "Our success in France," says the historian, "lived and died with him." *

The war-lord earned his honors, and no donation of land was large, as long as it brought the duty of protecting it, hour by hour, against a terrible enemy. In France and in England, the nobles were, down to a late day, born and bred to war; and the duel, which in peace still held them to the risks of war, diminished the envy that, in trading and studious nations, would else have pried into their title. They were looked on as men who played high for a great stake.

Great estates are not sinecures, if they are to be kept great. A creative economy is the fuel of magnificence. In the same line of Warwick, the successor next but one to Beauchamp, was the stout earl of Henry VI. and Edward IV. Few esteemed themselves in the mode, whose heads were not adorned with the black ragged staff, his badge. At his house in London, six oxen were daily eaten at a breakfast; and every tavern was full of his meat; and who had any acquaintance in his family, should have as much boiled and roast as he could carry on a long dagger.

The new age brings new qualities into request, the virtues of pirates gave way to those of planters, merchants, senators, and scholars. Comity, social talent, and fine manners, no doubt, have had their part also. I have met somewhere with a historiette, which, whether more or less true in its particulars, carries a general truth. "How came the Duke of Bedford by his great landed estates? His ancestor having travelled on the continent, a lively, pleasant man, became the companion of a foreign prince wrecked on the Dorsetshire coast, where Mr. Russell lived. The prince recommended him to Henry VIII., who, liking his company, gave him a large share of the plundered church lands."

The pretence is that the noble is of unbroken descent from the Norman, and has never worked for eight hundred years. But the fact is otherwise. Where is Bohun? where is De Vere? The lawyer, the farmer, the silk-mercer, lies *perdu* under the

* Fuller's Worthies, II. p. 472.

coronet, and winks to the antiquary to say nothing; especially skilful lawyers, nobody's sons, who did some piece of work at a nice moment for government, and were rewarded with ermine.

The national tastes of the English do not lead them to the life of the courtier, but to secure the comfort and independence of their homes. The aristocracy are marked by their predilection for country-life. They are called the county-families. They have often no residence in London, and only go thither a short time, during the season, to see the opera; but they concentrate the love and labor of many generations on the building, planting, and decoration of their homesteads. Some of them are too old and too proud to wear titles, or, as Sheridan said of Coke, "disdain to hide their head in a coronet"; and some curious examples are cited to show the stability of English families. Their proverb is, that, fifty miles from London, a family will last a hundred years; at a hundred miles, two hundred years; and so on; but I doubt that steam, the enemy of time, as well as of space, will disturb these ancient rules. Sir Henry Wotton says of the first Duke of Buckingham: "He was born at Brookeby in Leicestershire, where his ancestors had chiefly continued about the space of four hundred years, rather without obscurity, than with any great lustre." * Wraxall says, that, in 1781, Lord Surrey, afterwards Duke of Norfolk, told him, that when the year 1783 should arrive, he meant to give a grand festival to all the descendants of the body of Jockey of Norfolk, to mark the day when the dukedom should have remained three hundred years in their house, since its creation by Richard III. Pepys tells us, in writing of an Earl Oxford, in 1666, that the honor had now remained in that name and blood six hundred years.

This long descent of families and this cleaving through ages to the same spot of ground captivates the imagination. It has too a connection with the names of the towns and districts of the country.

The names are excellent, — an atmosphere of legendary melody spread over the land. Older than all epics and histories, which clothe a nation, this undershirt sits close to the body. What history too, and what stores of primitive and savage observation it infolds! Cambridge is the bridge of the Cam; Sheffield the field of the river Sheaf; Leicester the *castra* or camp of the Lear or Leir (now Soar); Rochdale, of the Roch; Exeter or Excester, the *castra* of the Ex; Exmouth, Dart-

* Reliquiæ Wottonianæ, p. 208.

mouth, Sidmouth, Teignmouth, the mouths of the Ex, Dart, Sid, and Teign rivers. Waltham is strong town; Radcliffe is red cliff; and so on: — a sincerity and use in naming very striking to an American, whose country is whitewashed all over by unmeaning names, the cast-off clothes of the country from which its emigrants came; or, named at a pinch from a psalm-tune. But the English are those "barbarians" of Jamblichus, who "are stable in their manners, and firmly continue to employ the same words, which also are dear to the gods."

'T is an old sneer, that the Irish peerage drew their names from playbooks. The English lords do not call their lands after their own names, but call themselves after their lands; as if the man represented the country that bred him; and they rightly wear the token of the glebe that gave them birth; suggesting that the tie is not cut, but that there in London, — the crags of Argyle, the kail of Cornwall, the downs of Devon, the iron of Wales, the clays of Stafford, are neither forgetting nor forgotten, but know the man who was born by them, and who, like the long line of his fathers, has carried that crag, that shore, dale, fen, or woodland, in his blood and manners. It has, too, the advantage of suggesting responsibleness. A susceptible man could not wear a name which represented in a strict sense a city or a county of England, without hearing in it a challenge to duty and honor.

The predilection of the patricians for residence in the country, combined with the degree of liberty possessed by the peasant, makes the safety of the English hall. Mirabeau wrote prophetically from England, in 1784: "If revolution break out in France, I tremble for the aristocracy: their chateaux will be reduced to ashes, and their blood spilt in torrents. The English tenant would defend his lord to the last extremity." The English go to their estates for grandeur. The French live at court, and exile themselves to their estates for economy. As they do not mean to live with their tenants, they do not conciliate them, but wring from them the last sous. Evelyn writes from Blois, in 1644: "The wolves are here in such numbers, that they often come and take children out of the streets; yet will not the Duke, who is sovereign here, permit them to be destroyed."

In evidence of the wealth amassed by ancient families, the traveller is shown the palaces in Piccadilly, Burlington House, Devonshire House, Lansdowne House in Berkshire Square, and, lower down in the city, a few noble houses which still withstand in all their amplitude the encroachment of streets. The Duke of Bedford includes or included a mile square in the heart of London, where the British Museum, once Montague House, now stands, and the land occupied by Woburn Square, Bedford Square, Russell Square. The Marquis of Westminster built within a few years the series of squares called Belgravia. Stafford House is the noblest palace in London. Northumberland House holds its place by Charing Cross. Chesterfield House remains in Audley Street. Sion House and Holland House are in the suburbs. But most of the historical houses are masked or lost in the modern uses to which trade or charity has converted them. A multitude of town palaces contain inestimable galleries of art.

In the country, the size of private estates is more impressive. From Barnard Castle I rode on the highway twenty-three miles from High Force, a fall of the Tees, towards Darlington, past Raby Castle, through the estate of the Duke of Cleveland. The Marquis of Breadalbane rides out of his house a hundred miles in a straight line to the sea, on his own property. The Duke of Sutherland owns the county of Sutherland, stretching across Scotland from sea to sea. The Duke of Devonshire, besides his other estates, owns 96,000 acres in the county of Derby. The Duke of Richmond has 40,000 acres at Goodwood, and 300,000 at Gordon Castle. The Duke of Norfolk's park in Sussex is fifteen miles in circuit. An agriculturist bought lately the island of Lewes, in Hebrides, containing 500,000 acres. The possessions of the Earl of Lonsdale gave him eight seats in Parliament. This is the Heptarchy again: and before the Reform of 1832, one hundred and fifty-four persons sent three hundred and seven members to Parliament. The borough-mongers governed England.

These large domains are growing larger. The great estates are absorbing the small freeholds. In 1786, the soil of England was owned by 250,000 corporations and proprietors; and, in 1822, by 32,000. These broad estates find room in this narrow island. All over England, scattered at short intervals among ship-yards, mills, mines, and forges, are the paradises of the nobles, where the livelong repose and refinement are heightened by the contrast with the roar of industry and necessity, out of which you have stepped aside.

I was surprised to observe the very small attendance usually in the House of Lords. Out of 573 peers, on ordinary days, only twenty or thirty. Where are they? I asked. "At home on their estates, devoured by *ennui*, or in the Alps, or up the Rhine, in the Harz Mountains, or in Egypt, or in India, on the Ghauts." But, with such interests at stake, how can these men afford to neglect them? "O," replied my friend, "why should they work for themselves, when every man in England works for them, and will suffer before they come to harm?" The hardest radical instantly uncovers, and changes his tone to a lord. It was remarked on the 10th April, 1848 (the day of the Chartist demonstration), that the upper classes were, for the first time, actively interesting themselves in their own defence, and men of rank were sworn special constables, with the rest. "Besides, why need they sit out the debate? Has not the Duke of Wellington, at this moment, their proxies, — the proxies of fifty peers in his pocket, to vote for them, if there be an emergency?"

It is however true, that the existence of the House of Peers as a branch of the government entitles them to fill half the Cabinet; and their weight of property and station give them a virtual nomination of the other half; whilst they have their share in the subordinate offices, as a school of training. This monopoly of political power has given them their intellectual and social eminence in Europe. A few law lords and a few political lords take the brunt of public business. In the army, the nobility fill a large part of the high commissions, and give to these a tone of expense and splendor, and also of exclusiveness. They have borne their full share of duty and danger in this service; and there are few noble families which have not paid in some of their members, the debt of life or limb, in the sacrifices of the Russian war. For the rest, the nobility have the lead in matters of state, and of expense; in questions of taste, in social usages, in convivial and domestic hospitalities. In general, all that is required of them is to sit securely, to preside at public meetings, to countenance charities, and to give the example of that decorum so dear to the British heart.

If one asks, in the critical spirit of the day, what service this class have rendered? — uses appear, or they would have perished long ago. Some of these are easily enumerated, others more subtle make a part of unconscious history. Their institution is one step in the progress of society. For a race yields a nobility in some form, however we name the lords, as surely as it yields women.

The English nobles are high-spirited, active, educated men,

born to wealth and power, who have run through every country, and kept in every country the best company, have seen every secret of art and nature, and, when men of any ability or ambition, have been consulted in the conduct of every important action. You cannot wield great agencies without lending yourself to them, and when it happens that the spirit of the earl meets his rank and duties, we have the best examples of behavior. Power of any kind readily appears in the manners; and beneficent power, *le talent de bien faire,* gives a majesty which cannot be concealed or resisted.

These people seem to gain as much as they lose by their position. They survey society, as from the top of St. Paul's, and if they never hear plain truth from men, they see the best of everything, in every kind, and they see things so grouped and amassed as to infer easily the sum and genius, instead of tedious particularities. Their good behavior deserves all its fame, and they have that simplicity, and that air of repose, which are the finest ornament of greatness.

The upper classes have only birth, say the people here, and not thoughts. Yes, but they have manners, and, 't is wonderful, how much talent runs into manners: — nowhere and never so much as in England. They have the sense of superiority, the absence of all the ambitious effort which disgusts in the aspiring classes, a pure tone of thought and feeling, and the power to command, among their other luxuries, the presence of the most accomplished men in their festive meetings.

Loyalty is in the English a sub-religion. They wear the laws as ornaments, and walk by their faith in their painted May-Fair, as if among the forms of gods. The economist of 1855 who asks, of what use are the lords? may learn of Franklin to ask, of what use is a baby? They have been a social church proper to inspire sentiments mutually honoring the lover and the loved. Politeness is the ritual of society, as prayers are of the church; a school of manners, and a gentle blessing to the age in which it grew. 'T is a romance adorning English life with a larger horizon; a midway heaven, fulfilling to their sense their fairy tales and poetry. This, just as far as the breeding of the nobleman, really made him brave, handsome, accomplished, and great-hearted.

On general grounds, whatever tends to form manners, or to finish men, has a great value. Every one who has tasted the delight of friendship, will respect every social guard which our manners can establish, tending to secure from the intrusion of frivolous and distasteful people. The jealousy of every class to guard itself, is a testimony to the reality they have found in life. When a man once knows that he has done justice to himself, let him dismiss all terrors of aristocracy as superstitions, so far as he is concerned. He who keeps the door of a mine, whether of cobalt, or mercury, or nickle, or plumbago, securely knows that the world cannot do without him. Everybody who is real is open and ready for that which is also real.

Besides, these are they who make England that strong-box and museum it is; who gather and protect works of art, dragged from amidst burning cities and revolutionary countries, and brought hither out of all the world. I look with respect at houses six, seven, eight hundred, or, like Warwick Castle, nine hundred years old. I pardoned high park fences, when I saw, that, besides does and pheasants, these have preserved Arundel marbles, Townley galleries, Howard and Spenserian libraries, Warwick and Portland vases, Saxon manuscripts, monastic architectures, millennial trees, and breeds of cattle elsewhere extinct. In these manors, after the frenzy of war and destruction subsides a little, the antiquary finds the frailest Roman jar, or crumbling Egyptian mummy-case, without so much as a new layer of dust, keeping the series of history unbroken, and waiting for its interpreter, who is sure to arrive. These lords are the treasurers and librarians of mankind, engaged by their pride and wealth to this function.

Yet there were other works for British dukes to do. George Loudon, Quintinye, Evelyn, had taught them to make gardens. Arthur Young, Bakewell, and Mechi have made them agricultural. Scotland was a camp until the day of Culloden. The Dukes of Athol, Sutherland, Buccleugh, and the Marquis of Breadalbane have introduced the rape-culture, the sheep-farm, wheat, drainage, the plantation of forests, the artificial replenishment of lakes and ponds with fish, the renting of game-preserves. Against the cry of the old tenantry, and the sympathetic cry of the English press, they have rooted out and planted anew, and now six millions of people live, and live better on the same land that fed three millions.

The English barons, in every period, have been brave and great, after the estimate and opinion of their times. The grand old halls scattered up and down in England are dumb vouchers to the state and broad hospitality of their ancient lords. Shakespeare's portraits of good Duke Humphrey, of

Warwick, of Northumberland, of Talbot, were drawn in strict consonance with the traditions. A sketch of the Earl of Shrewsbury, from the pen of Queen Elizabeth's Archbishop Parker;* Lord Herbert of Cherbury's autobiography; the letters and essays of Sir Philip Sidney; the anecdotes preserved by the antiquaries Fuller and Collins; some glimpses at the interiors of noble houses, which we owe to Pepys and Evelyn; the details which Ben Jonson's masques (performed at Kenilworth, Althorpe, Belvoir, and other noble houses) record or suggest; down to Aubrey's passages of the life of Hobbes in the house of the Earl of Devon, are favorable pictures of a romantic style of manners. Penshurst still shines for us, and its Christmas revels, "where logs not burn, but men." At Wilton House, the "Arcadia" was written, amidst conversations with Fulke Greville, Lord Brooke, a man of no vulgar mind, as his own poems declare him. I must hold Ludlow Castle an honest house, for which Milton's "Comus" was written, and the company nobly bred which performed it with knowledge and sympathy. In the roll of nobles are found poets, philosophers, chemists, astronomers, also men of solid virtues and of lofty sentiments; often they have been the friends and patrons of genius and learning, and especially of the fine arts; and at this moment, almost every great house has its sumptuous picture-gallery.

Of course, there is another side to this gorgeous show. Every victory was the defeat of a party only less worthy. Castles are proud things, but 't is safest to be outside of them. War is a foul game, and yet war is not the worst part of aristocratic history. In later times, when the baron, educated only for war, with his brains paralyzed by his stomach, found himself idle at home, he grew fat and wanton, and a sorry brute. Grammont, Pepys, and Evelyn show the kennels to which the king and court went in quest of pleasure. Prostitutes taken from the theatres were made duchesses, their bastards dukes and earls. "The young men sat uppermost, the old serious lords were out of favor." The discourse that the king's companions had with him was "poor and frothy." No man who valued his head might do what these pot-companions familiarly did with the king. In logical sequence of these dignified revels, Pepys can tell the beggarly shifts to which the king was reduced, who could not find paper at his

* Dibdin's Literary Reminiscences, Vol. I. xii.

council table, and "no handkerchers" in his wardrobe, "and but three bands to his neck," and the linen-draper and the stationer were out of pocket, and refusing to trust him, and the baker will not bring bread any longer. Meantime, the English Channel was swept, and London threatened by the Dutch fleet, manned too by English sailors, who, having been cheated of their pay for years by the king, enlisted with the enemy.

The Selwyn correspondence in the reign of George III., discloses a rottenness in the aristocracy, which threatened to decompose the state. The sycophancy and sale of votes and honor, for place and title; lewdness, gaming, smuggling, bribery, and cheating; the sneer at the childish indiscretion of quarrelling with ten thousand a year; the want of ideas; the splendor of the titles, and the apathy of the nation, are instructive, and make the reader pause and explore the firm bounds which confined these vices to a handful of rich men. In the reign of the Fourth George, things do not seem to have mended, and the rotten debauchee let down from a window by an inclined plane into his coach to take the air, was a scandal to Europe which the ill fame of his queen and of his family did nothing to retrieve.

Under the present reign, the perfect decorum of the Court is thought to have put a check on the gross vices of the aristocracy; yet gaming, racing, drinking, and mistresses bring them down, and the democrat can still gather scandals, if he will. Dismal anecdotes abound, verifying the gossip of the last generation of dukes served by bailiffs, with all their plate in pawn; of great lords living by the showing of their houses; and of an old man wheeled in his chair from room to room, whilst his chambers are exhibited to the visitor for money: of ruined dukes and earls living in exile for debt. The historic names of the Buckinghams, Beauforts, Marlboroughs, and Hertfords have gained no new lustre, and now and then darker scandals break out, ominous as the new chapters added under the Orleans dynasty to the "*Causes Célèbres*" in France. Even peers, who are men of worth and public spirit, are overtaken and embarrassed by their vast expense. The respectable Duke of Devonshire, willing to be the Mecænas and Lucullus of his island, is reported to have said that he cannot live at Chatsworth but one month in the year. Their many houses eat them up. They cannot sell them, because they are entailed. They will not let them, for pride's sake, but keep them empty, aired, and the grounds mown and dressed, at a cost of four or five thousand pounds a year. The spending is for a great part in servants, in many houses exceeding a hundred.

Most of them are only chargeable with idleness, which, because it squanders such vast power of benefit, has the mischief of crime. "They might be little Providences on earth," said my friend, "and they are, for the most part, jockeys and fops." Campbell says: "Acquaintance with the nobility, I could never keep up. It requires a life of idleness, dressing, and attendance on their parties." I suppose, too, that a feeling of self-respect is driving cultivated men out of this society, as if the noble were slow to receive the lessons of the times, and had not learned to disguise his pride of place. A man of wit, who is also one of the celebrities of wealth and fashion, confessed to his friend, that he could not enter their houses without being made to feel that they were great lords, and he a low plebeian. With the tribe of *artistes*, including the musical tribe, the patrician morgue keeps no terms, but excludes them. When Julia Grisi and Mario sang at the houses of the Duke of Wellington and other grandees, a ribbon was stretched between the singer and the company.

When every noble was a soldier, they were carefully bred to great personal prowess. The education of a soldier is a simpler affair than that of an earl in the nineteenth century. And this was very seriously pursued; they were expert in every species of equitation, to the most dangerous practices, and this down to the accession of William of Orange. But graver men appear to have trained their sons for civil affairs. Elizabeth extended her thought to the future; and Sir Philip Sidney in his letter to his brother, and Milton and Evelyn, gave plain and hearty counsel. Already, too, the English noble and squire were preparing for the career of the country-gentleman, and his peaceable expense. They went from city to city, learning receipts to make perfumes, sweet powders, pomanders, antidotes, gathering seeds, gems, coins, and divers curiosities, preparing for a private life thereafter, in which they should take pleasure in these recreations.

All advantages given to absolve the young patrician from intellectual labor are of course mistaken. "In the university, noblemen are exempted from the public exercises for the degree, &c., by which they attain a degree called *honorary*. At the same time the fees they have to pay for matriculation, and on all other occasions, are much higher." * Fuller records "the observation of foreigners, that Englishmen, by making their children gentlemen, before they are men, cause they are so seldom wise men." This cockering justifies Dr. Johnson's bitter apology for primogeniture, "that it makes but one fool in a family."

The revolution in society has reached this class. The great powers of industrial art have no exclusion of name or blood. The tools of our time, namely, steam, ships, printing, money, and popular education, belong to those who can handle them; and their effect has been, that advantages once confined to men of family are now open to the whole middle class. The road that grandeur levels for his coach, toil can travel in his cart.

This is more manifest every day, but I think it is true throughout English history. English history, wisely read, is the vindication of the brain of that people. Here, at last, were climate and condition friendly to the working faculty. Who now will work and dare, shall rule. This is the charter, or the chartism, which fogs, and seas, and rains proclaimed, — that intellect and personal force should make the law; that industry and administrative talent should administer; that work should wear the crown. I know that not this, but something else is pretended. The fiction with which the noble and the bystander equally please themselves is, that the former is of unbroken descent from the Norman, and so has never worked for eight hundred years. All the families are new, but the name is old, and they have made a covenant with their memories not to disturb it. But the analysis of the peerage and gentry shows the rapid decay and extinction of old families, the continual recruiting of these from new blood. The doors, though ostentatiously guarded, are really open, and hence the power of the bribe. All the barriers to rank only whet the thirst, and enhance the prize. "Now," said Nelson, when clearing for battle, "a peerage, or Westminster Abbey!" "I have no illusion left," said Sidney Smith, "but the Archbishop of Canterbury." "The lawyers," said Burke, "are only birds of passage in this House of Commons," and then added, with a new figure, "they have their best bower anchor in the House of Lords."

Another stride that has been taken, appears in the perishing of heraldry. Whilst the privileges of nobility are passing to

* Huber, History of English Universities.

the middle class, the badge is discredited, and the titles of lordship are getting musty and cumbersome. I wonder that sensible men have not been already impatient of them. They belong, with wigs, powder, and scarlet coats, to an earlier age, and may be advantageously consigned, with paint and tattoo, to the dignitaries of Australia and Polynesia.

A multitude of English, educated at the universities, bred into their society with manners, ability, and the gifts of fortune, are every day confronting the peers on a footing of equality, and outstripping them, as often, in the race of honor and influence. That cultivated class is large and ever enlarging. It is computed that, with titles and without, there are seventy thousand of these people coming and going in London, who make up what is called high society. They cannot shut their eyes to the fact that an untitled nobility possess all the power without the inconveniences that belong to rank, and the rich Englishman goes over the world at the present day, drawing more than all the advantages which the strongest of his kings could command.

CHAPTER XII.

UNIVERSITIES.

OF British universities, Cambridge has the most illustrious names on its list. At the present day, too, it has the advantage of Oxford, counting in its *alumni* a greater number of distinguished scholars. I regret that I had but a single day wherein to see King's College Chapel, the beautiful lawns and gardens of the colleges, and a few of its gownsmen.

But I availed myself of some repeated invitations to Oxford, where I had introductions to Dr. Daubeny, Professor of Botany, and to the Regius Professor of Divinity, as well as to a valued friend, a Fellow of Oriel, and went thither on the last day of March, 1848. I was the guest of my friend in Oriel, was housed close upon that college, and I lived on college hospitalities.

My new friends showed me their cloisters, the Bodleian Library, the Randolph Gallery, Merton Hall, and the rest. I saw several faithful, high-minded young men, some of them in the mood of making sacrifices for peace of mind, — a topic, of course, on which I had no counsel to offer. Their affectionate and gregarious ways reminded me at once of the habits of *our* Cambridge men, though I imputed to these English an advantage in their secure and polished manners. The halls are rich with oaken wainscoting and ceiling. The pictures of the founders hang from the walls; the tables glitter with plate. A youth came forward to the upper table, and pronounced the ancient form of grace before meals, which, I suppose, has been in use here for ages, *Benedictus benedicat; benedicitur, benedicatur.*

It is a curious proof of the English use and wont, or of their good-nature, that these young men are locked up every night at nine o'clock, and the porter at each hall is required to give the name of any belated student who is admitted after that hour. Still more descriptive is the fact, that out of twelve hundred young men, comprising the most spirited of the aristocracy, a duel has never occurred.

Oxford is old, even in England, and conservative. Its foundations date from Alfred, and even from Arthur, if, as is alleged, the Pheryllt of the Druids had a seminary here. In the reign of Edward I., it is pretended, here were thirty thousand students; and nineteen most noble foundations were then established. Chaucer found it as firm as if it had always stood; and it is in British story, rich with great names, the school of the island, and the link of England to the learned of Europe. Hither came Erasmus, with delight, in 1497. Albericus Gentilis, in 1580, was relieved and maintained by the university. Albert Alaskie, a noble Polonian, Prince of Sirad, who visited England to admire the wisdom of Queen Elizabeth, was entertained with stage-plays in the Refectory of Christ-church, in 1583. Isaac Casaubon, coming from Henri Quatre of France, by invitation of James I., was admitted to Christ's College, in July, 1613. I saw the Ashmolean Museum, whither Elias Ashmole, in 1682, sent twelve cart-loads of rarities. Here indeed was the Olympia of all Antony Wood's and Aubrey's games and heroes, and every inch of ground has its lustre. For Wood's *Athenæ Oxonienses*, or calendar of the writers of Oxford for two hundred years, is a lively record of English manners and merits, and as much a national monument as Purchas's Pilgrims or Hansard's Register. On every side, Oxford is redolent of age and authority. Its gates shut of themselves against modern innovation. It is still governed by the statutes of Archbishop Laud. The books in Merton Library are still chained to the wall. Here, on August 27, 1660, John Milton's *Pro Populo Anglicano Defensio* and *Iconoclastes* were committed to the flames. I saw the school-court or quadrangle, where, in 1683, the Convocation caused the Leviathan of Thomas Hobbes to be publicly burnt. I do not know whether this learned body have yet heard of the Declaration of American Independence, or whether the Ptolemaic astronomy does not still hold its ground against the novelties of Copernicus.

As many sons, almost so many benefactors. It is usual for a nobleman, or indeed for almost every wealthy student, on quitting college, to leave behind him some article of plate; and gifts of all values, from a hall, or a fellowship, or a library, down to a picture or a spoon, are continually accruing, in the course of a century. My friend Doctor J. gave me the following anecdote. In Sir Thomas Lawrence's collection at London were the cartoons of Raphael and Michel Angelo. This inestimable prize was offered to Oxford University for seven thousand pounds. The offer was accepted, and the committee charged with the affair had collected three thousand pounds, when among other friends they called on Lord Eldon. Instead of a hundred pounds, he surprised them by putting down his name for three thousand pounds. They told him, they should now very easily raise the remainder. "No," he said, "your men have probably already contributed all they can spare; I can as well give the rest": and he withdrew his check for three thousand, and wrote four thousand pounds. I saw the whole collection in April, 1848.

In the Bodleian Library, Dr. Bandinel showed me the manuscript Plato, of the date of A. D. 896, brought by Dr. Clarke from Egypt; a manuscript Virgil, of the same century; the first Bible printed at Mentz (I believe in 1450); and a duplicate of the same, which had been deficient in about twenty leaves at the end. But, one day, being in Venice, he bought a room full of books and manuscripts, — every scrap and fragment, — for four thousand louis d'ors, and had the doors locked and sealed by the consul. On proceeding, afterwards, to examine his purchase, he found the twenty deficient pages of his Mentz Bible, in perfect order; brought them to Oxford, with the rest of his purchase, and placed them in the volume; but has too much awe for the Providence that appears in bibliography also, to suffer the reunited parts to be rebound. The oldest building here is two hundred years younger than the frail manuscript brought by Dr. Clarke from Egypt. No candle or fire is ever lighted in the Bodleian. Its catalogue is the standard catalogue on the desk of every library in Oxford. In each several college, they underscore in red ink on this catalogue the titles of books contained in the library of that college, — the theory being that the Bodleian has all books. This rich library spent during the last year (1847) for the purchase of books £ 1668.

The logical English train a scholar as they train an engineer. Oxford is a Greek factory, as Wilton mills weave carpet, and Sheffield grinds steel. They know the use of a tutor, as they know the use of a horse ; and they draw the greatest amount of benefit out of both. The reading men are kept by hard walking, hard riding, and measured eating and drinking, at the top of their condition, and two days before the examination, do no work, but lounge, ride, or run, to be fresh on the college doomsday. Seven years' residence is the theoretic period for a master's degree. In point of fact, it has long been three years' residence, and four years more of standing. This "three years" is about twenty-one months in all.*

"The whole expense," says Professor Sewel, "of ordinary college tuition at Oxford, is about sixteen guineas a year." But this plausible statement may deceive a reader unacquainted with the fact, that the principal teaching relied on is private tuition. And the expenses of private tuition are reckoned at from £ 50 to £ 70 a year, or $ 1000 for the whole course of three years and a half. At Cambridge $ 750 a year is economical, and $ 1500 not extravagant.†

The number of students and of residents, the dignity of the authorities, the value of the foundations, the history and the architecture, the known sympathy of entire Britain in what is done there, justify a dedication to study in the undergraduate, such as cannot easily be in America, where his college is half suspected by the Freshman to be insignificant in the scale beside trade and politics. Oxford is a little aristocracy in itself, numerous and dignified enough to rank with other estates in the realm ; and where fame and secular promotion are to be had for study, and in a direction which has the unanimous respect of all cultivated nations.

This aristocracy, of course, repairs its own losses ; fills places,

* Huber, II. p. 304.

† Bristed, Five Years at an English University.

as they fall vacant, from the body of students. The number of fellowships at Oxford is 540, averaging £200 a year, with lodging and diet at the college. If a young American, loving learning, and hindered by poverty, were offered a home, a table, the walks, and the library, in one of these academical palaces, and a thousand dollars a year as long as he chose to remain a bachelor, he would dance for joy. Yet these young men thus happily placed, and paid to read, are impatient of their few checks, and many of them preparing to resign their fellowships. They shuddered at the prospect of dying a Fellow, and they pointed out to me a paralytic old man, who was assisted into the hall. As the number of undergraduates at Oxford is only about 1200 or 1300, and many of these are never competitors, the chance of a fellowship is very great. The income of the nineteen colleges in conjectured at £150,000 a year.

The effect of this drill is the radical knowledge of Greek and Latin, and of mathematics, and the solidity and taste of English criticism. Whatever luck there may be in this or that award, an Eton captain can write Latin longs and shorts, can turn the Court-Guide into hexameters, and it is certain that a Senior Classic can quote correctly from the *Corpus Poetarum*, and is critically learned in all the humanities. Greek erudition exists on the Isis and Cam, whether the Maud man or the Brazen Nose man be properly ranked or not; the atmosphere is loaded with Greek learning; the whole river has reached a certain height, and kills all that growth of weeds, which this Castalian water kills. The English nature takes culture kindly. So Milton thought. It refines the Norseman. Access to the Greek mind lifts his standard of taste. He has enough to think of, and, unless of an impulsive nature, is indisposed from writing or speaking, by the fulness of his mind, and the new severity of his taste. The great silent crowd of thorough-bred Grecians always known to be around him, the English writer cannot ignore. They prune his orations, and point his pen. Hence, the style and tone of English journalism. The men have learned accuracy and comprehension, logic, and pace, or speed of working. They have bottom, endurance, wind. When born with good constitutions, they make those eupeptic studying-mills, the cast-iron men, the *dura ilia*, whose powers of performance compare with ours, as the steam-hammer with the music-box; — Cokes, Mansfields, Seldens, and Bentleys, and when it happens that a superior brain puts a rider on this admirable horse, we obtain those masters of the world who combine the highest energy in affairs, with a supreme culture.

It is contended by those who have been bred at Eton, Harrow, Rugby, and Westminster, that the public sentiment within each of those schools is high-toned and manly; that, in their playgrounds, courage is universally admired, meanness despised, manly feelings and generous conduct are encouraged: that an unwritten code of honor deals to the spoiled child of rank and to the child of upstart wealth an even-handed justice, purges their nonsense out of both, and does all that can be done to make them gentlemen.

Again, at the universities, it is urged, that all goes to form what England values as the flower of its national life, — a well-educated gentleman. The German Huber, in describing to his countrymen the attributes of an English gentleman, frankly admits, that "in Germany, we have nothing of the kind. A gentleman must possess a political character, an independent and public position, or, at least, the right of assuming it. He must have average opulence, either of his own, or in his family. He should also have bodily activity and strength, unattainable by our sedentary life in public offices. The race of English gentlemen presents an appearance of manly vigor and form, not elsewhere to be found among an equal number of persons. No other nation produces the stock. And in England, it has deteriorated. The university is a decided presumption in any man's favor. And so eminent are the members that a glance at the calendars will show that in all the world one cannot be in better company than on the books of one of the larger Oxford or Cambridge colleges." *

These seminaries are finishing schools for the upper classes, and not for the poor. The useful is exploded. The definition of a public school is "a school which excludes all that could fit a man for standing behind a counter." †

No doubt, the foundations have been perverted. Oxford, which equals in wealth several of the smaller European states, shuts up the lectureships which were made "public for all men thereunto to have concourse"; misspends the revenues bestowed for such youths "as should be most meet for towardness, poverty, and painfulness"; there is gross favoritism; many chairs and many fellowships are made beds of ease; and 't is likely that the university will know how to resist and

* Huber, History of the English Universities. Newman's Translation.
† See Bristed, Five Years in an English University. New York, 1852.

make inoperative the terrors of parliamentary inquiry; no doubt, their learning is grown obsolete; — but Oxford also has its merits, and I found here also proof of the national fidelity and thoroughness. Such knowledge as they prize they possess and impart. Whether in course or by indirection, whether by a cramming tutor or by examiners with prizes and foundation scholarships, education according to the English notion of it is arrived at. I looked over the Examination Papers of the year 1848, for the various scholarships and fellowships, the Lusby, the Hertford, the Dean-Ireland, and the University (copies of which were kindly given me by a Greek professor), containing the tasks which many competitors had victoriously performed, and I believed they would prove too severe tests for the candidates for a Bachelor's degree in Yale or Harvard. And, in general, here was proof of a more searching study in the appointed directions, and the knowledge pretended to be conveyed was conveyed. Oxford sends out yearly twenty or thirty very able men, and three or four hundred well-educated men.

The diet and rough exercise secure a certain amount of old Norse power. A fop will fight, and, in exigent circumstances, will play the manly part. In seeing these youths, I believed I saw already an advantage in vigor and color and general habit, over their contemporaries in the American colleges. No doubt much of the power and brilliancy of the reading-men is merely constitutional or hygienic. With a hardier habit and resolute gymnastics, with five miles more walking, or five ounces less eating, or with a saddle and gallop of twenty miles a day, with skating and rowing-matches, the American would arrive at as robust exegesis, and cheery and hilarious tone. I should readily concede these advantages, which it would be easy to acquire, if I did not find also that they read better than we, and write better.

English wealth falling on their school and university training, makes a systematic reading of the best authors, and to the end of a knowledge how the things whereof they treat really stand: whilst pamphleteer or journalist reading for an argument for a party, or reading to write, or, at all events, for some by-end imposed on them, must read meanly and fragmentarily. Charles I. said, that he understood English law as well as a gentleman ought to understand it.

Then they have access to books; the rich libraries collected at every one of many thousands of houses, give an advantage not to be attained by a youth in this country, when one thinks how much more and better may be learned by a scholar, who, immediately on hearing of a book, can consult it, than by one who is on the quest, for years, and reads inferior books, because he cannot find the best.

Again, the great number of cultivated men keep each other up to a high standard. The habit of meeting well-read and knowing men teaches the art of omission and selection.

Universities are, of course, hostile to geniuses, which seeing and using ways of their own, discredit the routine : as churches and monasteries persecute youthful saints. Yet we all send our sons to college, and, though he be a genius, he must take his chance. The university must be retrospective. The gale that gives direction to the vanes on all its towers blows out of antiquity. Oxford is a library, and the professors must be librarians. And I should as soon think of quarrelling with the janitor for not magnifying his office by hostile sallies into the street, like the Governor of Kertch or Kinburn, as of quarrelling with the professors for not admiring the young neologists who pluck the beards of Euclid and Aristotle, or for not attempting themselves to fill their vacant shelves as original writers.

It is easy to carp at colleges, and the college, if we will wait for it, will have its own turn. Genius exists there also, but will not answer a call of a committee of the House of Commons. It is rare, precarious, eccentric, and darkling. England is the land of mixture and surprise, and when you have settled it that the universities are moribund, out comes a poetic influence from the heart of Oxford, to mould the opinions of cities, to build their houses as simply as birds their nests, to give veracity to art, and charm mankind, as an appeal to moral order always must. But besides this restorative genius, the best poetry of England of this age, in the old forms, comes from two graduates of Cambridge.

CHAPTER XIII.

RELIGION.

NO people, at the present day, can be explained by their national religion. They do not feel responsible for it; it lies far outside of them. Their loyalty to truth, and their labor and expenditure rest on real foundations, and not on a national church. And English life, it is evident, does not grow out of the Athanasian creed, or the Articles, or the Eucharist. It is with religion as with marriage. A youth marries in haste; afterwards, when his mind is opened to the reason of the conduct of life, he is asked, what he thinks of the institution of marriage, and of the right relations of the sexes? 'I should have much to say,' he might reply, 'if the question were open, but I have a wife and children, and all question is closed for me.' In the barbarous days of a nation, some *cultus* is formed or imported; altars are built, tithes are paid, priests ordained. The education and expenditure of the country take that direction, and when wealth, refinement, great men, and ties to the world, supervene, its prudent men say, why fight against Fate, or lift these absurdities which are now mountainous? Better find some niche or crevice in this mountain of stone which religious ages have quarried and carved, wherein to bestow yourself, than attempt anything ridiculously and dangerously above your strength, like removing it.

In seeing old castles and cathedrals, I sometimes say, as to-day, in front of Dundee Church tower, which is eight hundred years old, 'this was built by another and a better race than any that now look on it.' And, plainly, there has been great power of sentiment at work in this island, of which these buildings are the proofs: as volcanic basalts show the work of fire which has been extinguished for ages. England felt the full heat of the Christianity which fermented Europe, and drew, like the chemistry of fire, a firm line between barbarism and culture. The power of the religious sentiment put an end to human sacrifices, checked appetite, inspired the crusades, inspired resistance to tyrants, inspired self-respect, set bounds to serfdom and slavery, founded liberty, created the religious architecture, — York, Newstead, Westminster, Fountains Abbey, Ripon, Beverley, and Dundee, — works to which the key is lost, with the sentiment which created them; inspired the English Bible, the liturgy, the monkish histories, the chronicle of Richard of Devizes. The priest translated the Vulgate, and translated the sanctities of old hagiology into English virtues on English ground. It was a certain affirmative or aggressive state of the Caucasian races. Man awoke refreshed by the sleep of ages. The violence of the northern savages exasperated Christianity into power. It lived by the love of the people. Bishop Wilfrid manumitted two hundred and fifty serfs, whom he found attached to the soil. The clergy obtained respite from labor for the boor on the Sabbath, and on church festivals. "The lord who compelled his boor to labor between sunset on Saturday and sunset on Sunday, forfeited him altogether." The priest came out of the people, and sympathized with his class. The church was the mediator, check, and democratic principle in Europe. Latimer, Wicliffe, Arundel, Cobham, Antony Parsons, Sir Harry Vane, George Fox, Penn, Bunyan, are the democrats, as well as the saints of their times. The Catholic Church, thrown on this toiling, serious people, has made in fourteen centuries a massive system, close fitted to the manners and genius of the country, at once domestical and stately. In the long time, it has blended with everything in heaven above and the earth beneath. It moves through a zodiac of feasts and fasts, names every day of the year, every town and market and headland and monument, and has coupled itself with the almanac, that no court can be held, no field ploughed, no horse shod, without some leave from the church. All maxims of prudence or shop or farm are fixed and dated by the church. Hence, its strength in the agricultural districts. The distribution of land into parishes enforces a church sanction to every civil privilege; and the gradation of the clergy, — prelates for the rich, and curates for the poor, — with the fact that a classical education has been secured to the clergyman, makes them "the link which unites the sequestered peasantry with the intellectual advancement of the age." *

The English Church has many certificates to show, of humble effective service in humanizing the people, in cheering and refining men, feeding, healing, and educating. It has the seal of martyrs and confessors; the noblest books; a sublime

* Wordsworth.

architecture; a ritual marked by the same secular merits, nothing cheap or purchasable.

From this slow-grown church important reactions proceed; much for culture, much for giving a direction to the nation's affection and will to-day. The carved and pictured chapel — its entire surface animated with image and emblem — made the parish-church a sort of book and Bible to the people's eye.

Then, when the Saxon instinct had secured a service in the vernacular tongue, it was the tutor and university of the people. In York minster, on the day of the enthronization of the new archbishop, I heard the service of evening prayer read and chanted in the choir. It was strange to hear the pretty pastoral of the betrothal of Rebecca and Isaac, in the morning of the world, read with circumstantiality in York minster, on the 13th January, 1848, to the decorous English audience, just fresh from the Times newspaper and their wine; and listening with all the devotion of national pride. That was binding old and new to some purpose. The reverence for the Scriptures is an element of civilization, for thus has the history of the world been preserved, and is preserved. Here in England every day a chapter of Genesis, and a leader in the Times.

Another part of the same service on this occasion was not insignificant. Handel's coronation anthem, *God save the King*, was played by Dr. Camidge on the organ, with sublime effect. The minster and the music were made for each other. It was a hint of the part the church plays as a political engine. From his infancy, every Englishman is accustomed to hear daily prayers for the queen, for the royal family, and the Parliament, by name; and this life-long consecration of these personages cannot be without influence on his opinions.

The universities, also, are parcel of the ecclesiastical system, and their first design is to form the clergy. Thus the clergy for a thousand years have been the scholars of the nation.

The national temperament deeply enjoys the unbroken order and tradition of its church; the liturgy, ceremony, architecture; the sober grace, the good company, the connection with the throne, and with history, which adorn it. And whilst it endears itself thus to men of more taste than activity, the stability of the English nation is passionately enlisted to its support, from its inextricable connection with the cause of public order, with politics and with the funds.

Good churches are not built by bad men; at least there

must be probity and enthusiasm somewhere in society. These minsters were neither built nor filled by atheists. No church has had more learned, industrious, or devoted men; plenty of "clerks and bishops, who, out of their gowns, would turn their backs on no man." * Their architecture still glows with faith in immortality. Heats and genial periods arrive in history, or, shall we say, plenitudes of Divine Presence, by which high tides are caused in the human spirit, and great virtues and talents appear, as in the eleventh, twelfth, thirteenth, and again in the sixteenth and seventeenth centuries, when the nation was full of genius and piety.

But the age of the Wicliffes, Cobhams, Arundels, Beckets; of the Latimers, Mores, Cranmers; of the Taylors, Leightons, Herberts; of the Sherlocks, and Butlers, is gone. Silent revolutions in opinion have made it impossible that men like these should return or find a place in their once sacred stalls. The spirit that dwelt in this church has glided away to animate other activities; and they who come to the old shrines find apes and players rustling the old garments.

The religion of England is part of good breeding. When you see on the Continent the well-dressed Englishman come into his ambassador's chapel, and put his face for silent prayer into his smooth-brushed hat, one cannot help feeling how much national pride prays with him, and the religion of a gentleman. So far is he from attaching any meaning to the words, that he believes himself to have done almost the generous thing, and that it is very condescending in him to pray to God. A great duke said on the occasion of a victory, in the House of Lords, that he thought the Almighty God had not been well used by them, and that it would become their magnanimity, after so great successes, to take order that a proper acknowledgment be made. It is the church of the gentry; but it is not the church of the poor. The operatives do not own it, and gentlemen lately testified in the House of Commons that in their lives they never saw a poor man in a ragged coat inside a church.

The torpidity on the side of religion of the vigorous English understanding shows how much wit and folly can agree in one brain. Their religion is a quotation; their church is a doll; and any examination is interdicted with screams of terror. In good company, you expect them to laugh at the fanaticism of the vulgar; but they do not; they are the vulgar.

* Fuller.

The English, in common perhaps with Christendom in the nineteenth century, do not respect power, but only performance; value ideas only for an economic result. Wellington esteems a saint only as far as he can be an army chaplain: "Mr. Briscoll, by his admirable conduct and good sense, got the better of Methodism, which had appeared among the soldiers, and once among the officers." They value a philosopher as they value an apothecary who brings bark or a drench; and inspiration is only some blowpipe, or a finer mechanical aid.

I suspect that there is in an Englishman's brain a valve that can be closed at pleasure, as an engineer shuts off steam. The most sensible and well-informed men possess the power of thinking just so far as the bishop in religious matters, and as the chancellor of the exchequer in politics. They talk with courage and logic, and show you magnificent results, but the same men who have brought free trade or geology to their present standing, look grave and lofty, and shut down their valve, as soon as the conversation approaches the English Church. After that, you talk with a box-turtle.

The action of the university, both in what is taught, and in the spirit of the place, is directed more on producing an English gentleman, than a saint or a psychologist. It ripens a bishop, and extrudes a philosopher. I do not know that there is more cabalism in the Anglican, than in other churches, but the Anglican clergy are identified with the aristocracy. They say, here, that, if you talk with a clergyman, you are sure to find him well bred, informed, and candid. He entertains your thought or your project with sympathy and praise. But if a second clergyman come in, the sympathy is at an end: two together are inaccessible to your thought, and, whenever it comes to action, the clergyman invariably sides with his church.

The Anglican church is marked by the grace and good sense of its forms, by the manly grace of its clergy. The gospel it preaches is, 'By taste are ye saved.' It keeps the old structures in repair, spends a world of money in music and building; and in buying Pugin, and architectural literature. It has a general good name for amenity and mildness. It is not in ordinary a persecuting church; it is not inquisitorial, not even inquisitive, is perfectly well bred, and can shut its eyes on all proper occasions. If you let it alone, it will let you alone. But its instinct is hostile to all change in politics, literature, or social arts. The church has not been the founder of the London University of the Mechanics' Institutes, of the Free School, or whatever aims at diffusion of knowledge. The Platonists of Oxford are as bitter against this heresy, as Thomas Taylor.

The doctrine of the Old Testament is the religion of England. The first leaf of the New Testament it does not open. It believes in a Providence which does not treat with levity a pound sterling. They are neither transcendentalists nor Christians. They put up no Socratic prayer, much less any saintly prayer for the queen's mind; ask neither for light nor right, but say bluntly, "Grant her in health and wealth long to live." And one traces this Jewish prayer in all English private history, from the prayers of King Richard, in Richard of Devizes' Chronicle, to those in the diaries of Sir Samuel Romilly, and of Haydon the painter. "Abroad with my wife," writes Pepys piously, "the first time that ever I rode in my own coach; which do make my heart rejoice and praise God, and pray him to bless it to me, and continue it." The bill for the naturalization of the Jews (in 1753) was resisted by petitions from all parts of the kingdom, and by petition from the city of London, reprobating this bill, as "tending extremely to the dishonor of the Christian religion, and extremely injurious to the interests and commerce of the kingdom in general, and of the city of London in particular."

But they have not been able to congeal humanity by act of Parliament. "The heavens journey still and sojourn not," and arts, wars, discoveries, and opinion go onward at their own pace. The new age has new desires, new enemies, new trades, new charities, and reads the Scriptures with new eyes. The chatter of French politics, the steam-whistle, the hum of the mill, and the noise of embarking emigrants, had quite put most of the old legends out of mind; so that when you came to read the liturgy to a modern congregation, it was almost absurd in its unfitness, and suggested a masquerade of old costumes.

No chemist has prospered in the attempt to crystallize a religion. It is endogenous, like the skin, and other vital organs. A new statement every day. The prophet and apostle knew this, and the nonconformist confutes the conformists, by quoting the texts they must allow. It is the condition of a religion, to require religion for its expositor. Prophet and apostle can only be rightly understood by prophet and apostle. The statesman knows that the religious element will not fail, any more than the supply of fibrine and chyle; but it is in its nature constructive, and will organize such a church as it wants. The wise legislator will spend on temples, schools, libraries, colleges, but will shun the enriching of priests. If, in any manner, he can leave the election and paying of the priest to the people, he will do well. Like the Quakers, he may resist the separation of a class of priests, and create opportunity and expectation in the society, to run to meet natural endowment, in this kind. But, when wealth accrues to a chaplaincy, a bishopric, or rectorship, it requires moneyed men for its stewards, who will give it another direction than to the mystics of their day. Of course, money will do after its kind, and will steadily work to unspiritualize and unchurch the people to whom it was bequeathed. The class certain to be excluded from all preferment are the religious, — and driven to other churches; — which is nature's *vis medicatrix.*

The curates are ill paid, and the prelates are overpaid. This abuse draws into the church the children of the nobility, and other unfit persons, who have a taste for expense. Thus a bishop is only a surpliced merchant. Through his lawn, I can see the bright buttons of the shopman's coat glitter. A wealth like that of Durham makes almost a premium on felony. Brougham, in a speech in the House of Commons on the Irish elective franchise, said, "How will the reverend bishops of the other house be able to express their due abhorrence of the crime of perjury, who solemnly declare in the presence of God, that when they are called upon to accept a living, perhaps of £4000 a year, at that very instant, they are moved by the Holy Ghost to accept the office and administration thereof, and for no other reason whatever?" The modes of initiation are more damaging than custom-house oaths. The Bishop is elected by the Dean and Prebends of the cathedral. The Queen sends these gentlemen a *congê d'élire*, or leave to elect; but also sends them the name of the person whom they are to elect. They go into the cathedral, chant and pray, and beseech the Holy Ghost to assist them in their choice; and, after these invocations, invariably find that the dictates of the Holy Ghost agree with the recommendations of the Queen.

But you must pay for conformity. All goes well as long as you run with conformists. But you, who are honest man in other particulars, know, that there is alive somewhere a man whose honesty reaches to this point also, that he shall not kneel to false gods, and, on the day when you meet him, you sink into the class of counterfeits. Besides, this succumbing has grave penalties. If you take in a lie, you must take in all that belongs to it. England accepts this ornamented national church, and it glazes the eyes, bloats the flesh, gives the voice a stertorous clang, and clouds the understanding of the receivers.

The English Church, undermined by German criticism, had nothing left but tradition, and was led logically back to Romanism. But that was an element which only hot heads could breathe : in view of the educated class, generally, it was not a fact to front the sun ; and the alienation of such men from the church became complete.

Nature, to be sure, had her remedy. Religious persons are driven out of the Established Church into sects, which instantly rise to credit, and hold the Establishment in check. Nature has sharper remedies, also. The English, abhorring change in all things, abhorring it most in matters of religion, cling to the last rag of form, and are dreadfully given to cant. The English (and I wish it were confined to them, but 't is a taint in the Anglo-Saxon blood in both hemispheres), the English and the Americans cant beyond all other nations. The French relinquish all that industry to them. What is so odious as the polite bows to God, in our books and newspapers? The popular press is flagitious in the exact measure of its sanctimony, and the religion of the day is a theatrical Sinai, where the thunders are supplied by the property-man. The fanaticism and hypocrisy create satire. Punch finds an inexhaustible material. Dickens writes novels on Exeter Hall humanity. Thackeray exposes the heartless high life. Nature revenges herself more summarily by the heathenism of the lower classes. Lord Shaftesbury calls the poor thieves together, and reads sermons to them, and they call it 'gas.' George Borrow summons the Gypsies to hear his discourse on the Hebrews in Egypt, and reads to them the Apostles' Creed in Romany. "When I had concluded," he says, "I looked around me. The features of the assembly were twisted, and the eyes of all turned upon me with a frightful squint: not an individual present but squinted; the genteel Pepa, the good-humored Chicharona, the Cosdami, all squinted: the Gypsy jockey squinted worst of all."

The church at this moment is much to be pitied. She has

nothing left but possession. If a bishop meets an intelligent gentleman, and reads fatal interrogations in his eyes, he has no resource but to take wine with him. False position introduces cant, perjury, simony, and ever a lower class of mind and character into the clergy ; and, when the hierarchy is afraid of science and education, afraid of piety, afraid of tradition, and afraid of theology, there is nothing left but to quit a church which is no longer one.

But the religion of England, — is it the Established Church? no ; is it the sects? no ; they are only perpetuations of some private man's dissent, and are to the Established Church as cabs are to a coach, cheaper and more convenient, but really the same thing. Where dwells the religion? Tell me first where dwells electricity, or motion, or thought or gesture. They do not dwell or stay at all. Electricity cannot be made fast, mortared up and ended, like London Monument, or the Tower, so that you shall know where to find it, and keep it fixed, as the English do with their things, forevermore ; it is passing, glancing, gesticular ; it is a traveller, a newness, a surprise, a secret, which perplexes them, and puts them out. Yet, if religion be the doing of all good, and for its sake the suffering of all evil, *souffrir de tout le monde et ne faire souffrir personne*, that divine secret has existed in England from the days of Alfred to those of Romilly, of Clarkson, and of Florence Nightingale, and in thousands who have no fame.

CHAPTER XIV.

LITERATURE.

A STRONG common sense, which it is not easy to unseat or disturb, marks the English mind for a thousand years ; a rude strength newly applied to thought, as of sailors and soldiers who had lately learned to read. They have no fancy, and never are surprised into a covert or witty word, such as pleased the Athenians and Italians, and was convertible into a fable not long after ; but they delight in strong earthy expression, not mistakable, coarsely true to the human body, and, though spoken among princes, equally fit and welcome to the mob. This homeliness, veracity, and plain style appear in the earliest extant works, and in the latest. It imports into songs and ballads the smell of the earth, the breath of cattle, and, like a Dutch painter, seeks a household charm, though by pails and pans. They ask their constitutional utility in verse. The kail and herrings are never out of sight. The poet nimbly recovers himself from every sally of the imagination. The English muse loves the farm-yard, the lane and market. She says, with De Staël, "I tramp in the mire with wooden shoes, whenever they would force me into the clouds." For, the Englishman has accurate perceptions; takes hold of things by the right end, and there is no slipperiness in his grasp. He loves the axe, the spade, the oar, the gun, the steam-pipe: he has built the engine he uses. He is materialist, economical, mercantile. He must be treated with sincerity and reality, with muffins and not the promise of muffins; and prefers his hot chop, with perfect security and convenience in the eating of it, to the chances of the amplest and Frenchiest bill of fare, engraved on embossed paper. When he is intellectual, and a poet or a philosopher, he carries the same hard truth and the same keen machinery into the mental sphere. His mind must stand on a fact. He will not be baffled, or catch at clouds, but the mind must have a symbol palpable and resisting. What he relishes in Dante, is the vice-like tenacity with which he holds a mental image before the eyes, as if it were a scutcheon painted on a shield. Byron "liked something craggy to break his mind upon." A taste for plain strong speech, what is called a biblical style, marks the English. It is in Alfred, and the Saxon Chronicle, and in the Sagas of the Northmen. Latimer was homely. Hobbes was perfect in the "noble vulgar speech." Donne, Bunyan, Milton, Taylor, Evelyn, Pepys, Hooker, Cotton, and the translators, wrote it. How realistic or materialistic in treatment of his subject is Swift. He describes his fictitious persons as if for the police. Defoe has no insecurity or choice. Hudibras has the same hard mentality, — keeping the truth at once to the senses, and to the intellect.

It is not less seen in poetry. Chaucer's hard painting of his Canterbury pilgrims satisfies the senses. Shakespeare, Spenser, and Milton, in their loftiest ascents, have this national grip and exactitude of mind. This mental materialism makes the value of English transcendental genius; in these writers, and in Herbert, Henry More, Donne, and Sir Thomas Browne. The Saxon materialism and narrowness, exalted into the sphere of intellect, makes the very genius of Shakespeare and Milton. When it reaches the pure element, it treads the clouds as securely as the adamant. Even in its elevations, materialistic, its poetry is common sense inspired; or iron raised to white heat.

The marriage of the two qualities is in their speech. It is a tacit rule of the language to make the frame or skeleton, of Saxon words, and, when elevation or ornament is sought, to interweave Roman; but sparingly; nor is a sentence made of Roman words alone, without loss of strength. The children and laborers use the Saxon unmixed. The Latin unmixed is abandoned to the colleges and Parliament. Mixture is a secret of the English island; and, in their dialect, the male principle is the Saxon; the female, the Latin; and they are combined in every discourse. A good writer, if he has indulged in a Roman roundness, makes haste to chasten and nerve his period by English monosyllables.

When the Gothic nations came into Europe, they found it lighted with the sun and moon of Hebrew and of Greek genius. The tablets of their brain, long kept in the dark, were finely sensible to the double glory. To the images from this twin source (of Christianity and art), the mind became fruitful as by the incubation of the Holy Ghost. The English mind flowered in every faculty. The common sense was surprised and inspired. For two centuries, England was philosophic, religious, poetic. The mental furniture seemed of larger scale; the memory capacious like the storehouse of the rains; the ardor and endurance of study; the boldness and facility of their mental construction; their fancy, and imagination, and easy spanning of vast distances of thought; the enterprise or accosting of new subjects; and, generally, the easy exertion of power, astonish, like the legendary feats of Guy of Warwick. The union of Saxon precision and Oriental soaring, of which Shakespeare is the perfect example, is shared in less degree by the writers of two centuries. I find not only the great masters out of all rivalry and reach, but the whole writing of the time charged with a masculine force and freedom.

There is a hygienic simpleness, rough vigor, and closeness to the matter in hand, even in the second and third class of writers; and, I think, in the common style of the people, as one finds it in the citation of wills, letters, and public documents, in proverbs, and forms of speech. The more hearty and sturdy expression may indicate that the savageness of the Norseman was not all gone. Their dynamic brains hurled off their words, as the revolving stone hurls off scraps of grit. I could cite from the seventeenth century sentences and phrases of edge not to be matched in the nineteenth. Their poets by simple force of mind equalized themselves with the accumulated science of ours. The country gentlemen had a posset or drink they called October; and the poets, as if by this hint, knew how to distil the whole season into their autumnal verses: and, as nature, to pique the more, sometimes works up deformities into beauty, in some rare Aspasia, or Cleopatra; and, as the Greek art wrought many a vase or column, in which too long, or too lithe, or nodes, or pits and flaws, are made a beauty of; so these were so quick and vital, that they could charm and enrich by mean and vulgar objects.

A man must think that age well taught and thoughtful, by which masques and poems, like those of Ben Jonson, full of heroic sentiment in a manly style, were received with favor. The unique fact in literary history, the unsurprised reception of Shakespeare, — the reception proved by his making his fortune; and the apathy proved by the absence of all contemporary panegyric, — seems to demonstrate an elevation in the mind of the people. Judge of the splendor of a nation, by the insignificance of great individuals in it. The manner in which they learned Greek and Latin, before our modern facilities were yet ready, without dictionaries, grammars, or indexes, by lectures of a professor, followed by their own searchings, — required a more robust memory, and co-operation of all the faculties; and their scholars, Camden, Usher, Selden, Mede, Gataker, Hooker, Taylor, Burton, Bentley, Brian Walton, acquired the solidity and method of engineers.

The influence of Plato tinges the British genius. Their minds loved analogy; were cognizant of resemblances, and climbers on the staircase of unity. 'T is a very old strife between those who elect to see identity, and those who elect to see discrepancies; and it renews itself in Britain. The poets, of course, are of one part; the men of the world, of the other. But Britain had many disciples of Plato, — More, Hooker, Bacon, Sidney, Lord Brooke, Herbert, Browne, Donne, Spenser, Chapman, Milton, Crashaw, Norris, Cudworth, Berkeley, Jeremy Taylor.

Lord Bacon has the English duality. His centuries of observations, on useful science, and his experiments, I suppose, were worth nothing. One hint of Franklin, or Watt, or Dalton, or Davy, or any one who had a talent for experiment, was worth all his lifetime of exquisite trifles. But he drinks of a diviner stream, and marks the influx of idealism into England. Where that goes, is poetry, health, and progress. The rules of its genesis or its diffusion are not known. That knowledge, if we had it, would supersede all we call science of the mind. It seems an affair of race, or of meta-chemistry ; — the vital point being, — how far the sense of unity, or instinct of seeking resemblances, predominated. For, wherever the mind takes a step, it is, to put itself at one with a larger class, discerned beyond the lesser class with which it has been conversant. Hence, all poetry, and all affirmative action comes.

Bacon, in the structure of his mind, held of the analogists, of the idealists, or (as we popularly say, naming from the best example) Platonists. Whoever discredits analogy, and requires heaps of facts, before any theories can be attempted, has no poetic power, and nothing original or beautiful will be produced by him. Locke is as surely the influx of decomposition and of prose, as Bacon and the Platonists, of growth. The Platonic is the poetic tendency ; the so-called scientific is the negative and poisonous. 'T is quite certain, that Spenser, Burns, Byron, and Wordsworth will be Platonists ; and that the dull men will be Lockists. Then politics and commerce will absorb from the educated class men of talents without genius, precisely because such have no resistance.

Bacon, capable of ideas, yet devoted to ends, required in his map of the mind, first of all, universality, or *prima philosophia*, the receptacle for all such profitable observations, and axioms as fall not within the compass of any of the special parts of philosophy, but are more common, and of a higher stage. He held this element essential : it is never out of mind : he never spares rebukes for such as neglect it ; believing that no perfect discovery can be made in a flat or level, but you must ascend to a higher science. "If any man thinketh philosophy and universality to be idle studies, he does not consider that all professions are from thence served and supplied, and this I take to be a great cause that has hindered the progression of learning, because these fundamental knowledges have been studied but in passage." He explained himself by giving various quaint examples of the summary or common laws, of which each science has its own illustration. He complains, that "he finds this part of learning very deficient, the profounder sort of wits drawing a bucket now and then for their own use, but the spring-head unvisited. This was the *dry light* which did scorch and offend most men's watery natures." Plato had signified the same sense, when he said: "All the great arts require a subtle and speculative research into the law of nature, since loftiness of thought and perfect mastery over every subject seem to be derived from some such source as this. This Pericles had, in addition to a great natural genius. For, meeting with Anaxagoras, who was a person of this kind, he attached himself to him, and nourished himself with sublime speculations on the absolute intelligence; and imported thence into the oratorical art whatever could be useful to it."

A few generalizations always circulate in the world, whose authors we do not rightly know, which astonish, and appear to be avenues to vast kingdoms of thought, and these are in the world *constants*, like the Copernican and Newtonian theories in physics. In England, these may be traced usually to Shakespeare, Bacon, Milton, or Hooker, even to Van Helmont and Behmen, and do all have a kind of filial retrospect to Plato and the Greeks. Of this kind is Lord Bacon's sentence, that "nature is commanded by obeying her"; his doctrine of poetry, which "accommodates the shows of things to the desires of the mind"; or the Zoroastrian definition of poetry, mystical, yet exact, "apparent pictures of unapparent natures"; Spenser's creed, that "soul is form, and doth the body make"; the theory of Berkeley, and we have no certain assurance of the existence of matter; Doctor Samuel Clarke's argument for theism from the nature of space and time; Harrington's political rule, that power must rest on land, — a rule which requires to be liberally interpreted; the theory of Swedenborg, so cosmically applied by him, that the man makes his heaven and hell; Hegel's study of civil history, as the conflict of ideas and the victory of the deeper thought; the identity-philosophy of Schelling, couched in the statement that "all difference is quantitative." So the very announcement of the theory of gravitation, of Kepler's three harmonic laws, and even of Dalton's doctrine of definite proportions, finds a sudden response in the mind, which remains a superior evidence to empirical demonstrations. I cite these generalizations, some of which are more recent, merely to indicate a class. Not these particulars, but the mental plane or the atmosphere from which they emanate, was the home and element of the writers and readers in what we loosely call the Elizabethan age (say in literary history, the period from 1575 to 1625), yet a period almost short enough to justify Ben Jonson's remark on Lord Bacon : "About his time, and within his view, were born all the wits that could honor a nation, or help study."

Such richness of genius had not existed more than once before. These heights could not be maintained. As we find stumps of vast trees in our exhausted soils, and have received traditions of their ancient fertility to tillage, so history reckons epochs in which the intellect of famed races became effete. So it fared with English genius. These heights were followed by a meanness, and a descent of the mind into lower levels ; the loss of wings ; no high speculation. Locke, to whom the meaning of ideas was unknown, became the type of philosophy, and his "understanding" the measure, in all nations, of the English intellect. His countrymen forsook the lofty sides of Parnassus, on which they had once walked with echoing steps, and disused the studies once so beloved ; the powers of thought fell into neglect. The later English want the faculty of Plato and Aristotle, of grouping men in natural classes by an insight of general laws, so deep, that the rule is deduced with equal precision from few subjects or from one, as from multitudes of lives. Shakespeare is supreme in that, as in all the great mental energies. The Germans generalize : the English cannot interpret the German mind. German science comprehends the English. The absence of the faculty in England is shown by the timidity which accumulates mountains of facts, as a bad general wants myriads of men and miles of redoubts, to compensate the inspirations of courage and conduct.

The English shrink from a generalization. "They do not look abroad into universality, or they draw only a bucket-full at the fountain of the First Philosophy for their occasion, and do not go to the spring-head." Bacon, who said this, is almost unique among his countrymen in that faculty, at least among the prose-writers. Milton, who was the stair or high table-land to let down the English genius from the summits of Shakespeare, used this privilege sometimes in poetry, more rarely in prose. For a long interval afterwards, it is not found. Burke was addicted to generalizing, but his was a shorter line ; as his thoughts have less depth, they have less compass. Hume's abstractions are not deep or wise. He owes his fame to one keen observation, that no copula had been detected between any cause and effect, either in physics or in thought; that the term cause and effect was loosely or gratuitously applied to what we know only as consecutive, not at all as casual. Dr. Johnson's written abstractions have little value: the tone of feeling in them makes their chief worth.

Mr. Hallam, a learned and elegant scholar, has written the history of European literature for three centuries, — a performance of great ambition, inasmuch as a judgment was to be attempted on every book. But his eye does not reach to the ideal standards; the verdicts are all dated from London: all new thought must be cast into the old moulds. The expansive element which creates literature is steadily denied. Plato is resisted, and his school. Hallam is uniformly polite, but with deficient sympathy; writes with resolute generosity, but is unconscious of the deep worth which lies in the mystics, and which often outvalues as a seed of power and a source of revolution all the correct writers and shining reputations of their day. He passes in silence, or dismisses with a kind of contempt, the profounder masters: a lover of ideas is not only uncongenial, but unintelligible. Hallam inspires respect by his knowledge and fidelity, by his manifest love of good books, and he lifts himself to own better than almost any the greatness of Shakespeare, and better than Johnson he appreciates Milton. But in Hallam, or in the firmer intellectual nerve of Mackintosh, one still finds the same type of English genius. It is wise and rich, but it lives on its capital. It is retrospective. How can it discern and hail the new forms that are looming up on the horizon, — new and gigantic thoughts which cannot dress themselves out of any old wardrobe of the past?

The essays, the fiction, and the poetry of the day have the like municipal limits. Dickens, with preternatural apprehension of the language of manners, and the varieties of street life, with pathos and laughter, with patriotic and still enlarging generosity, writes London tracts. He is a painter of English details, like Hogarth; local and temporary in his tints and style, and local in his aims. Bulwer, an industrious writer, with occasional ability, is distinguished for his reverence of intellect as a temporality, and appeals to the worldly ambition of the student. His romances tend to fan these low flames. Their novelists despair of the heart. Thackeray finds that God has made no allowance for the poor thing in his universe; — more 's the pity, he thinks; — but 't is not for us to be wiser: we must renounce ideals, and accept London.

The brilliant Macaulay, who expresses the tone of the English governing classes of the day, explicitly teaches, that *good* means good to eat, good to wear, material commodity; that the glory of modern philosophy is its direction on "fruit"; to yield economical inventions; and that its merit is to avoid ideas, and avoid morals. He thinks it the distinctive merit of the Baconian philosophy, in its triumph over the old Platonic, its disentangling the intellect from theories of the all-Fair and all-Good, and pinning it down to the making a better sick-chair and a better wine-whey for an invalid; — this not ironically, but in good faith; — that, "solid advantage," as he calls it, meaning always sensual benefit, is the only good. The eminent benefit of astronomy is the better navigation it creates to enable the fruit-ships to bring home their lemons and wine to the London grocer. It was a curious result, in which the civility and religion of England for a thousand years, ends, in denying morals, and reducing the intellect to a sauce-pan. The critic hides his scepticism under the English cant of practical. To convince the reason, to touch the conscience, is romantic pretension. The fine arts fall to the ground. Beauty, except as luxurious commodity, does not exist. It is very certain, I may say in passing, that if Lord Bacon had been only the sensualist his critic pretends, he would never have acquired the fame which now entitles him to this patronage. It is because he had imagination, the leisures of the spirit, and basked in an element of contemplation out of all modern English atmospheric gauges, that he is impressive to the imaginations of men, and has become a potentate not to be ignored. Sir David Brewster sees the high place of Bacon, without finding Newton indebted to him, and thinks it a mistake. Bacon occupies it by specific gravity or levity, not by any feat he did, or by any tutoring more or less of Newton, &c., but an effect of the same cause which showed itself more pronounced afterwards in Hooke, Boyle, and Halley.

Coleridge, a catholic mind, with a hunger for ideas, with eyes looking before and after to the highest bards and sages, and who wrote and spoke the only high criticism in his time, — is one of those who save England from the reproach of no longer possessing the capacity to appreciate what rarest wit the island has yielded. Yet the misfortune of his life, his vast attempts but most inadequate performings, failing to accomplish any one masterpiece, seems to mark the closing of an era. Even in him, the traditional Englishman was too strong for the philosopher, and he fell into *accommodations:* and, as Burke had striven to idealize the English State, so Coleridge 'narrowed his mind' in the attempt to reconcile the gothic rule and dogma of the Anglican Church, with eternal ideas. But for Coleridge, and a lurking taciturn minority, uttering itself in occasional criticism, oftener in private discourse, one would say, that in Germany and in America, is the best mind in England rightly respected. It is the surest sign of national decay, when the Bramins can no longer read or understand the Braminical philosophy.

In the decomposition and asphyxia that followed all this materialism, Carlyle was driven by his disgust at the pettiness and the cant, into the preaching of Fate. In comparison with all this rottenness, any check, any cleansing, though by fire, seemed desirable and beautiful. He saw little difference in the gladiators, or the "causes" for which they combated; the one comfort was, that they were all going speedily into the abyss together: And his imagination, finding no nutriment in any creation, avenged itself by celebrating the majestic beauty of the laws of decay. The necessities of mental structure force all minds into a few categories, and where impatience of the tricks of men makes Nemesis amiable, and builds altars to the negative Deity, the inevitable recoil is to heroism or the gallantry of the private heart, which decks its immolation with glory, in the unequal combat of will against fate.

Wilkinson, the editor of Swedenborg, the annotator of Fourier, and the champion of Hahnemann, has brought to metaphysics and to physiology a native vigor, with a catholic perception of relations, equal to the highest attempts, and a rhetoric like the armory of the invincible knights of old. There is in the action of his mind a long Atlantic roll not known except in deepest waters, and only lacking what ought to accompany such powers, a manifest centrality. If his mind does not rest in immovable biases, perhaps the orbit is larger, and the return is not yet: but a master should inspire a confidence that he will adhere to his convictions, and give his present studies always the same high place.

It would be easy to add exceptions to the limitary tone of English thought, and much more easy to adduce examples of excellence in particular veins; and if, going out of the region of dogma, we pass into that of general culture, there is no end to the graces and amenities, wit, sensibility, and erudition, of the learned class. But the artificial succor which marks all

English performance, appears in letters also: much of their æsthetic production is antiquarian and manufactured, and literary reputations have been achieved by forcible men, whose relation to literature was purely accidental, but who were driven by tastes and modes they found in vogue into their several careers. So, at this moment, every ambitious young man studies geology; so members of Parliament are made, and churchmen.

The bias of Englishmen to practical skill has reacted on the national mind. They are incapable of an inutility, and respect the five mechanic powers even in their song. The voice of their modern muse has a slight hint of the steam-whistle, and the poem is created as an ornament and finish of their monarchy, and by no means as the bird of a new morning which forgets the past world in the full enjoyment of that which is forming. They are with difficulty ideal; they are the most conditioned men, as if, having the best conditions, they could not bring themselves to forfeit them. Every one of them is a thousand years old, and lives by his memory; and when you say this, they accept it as praise.

Nothing comes to the book-shops but politics, travels, statistics, tabulation, and engineering, and even what is called philosophy and letters is mechanical in its structure, as if inspiration had ceased, as if no vast hope, no religion, no song of joy, no wisdom, no analogy, existed any more. The tone of colleges and of scholars and of literary society has this mortal air. I seem to walk on a marble floor, where nothing will grow. They exert every variety of talent on a lower ground, and may be said to live and act in a sub-mind. They have lost all commanding views in literature, philosophy, and science. A good Englishman shuts himself out of three fourths of his mind, and confines himself to one fourth. He has learning, good sense, power of labor, and logic: but a faith in the laws of the mind like that of Archimedes; a belief like that of Euler and Kepler, that experience must follow and not lead the laws of the mind; a devotion to the theory of politics, like that of Hooker, and Milton, and Harrington, the modern English mind repudiates.

I fear the same fault lies in their science, since they have known how to make it repulsive, and bereave nature of its charm; — though perhaps the complaint flies wider, and the vice attaches to many more than to British physicists. The eye of the naturalist must have a scope like nature itself, a susceptibility to all impressions, alive to the heart as well as to the logic of creation. But English science puts humanity to the door. It wants the connection which is the test of genius. The science is false by not being poetic. It isolates the reptile or mollusk it assumes to explain; whilst reptile or mollusk only exists in system, in relation. The poet only sees it as an inevitable step in the path of the Creator. But, in England, one hermit finds this fact, and another finds that, and lives and dies ignorant of its value. There are great exceptions, of John Hunter, a man of ideas; perhaps of Robert Brown, the botanist; and of Richard Owen, who has imported into Britain the German homologies, and enriched science with contributions of his own, adding sometimes the divination of the old masters to the unbroken power of labor in the English mind. But for the most part, the natural science in England is out of its loyal alliance with morals, and is as void of imagination and free play of thought, as conveyancing. It stands in strong contrast with the genius of the Germans, those semi-Greeks, who love analogy, and, by means of their height of view, preserve their enthusiasm, and think for Europe.

No hope, no sublime augury, cheers the student, no secure striding from experiment onward to a foreseen law, but only a casual dipping here and there, like diggers in California "prospecting for a placer" that will pay. A horizon of brass of the diameter of his umbrella shuts down around his senses. Squalid contentment with conventions, satire at the names of philosophy and religion, parochial and shop-till politics, and idolatry of usage, betray the ebb of life and spirit. As they trample on nationalities to reproduce London and Londoners in Europe and Asia, so they fear the hostility of ideas, of poetry, of religion, — ghosts which they cannot lay; and, having attempted to domesticate and dress the Blessed Soul itself in English broadcloth and gaiters, they are tormented with fear that herein lurks a force that will sweep their system away. The artists say, "Nature puts us out"; the scholars have become un-ideal. They parry earnest speech with banter and levity; they laugh you down, or they change the subject. "The fact is," say they over their wine, "all that about liberty, and so forth, is gone by; it won't do any longer." The practical and comfortable oppress them with inexorable claims, and the smallest fraction of power remains for heroism and poetry. No poet dares murmur of beauty out of the precinct of his rhymes. No priest dares hint at a Providence which does not respect English utility. The island is a roaring volcano of fate, of material values, of tariffs, and laws of repression, glutted markets and low prices.

In the absence of the highest aims, of the pure love of knowledge, and the surrender to nature, there is the suppression of the imagination, the priapism of the senses and the understanding ; we have the factitious instead of the natural ; tasteless expense, arts of comfort, and the rewarding as an illustrious inventor whosoever will contrive one impediment more to interpose between the man and his objects.

Thus poetry is degraded, and made ornamental. Pope and his school wrote poetry fit to put round frosted cake. What did Walter Scott write without stint ? a rhymed traveller's guide to Scotland. And the libraries of verses they print have this Birmingham character. How many volumes of well-bred metre we must jingle through, before we can be filled, taught, renewed ! We want the miraculous ; the beauty which we can manufacture at no mill, — can give no account of ; the beauty of which Chaucer and Chapman had the secret. The poetry of course is low and prosaic ; only now and then, as in Wordsworth, conscientious ; or in Byron, passional ; or in Tennyson, factitious. But if I should count the poets who have contributed to the Bible of existing England sentences of guidance and consolation which are still glowing and effective, — how few ! Shall I find my heavenly bread in the reigning poets ? Where is great design in modern English poetry ? The English have lost sight of the fact that poetry exists to speak the spiritual law, and that no wealth of description or of fancy is yet essentially new, and out of the limits of prose, until this condition is reached. Therefore the grave old poets, like the Greek artists, heeded their designs, and less considered the finish. It was their office to lead to the divine sources, out of which all this, and much more, readily springs ; and, if this religion is in the poetry, it raises us to some purpose, and we can well afford some staidness, or hardness, or want of popular tune in the verses.

The exceptional fact of the period is the genius of Wordsworth. He had no master but nature and solitude. "He wrote a poem," says Landor, "without the aid of war." His verse is the voice of sanity in a worldly and ambitious age. One regrets that his temperament was not more liquid and musical. He has written longer than he was inspired. But for the rest, he has no competitor.

Tennyson is endowed precisely in points where Wordsworth wanted. There is no finer ear than Tennyson's, nor more command of the keys of language. Color, like the dawn, flows over the horizon from his pencil, in waves so rich that we do not miss the central form. Through all his refinements, too, he has reached the public, — a certificate of good sense and general power, since he who aspires to be the English poet must be as large as London, not in the same kind as London, but in his own kind. But he wants a subject, and climbs no mount of vision to bring its secrets to the people. He contents himself with describing the Englishman as he is, and proposes no better. There are all degrees in poetry, and we must be thankful for every beautiful talent. But it is only a first success, when the ear is gained. The best office of the best poets has been to show how low and uninspired was their general style, and that only once or twice they have struck the high chord.

That expansiveness which is the essence of the poetic element, they have not. It was no Oxonian, but Hafiz, who said: "Let us be crowned with roses, let us drink wine, and break up the tiresome old roof of heaven into new forms." A stanza of the song of nature the Oxonian has no ear for, and he does not value the salient and curative influence of intellectual action, studious of truth, without a by-end.

By the law of contraries, I look for an irresistible taste for Orientalism in Britain. For a self-conceited modish life, made up of trifles, clinging to a corporeal civilization, hating ideas, there is no remedy like the Oriental largeness. That astonishes and disconcerts English decorum. For once there is thunder it never heard, light it never saw, and power which trifles with time and space. I am not surprised, then, to find an Englishman like Warren Hastings, who had been struck with the grand style of thinking in the Indian writings, deprecating the prejudices of his countrymen, while offering them a translation of the Bhagvat. "Might I," he says, "an unlettered man, venture to prescribe bounds to the latitude of criticism, I should exclude, in estimating the merit of such a production, all rules drawn from the ancient or modern literature of Europe, all references to such sentiments or manners as are become the standards of propriety for opinion and action in our own modes, and, equally, all appeals to our revealed tenets, of religion and moral duty." * He goes on to bespeak indul-

* Preface to Wilkins's Translation of the Bhagvat Geeta.

gence to "ornaments of fancy unsuited to our taste, and passages elevated to a tract of sublimity into which our habits of judgment will find it difficult to pursue them."

Meantime, I know that a retrieving power lies in the English race, which seems to make any recoil possible; in other words, there is at all times a minority of profound minds existing in the nation, capable of appreciating every soaring of intellect and every hint of tendency. While the constructive talent seems dwarfed and superficial, the criticism is often in the noblest tone, and suggests the presence of the invisible gods. I can well believe what I have often heard, that there are two nations in England; but it is not the Poor and the Rich; nor is it the Normans and Saxons; nor the Celt and the Goth. These are each always becoming the other; for Robert Owen does not exaggerate the power of circumstance. But the two complexions, or two styles of mind, — the perceptive class, and the practical finality class, — are ever in counterpoise, interacting mutually; one, in hopeless minorities; the other, in huge masses; one studious, contemplative, experimenting; the other, the ungrateful pupil, scornful of the source, whilst availing itself of the knowledge for gain; these two nations, of genius and of animal force, though the first consist of only a dozen souls, and the second of twenty millions, forever by their discord and their accord yield the power of the English State.

CHAPTER XV.

THE "TIMES."

THE power of the newspaper is familiar in America, and in accordance with our political system. In England, it stands in antagonism with the feudal institutions, and it is all the more beneficent succor against the secretive tendencies of a monarchy. The celebrated Lord Somers "knew of no good law proposed and passed in his time, to which the public papers had not directed his attention." There is no corner and no night. A relentless inquisition drags every secret to the day, turns the glare of this solar microscope on every malfaisance, so as to make the public a more terrible spy than any foreigner; and no weakness can be taken advantage of by an enemy, since the whole people are already forewarned. Thus England rids herself of those incrustations which have been the ruin of old states. Of course, this inspection is feared. No antique privilege, no comfortable monopoly, but sees surely that its days are counted; the people are familiarized with the reason of reform, and, one by one, take away every argument of the obstructives. "So your Grace likes the comfort of reading the newspapers," said Lord Mansfield to the Duke of Northumberland; "mark my words; you and I shall not live to see it, but this young gentleman (Lord Eldon) may, or it may be a little later; but a little sooner or later, these newspapers will most assuredly write the dukes of Northumberland out of their titles and possessions, and the country out of its king." The tendency in England towards social and political institutions like those of America, is inevitable, and the ability of its journals is the driving force.

England is full of manly, clever, well-bred men who possess the talent of writing off-hand pungent paragraphs, expressing with clearness and courage their opinion on any person or performance. Valuable or not, it is a skill that is rarely found, out of the English journals. The English do this, as they write poetry, as they ride and box, by being educated to it. Hundreds of clever Praeds, and Freres, and Froudes, and Hoods, and Hooks, and Maginns, and Mills, and Macaulays, make poems, or short essays for a journal, as they make speeches in Parliament and on the hustings, or, as they shoot and ride. It is a quite accidental and arbitrary direction of their general ability. Rude health and spirits, an Oxford education, and the habits of society are implied, but not a ray of genius. It comes of the crowded state of the professions, the violent interest which all men take in politics, the facility of experimenting in the journals, and high pay.

The most conspicuous result of this talent is the "Times" newspaper. No power in England is more felt, more feared, or more obeyed. What you read in the morning in that journal, you shall hear in the evening in all society. It has ears everywhere, and its information is earliest, completest, and surest. It has risen, year by year, and victory by victory, to its present authority. I asked one of its old contributors, whether it had once been abler than it is now? "Never," he said; "these are its palmiest days." It has shown those qualities which are dear to Englishmen, unflinching adherence to its objects, prodigal intellectual ability, and a towering assurance, backed by the perfect organization in its printing-house, and its world-wide network of correspondence and reports. It has its own history and famous trophies. In 1820, it adopted the cause of Queen Caroline, and carried it against the king. It adopted a poor-law system, and almost alone lifted it through. When Lord Brougham was in power, it decided against him, and pulled him down. It declared war against Ireland, and conquered it. It adopted the League against the Corn Laws, and, when Cobden had begun to despair, it announced his triumph. It denounced and discredited the French Republic of 1848, and checked every sympathy with it in England, until it had enrolled 200,000 special constables to watch the Chartists, and make them ridiculous on the 10th April. It first denounced and then adopted the new French Empire, and urged the French Alliance and its results. It has entered into each municipal, literary, and social question, almost with a controlling voice. It has done bold and seasonable service in exposing frauds which threatened the commercial community. Meantime, it attacks its rivals by perfecting its printing machinery, and will drive them out of circulation; for the only limit to the circulation of the "Times" is the impossibility of printing copies fast enough; since a daily paper can only be new and seasonable for a few hours. It will kill all but that paper which is diametrically in opposition; since many papers, first and last, have lived by their attacks on the leading journal.

The late Mr. Walter was printer of the "Times," and had gradually arranged the whole *materiel* of it in perfect system. It is told, that when he demanded a small share in the proprietary, and was refused, he said, "As you please, gentlemen; and you may take away the 'Times' from this office when you will; I shall publish the 'New Times' next Monday morning." The proprietors, who had already complained that his charges for printing were excessive, found that they were in his power, and gave him whatever he wished.

I went one day with a good friend to the "Times" office, which was entered through a pretty garden-yard, in Printing-House Square. We walked with some circumspection, as if we were entering a powder-mill; but the door was opened by a mild old woman, and, by dint of some transmission of cards, we were at last conducted into the parlor of Mr. Morris, a very gentle person, with no hostile appearances. The statistics are now quite out of date, but I remember he told us that the daily printing was then 35,000 copies; that on the 1st March, 1848, the greatest number ever printed, — 54,000 were issued; that, since February, the daily circulation had increased by 8000 copies. The old press they were then using printed five or six thousand sheets per hour; the new machine, for which they were then building an engine, would print twelve thousand per hour. Our entertainer confided us to a courteous assistant to show us the establishment, in which, I think, they employed a hundred and twenty men. I remember, I saw the reporters' room, in which they redact their hasty stenographs, but the editor's room, and who is in it, I did not see, though I shared the curiosity of mankind respecting it.

The staff of the "Times" has always been made up of able men. Old Walter, Sterling, Bacon, Barnes, Alsiger, Horance Twiss, Jones Loyd, John Oxenford, Mr. Mosely, Mr. Bailey, have contributed to its renown in their special departments. But it has never wanted the first pens for occasional assistance. Its private information is inexplicable, and recalls the stories of Fouché's police, whose omniscience made it believed that the Empress Josephine must be in his pay. It has mercantile and political correspondents in every foreign city; and its expresses outrun the despatches of the government. One hears anecdotes of the rise of its servants, as of the functionaries of the India House. I was told of the dexterity of one of its reporters, who, finding himself, on one occasion, where the magistrates had strictly forbidden reporters, put his hands into his coat-pocket, and with pencil in one hand, and tablet in the other, did his work.

The influence of this journal is a recognized power in Europe, and, of course, none is more conscious of it than its conductors. The tone of its articles has often been the occasion of comment from the official organs of the continental courts, and sometimes the ground of diplomatic complaint. What would the "Times" say? is a terror in Paris, in Berlin, in Vienna, in Copenhagen, and in Nepaul. Its consummate discretion and success exhibit the English skill of combination. The daily paper is the work of many hands, chiefly, it is said, of young men recently from the University, and perhaps reading law in chambers in London. Hence the academic elegance, and classic allusion, which adorn its columns. Hence, too, the heat and gallantry of its onset. But the steadiness of the aim suggests the belief that this fire is directed and fed by older engineers; as if persons of exact information, and with settled views of policy, supplied the writers with the basis of fact, and the object to be attained, and availed themselves of their younger energy and eloquence to plead the cause. Both the council and the executive departments gain by this division. Of two men of equal ability, the one who does not write, but keeps his eye on the course of public affairs, will have the higher judicial wisdom. But the parts are kept in concert; all the articles appear to proceed from a single will. The "Times" never disapproves of what itself has said, or cripples itself by apology for the absence of the editor, or the indiscretion of him who held the pen. It speaks out bluff and bold, and sticks to what it says. It draws from any number of learned and skilful contributors; but a more learned and skilful person supervises, corrects, and co-ordinates. Of this closet, the secret does not transpire. No writer is suffered to claim the authorship of any paper; everything good, from whatever quarter, comes out editorially; and thus, by making the paper everything, and those who write it nothing, the character and the awe of the journal gain.

The English like it for its complete information. A statement of fact in the "Times" is as reliable as a citation from Hansard. Then, they like its independence; they do not know, when they take it up, what their paper is going to say: but, above all, for the nationality and confidence of its tone. It thinks for them all; it is their understanding and day's ideal daguerreotyped. When I see them reading its columns, they seem to me becoming every moment more British. It has the national courage, not rash and petulant, but considerate and determined. No dignity or wealth is a shield from its assault. It attacks a duke as readily as a policeman, and with the most provoking airs of condescension. It makes rude work with the Board of Admiralty. The Bench of Bishops is still less safe. One bishop fares badly for his rapacity, and another for his bigotry, and a third for his courtliness. It addresses occasionally a hint to majesty itself, and sometimes a hint which is taken. There is an air of freedom even in their advertising columns, which speaks well for England to a foreigner. On the days when I arrived in London in 1847, I read among the daily announcements, one offering a reward of fifty pounds to any person who would put a nobleman, described by name and title, late a member of Parliament, into any county jail in England, he having been convicted of obtaining money under false pretences.

Was never such arrogancy as the tone of this paper. Every slip of an Oxonian or Cantabrigian who writes his first leader assumes that we subdued the earth before we sat down to write this particular "Times." One would think the world was on its knees to the "Times" Office, for its daily breakfast. But this arrogance is calculated. Who would care for it, if it "surmised," or "dared to confess," or "ventured to predict," &c. No ; *it is so,* and so it shall be.

The morality and patriotism of the "Times" claims only to be representative, and by no means ideal. It gives the argument, not of the majority, but of the commanding class. Its editors know better than to defend Russia, or Austria, or English vested rights, on abstract grounds. But they give a voice to the class who, at the moment, take the lead ; and they have an instinct for finding where the power now lies, which is eternally shifting its banks. Sympathizing with, and speaking for the class that rules the hour, yet, being apprised of every ground-swell, every Chartist resolution, every Church squabble, every strike in the mills, they detect the first tremblings of change. They watch the hard and bitter struggles of the authors of each liberal movement, year by year, — watching them only to taunt and obstruct them, — until, at last, when they see that these have established their fact, that power is on the point of passing to them, they strike in, with the voice of a monarch, astonish those whom they succor, as much as those whom they desert, and make victory sure. Of course, the aspirants see that the "Times" is one of the goods of fortune, not to be won but by winning their cause.

"Punch" is equally an expression of English good sense, as the "London Times." It is the comic version of the same sense. Many of its caricatures are equal to the best pamphlets, and will convey to the eye in an instant the popular view which was taken of each turn of public affairs. Its sketches are usually made by masterly hands, and sometimes with genius; the delight of every class, because uniformly guided by that taste which is tyrannical in England. It is a new trait of the nineteenth century, that the wit and humor of England, as in Punch, so in the humorists, Jerrold, Dickens, Thackeray, Hood, have taken the direction of humanity and freedom.

The "Times," like every important institution, shows the

way to a better. It is a living index of the colossal British power. Its existence honors the people who dare to print all they know, dare to know all the facts, and do not wish to be flattered by hiding the extent of the public disaster. There is always safety in valor. I wish I could add, that this journal aspired to deserve the power it wields, by guidance of the public sentiment to the right. It is usually pretended, in Parliament and elsewhere, that the English press has a high tone,— which it has not. It has an imperial tone, as of a powerful and independent nation. But as with other empires, its tone is prone to be official, and even officinal. The "Times" shares all the limitations of the governing classes, and wishes never to be in a minority. If only it dared to cleave to the right, to show the right to be the only expedient, and feed its batteries from the central heart of humanity, it might not have so many men of rank among its contributors, but genius would be its cordial and invincible ally; it might now and then bear the brunt of formidable combinations, but no journal is ruined by wise courage. It would be the natural leader of British reform; its proud function, that of being the voice of Europe, the defender of the exile and patriot against despots, would be more effectually discharged; it would have the authority which is claimed for that dream of good men not yet come to pass, an International Congress; and the least of its victories would be to give to England a new millennium of beneficent power.

CHAPTER XVI.

STONEHENGE.

IT had been agreed between my friend Mr. C. and me, that before I left England we should make an excursion together to Stonehenge, which neither of us had seen; and the project pleased my fancy with the double attraction of the monument and the companion. It seemed a bringing together of extreme points, to visit the oldest religious monument in Britain, in company with her latest thinker, and one whose influence may be traced in every contemporary book. I was glad to sum up a little my experiences, and to exchange a few reasonable words on the aspects of England, with a man on whose genius I set a very high value, and who had as much penetration, and as severe a theory of duty as any person in it. On Friday, 7th July, we took the Southwestern Railway through Hampshire to Salisbury, where we found a carriage to convey us to Amesbury. The fine weather and my friend's local knowledge of Hampshire, in which he is wont to spend a part of every summer, made the way short. There was much to say, too, of the travelling Americans, and their usual objects in London. I thought it natural, that they should give some time to works of art collected here, which they cannot find at home, and a little to scientific clubs and museums, which, at this moment, make London very attractive. But my philosopher was not contented. Art and 'high art' is a favorite target for his wit. "Yes, *Kunst* is a great delusion, and Goethe and Schiller wasted a great deal of good time on it" : — and he thinks he discovers that old Goethe found this out, and, in his later writings, changed his tone. As soon as men begin to talk of art, architecture, and antiquities, nothing good comes of it. He wishes to go through the British Museum in silence, and thinks a sincere man will see something, and say nothing. In these days, he thought, it would become an architect to consult only the grim necessity, and say, 'I can build you a coffin for such dead persons as you are, and for such dead purposes as you have, but you shall have no ornament.' For the science, he had, if possible, even less tolerance, and compared the savans of Somerset House to the boy who asked Confucius "how many stars in the sky?" Confucius replied, "he minded things near him"; then said the boy, "how many hairs are there in your eyebrows?" Confucius said, "he did n't know and did n't care."

Still speaking of the Americans, C. complained that they dislike the coldness and exclusiveness of the English, and run away to France, and go with their countrymen, and are amused, instead of manfully staying in London, and confronting Englishmen, and acquiring their culture, who really have much to teach them.

I told C. that I was easily dazzled, and was accustomed to concede readily all that an Englishman would ask ; I saw everywhere in the country proofs of sense and spirit, and success of every sort : I like the people : they are as good as they are handsome ; they have everything, and can do everything : but meantime, I surely know, that, as soon as I return to Massachusetts, I shall lapse at once into the feeling, which the geography of America inevitably inspires, that we play the game with immense advantage ; that there and not here is the seat and centre of the British race ; and that no skill or activity can long compete with the prodigious natural advantages of that country, in the hands of the same race ; and that England, an old and exhausted island, must one day be contented, like other parents, to be strong only in her children. But this was a proposition which no Englishman of whatever condition can easily entertain.

We left the train at Salisbury, and took a carriage to Amesbury, passing by Old Sarum, a bare, treeless hill, once containing the town which sent two members to Parliament, — now, not a hut ; — and, arriving at Amesbury, stopped at the George Inn. After dinner, we walked to Salisbury Plain. On the broad downs, under the gray sky, not a house was visible, nothing but Stonehenge, which looked like a group of brown dwarfs in the wide expanse, — Stonehenge and the barrows, — which rose like green bosses about the plain, and a few hayricks. On the top of a mountain, the old temple would not be more impressive. Far and wide a few shepherds with their flocks sprinkled the plain, and a bagman drove along the road. It looked as if the wide margin given in this crowded isle to this primeval temple were accorded by the veneration of the British race to the old egg out of which all their ecclesiastical structures and history had proceeded. Stonehenge is a circular colonnade with a diameter of a hundred feet, and enclosing a second and a third colonnade within. We walked round the stones, and clambered over them, to wont ourselves with their strange aspect and groupings, and found a nook sheltered from the wind among them, where C. lighted his cigar. It was pleasant to see, that, just this simplest of all simple structures, — two upright stones and a lintel laid across, — had long outstood all later churches, and all history, and were like what is most permanent on the face of the planet : these, and the barrows, — mere mounds (of which there are a hundred and sixty within a circle of three miles about Stonehenge), like the same mound on the plain of Troy, which still makes good to the passing mariner on Hellespont, the vaunt of Homer and the fame of Achilles. Within the enclosure grow buttercups, nettles, and, all around, wild thyme, daisy, meadow-sweet, golden-rod, thistle, and the carpeting grass. Over us, larks were soaring and singing, — as my friend said : " the larks which were hatched last year, and the wind which was hatched many thousand years ago." We counted and measured by paces the biggest stones, and soon knew as much as any man can suddenly know of the inscrutable temple. There are ninety-four stones, and there were once probably one hundred and sixty. The temple is circular, and uncovered, and the situation fixed astronomically, — the grand entrances here, and at Abury, being placed exactly northeast, "as all the gates of the old cavern temples are." How came the stones here? for these *sarsens* or Druidical sandstones, are not found in this neighborhood. The *sacrificial stone*, as it is called, is the only one in all these blocks, that can resist the action of fire, and as I read in the books, must have been brought one hundred and fifty miles.

On almost every stone we found the marks of the mineralogist's hammer and chisel. The nineteen smaller stones of the inner circle are of granite. I, who had just come from Professor Sedgwick's Cambridge Museum of megatheria and mastodons, was ready to maintain that some cleverer elephants or mylodonta had borne off and laid these rocks one on another. Only the good beasts must have known how to cut a well-wrought tenon and mortise, and to smooth the surface of some of the stones. The chief mystery is, that any mystery should have been allowed to settle on so remarkable a monument, in a country on which all the muses have kept their eyes now for eighteen hundred years. We are not yet too late to learn much more than is known of this structure. Some diligent Fellowes or Layard will arrive, stone by stone, at the whole history, by that exhaustive British sense and perseverance, so whimsical in its choice of objects, which leaves its own Stonehenge or Choir Gaur to the rabbits, whilst it opens pyramids, and uncovers Nineveh. Stonehenge, in virtue of the simplicity of its plan, and its good preservation, is as if new and recent; and, a thousand years hence, men will thank this age for the accurate history it will yet eliminate. We walked in and out, and took again and again a fresh look at the uncanny stones. The old sphinx put our petty differences of nationality out of sight. To these conscious stones we two pilgrims were alike known and near. We could equally well revere their old British meaning. My philosopher was subdued and gentle. In this quiet house of destiny, he happened to say, "I plant cypresses wherever I go, and if I am in search of pain, I cannot go wrong." The spot, the gray blocks, and their rude order, which refuses to be disposed of, suggested to him the flight of ages, and the succession of religions. The old times of England impress C. much : he reads little, he says, in these last years, but "*Acta Sanctorum*," the fifty-three volumes of which are in the "London Library." He finds all English history therein. He can see, as he reads, the old saint of Iona sitting there, and writing, a man to men. The *Acta Sanctorum* show plainly that the men of those times believed in God, and in the immortality of the soul, as their abbeys and cathedrals testify: now, even the puritanism is all gone. London is pagan. He fancied that greater men had lived in England than any of her writers; and, in fact, about the time when those writers appeared, the last of these were already gone.

We left the mound in the twilight, with the design to return the next morning, and coming back two miles to our inn, we were met by little showers, and late as it was, men and women were out attempting to protect their spread wind-rows. The grass grows rank and dark in the showery England. At the inn, there was only milk for one cup of tea. When we called for more, the girl brought us three drops. My friend was annoyed who stood for the credit of an English inn, and still more, the next morning, by the dog-cart, sole procurable vehicle, in which we were to be sent to Wilton. I engaged the local antiquary, Mr. Brown, to go with us to Stonehenge, on our way, and show us what he knew of the "astronomical" and "sacrificial" stones. I stood on the last, and he pointed to the upright, or rather, inclined stone, called the "astronomical," and bade me notice that its top ranged with the sky-line. "Yes." Very well. Now, at the summer solstice, the sun rises exactly over the top of that stone, and, at the Druidical temple at Abury, there is also an astronomical stone, in the same relative positions.

In the silence of tradition, this one relation to science becomes an important clew; but we were content to leave the problem, with the rocks. Was this the "Giants' Dance" which Merlin brought from Killaraus, in Ireland, to be Uther Pendragon's monument to the British nobles whom Hengist slaughtered here, as Geoffrey of Monmouth relates? or was it a Roman work, as Inigo Jones explained to King James; or identical in design and style with the East Indian temples of the sun; as Davies in the Celtic Researches maintains? Of all the writers, Stukeley is the best. The heroic antiquary, charmed with the geometric perfections of his ruin, connects it with the oldest monuments and religion of the world, and, with the courage of his tribe, does not stick to say, "the

Deity who made the world by the scheme of Stonehenge." He finds that the *cursus* * on Salisbury Plain stretches across the downs, like a line of latitude upon the globe, and the meridian line of Stonehenge passes exactly through the middle of this *cursus*. But here is the high point of the theory: the Druids had the magnet; laid their courses by it; their cardinal points in Stonehenge, Ambresbury, and elsewhere, which vary a little from true east and west, followed the variations of the compass. The Druids were Phœnicians. The name of the magnet is *lapis Heracleus,* and Hercules was the god of the Phœnicians. Hercules, in the legend, drew his bow at the sun, and the sun-god gave him a golden cup, with which he sailed over the ocean. What was this, but a compass-box? This cup or little boat, in which the magnet was made to float on water, and so show the north, was probably its first form, before it was suspended on a pin. But science was an *arcanum*, and, as Britain was a Phœnician secret, so they kept their compass a secret, and it was lost with the Tyrian commerce. The golden fleece, again, of Jason, was the compass, — a bit of loadstone, easily supposed to be the only one in the world, and therefore naturally awakening the cupidity and ambition of the young heroes of a maritime nation to join in an expedition to obtain possession of this wise stone. Hence the fable that the ship Argo was loquacious and oracular. There is also some curious coincidence in the names. Apollodorus makes *Magnes* the son of *Æolus*, who married *Nais.* On hints like these, Stukeley builds again the grand colonnade into historic harmony, and computing backward by the known variations of the compass, bravely assigns the year 406 before Christ for the date of the temple.

For the difficulty of handling and carrying stones of this size, the like is done in all cities, every day, with no other aid than horse-power. I chanced to see a year ago men at work on the substructure of a house in Bowdoin Square, in Boston, swinging a block of granite of the size of the largest of the Stonehenge columns with an ordinary derrick. The men were common masons, with paddies to help, nor did they think they were doing anything remarkable. I suppose there

* Connected with Stonehenge are an avenue and a *cursus*. The avenue is a narrow road of raised earth, extending 594 yards in a straight line from the grand entrance, then dividing into two branches, which lead, severally, to a row of barrows; and to the *cursus*, — an artificially formed flat tract of ground. This is half a mile northeast from Stonehenge, bounded by banks and ditches, 3036 yards long, by 110 broad.

were as good men a thousand years ago. And we wonder how Stonehenge was built and forgotten. After spending half an hour on the spot, we set forth in our dog-cart over the downs for Wilton, C. not suppressing some threats and evil omens on the proprietors, for keeping these broad plains a wretched sheep-walk when so many thousands of Englishmen were hungry and wanted labor. But I heard afterwards that it is not an economy to cultivate this land, which only yields one crop on being broken up, and is then spoiled.

We came to Wilton and to Wilton Hall,—the renowned seat of the Earls of Pembroke, a house known to Shakespeare and Massinger, the frequent home of Sir Philip Sidney where he wrote the Arcadia; where he conversed with Lord Brooke, a man of deep thought, and a poet, who caused to be engraved on his tombstone, "Here lies Fulke Greville Lord Brooke, the friend of Sir Philip Sidney." It is now the property of the Earl of Pembroke, and the residence of his brother, Sidney Herbert, Esq., and is esteemed a noble specimen of the English manor-hall. My friend had a letter from Mr. Herbert to his housekeeper, and the house was shown. The state drawing-room is a double cube, thirty feet high, by thirty wide, by sixty feet long: the adjoining room is a single cube, of thirty feet every way. Although these apartments and the long library were full of good family portraits, Vandykes and other; and though there were some good pictures, and a quadrangle cloister full of antique and modern statuary, — to which C., catalogue in hand, did all too much justice,—yet the eye was still drawn to the windows, to a magnificent lawn, on which grew the finest cedars in England. I had not seen more charming grounds. We went out, and walked over the estate. We crossed a bridge built by Inigo Jones over a stream, of which the gardener did not know the name, (*Qu.* Alph?) watched the deer; climbed to the lonely sculptured summer-house, on a hill backed by a wood; came down into the Italian garden, and into a French pavilion, garnished with French busts; and so, again to the house, where we found a table laid for us with bread, meats, peaches, grapes, and wine.

On leaving Wilton House, we took the coach for Salisbury. The Cathedral which was finished six hundred years ago has even a spruce and modern air, and its spire is the highest in England. I know not why, but I had been more struck with one of no fame at Coventry, which rises three hundred feet from the ground, with the lightness of a mullein-plant, and not at all

13*

implicated with the church. Salisbury is now esteemed the culmination of the Gothic art in England, as the buttresses are fully unmasked, and honestly detailed from the sides of the pile. The interior of the Cathedral is obstructed by the organ in the middle, acting like a screen. I know not why in real architecture the hunger of the eye for length of line is so rarely gratified. The rule of art is that a colonnade is more beautiful the longer it is, and that *ad infinitum.* And the nave of a church is seldom so long that it need be divided by a screen.

We loitered in the church, outside the choir, whilst service was said. Whilst we listened to the organ, my friend remarked, the music is good and yet not quite religious, but somewhat as if a monk were panting to some fine Queen of Heaven. C. was unwilling, and we did not ask to have the choir shown us, but returned to our inn, after seeing another old church of the place. We passed in the train Clarendon Park, but could see little but the edge of a wood, though C. had wished to pay closer attention to the birthplace of the Decrees of Clarendon. At Bishopstoke we stopped, and found Mr. H., who received us in his carriage, and took us to his house at Bishops Waltham.

On Sunday, we had much discourse on a very rainy day. My friends ask, whether there were any Americans? — any with an American idea, — any theory of the right future of that country? Thus challenged, I bethought myself neither of caucuses nor congress, neither of presidents nor of cabinet-ministers, nor of such as would make of America another Europe. I thought only of the simplest and purest minds; I said, 'Certainly yes; but those who hold it are fanatics of a dream which I should hardly care to relate to your English ears, to which it might be only ridiculous, — and yet it is the only true.' So I opened the dogma of no government and non-resistance, and anticipated the objections and the fun, and procured a kind of hearing for it. I said, it is true that I have never seen in any country a man of sufficient valor to stand for this truth, and yet it is plain to me that no less valor than this can command my respect. I can easily see the bankruptcy of the vulgar musket-worship, — though great men be musket-worshippers; and 't is certain, as God liveth, the gun that does not need another gun, the law of love and justice alone, can effect a clean revolution. I fancied that one or two of my anecdotes made some impression on C., and I insisted that the manifest absurdity of the view to English feasibility could make no difference to a gentleman; that as to our secure tenure of our mutton-chop and spinage in London or in Boston, the soul might quote Talleyrand, "*Monsieur, je n'en vois pas la nécessité.*" * As I had thus taken in the conversation the saint's part, when dinner was announced, C. refused to go out before me, — "he was altogether too wicked." I planted my back against the wall, and our host wittily rescued us from the dilemma, by saying, he was the wickedest, and would walk out first, then C. followed, and I went last.

On the way to Winchester, whither our host accompanied us in the afternoon, my friends asked many questions respecting American landscape, forests, houses, — my house, for example. It is not easy to answer these queries well. There I thought, in America, lies nature sleeping, overgrowing, almost conscious, too much by half for man in the picture, and so giving a certain *tristesse*, like the rank vegetation of swamps and forests seen at night, steeped in dews and rains, which it loves; and on it man seems not able to make much impression. There, in that great sloven continent, in high Alleghany pastures, in the sea-wide, sky-skirted prairie, still sleeps and murmurs and hides the great mother, long since driven away from the trim hedge-rows and over-cultivated garden of England. And, in England, I am quite too sensible of this. Every one is on his good behavior, and must be dressed for dinner at six. So I put off my friends with very inadequate details, as best I could.

Just before entering Winchester, we stopped at the Church of Saint Cross, and, after looking through the quaint antiquity, we demanded a piece of bread and a draught of beer, which the founder, Henry de Blois, in 1136, commanded should be given to every one who should ask it at the gate. We had both, from the old couple who take care of the church. Some twenty people, every day, they said, make the same demand. This hospitality of seven hundred years' standing did not hinder C. from pronouncing a malediction on the priest who receives £ 2000 a year, that were meant for the poor, and spends a pittance on this small beer and crumbs.

In the Cathedral, I was gratified, at least by the ample dimensions. The length of line exceeds that of any other English church; being 556 feet by 250 in breadth of transept. I think I prefer this church to all I have seen, except Westminster and York. Here was Canute buried, and here Alfred the

* "*Mais, Monseigneur, il faut que j'existe.*"

Great was crowned and buried, and here the Saxon kings: and, later, in his own church, William of Wykeham. It is very old: part of the crypt into which we went down and saw the Saxon and Norman arches of the old church on which the present stands, was built fourteen or fifteen hundred years ago. Sharon Turner says: "Alfred was buried at Winchester, in the Abbey he had founded there, but his remains were removed by Henry I. to the new Abbey in the meadows at Hyde, on the northern quarter of the city, and laid under the high altar. The building was destroyed at the Reformation, and what is left of Alfred's body now lies covered by modern buildings, or buried in the ruins of the old." * William of Wykeham's shrine tomb was unlocked for us, and C. took hold of the recumbent statue's marble hands, and patted them affectionately, for he rightly values the brave man who built Windsor, and this Cathedral, and the School here, and New College at Oxford. But it was growing late in the afternoon. Slowly we left the old house, and parting with our host, we took the train for London.

CHAPTER XVII.

PERSONAL.

IN these comments on an old journey now revised after seven busy years have much changed men and things in England, I have abstained from reference to persons, except in the last chapter, and in one or two cases where the fame of the parties seemed to have given the public a property in all that concerned them. I must further allow myself a few notices, if only as an acknowledgment of debts that cannot be paid. My journeys were cheered by so much kindness from new friends, that my impression of the island is bright with agreeable memories both of public societies and of households; and, what is nowhere better found than in England, a cultivated person fitly surrounded by a happy home, "with honor, love, obedience, troops of friends," is of all institutions the best. At the landing in Liverpool, I found my Manchester correspondent awaiting me, a gentleman whose kind reception was followed by a train of friendly and effective attentions

* History of the Anglo-Saxons, I. 599.

which never rested whilst I remained in the country. A man of sense and of letters, the editor of a powerful local journal, he added to solid virtues an infinite sweetness and *bonhommie*. There seemed a pool of honey about his heart which lubricated all his speech and action with fine jets of mead. An equal good-fortune attended many later accidents of my journey, until the sincerity of English kindness ceased to surprise. My visit fell in the fortunate days when Mr. Bancroft was the American Minister in London, and at his house, or through his good offices, I had easy access to excellent persons and to privileged places. At the house of Mr. Carlyle, I met persons eminent in society and in letters. The privileges of the Athenæum and of the Reform Clubs were hospitably opened to me, and I found much advantage in the circles of the "Geologic," the "Antiquarian," and the "Royal Societies." Every day in London gave me new opportunities of meeting men and women who give splendor to society. I saw Rogers, Hallam, Macaulay, Milnes, Milman, Barry Cornwall, Dickens, Thackeray, Tennyson, Leigh Hunt, D'Israeli, Helps, Wilkinson, Bailey, Kenyon, and Forster: the younger poets, Clough, Arnold, and Patmore; and, among the men of science, Robert Brown, Owen, Sedgwick, Faraday, Buckland, Lyell, De la Beche, Hooker, Carpenter, Babbage, and Edward Forbes. It was my privilege also to converse with Miss Baillie, with Lady Morgan, with Mrs. Jameson, and Mrs. Somerville. A finer hospitality made many private houses not less known and dear. It is not in distinguished circles that wisdom and elevated characters are usually found, or, if found, not confined thereto; and my recollections of the best hours go back to private conversations in different parts of the kingdom, with persons little known. Nor am I insensible to the courtesy which frankly opened to me some noble mansions, if I do not adorn my page with their names. Among the privileges of London, I recall with pleasure two or three signal days, one at Kew, where Sir William Hooker showed me all the riches of the vast botanic garden; one at the Museum, where Sir Charles Fellowes explained in detail the history of his Ionic trophy-monument; and still another, on which Mr. Owen accompanied my countryman Mr. H. and myself through the Hunterian Museum.

The like frank hospitality, bent on real service, I found among the great and the humble, wherever I went; in Birmingham, in Oxford, in Leicester, in Nottingham, in Sheffield, in Manchester, in Liverpool. At Edinburgh, through the kindness of Dr. Samuel Brown, I made the acquaintance of DeQuincey, of Lord Jeffrey, of Wilson, of Mrs. Crowe, of the Messrs. Chambers, and of a man of high character and genius, the short-lived painter David Scott.

At Ambleside, in March, 1848, I was for a couple of days the guest of Miss Martineau, then newly returned from her Egyptian tour. On Sunday afternoon, I accompanied her to Rydal Mount. And as I have recorded a visit to Wordsworth, many years before, I must not forget this second interview. We found Mr. Wordsworth asleep on the sofa. He was at first silent and indisposed, as an old man, suddenly waked, before he had ended his nap; but soon became full of talk on the French news. He was nationally bitter on the French: bitter on Scotchmen, too. No Scotchman, he said, can write English. He detailed the two models, on one or the other of which all the sentences of the historian Robertson are framed. Nor could Jeffrey, nor the Edinburgh Reviewers write English, nor can . . . . who is a pest to the English tongue. Incidentally he added, Gibbon cannot write English. The *Edinburgh Review* wrote what would tell and what would sell. It had however changed the tone of its literary criticism from the time when a certain letter was written to the editor by Coleridge. Mrs. W. had the Editor's answer in her possession. Tennyson he thinks a right poetic genius, though with some affectation. He had thought an elder brother of Tennyson at first the better poet, but must now reckon Alfred the true one. . . . . In speaking of I know not what style, he said, "To be sure it was the manner, but then you know the matter always comes out of the manner." . . . . He thought Rio Janeiro the best place in the world for a great capital city. . . . . We talked of English national character. I told him it was not creditable that no one in all the country knew anything of Thomas Taylor, the Platonist, whilst in every American library his translations are found. I said, if Plato's Republic were published in England as a new book to-day, do you think it would find any readers? — he confessed, it would not: "And yet," he added after a pause, with that complacency which never deserts a true-born Englishman, — "and yet we have embodied it all."

His opinions of French, English, Irish, and Scotch seemed rashly formulized from little anecdotes of what had befallen himself and members of his family, in a diligence or stage-coach. His face sometimes lighted up, but his conversation was not marked by special force or elevation. Yet perhaps it is a high compliment to the cultivation of the English generally, when we find such a man not distinguished. He had a healthy look, with a weather-beaten face, his face corrugated, especially the large nose.

Miss Martineau, who lived near him, praised him to me, not for his poetry, but for thrift and economy; for having afforded to his country neighbors an example of a modest household, where comfort and culture were secured without any display. She said, that, in his early housekeeping at the cottage where he first lived, he was accustomed to offer his friends bread and plainest fare: if they wanted anything more, they must pay him for their board. It was the rule of the house. I replied, that it evinced English pluck more than any anecdote I knew. A gentleman in the neighborhood told the story of Walter Scott's once staying a week with Wordsworth, and slipping out every day under pretence of a walk, to the Swan Inn, for a cold cut and porter; and one day passing with Wordsworth the inn, he was betrayed by the landlord's asking him if he had come for his porter. Of course, this trait would have another look in London, and there you will hear from different literary men, that Wordsworth had no personal friend, that he was not amiable, that he was parsimonious, &c. Landor, always generous, says that he never praised anybody. A gentleman in London showed me a watch that once belonged to Milton, whose initials are engraved on its face. He said, he once showed this to Wordsworth, who took it in one hand, then drew out his own watch, and held it up with the other, before the company, but no one making the expected remark, he put back his own in silence. I do not attach much importance to the disparagement of Wordsworth among London scholars. Who reads him well will know, that in following the strong bent of his genius, he was careless of the many, careless also of the few, self-assured that he should "create the taste by which he is to be enjoyed." He lived long enough to witness the revolution he had wrought, and "to see what he foresaw." There are torpid places in his mind, there is something hard and sterile in his poetry, want of grace and variety, want of due catholicity and cosmopolitan scope: he had conformities to English politics and traditions; he had egotistic puerilities in the choice and treatment of his subjects; but let us say of him, that, alone in his time, he treated the human mind well, and with an absolute trust. His adherence to his poetic creed rested on real inspirations. The Ode on Immortality is the high-water mark which the intellect has reached in this age. New means were employed, and new realms added to the empire of the muse, by his courage.

CHAPTER XVIII.

RESULT.

ENGLAND is the best of actual nations. It is no ideal framework, it is an old pile built in different ages, with repairs, additions, and makeshifts; but you see the poor best you have got. London is the epitome of our times, and the Rome of to-day. Broad-fronted broad-bottomed Teutons, they stand in solid phalanx foursquare to the points of compass; they constitute the modern world, they have earned their vantage-ground, and held it through ages of adverse possession. They are well marked and differing from other leading races. England is tender-hearted. Rome was not. England is not so public in its bias; private life is its place of honor. Truth in private life, untruth in public, marks these home-loving men. Their political conduct is not decided by general views, but by internal intrigues and personal and family interest. They cannot readily see beyond England. The history of Rome and Greece, when written by their scholars, degenerates into English party pamphlets. They cannot see beyond England, nor in England can they transcend the interests of the governing classes. "English principles" mean a primary regard to the interests of property. England, Scotland, and Ireland combine to check the colonies. England and Scotland combine to check Irish manufactures and trade. England rallies at home to check Scotland. In England, the strong classes check the weaker. In the home population of near thirty millions, there are but one million voters. The Church punishes dissent, punishes education. Down to a late day, marriages performed by dissenters were illegal. A bitter class-legislation gives power to those who are rich enough to buy a law. The game-laws are a proverb of oppression. Pauperism incrusts and clogs the state, and in hard times becomes hideous. In bad seasons, the porridge was diluted. Multitudes lived miserably by shell-fish and sea-ware. In cities, the children are trained to beg, until they shall be old enough to rob. Men and women were convicted of poisoning scores of children for burial fees. In Irish districts, men deteriorated in size and shape. The nose sunk, the gums were exposed, with diminished brain and brutal form. During the Australian emigration, multitudes were rejected by the commissioners as being too emaciated for useful colonists. During the Russian war, few of those that offered as recruits were found up to the medical standard, though it had been reduced.

The foreign policy of England, though ambitious and lavish of money, has not often been generous or just. It has a principal regard to the interest of trade, checked however by the aristocratic bias of the ambassador, which usually puts him in sympathy with the continental Courts. It sanctioned the partition of Poland, it betrayed Genoa, Sicily, Parga, Greece, Turkey, Rome, and Hungary.

Some public regards they have. They have abolished slavery in the West Indies, and put an end to human sacrifices in the East. At home they have a certain statute hospitality. England keeps open doors, as a trading country must, to all nations. It is one of their fixed ideas, and wrathfully supported by their laws in unbroken sequence for a thousand years. In *Magna Charta* it was ordained, that all "merchants shall have safe and secure conduct to go out and come into England, and to stay there, and to pass as well by land as by water, to buy and sell by the ancient allowed customs, without any evil toll, except in time of war, or when they shall be of any nation at war with us." It is a statute and obliged hospitality, and peremptorily maintained. But this shop-rule had one magnificent effect. It extends its cold unalterable courtesy to political exiles of every opinion, and is a fact which might give additional light to that portion of the planet seen from the farthest star. But this perfunctory hospitality puts no sweetness into their unaccommodating manners, no check on that puissant nationality which makes their existence incompatible with all that is not English.

What we must say about a nation is a superficial dealing with symptoms. We cannot go deep enough into the biography of the spirit who never throws himself entire into one hero, but delegates his energy in parts or spasms to vicious and defective individuals. But the wealth of the source is seen in the plenitude of English nature. What variety of power and talent; what facility and plenteousness of knighthood, lordship, ladyship, royalty, loyalty; what a proud chivalry is indicated in "Collins's Peerage," through eight hundred years! What dignity resting on what reality and stoutness! What courage in war, what sinew in labor, what cunning workmen, what inventors and engineers, what seamen and pilots, what clerks and scholars! No one man and no few men can represent them. It is a people of myriad personalities. Their many-headedness is owing to the advantageous position of the middle class, who are always the source of letters and science. Hence the vast plenty of their æsthetic production. As they are many-headed, so they are many-nationed: their colonization annexes archipelagoes and continents, and their speech seems destined to be the universal language of men. I have noted the reserve of power in the English temperament. In the island, they never let out all the length of all the reins, there is no Berserkir rage, no abandonment or ecstasy of will or intellect, like that of the Arabs in the time of Mahomet, or like that which intoxicated France in 1789. But who would see the uncoiling of that tremendous spring, the explosion of their well-husbanded forces, must follow the swarms which, pouring now for two hundred years from the British islands, have sailed, and rode, and traded, and planted, through all climates, mainly following the belt of empire, the temperate zones, carrying the Saxon seed, with its instinct for liberty and law, for arts and for thought, — acquiring under some skies a more electric energy than the native air allows, — to the conquest of the globe. Their colonial policy, obeying the necessities of a vast empire, has become liberal. Canada and Australia have been contented with substantial independence. They are expiating the wrongs of India, by benefits: first, in works for the irrigation of the peninsula, and roads and telegraphs; and secondly, in the instruction of the people, to qualify them for self-government, when the British power shall be finally called home.

Their mind is in a state of arrested development, — a divine cripple like Vulcan; a blind *savant* like Huber and Sanderson. They do not occupy themselves on matters of general and lasting import, but on a corporeal civilization, on goods that perish in the using. But they read with good intent, and what they learn they incarnate. The English mind turns every abstraction it can receive into a portable utensil, or a working institution. Such is their tenacity, and such their practical turn, that they hold all they gain. Hence we say, that only the

English race can be trusted with freedom, — freedom which is double-edged and dangerous to any but the wise and robust. The English designate the kingdoms emulous of free institutions as the sentimental nations. Their own culture is not an outside varnish, but is thorough and secular in families and the race. They are oppressive with their temperament, and all the more that they are refined. I have sometimes seen them walk with my countrymen when I was forced to allow them every advantage, and their companions seemed bags of bones.

There is cramp limitation in their habit of thought, sleepy routine, and a tortoise's instinct to hold hard to the ground with his claws, lest he should be thrown on his back. There is a drag of inertia which resists reform in every shape; law-reform, army-reform, extension of suffrage, Jewish franchise, Catholic emancipation, — the abolition of slavery, of impressment, penal code, and entails. They praise this drag, under the formula, that it is the excellence of the British constitution, that no law can anticipate the public opinion. These poor tortoises must hold hard, for they feel no wings sprouting at their shoulders. Yet somewhat divine warms at their heart, and waits a happier hour. It hides in their sturdy will. "Will," said the old philosophy, "is the measure of power," and personality is the token of this race. *Quid vult valde vult.* What they do they do with a will. You cannot account for their success by their Christianity, commerce, charter, common law, Parliament, or letters, but by the contumacious sharp-tongued energy of English *naturel*, with a poise impossible to disturb, which makes all these its instruments. They are slow and reticent, and are like a dull good horse which lets every nag pass him, but with whip and spur will run down every racer in the field. They are right in their feeling, though wrong in their speculation.

The feudal system survives in the steep inequality of property and privilege, in the limited franchise, in the social barriers which confine patronage and promotion to a caste, and still more in the submissive ideas pervading these people. The fagging of the schools is repeated in the social classes. An Englishman shows no mercy to those below him in the social scale, as he looks for none from those above him; any forbearance from his superiors surprises him, and they suffer in his good opinion. But the feudal system can be seen with less pain on large historical grounds. It was pleaded in mitigation of the rotten borough, that it worked well, that substantial justice was done. Fox, Burke, Pitt, Erskine, Wilberforce, Sheridan, Romilly, or whatever national man, were by this means sent to Parliament, when their return by large constituencies would have been doubtful. So now we say, that the right measures of England are the men it bred; that it has yielded more able men in five hundred years than any other nation; and, though we must not play Providence, and balance the chances of producing ten great men against the comfort of ten thousand mean men, yet retrospectively we may strike the balance, and prefer one Alfred, one Shakespeare, one Milton, one Sidney, one Raleigh, one Wellington, to a million foolish democrats.

The American system is more democratic, more humane; yet the American people do not yield better or more able men, or more inventions or books or benefits, than the English. Congress is not wiser or better than Parliament. France has abolished its suffocating old *régime*, but is not recently marked by any more wisdom or virtue.

The power of performance has not been exceeded, — the creation of value. The English have given importance to individuals, a principal end and fruit of every society. Every man is allowed and encouraged to be what he is, and is guarded in the indulgence of his whim. "Magna Charta," said Rushworth, "is such a fellow that he will have no sovereign." By this general activity, and by this sacredness of individuals, they have in seven hundred years evolved the principles of freedom. It is the land of patriots, martyrs, sages, and bards, and if the ocean out of which it emerged should wash it away, it will be remembered as an island famous for immortal laws, for the announcements of original right which make the stone tables of liberty.

CHAPTER XIX.

SPEECH AT MANCHESTER.

A FEW days after my arrival at Manchester, in November, 1847, the Manchester Athenæum gave its annual Banquet in the Free-Trade Hall. With other guests, I was invited to be present, and to address the company. In looking over recently a newspaper report of my remarks, I incline to reprint it, as fitly expressing the feeling with which I entered England, and which agrees well enough with the more deliberate results of better acquaintance recorded in the foregoing pages. Sir Archibald Alison, the historian, presided, and opened the meeting with a speech. He was followed by Mr. Cobden, Lord Brackley, and others, among whom was Mr. Cruikshank, one of the contributors to "Punch." Mr. Dickens's letter of apology for his absence was read. Mr. Jerrold, who had been announced, did not appear. On being introduced to the meeting I said:—

Mr. Chairman and Gentlemen: It is pleasant to me to meet this great and brilliant company, and doubly pleasant to see the faces of so many distinguished persons on this platform. But I have known all these persons already. When I was at home, they were as near to me as they are to you. The arguments of the League and its leader are known to all the friends of free trade. The gayeties and genius, the political, the social, the parietal wit of "Punch" go duly every fortnight to every boy and girl in Boston and New York. Sir, when I came to sea, I found the "History of Europe"* on the ship's cabin table, the property of the captain;—a sort of programme or play-bill to tell the seafaring New-Englander what he shall find on his landing here. And as for Dombey, sir, there is no land where paper exists to print on, where it is not found; no man who can read, that does not read it, and, if he cannot, he finds some charitable pair of eyes that can, and hears it.

But these things are not for me to say; these compliments, though true, would better come from one who felt and under-

* By Sir A. Alison.

stood these merits more. I am not here to exchange civilities with you, but rather to speak of that which I am sure interests these gentlemen more than their own praises; of that which is good in holidays and working-days, the same in one century and in another century. That which lures a solitary American in the woods with the wish to see England, is the moral peculiarity of the Saxon race, — its commanding sense of right and wrong, — the love and devotion to that, — this is the imperial trait, which arms them with the sceptre of the globe. It is this which lies at the foundation of that aristocratic character, which certainly wanders into strange vagaries, so that its origin is often lost sight of, but which, if it should lose this, would find itself paralyzed; and in trade, and in the mechanic's shop, gives that honesty in performance, that thoroughness and solidity of work, which is a national characteristic. This conscience is one element, and the other is that loyal adhesion, that habit of friendship, that homage of man to man, running through all classes, — the electing of worthy persons to a certain fraternity, to acts of kindness and warm and stanch support, from year to year, from youth to age, — which is alike lovely and honorable to those who render and those who receive it; — which stands in strong contrast with the superficial attachments of other races, their excessive courtesy, and short-lived connection.

You will think me very pedantic, gentlemen, but holiday though it be, I have not the smallest interest in any holiday, except as it celebrates real and not pretended joys; and I think it just, in this time of gloom and commercial disaster, of affliction and beggary in these districts, that on these very accounts I speak of, you should not fail to keep your literary anniversary. I seem to hear you say, that, for all that is come and gone yet, we will not reduce by one chaplet or one oak-leaf the braveries of our annual feast. For I must tell you, I was given to understand in my childhood, that the British island from which my forefathers came, was no lotus-garden, no paradise of serene sky and roses and music and merriment all the year round, no, but a cold, foggy, mournful country, where nothing grew well in the open air, but robust men and virtuous women, and these of a wonderful fibre and endurance; that their best parts were slowly revealed; their virtues did not come out until they quarrelled: they did not strike twelve the first time; good lovers, good haters, and you could know little about them till you had seen them long, and little good of them till you had seen them in action; that in prosperity they were moody and dumpish, but in adversity they were grand. Is it not true, sir, that the wise ancients did not praise the ship parting with flying colors from the port, but only that brave sailer which came back with torn sheets and battered sides, stript of her banners, but having ridden out the storm? And so, gentlemen, I feel in regard to this aged England, with the possessions, honors and trophies, and also with the infirmities of a thousand years gathering around her, irretrievably committed as she now is to many old customs which cannot be suddenly changed; pressed upon by the transitions of trade, and new and all incalculable modes, fabrics, arts, machines, and competing populations, — I see her not dispirited, not weak, but well remembering that she has seen dark days before; indeed, with a kind of instinct that she sees a little better in a cloudy day, and that in storm of battle and calamity, she has a secret vigor and a pulse like a cannon. I see her in her old age, not decrepit, but young, and still daring to believe in her power of endurance and expansion. Seeing this, I say, All hail! mother of nations, mother of heroes, with strength still equal to the time; still wise to entertain and swift to execute the policy which the mind and heart of mankind requires in the present hour, and thus only hospitable to the foreigner, and truly a home to the thoughtful and generous who are born in the soil. So be it! so let it be! If it be not so, if the courage of England goes with the chances of a commercial crisis, I will go back to the capes of Massachusetts, and my own Indian stream, and say to my countrymen, the old race are all gone, and the elasticity and hope of mankind must henceforth remain on the Alleghany ranges, or nowhere.

CONDUCT OF LIFE.

FATE.

Delicate omens traced in air
To the lone bard true witness bare;
Birds with auguries on their wings
Chanted undeceiving things
Him to beckon, him to warn;
Well might then the poet scorn
To learn of scribe or courier
Hints writ in vaster character;
And on his mind, at dawn of day,
Soft shadows of the evening lay.
For the prevision is allied
Unto the thing so signified·
Or say, the foresight that awaits
Is the same Genius that creates.

FATE.

IT chanced during one winter, a few years ago, that our cities were bent on discussing the theory of the Age. By an odd coincidence, four or five noted men were each reading a discourse to the citizens of Boston or New York, on the Spirit of the Times. It so happened that the subject had the same prominence in some remarkable pamphlets and journals issued in London in the same season. To me, however, the question of the times resolved itself into a practical question of the conduct of life. How shall I live? We are incompetent to solve the times. Our geometry cannot span the huge orbits of the prevailing ideas, behold their return, and reconcile their opposition. We can only obey our own polarity. 'T is fine for us to speculate and elect our course, if we must accept an irresistible dictation.

In our first steps to gain our wishes, we come upon immovable limitations. We are fired with the hope to reform men. After many experiments, we find that we must begin earlier, — at school. But the boys and girls are not docile; we can make nothing of them. We decide that they are not of good stock. We must begin our reform earlier still, — at generation: that is to say, there is Fate, or laws of the world.

But if there be irresistible dictation, this dictation understands itself. If we must accept Fate, we are not less compelled to affirm liberty, the significance of the individual, the grandeur of duty, the power of character. This is true, and that other is true. But our geometry cannot span these extreme points, and reconcile them. What to do? By obeying each thought frankly, by harping, or, if you will, pounding on each string, we learn at last its power. By the same obedience to other thoughts, we learn theirs, and then comes some reasonable hope of harmonizing them. We are sure, that, though we know not how, necessity does comport with liberty, the individual with the world, my polarity with the spirit of the times. The riddle of the age has for each a private solution. If one would study his own time, it must be by this method of taking up in turn each of the leading topics which belong to our scheme of human life, and, by firmly stating all that is agreeable to experience on one, and doing the same justice to the opposing facts in the others, the true limitations will appear. Any excess of emphasis, on one part, would be corrected, and a just balance would be made.

But let us honestly state the facts. Our America has a bad name for superficialness. Great men, great nations, have not been boasters and buffoons, but perceivers of the terror of life, and have manned themselves to face it. The Spartan, embodying his religion in his country, dies before its majesty without a question. The Turk, who believes his doom is written on the iron leaf in the moment when he entered the world, rushes on the enemy's sabre with undivided will. The Turk, the Arab, the Persian, accepts the foreordained fate.

> "On two days, it steads not to run from thy grave,
> The appointed, and the unappointed day;
> On the first, neither balm nor physician can save,
> Nor thee, on the second, the Universe slay."

The Hindoo, under the wheel, is as firm. Our Calvinists, in the last generation, had something of the same dignity. They felt that the weight of the Universe held them down to their place. What could *they* do? Wise men feel that there is something which cannot be talked or voted away, — a strap or belt which girds the world.

> "The Destiny, minister general,
> That executeth in the world o'er all,
> The purveyance which God hath seen beforne,
> So strong it is, that though the world had sworn
> The contrary of a thing by yea or nay,
> Yet sometime it shall fallen on a day
> That falleth not oft in a thousand year;
> For, certainly, our appetités here,
> Be it of war, or peace, or hate, or love,
> All this is ruled by the sight above."
>
> CHAUCER: *The Knighte's Tale.*

The Greek Tragedy expressed the same sense: "Whatever is fated, that will take place. The great immense mind of Jove is not to be transgressed."

Savages cling to a local god of one tribe or town. The broad ethics of Jesus were quickly narrowed to village theologies, which preach an election or favoritism. And, now and then, an amiable parson, like Jung Stilling, or Robert Huntington, believes in a pistareen-Providence, which, whenever the good man wants a dinner, makes that somebody shall knock at his door, and leave a half-dollar. But Nature is no sentimentalist, — does not cosset or pamper us. We must see that the world is rough and surly, and will not mind drowning a man or a woman; but swallows your ship like a grain of dust. The cold, inconsiderate of persons, tingles your blood, benumbs your feet, freezes a man like an apple. The diseases, the elements, fortune, gravity, lightning, respect no persons. The way of Providence is a little rude. The habit of snake and spider, the snap of the tiger, and other leapers and bloody jumpers, the crackle of the bones of his prey in the coil of the anaconda, — these are in the system, and our habits are like theirs. You have just dined, and, however scrupulously the slaughter-house is concealed in the graceful distance of miles, there is complicity, — expensive races, — race living at the expense of race. The planet is liable to shocks from comets, perturbations from planets, rendings from earthquake and volcano, alterations of climate, precessions of equinoxes. Rivers dry up by opening of the forest. The sea changes its bed. Towns and counties fall into it. At Lisbon, an earthquake killed men like flies. At Naples, three years ago, ten thousand persons were crushed in a few minutes. The scurvy at sea; the sword of the climate in the west of Africa, at Cayenne, at Panama, at New Orleans, cut off men like a massacre. Our Western prairie shakes with fever and ague. The cholera, the small-pox, have proved as mortal to some tribes, as a frost to the crickets, which, having filled the summer with noise, are silenced by a fall of the temperature of one night. Without uncovering what does not concern us, or counting how many species of parasites hang on a bombyx; or groping after intestinal parasites, or infusory biters, or the obscurities of alternate generation; — the forms of the shark, the *labrus*, the jaw of the sea-wolf paved with crushing teeth, the weapons of the grampus, and other warriors hidden in the sea, — are hints of ferocity in the interiors of nature. Let us not deny it up and down. Providence has a wild, rough, incalculable road to its end, and it is of no use to try to whitewash its huge, mixed instrumentalities, or to dress up that terrific benefactor in a clean shirt and white neckcloth of a student in divinity.

Will you say, the disasters which threaten mankind are exceptional, and one need not lay his account for cataclysms every day? Ay, but what happens once may happen again, and so long as these strokes are not to be parried by us, they must be feared.

But these shocks and ruins are less destructive to us, than the stealthy power of other laws which act on us daily. An expense of ends to means is fate;—organization tyrannizing over character. The menagerie, or forms and powers of the spine, is a book of fate: the bill of the bird, the skull of the snake, determines tyrannically its limits. So is the scale of races, of temperaments; so is sex; so is climate; so is the reaction of talents imprisoning the vital power in certain directions. Every spirit makes its house; but afterwards the house confines the spirit.

The gross lines are legible to the dull: the cabman is phrenologist so far: he looks in your face to see if his shilling is sure. A dome of brow denotes one thing; a pot-belly another; a squint, a pug-nose, mats of hair, the pigment of the epidermis, betray character. People seem sheathed in their tough organization. Ask Spurzheim, ask the doctors, ask Quetelet, if temperaments decide nothing? or if there be anything they do not decide? Read the description in medical books of the four temperaments, and you will think you are reading your own thoughts which you had not yet told. Find the part which black eyes, and which blue eyes, play severally in the company. How shall a man escape from his ancestors, or draw off from his veins the black drop which he drew from his father's or his mother's life? It often appears in a family, as if all the qualities of the progenitors were potted in several jars,—some ruling quality in each son or daughter of the house,—and sometimes the unmixed temperament, the rank unmitigated elixir, the family vice, is drawn off in a separate individual, and the others are proportionally relieved. We sometimes see a change of expression in our companion, and say, his father, or his mother, comes to the windows of his eyes, and sometimes a remote relative. In different hours, a man represents each of several of his ancestors, as if there were seven or eight of us rolled up in each man's skin,—seven or eight ancestors at least,—and they constitute the variety of notes for that new piece of music which his life is. At the corner of the street, you read the possibility of each passenger, in the facial angle, in the complexion, in the depth of his eye. His parentage determines it. Men are what their mothers made them. You may as well ask a loom which weaves huckaback, why it does not make cashmere, as expect poetry from this engineer, or a chemical discovery from that jobber. Ask the digger in the ditch to explain Newton's laws; the fine organs of his brain have been pinched by overwork and squalid poverty from father to son, for a hundred years. When each comes forth from his mother's womb, the gate of gifts closes behind him. Let him value his hands and feet, he has but one pair. So he has but one future, and that is already predetermined in his lobes, and described in that little fatty face, pig-eye, and squat form. All the privilege and all the legislation of the world cannot meddle or help to make a poet or a prince of him.

Jesus said, "When he looketh on her, he hath committed adultery." But he is an adulterer before he has yet looked on the woman, by the superfluity of animal, and the defect of thought in his constitution. Who meets him, or who meets her, in the street, sees that they are ripe to be each other's victim.

In certain men, digestion and sex absorb the vital force, and the stronger these are, the individual is so much weaker. The more of these drones perish, the better for the hive. If, later, they give birth to some superior individual, with force enough to add to this animal a new aim, and a complete apparatus to work it out, all the ancestors are gladly forgotten. Most men and most women are merely one couple more. Now and then, one has a new cell or camarilla opened in his brain, — an architectural, a musical, or a philological knack, some stray taste or talent for flowers, or chemistry, or pigments, or story-telling, a good hand for drawing, a good foot for dancing, an athletic frame for wide journeying, &c., — which skill nowise alters rank in the scale of nature, but serves to pass the time, the life of sensation going on as before. At last, these hints and tendencies are fixed in one, or in a succession. Each absorbs so much food and force as to become itself a new centre. The new talent draws off so rapidly the vital force, that not enough remains for the animal functions, hardly enough for health; so that, in the second generation, if the like genius appear, the health is visibly deteriorated, and the generative force impaired.

People are born with the moral or with the material bias; — uterine brothers with this diverging destination: and I suppose, with high magnifiers, Mr. Frauenhofer or Dr. Carpenter might come to distinguish in the embryo at the fourth day, this is a Whig, and that a Free-soiler.

It was a poetic attempt to lift this mountain of Fate, to reconcile this despotism of race with liberty, which led the Hindoos to say, "Fate is nothing but the deeds committed in a prior state of existence." I find the coincidence of the extremes of Eastern and Western speculation in the daring statement of Schelling, "There is in every man a certain feeling, that he has been what he is from all eternity, and by no means became such in time." To say it less sublimely, — in the history of the individual is always an account of his condition, and he knows himself to be a party to his present estate.

A good deal of our politics is physiological. Now and then, a man of wealth in the heyday of youth adopts the tenet of broadest freedom. In England, there is always some man of wealth and large connection planting himself, during all his years of health, on the side of progress, who, as soon as he begins to die, checks his forward play, calls in his troops, and becomes conservative. All conservatives are such from personal defects. They have been effeminated by position or nature, born halt and blind, through luxury of their parents, and can only, like invalids, act on the defensive. But strong natures, backwoodsmen, New Hampshire giants, Napoleons, Burkes, Broughams, Websters, Kossuths, are inevitable patriots, until their life ebbs, and their defects and gout, palsy and money, warp them.

The strongest idea incarnates itself in majorities and nations, in the healthiest and strongest. Probably, the election goes by avoirdupois weight, and, if you could weigh bodily the tonnage of any hundred of the Whig and the Democratic party in a town on the Dearborn balance, as they passed the hayscales, you could predict with certainty which party would carry it. On the whole, it would be rather the speediest way of deciding the vote, to put the selectmen or the mayor and aldermen at the hayscales.

In science, we have to consider two things : power and circumstance. All we know of the egg, from each successive discovery, is, *another vesicle ;* and if, after five hundred years, you get a better observer, or a better glass, he finds within the last observed another. In vegetable and animal tissue, it is just alike, and all that the primary power or spasm operates, is, still, vesicles, vesicles. Yes, — but the tyrannical Circumstance! A vesicle in new circumstances, a vesicle lodged in darkness, Oken thought, became animal; in light, a plant.

Lodged in the parent animal, it suffers changes, which end in unsheathing miraculous capability in the unaltered vesicle, and it unlocks itself to fish, bird, or quadruped, head and foot, eye and claw. The Circumstance is Nature. Nature is what you may do. There is much you may not. We have two things, — the circumstance and the life. Once we thought, positive power was all. Now we learn, that negative power, or circumstance, is half. Nature is the tyrannous circumstance, the thick skull, the sheathed snake, the ponderous, rock-like jaw; necessitated activity; violent direction; the conditions of a tool, like the locomotive, strong enough on its track, but which can do nothing but mischief off of it; or skates, which are wings on the ice, but fetters on the ground.

The book of Nature is the book of Fate. She turns the gigantic pages, — leaf after leaf, — never re-turning one. One leaf she lays down, a floor of granite; then a thousand ages, and a bed of slate; a thousand ages, and a measure of coal; a thousand ages, and a layer of marl and mud: vegetable forms appear: her first misshapen animals, zoophyte, trilobium, fish; then, saurians, — rude forms, in which she has only blocked her future statue, concealing under these unwieldy monsters the fine type of her coming king. The face of the planet cools and dries, the races meliorate, and man is born. But when a race has lived its term, it comes no more again.

The population of the world is a conditional population; not the best, but the best that could live now; and the scale of tribes, and the steadiness with which victory adheres to one tribe, and defeat to another, is as uniform as the superposition of strata. We know in history what weight belongs to race. We see the English, French, and Germans planting themselves on every shore and market of America and Australia, and monopolizing the commerce of these countries. We like the nervous and victorious habit of our own branch of the family. We follow the step of the Jew, of the Indian, of the Negro. We see how much will has been expended to extinguish the Jew, in vain. Look at the unpalatable conclusions of Knox, in his "Fragment of Races," — a rash and unsatisfactory writer, but charged with pungent and unforgetable truths. "Nature respects race, and not hybrids." "Every race has its own *habitat*." "Detach a colony from the race, and it deteriorates to the crab." See the shades of the picture. The German and Irish millions, like the Negro, have a great deal of guano in their destiny. They are ferried over the Atlantic, and carted over America, to ditch and to drudge, to make corn cheap, and then to lie down prematurely to make a spot of green grass on the prairie.

One more fagot of these adamantine bandages, is, the new science of Statistics. It is a rule, that the most casual and extraordinary events — if the basis of population is broad enough — become matter of fixed calculation. It would not be safe to say when a captain like Bonaparte, a singer like Jenny Lind, or a navigator like Bowditch, would be born in Boston: but, on a population of twenty or two hundred millions, something like accuracy may be had.*

'T is frivolous to fix pedantically the date of particular inventions. They have all been invented over and over fifty times. Man is the arch machine, of which all these shifts drawn from himself are toy models. He helps himself on each emergency by copying or duplicating his own structure, just so far as the need is. 'T is hard to find the right Homer, Zoroaster, or Menu; harder still to find the Tubal Cain, or Vulcan, or Cadmus, or Copernicus, or Fust, or Fulton, the indisputable inventor. There are scores and centuries of them. "The air is full of men." This kind of talent so abounds, this constructive tool-making efficiency, as if it adhered to the chemic atoms, as if the air he breathes were made of Vaucansons, Franklins, and Watts.

Doubtless, in every million there will be an astronomer, a mathematician, a comic poet, a mystic. No one can read the history of astronomy, without perceiving that Copernicus, Newton, Laplace, are not new men, or a new kind of men, but that Thales, Anaximenes, Hipparchus, Empedocles, Aristarchus, Pythagoras, Œnipodes, had anticipated them: each had the same tense geometrical brain, apt for the same vigorous computation and logic, a mind parallel to the movement of the world. The Roman mile probably rested on a measure of a degree of the meridian. Mahometan and Chinese know what we know of leap-year, of the Gregorian calendar, and of the precession of the equinoxes. As, in every barrel of cowries, brought to New Bedford, there shall be one *orangia*, so there will, in a dozen millions of Malays and Mahometans, be

* "Everything which pertains to the human species, considered as a whole, belongs to the order of physical facts. The greater the number of individuals, the more does the influence of the individual will disappear, leaving predominance to a series of general facts dependent on causes by which society exists, and is preserved." — QUETELET.

one or two astronomical skulls. In a large city, the most casual things, and things whose beauty lies in their casualty, are produced as punctually and to order as the baker's muffin for breakfast. Punch makes exactly one capital joke a week; and the journals contrive to furnish one good piece of news every day.

And not less work the laws of repression, the penalties of violated functions. Famine, typhus, frost, war, suicide, and effete races, must be reckoned calculable parts of the system of the world.

These are pebbles from the mountain, hints of the terms by which our life is walled up, and which show a kind of mechanical exactness, as of a loom or mill, in what we call casual or fortuitous events.

The force with which we resist these torrents of tendency looks so ridiculously inadequate, that it amounts to little more than a criticism or a protest made by a minority of one, under compulsion of millions. I seemed, in the height of a tempest, to see men overboard struggling in the waves, and driven about here and there. They glanced intelligently at each other, but 't was little they could do for one another; 't was much if each could keep afloat alone. Well, they had a right to their eye-beams, and all the rest was Fate.

We cannot trifle with this reality, this cropping-out in our planted gardens of the core of the world. No picture of life can have any veracity that does not admit the odious facts. A man's power is hooped in by a necessity, which, by many experiments, he touches on every side, until he learns its arc.

The element running through entire nature, which we popularly call Fate, is known to us as limitation. Whatever limits us, we call Fate. If we are brute and barbarous, the fate takes a brute and dreadful shape. As we refine, our checks become finer. If we rise to spiritual culture, the antagonism takes a spiritual form. In the Hindoo fables, Vishnu follows Maya through all her ascending changes, from insect and craw-fish up to elephant; whatever form she took, he took the male form of that kind, until she became at last woman and goddess, and he a man and a god. The limitations refine as the soul purifies, but the ring of necessity is always perched at the top.

When the gods in the Norse heaven were unable to bind the Fenris Wolf with steel or with weight of mountains, — the one he snapped and the other he spurned with his heel, — they put round his foot a limp band softer than silk or cobweb, and this held him: the more he spurned it, the stiffer it drew. So soft and so stanch is the ring of Fate. Neither brandy, nor nectar, nor sulphuric ether, nor hell-fire, nor ichor, nor poetry, nor genius, can get rid of this limp band. For if we give it the high sense in which the poets use it, even thought itself is not above Fate: that too must act according to eternal laws, and all that is wilful and fantastic in it is in opposition to its fundamental essence.

And last of all, high over thought, in the world of morals, Fate appears as vindicator, levelling the high, lifting the low, requiring justice in man, and always striking soon or late, when justice is not done. What is useful will last; what is hurtful will sink. "The doer must suffer," said the Greeks: "you would soothe a Deity not to be soothed." "God himself cannot procure good for the wicked," said the Welsh triad. "God may consent, but only for a time," said the bard of Spain. The limitation is impassable by any insight of man. In its last and loftiest ascensions, insight itself, and the freedom of the will, is one of its obedient members. But we must not run into generalizations too large, but show the natural bounds or essential distinctions, and seek to do justice to the other elements as well.

Thus we trace Fate, in matter, mind, and morals, — in race, in retardations of strata, and in thought and character as well. It is everywhere bound or limitation. But Fate has its lord; limitation its limits; is different seen from above and from below; from within and from without. For, though fate is immense, so is power, which is the other fact in the dual world, immense. If Fate follows and limits power, power attends and antagonizes Fate. We must respect Fate as natural history, but there is more than natural history. For who and what is this criticism that pries into the matter? Man is not order of nature, sack and sack, belly and members, link in a chain, nor any ignominious baggage, but a stupendous antagonism, a dragging together of the poles of the Universe. He betrays his relation to what is below him, — thick-skulled, small-brained, fishy, quadrumanous, — quadruped ill-disguised, hardly escaped into biped, and has paid for the new powers by loss of some of the old ones. But the lightning which explodes and fashions planets, maker of planet and suns, is in him. On one side, elemental order, sandstone and granite, rock-ledges, peat-bog, forest, sea and shore ; and, on the other part, thought, the spirit which composes and decomposes nature, — here they are, side by side, god and devil, mind and matter, king and conspirator, belt and spasm, riding peacefully together in the eye and brain of every man.

Nor can he blink the freewill. To hazard the contradiction, — freedom is necessary. If you please to plant yourself on the side of Fate, and say, Fate is all ; then we say, a part of Fate is the freedom of man. Forever wells up the impulse of choosing and acting in the soul. Intellect annuls Fate. So far as a man thinks, he is free. And though nothing is more disgusting than the crowing about liberty by slaves, as most men are, and the flippant mistaking for freedom of some paper preamble like a "Declaration of Independence," or the statute right to vote, by those who have never dared to think or to act, yet it is wholesome to man to look not at Fate, but the other way : the practical view is the other. His sound relation to these facts is to use and command, not to cringe to them. "Look not on nature, for her name is fatal," said the oracle. The too much contemplation of these limits induces meanness. They who talk much of destiny, their birth-star, &c., are in a lower dangerous plane, and invite the evils they fear.

I cited the instinctive and heroic races as proud believers in Destiny. They conspire with it ; a loving resignation is with the event. But the dogma makes a different impression, when it is held by the weak and lazy. 'T is weak and vicious people who cast the blame on Fate. The right use of Fate is to bring up our conduct to the loftiness of nature. Rude and invincible except by themselves are the elements. So let man be. Let him empty his breast of his windy conceits, and show his lordship by manners and deeds on the scale of nature. Let him hold his purpose as with the tug of gravitation. No power, no persuasion, no bribe shall make him give up his point. A man ought to compare advantageously with a river, an oak, or a mountain. He shall have not less the flow, the expansion, and the resistance of these.

'T is the best use of Fate to teach a fatal courage. Go face the fire at sea, or the cholera in your friend's house, or the burglar in your own, or what danger lies in the way of duty, knowing you are guarded by the cherubim of Destiny. If you believe in Fate to your harm, believe it, at least, for your good.

For, if Fate is so prevailing, man also is part of it, and can confront fate with fate. If the Universe have these savage accidents, our atoms are as savage in resistance. We should be crushed by the atmosphere, but for the reaction of the air within the body. A tube made of a film of glass can resist the shock of the ocean, if filled with the same water. If there be omnipotence in the stroke, there is omnipotence of recoil.

1. But Fate against Fate is only parrying and defence: there are, also, the noble creative forces. The revelation of Thought takes man out of servitude into freedom. We rightly say of ourselves, we were born, and afterward we were born again, and many times. We have successive experiences so important, that the new forgets the old, and hence the mythology of the seven or the nine heavens. The day of days, the great day of the feast of life, is that in which the inward eye opens to the Unity in things, to the omnipresence of law; — sees that what is must be, and ought to be, or is the best. This beatitude dips from on high down on us, and we see. It is not in us so much as we are in it. If the air come to our lungs, we breathe and live; if not, we die. If the light come to our eyes, we see; else not. And if truth come to our mind, we suddenly expand to its dimensions, as if we grew to worlds. We are as lawgivers; we speak for Nature; we prophesy and divine.

This insight throws us on the party and interest of the Universe, against all and sundry; against ourselves, as much as others. A man speaking from insight affirms of himself what is true of the mind: seeing its immortality, he says, I am immortal; seeing its invincibility, he says, I am strong. It is not in us, but we are in it. It is of the maker, not of what is made. All things are touched and changed by it. This uses, and is not used. It distances those who share it, from those who share it not. Those who share it not are flocks and herds. It dates from itself; — not from former men or better men, — gospel, or constitution, or college, or custom. Where it shines, Nature is no longer intrusive, but all things make a musical or pictorial impression. The world of men show like a comedy without laughter: populations, interests, government, history; 't is all toy figures in a toy house. It does not overvalue particular truths. We hear eagerly every thought and word quoted from an intellectual man. But, in his presence, our own mind is roused to activity, and we forget very fast what he says, much more interested in the new play of our own thought, than in any thought of his. 'T is the majesty into which we have suddenly mounted, the impersonality, the scorn of egotisms, the sphere of laws, that engage us. Once we were stepping a little this way, and a little that way; now, we are as men in a balloon, and do not think so much of the point we have left, or the point we would make, as of the liberty and glory of the way.

Just as much intellect as you add, so much organic power. He who sees through the design, presides over it, and must will that which must be. We sit and rule, and, though we sleep, our dream will come to pass. Our thought, though it were only an hour old, affirms an oldest necessity, not to be separated from thought, and not to be separated from will. They must always have co-existed. It apprises us of its sovereignty and godhead, which refuse to be severed from it. It is not mine or thine, but the will of all mind. It is poured into the souls of all men, as the soul itself which constitutes them men. I know not whether there be, as is alleged, in the upper region of our atmosphere, a permanent westerly current, which carries with it all atoms which rise to that height, but I see, that when souls reach a certain clearness of perception, they accept a knowledge and motive above selfishness. A breath of will blows eternally through the universe of souls in the direction of the Right and Necessary. It is the air which all intellects inhale and exhale, and it is the wind which blows the worlds into order and orbit.

Thought dissolves the material universe, by carrying the mind up into a sphere where all is plastic. Of two men, each obeying his own thought, he whose thought is deepest will be the strongest character. Always one man more than another represents the will of Divine Providence to the period.

2. If thought makes free, so does the moral sentiment. The mixtures of spiritual chemistry refuse to be analyzed. Yet we can see that with the perception of truth is joined the desire that it shall prevail. That affection is essential to will. Moreover, when a strong will appears, it usually results from a certain unity of organization, as if the whole energy of body and mind flowed in one direction. All great force is real and elemental. There is no manufacturing a strong will. There must be a pound to balance a pound. Where power is shown in will, it must rest on the universal force. Alaric and Bonaparte must believe they rest on a truth, or their will can be bought or bent. There is a bribe possible for any finite will.

But the pure sympathy with universal ends is an infinite force, and cannot be bribed or bent. Whoever has had experience of the moral sentiment cannot choose but believe in unlimited power. Each pulse from that heart is an oath from the Most High. I know not what the word *sublime* means, if it be not the intimations in this infant of a terrific force. A text of heroism, a name and anecdote of courage, are not arguments, but sallies of freedom. One of these is the verse of the Persian Hafiz, "'T is written on the gate of heaven, 'Woe unto him who suffers himself to be betrayed by Fate!'" Does the reading of history make us fatalists? What courage does not the opposite opinion show! A little whim of will to be free gallantly contending against the universe of chemistry.

But insight is not will, nor is affection will. Perception is cold, and goodness dies in wishes; as Voltaire said, 't is the misfortune of worthy people that they are cowards; "*un des plus grands malheurs des honnêtes gens c'est qu'ils sont des lâches.*" There must be a fusion of these two to generate the energy of will. There can be no driving force, except through the conversion of the man into his will, making him the will, and the will him. And one may say boldly, that no man has a right perception of any truth, who has not been reacted on by it, so as to be ready to be its martyr.

The one serious and formidable thing in nature is a will. Society is servile from want of will, and therefore the world wants saviours and religions. One way is right to go: the hero sees it, and moves on that aim, and has the world under him for root and support. He is to others as the world. His approbation is honor; his dissent, infamy. The glance of his eye has the force of sunbeams. A personal influence towers up in memory only worthy, and we gladly forget numbers, money, climate, gravitation, and the rest of Fate.

We can afford to allow the limitation, if we know it is the meter of the growing man. We stand against Fate, as children stand up against the wall in their father's house, and notch their height from year to year. But when the boy grows to man, and is master of the house, he pulls down that wall, and builds a new and bigger. 'T is only a question of time. Every brave youth is in training to ride and rule this dragon. His science is to make weapons and wings of these passions and retarding forces. Now whether, seeing these two things, fate and power, we are permitted to believe in unity? The bulk of mankind believe in two gods. They are under one dominion here in the house, as friend and parent, in social circles, in letters, in art, in love, in religion: but in mechanics, in dealing with steam and climate, in trade, in politics, they think they come under another; and that it would be a practical blunder to transfer the method and way of working of one sphere, into the other. What good, honest, generous men at home, will be wolves and foxes on change! What pious men in the parlor will vote for what reprobates at the polls! To a certain point, they believe themselves the care of a Providence. But, in a steamboat, in an epidemic, in war, they believe a malignant energy rules.

But relation and connection are not somewhere and sometimes, but everywhere and always. The divine order does not stop where their sight stops. The friendly power works on the same rules, in the next farm, and the next planet. But, where they have not experience, they run against it, and hurt themselves. Fate, then, is a name for facts not yet passed under the fire of thought; — for causes which are unpenetrated.

But every jet of chaos which threatens to exterminate us, is convertible by intellect into wholesome force. Fate is unpenetrated causes. The water drowns ship and sailor, like a grain of dust. But learn to swim, trim your bark, and the wave which drowned it will be cloven by it, and carry it, like its own foam, a plume and a power. The cold is inconsiderate of persons, tingles your blood, freezes a man like a dewdrop. But learn to skate, and the ice will give you a graceful, sweet, and poetic motion. The cold will brace your limbs and brain to genius, and make you foremost men of time. Cold and sea will train an imperial Saxon race, which nature cannot bear to lose, and, after cooping it up for a thousand years in yonder England, gives a hundred Englands, a hundred Mexicos. All the bloods it shall absorb and domineer: and more than Mexicos, — the secrets of water and steam, the spasms of electricity, the ductility of metals, the chariot of the air, the ruddered balloon, are awaiting you.

The annual slaughter from typhus far exceeds that of war; but right drainage destroys typhus. The plague in the sea-service from scurvy is healed by lemon-juice and other diets portable or procurable: the depopulation by cholera and small-pox is ended by drainage and vaccination; and every other pest is not less in the chain of cause and effect, and may be fought off. And, whilst art draws out the venom, it commonly extorts some benefit from the vanquished enemy. The mischievous torrent is taught to drudge for man: the wild beasts he makes useful for food, or dress, or labor; the chemic explosions are controlled like his watch. These are now the steeds on which he rides. Man moves in all modes, by legs of horses, by wings of wind, by steam, by gas of balloon, by electricity, and stands on tiptoe threatening to hunt the eagle in his own element. There 's nothing he will not make his carrier.

Steam was, till the other day, the devil which we dreaded. Every pot made by any human potter or brazier had a hole in its cover, to let off the enemy, lest he should lift pot and roof, and carry the house away. But the Marquis of Worcester, Watt, and Fulton bethought themselves, that, where was power, was not devil, but was God; that it must be availed of, and not by any means let off and wasted. Could he lift pots and roofs and houses so handily? he was the workman they were in search of. He could be used to lift away, chain, and compel other devils far more reluctant and dangerous, namely, cubic miles of earth, mountains, weight or resistance of water, machinery, and the labors of all men in the world; and time he shall lengthen, and shorten space.

It has not fared much otherwise with higher kinds of steam. The opinion of the million was the terror of the world, and it was attempted, either to dissipate it, by amusing nations, or to pile it over with strata of society, — a layer of soldiers; over that, a layer of lords; and a king on the top; with clamps and hoops of castles, garrisons, and police. But, sometimes, the religious principle would get in, and burst the hoops, and ride every mountain laid on top of it. The Fultons and Watts of politics, believing in unity, saw that it was a power, and, by satisfying it, (as justice satisfies everybody,) through a different disposition of society, — grouping it on a level, instead of piling it into a mountain, — they have contrived to make of this terror the most harmless and energetic form of a State.

Very odious, I confess, are the lessons of Fate. Who likes to have a dapper phrenologist pronouncing on his fortunes? Who likes to believe that he has hidden in his skull, spine, and pelvis, all the vices of a Saxon or Celtic race, which will be sure to pull him down — with what grandeur of hope and resolve he is fired, — into a selfish, huckstering, servile, dodging animal? A learned physician tells us, the fact is invariable with the Neapolitan, that, when mature, he assumes the forms of the unmistakable scoundrel. That is a little overstated, — but may pass.

But these are magazines and arsenals. A man must thank his defects, and stand in some terror of his talents. A transcendent talent draws so largely on his forces, as to lame him; a defect pays him revenues on the other side. The sufferance, which is the badge of the Jew, has made him, in these days, the ruler of the rulers of the earth. If Fate is ore and quarry, if evil is good in the making, if limitation is power that shall be, if calamities, oppositions, and weights are wings and means, — we are reconciled.

Fate involves the melioration. No statement of the Universe can have any soundness, which does not admit its ascending effort. The direction of the whole, and of the parts, is toward benefit, and in proportion to the health. Behind every individual closes organization: before him, opens liberty, — the Better, the Best. The first and worst races are dead. The second and imperfect races are dying out, or remain for the maturing of higher. In the latest race, in man, every generosity, every new perception, the love and praise he extorts from his fellows, are certificates of advance out of fate into freedom. Liberation of the will from the sheaths and clogs of organization which he has outgrown, is the end and aim of this world. Every calamity is a spur and valuable hint; and where his endeavors do not yet fully avail, they tell as tendency. The whole circle of animal life, — tooth against tooth, — devouring war, war for food, a yelp of pain and a grunt of triumph, until, at last, the whole menagerie, the whole chemical mass is mellowed and refined for higher use, — pleases at a sufficient perspective.

But to see how fate slides into freedom, and freedom into fate, observe how far the roots of every creature run, or find, if you can, a point where there is no thread of connection. Our life is consentaneous and far-related. This knot of nature is so well tied, that nobody was ever cunning enough to find the two ends. Nature is intricate, overlapped, interweaved, and endless. Christopher Wren said of the beautiful King's College chapel, "that, if anybody would tell him where to lay the first stone, he would build such another." But where shall we find the first atom in this house of man, which is all consent, inosculation, and balance of parts?

The web of relation is shown in *habitat*, shown in hybernation. When hybernation was observed, it was found, that, whilst some animals became torpid in winter, others were torpid in summer: hybernation then was a false name. The *long sleep* is not an effect of cold, but is regulated by the supply of food proper to the animal. It becomes torpid when the fruit or prey it lives on is not in season, and regains its activity when its food is ready.

Eyes are found in light; ears in auricular air; feet on land; fins in water; wings in air; and, each creature where it was meant to be, with a mutual fitness. Every zone has its own *Fauna*. There is adjustment between the animal and its food, its parasite, its enemy. Balances are kept. It is not allowed to diminish in numbers, nor to exceed. The like adjustments exist for man. His food is cooked, when he arrives; his coal in the pit; his house ventilated; the mud of the deluge dried; his companions arrived at the same hour, and awaiting him with love, concert, laughter, and tears. These are coarse adjustments, but the invisible are not less. There are more belongings to every creature than his air and his food. His instincts must be met, and he has predisposing power that bends and fits what is near him to his use. He is not possible until the invisible things are right for him, as well as the visible. Of what changes, then, in sky and earth, and in finer skies and earths, does the appearance of some Dante or Columbus apprise us!

How is this effected? Nature is no spendthrift, but takes the shortest way to her ends. As the general says to his soldiers, "If you want a fort, build a fort," so nature makes every creature do its own work and get its living, — is it planet, animal, or tree. The planet makes itself. The animal cell makes itself; — then, what it wants. Every creature — wren or dragon — shall make its own lair. As soon as there is life, there is self-direction, and absorbing and using of material. Life is freedom, — life in the direct ratio of its amount. You may be sure, the new-born man is not inert. Life works both voluntarily and supernaturally in its neighborhood. Do you suppose, he can be estimated by his weight in pounds, or, that he is contained in his skin, — this reaching, radiating, jaculating fellow? The smallest candle fills a mile with its rays, and the papillæ of a man run out to every star.

When there is something to be done, the world knows how to get it done. The vegetable eye makes leaf, pericarp, root, bark, or thorn, as the need is; the first cell converts itself into stomach, mouth, nose, or nail, according to the want: the world throws its life into a hero or a shepherd; and puts him where he is wanted. Dante and Columbus were Italians, in their time: they would be Russians or Americans to-day. Things ripen, new men come. The adaptation is not capricious. The ulterior aim, the purpose beyond itself, the correlation by which planets subside and crystallize, then animate beasts and men, will not stop, but will work into finer particulars, and from finer to finest.

The secret of the world is, the tie between person and event. Person makes event, and event person. The "times," "the age," what is that, but a few profound persons and a few active persons who epitomize the times? — Goethe, Hegel, Metternich, Adams, Calhoun, Guizot, Peel, Cobden, Kossuth, Rothschild, Astor, Brunel, and the rest. The same fitness must be presumed between a man and the time and event, as between the sexes, or between a race of animals and the food it eats, or the inferior races it uses. He thinks his fate alien, because the copula is hidden. But the soul contains the event that shall befall it, for the event is only the actualization of its thoughts; and what we pray to ourselves for is always granted. The event is the print of your form. It fits you like your skin. What each does is proper to him. Events are the children of his body and mind. We learn that the soul of Fate is the soul of us, as Hafiz sings,

> Alas! till now I had not known,
> My guide and fortune's guide are one.

All the toys that infatuate men, and which they play for, — houses, land, money, luxury, power, fame, are the selfsame thing, with a new gauze or two of illusion overlaid. And of all the drums and rattles by which men are made willing to have their heads broke, and are led out solemnly every morning to parade, — the most admirable is this by which we are brought to believe that events are arbitrary, and independent of actions. At the conjurer's, we detect the hair by which he moves his puppet, but we have not eyes sharp enough to descry the thread that ties cause and effect.

Nature magically suits the man to his fortunes, by making these the fruit of his character. Ducks take to the water, eagles to the sky, waders to the sea margin, hunters to the forest, clerks to counting-rooms, soldiers to the frontier. Thus events grow on the same stem with persons; are sub-persons. The pleasure of life is according to the man that lives it, and not according to the work or the place. Life is an ecstasy. We know what madness belongs to love, — what power to paint a vile object in hues of heaven. As insane persons are indifferent to their dress, diet, and other accommodations, and, as we do in dreams, with equanimity, the most absurd acts, so, a drop more of wine in our cup of life will reconcile us to strange company and work. Each creature puts forth from itself its own condition and sphere, as the slug sweats out its slimy house on the pear-leaf, and the woolly aphides on the apple perspire their own bed, and the fish its shell. In youth, we clothe ourselves with rainbows, and go as brave as the zodiac. In age, we put out another sort of perspiration, — gout, fever, rheumatism, caprice, doubt, fretting, and avarice.

A man's fortunes are the fruit of his character. A man's friends are his magnetisms. We go to Herodotus and Plutarch for examples of Fate ; but we are examples. "*Quisque suos patimur manes.*" The tendency of every man to enact all that is in his constitution is expressed in the old belief, that the efforts which we make to escape from our destiny only serve to lead us into it : and I have noticed, a man likes better to be complimented on his position, as the proof of the last or total excellence, than on his merits.

A man will see his character emitted in the events that seem to meet, but which exude from and accompany him. Events expand with the character. As once he found himself among toys, so now he plays a part in colossal systems, and his growth is declared in his ambition, his companions, and his performance. He looks like a piece of luck, but is a piece of causation ; the mosaic, angulated and ground to fit into the gap he fills. Hence in each town there is some man who is, in his brain and performance, an explanation of the tillage, production, factories, banks, churches, ways of living, and society, of that town. If you do not chance to meet him, all that you see will leave you a little puzzled : if you see him, it will become plain. We know in Massachusetts who built New Bedford, who built Lynn, Lowell, Lawrence, Clinton, Fitchburg, Holyoke, Portland, and many another noisy mart. Each of these men, if they were transparent, would seem to you not so much men, as walking cities, and, wherever you put them, they would build one.

History is the action and reaction of these two, — Nature and Thought ; two boys pushing each other on the curb-stone of the pavement. Everything is pusher or pushed : and matter and mind are in perpetual tilt and balance, so. Whilst the man is weak, the earth takes up to him. He plants his brain and affections. By and by he will take up the earth, and have his gardens and vineyards in the beautiful order and productiveness of his thought. Every solid in the universe is ready to become fluid on the approach of the mind, and the power to flux it is the measure of the mind. If the wall remain adamant, it accuses the want of thought. To a subtler force, it will stream into new forms, expressive of the character of the mind. What is the city in which we sit here, but an aggregate of incongruous materials, which have obeyed the will of some man? The granite was reluctant, but his hands were stronger, and it came. Iron was deep in the ground, and well combined with stone, but could not hide from his fires. Wood, lime, stuffs, fruits, gums, were dispersed over the earth and sea, in vain. Here they are, within reach of every man's day-labor, — what he wants of them. The whole world is the flux of matter over the wires of thought to the poles or points where it would build. The races of men rise out of the ground preoccupied with a thought which rules them, and divided into parties ready armed and angry to fight for this metaphysical abstraction. The quality of the thought differences the Egyptian and the Roman, the Austrian and the American. The men who come on the stage at one period are all found to be related to each other. Certain ideas are in the air. We are all impressionable, for we are made of them; all impressionable, but some more than others, and these first express them. This explains the curious contemporaneousness of inventions and discoveries. The truth is in the air, and the most impressionable brain will announce it first, but all will announce it a few minutes later. So women, as most susceptible, are the best index of the coming hour. So the great man, that is, the man most imbued with the spirit of the time, is the impressionable man, — of a fibre irritable and delicate, like iodine to light. He feels the infinitesimal attractions. His mind is righter than others, because he yields to a current so feeble as can be felt only by a needle delicately poised.

The correlation is shown in defects. Möller, in his Essay on Architecture, taught that the building which was fitted accurately to answer its end, would turn out to be beautiful, though beauty had not been intended. I find the like unity in human structures rather virulent and pervasive; that a crudity in the blood will appear in the argument; a hump in the shoulder will appear in the speech and handiwork. If his mind could be seen, the hump would be seen. If a man has a seesaw in his voice, it will run into his sentences, into his poem, into the structure of his fable, into his speculation, into his charity. And, as every man is hunted by his own demon, vexed by his own disease, this checks all his activity.

So each man, like each plant, has his parasites. A strong, astringent, bilious nature has more truculent enemies than the slugs and moths that fret my leaves. Such an one has curculios, borers, knife-worms: a swindler ate him first, then a client, then a quack, then smooth, plausible gentlemen, bitter and selfish as Moloch.

This correlation really existing can be divined. If the threads are there, thought can follow and show them. Especially when a soul is quick and docile; as Chaucer sings: —

"Or if the soul of proper kind
Be so perfect as men find,
That it wot what is to come,
And that he warneth all and some
Of every of their aventures,
By previsions or figures;
But that our flesh hath not might
It to understand aright
For it is warned too darkly."

Some people are made up of rhyme, coincidence, omen, periodicity, and presage: they meet the person they seek; what their companion prepares to say to them, they first say to him; and a hundred signs apprise them of what is about to befall.

Wonderful intricacy in the web, wonderful constancy in the design, this vagabond life admits. We wonder how the fly finds its mate, and yet year after year we find two men, two women, without legal or carnal tie, spend a great part of their best time within a few feet of each other. And the moral is, that what we seek we shall find; what we flee from flees from us; as Goethe said, "what we wish for in youth, comes in heaps on us in old age," too often cursed with the granting of our prayer: and hence the high caution, that, since we are sure of having what we wish, we beware to ask only for high things.

One key, one solution to the mysteries of human condition, one solution to the old knots of fate, freedom and foreknowledge, exists, the propounding, namely, of the double consciousness. A man must ride alternately on the horses of his private and his public nature, as the equestrians in the circus throw themselves nimbly from horse to horse, or plant one foot on the back of one, and the other foot on the back of the other. So when a man is the victim of his fate, has sciatica in his loins, and cramp in his mind; a club-foot and a club in his wit; a sour face, and a selfish temper; a strut in his gait, and a conceit in his affection; or is ground to powder by the vice of his race; he is to rally on his relation to the Universe, which his ruin benefits. Leaving the demon who suffers, he is to take sides with the Deity who secures universal benefit by his pain.

To offset the drag of temperament and race, which pulls down, learn this lesson, namely, that by the cunning co-presence of two elements, which is throughout nature, whatever lames or paralyzes you, draws in with it the divinity, in some form, to repay. A good intention clothes itself with sudden power. When a god wishes to ride, any chip or pebble will bud and shoot out winged feet, and serve him for a horse.

Let us build altars to the Blessed Unity which holds nature and souls in perfect solution, and compels every atom to serve an universal end. I do not wonder at a snow-flake, a shell, a summer landscape, or the glory of the stars; but at the necessity of beauty under which the universe lies; that all is and must be pictorial; that the rainbow, and the curve of the horizon, and the arch of the blue vault, are only results from the organism of the eye. There is no need for foolish amateurs to fetch me to admire a garden of flowers, or a sun-gilt cloud, or a waterfall, when I cannot look without seeing splendor and grace. How idle to choose a random sparkle here or there, when the indwelling necessity plants the rose of beauty on the brow of chaos, and discloses the central intention of Nature to be harmony and joy.

Let us build altars to the Beautiful Necessity. If we thought men were free in the sense, that, in a single exception one fantastical will could prevail over the law of things, it were all one as if a child's hand could pull down the sun. If, in the least particular, one could derange the order of nature, — who would accept the gift of life?

Let us build altars to the Beautiful Necessity, which secures that all is made of one piece; that plaintiff and defendant, friend and enemy, animal and planet, food and eater, are of one kind. In astronomy is vast space, but no foreign system; in geology, vast time, but the same laws as to-day

Why should we be afraid of Nature, which is no other than "philosophy and theology embodied"? Why should we fear to be crushed by savage elements, we who are made up of the same elements? Let us build to the Beautiful Necessity, which makes man brave in believing that he cannot shun a danger that is appointed, nor incur one that is not; to the Necessity which rudely or softly educates him to the perception that there are no contingencies; that Law rules throughout existence, a Law which is not intelligent but intelligence, — not personal nor impersonal, — it disdains words and passes understanding; it dissolves persons; it vivifies nature; yet solicits the pure in heart to draw on all its omnipotence.

II.

POWER.

His tongue was framed to music,
And his hand was armed with skill,
His face was the mould of beauty,
And his heart the throne of will.

POWER.

THERE is not yet any inventory of a man's faculties, any more than a bible of his opinions. Who shall set a limit to the influence of a human being? There are men, who, by their sympathetic attractions, carry nations with them, and lead the activity of the human race. And if there be such a tie, that, wherever the mind of man goes, nature will accompany him, perhaps there are men whose magnetisms are of that force to draw material and elemental powers, and, where they appear, immense instrumentalities organize around them. Life is a search after power; and this is an element with which the world is so saturated, — there is no chink or crevice in which it is not lodged, — that no honest seeking goes unrewarded. A man should prize events and possessions as the ore in which this fine mineral is found; and he can well afford to let events and possessions, and the breath of the body go, if their value has been added to him in the shape of power. If he have secured the elixir, he can spare the wide gardens from which it was distilled. A cultivated man, wise to know and bold to perform, is the end to which nature works, and the education of the will is the flowering and result of all this geology and astronomy.

All successful men have agreed in one thing, — they were *causationists*. They believed that things went not by luck, but by law; that there was not a weak or a cracked link in the chain that joins the first and last of things. A belief in causality, or strict connection between every pulse-beat and the principle of being, and, in consequence, belief in compensation, or, that nothing is got for nothing, — characterizes all valuable minds, and must control every effort that is made by an industrious one. The most valiant men are the best believers in the tension of the laws. "All the great captains," said

Bonaparte, "have performed vast achievements by conforming with the rules of the art, — by adjusting efforts to obstacles."

The key to the age may be this, or that, or the other, as the young orators describe; the key to all ages is — Imbecility; imbecility in the vast majority of men, at all times, and, even in heroes, in all but certain eminent moments; victims of gravity, custom, and fear. This gives force to the strong, — that the multitude have no habit of self-reliance or original action.

We must reckon success a constitutional trait. Courage, — the old physicians taught (and their meaning holds, if their physiology is a little mythical), — courage, or the degree of life, is as the degree of circulation of the blood in the arteries. "During passion, anger, fury, trials of strength, wrestling, fighting, a large amount of blood is collected in the arteries, the maintenance of bodily strength requiring it, and but little is sent into the veins. This condition is constant with intrepid persons." Where the arteries hold their blood, is courage and adventure possible. Where they pour it unrestrained into the veins, the spirit is low and feeble. For performance of great mark, it needs extraordinary health. If Eric is in robust health, and has slept well, and is at the top of his condition, and thirty years old, at his departure from Greenland, he will steer west, and his ships will reach Newfoundland. But take out Eric, and put in a stronger and bolder man, — Biorn, or Thorfin, — and the ships will, with just as much ease, sail six hundred, one thousand, fifteen hundred miles farther, and reach Labrador and New England. There is no chance in results. With adults, as with children, one class enter cordially into the game, and whirl with the whirling world; the others have cold hands, and remain bystanders; or are only dragged in by the humor and vivacity of those who can carry a dead weight. The first wealth is health. Sickness is poor-spirited, and cannot serve any one: it must husband its resources to live. But health or fulness answers its own ends, and has to spare, runs over, and inundates the neighborhoods and creeks of other men's necessities.

All power is of one kind, a sharing of the nature of the world. The mind that is parallel with the laws of nature will be in the current of events, and strong with their strength. One man is made of the same stuff of which events are made; is in sympathy with the course of things; can predict it. Whatever befalls, befalls him first; so that he is equal to whatever shall happen. A man who knows men, can talk well on politics, trade, law, war, religion. For, everywhere, men are led in the same manners.

The advantage of a strong pulse is not to be supplied by any labor, art, or concert. It is like the climate, which easily rears a crop, which no glass, or irrigation, or tillage, or manures, can elsewhere rival. It is like the opportunity of a city like New York, or Constantinople, which needs no diplomacy to force capital or genius or labor to it. They come of themselves, as the waters flow to it. So a broad, healthy, massive understanding seems to lie on the shore of unseen rivers, of unseen oceans, which are covered with barks, that, night and day, are drifted to this point. That is poured into its lap, which other men lie plotting for. It is in everybody's secret; anticipates everybody's discovery; and if it do not command every fact of the genius and the scholar, it is because it is large and sluggish, and does not think them worth the exertion which you do.

This affirmative force is in one, and is not in another, as one horse has the spring in him, and another in the whip. "On the neck of the young man," said Hafiz, "sparkles no gem so gracious as enterprise." Import into any stationary district, as into an old Dutch population in New York or Pennsylvania, or among the planters of Virginia, a colony of hardy Yankees, with seething brains, heads full of steam-hammer, pulley, crank, and toothed wheel, — and everything begins to shine with values. What enhancement to all the water and land in England, is the arrival of James Watt or Brunel! In every company, there is not only the active and passive sex, but in both men and women, a deeper and more important *sex of mind*, namely, the inventive or creative class of both men and women, and the uninventive or accepting class. Each *plus* man represents his set, and, if he have the accidental advantage of personal ascendency, — which implies neither more nor less of talent, but merely the temperamental or taming eye of a soldier or a schoolmaster, (which one has, and one has not, as one has a black moustache and one a blond,) then quite easily and without envy or resistance, all his coadjutors and feeders will admit his right to absorb them. The merchant works by book-keeper and cashier; the lawyer's authorities are hunted up by clerks; the geologist reports the surveys of his subalterns; Commander Wilkes appropriates the results of all the naturalists attached to the Expedition; Thorwaldsen's statue is finished by stone-cutters; Dumas has journeymen; and Shakespeare was theatre-manager, and used the labor of many young men, as well as the playbooks.

There is always room for a man of force, and he makes room for many. Society is a troop of thinkers, and the best heads among them take the best places. A feeble man can see the farms that are fenced and tilled, the houses that are built. The strong man sees the possible houses and farms. His eye makes estates, as fast as the sun breeds clouds.

When a new boy comes into school, when a man travels, and encounters strangers every day, or, when into an old club a new comer is domesticated, that happens which befalls, when a strange ox is driven into a pen or pasture where cattle are kept; there is at once a trial of strength between the best pair of horns and the new comer, and it is settled thenceforth which is the leader. So now, there is a measuring of strength, very courteous, but decisive, and an acquiescence thenceforward when these two meet. Each reads his fate in the other's eyes. The weaker party finds, that none of his information or wit quite fits the occasion. He thought he knew this or that: he finds that he omitted to learn the end of it. Nothing that he knows will quite hit the mark, whilst all the rival's arrows are good, and well thrown. But if he knew all the facts in the encyclopædia, it would not help him: for this is an affair of presence of mind, of attitude, of aplomb: the opponent has the sun and wind, and, in every cast, the choice of weapon and mark; and, when he himself is matched with some other antagonist, his own shafts fly well and hit. 'T is a question of stomach and constitution. The second man is as good as the first, — perhaps better; but has not stoutness or stomach, as the first has, and so his wit seems over-fine or under-fine.

Health is good, — power, life, that resists disease, poison, and all enemies, and is conservative, as well as creative. Here is question, every spring, whether to graft with wax, or whether with clay; whether to whitewash or to potash, or to prune; but the one point is the thrifty tree. A good tree, that agrees with the soil, will grow in spite of blight, or bug, or pruning, or neglect, by night and by day, in all weathers and all treatments. Vivacity, leadership, must be had, and we are not allowed to be nice in choosing. We must fetch the pump with dirty water, if clean cannot be had. If we will make bread, we must have contagion, yeast, emptyings, or what not, to induce fermentation into the dough: as the torpid artist seeks inspiration at any cost, by virtue or by vice, by friend or by fiend, by prayer or by wine. And we have a certain instinct, that where is great amount of life, though gross and peccant, it has its own checks and purifications, and will be found at last in harmony with moral laws.

We watch in children with pathetic interest, the degree in which they possess recuperative force. When they are hurt by us, or by each other, or go to the bottom of the class, or miss the annual prizes, or are beaten in the game, — if they lose heart, and remember the mischance in their chamber at home, they have a serious check. But if they have the buoyancy and resistance that preoccupies them with new interest in the new moment, — the wounds cicatrize, and the fibre is the tougher for the hurt.

One comes to value this *plus* health, when he sees that all difficulties vanish before it. A timid man listening to the alarmists in Congress, and in the newspapers, and observing the profligacy of party, — sectional interests urged with a fury which shuts its eyes to consequences, with a mind made up to desperate extremities, ballot in one hand, and rifle in the other, — might easily believe that he and his country have seen their best days, and he hardens himself the best he can against the coming ruin. But, after this has been foretold with equal confidence fifty times, and government six per cents have not declined a quarter of a mill, he discovers that the enormous elements of strength which are here in play make our politics unimportant. Personal power, freedom, and the resources of nature strain every faculty of every citizen. We prosper with such vigor, that, like thrifty trees, which grow in spite of ice, lice, mice, and borers, so we do not suffer from the profligate swarms that fatten on the national treasury. The huge animals nourish huge parasites, and the rancor of the disease attests the strength of the constitution. The same energy in the Greek *Demos* drew the remark, that the evils of popular government appear greater than they are; there is compensation for them in the spirit and energy it awakens. The rough-and-ready style which belongs to a people of sailors, foresters, farmers, and mechanics, has its advantages. Power educates the potentate. As long as our people quote English standards they dwarf their own proportions. A Western lawyer of eminence said to me he wished it were a penal offence to bring an English law-book into a court in this country, so pernicious had he found in his experience our deference to English precedent. The very word 'commerce' has only an English meaning, and is pinched to the cramp exigencies of English experience. The commerce of rivers, the commerce of railroads, and who knows but the commerce of air-balloons, must add an American extension to the pond-hole of admiralty. As long as our people quote English standards, they will miss the sovereignty of power; but let these rough riders, — legislators in shirt-sleeves, — Hoosier, Sucker, Wolverine, Badger, — or whatever hard head Arkansas, Oregon, or Utah sends, half orator, half assassin, to represent its wrath and cupidity at Washington, — let these drive as they may; and the disposition of territories and public lands, the necessity of balancing and keeping at bay the snarling majorities of German, Irish, and of native millions, will bestow promptness, address, and reason, at last, on our buffalo-hunter, and authority and majesty of manners. The instinct of the people is right. Men expect from good whigs, put into office by the respectability of the country, much less skill to deal with Mexico, Spain, Britain, or with our own malcontent members, than from some strong transgressor, like Jefferson, or Jackson, who first conquers his own government, and then uses the same genius to conquer the foreigner. The senators who dissented from Mr. Polk's Mexican war were not those who knew better, but those who, from political position, could afford it; not Webster, but Benton and Calhoun.

This power, to be sure, is not clothed in satin. 'T is the power of Lynch law, of soldiers and pirates; and it bullies the peaceable and loyal. But it brings its own antidote; and here is my point, — that all kinds of power usually emerge at the same time; good energy, and bad; power of mind, with physical health; the ecstasies of devotion, with the exasperations of debauchery. The same elements are always present, only sometimes these conspicuous, and sometimes those; what was yesterday foreground, being to-day background, — what was surface, playing now a not less effective part as basis. The longer the drought lasts, the more is the atmosphere surcharged with water. The faster the ball falls to the sun, the force to fly off is by so much augmented. And, in morals, wild liberty breeds iron conscience; natures with great impulses have great resources, and return from far. In politics, the sons of democrats will be whigs; whilst red republicanism, in the father, is a spasm of nature to engender an intolerable tyrant in the next age. On the other hand, conservatism, ever more timorous and narrow, disgusts the children, and drives them for a mouthful of fresh air into radicalism.

Those who have most of this coarse energy, — the 'bruisers,' who have run the gauntlet of caucus and tavern through the county or the state, have their own vices, but they have the good-nature of strength and courage. Fierce and unscrupulous, they are usually frank and direct, and above falsehood. Our politics fall into bad hands, and churchmen and men of refinement, it seems agreed, are not fit persons to send to Congress. Politics is a deleterious profession, like some poisonous handicrafts. Men in power have no opinions, but may be had cheap for any opinion, for any purpose, — and if it be only a question between the most civil and the most forcible, I lean to the last. These Hoosiers and Suckers are really better than the snivelling opposition. Their wrath is at least of a bold and manly cast. They see, against the unanimous declarations of the people, how much crime the people will bear; they proceed from step to step, and they have calculated but too justly upon their Excellencies, the New England governors and upon their Honors, the New England legislators. The messages of the governors and the resolutions of the legislatures are a proverb for expressing a sham virtuous indignation, which, in the course of events, is sure to be belied.

In trade, also, this energy usually carries a trace of ferocity. Philanthropic and religious bodies do not commonly make their executive officers out of saints. The communities hitherto founded by Socialists, — the Jesuits, the Port-Royalists, the American communities at New Harmony, at Brook Farm, at Zoar, are only possible, by installing Judas as steward. The rest of the offices may be filled by good burgesses. The pious and charitable proprietor has a foreman not quite so pious and charitable. The most amiable of country gentlemen has a certain pleasure in the teeth of the bulldog which guards his orchard. Of the Shaker society, it was formerly a sort of proverb in the country, that they always sent the devil to market. And in representations of the Deity, painting, poetry, and popular religion have ever drawn the wrath from Hell. It is an esoteric doctrine of society, that a little wickedness is good to make muscle; as if conscience were not good for hands and legs, as if poor decayed formalists of law and order cannot run like wild goats, wolves, and conies; that, as there is a use in medicine for poisons, so the world cannot move without rogues; that public spirit and the ready hand are as well found among the malignants. 'T is not very rare, the coincidence of sharp private and political practice, with public spirit, and good neighborhood.

I knew a burly Boniface who for many years kept a public-house in one of our rural capitals. He was a knave whom the town could ill spare. He was a social, vascular creature, grasping and selfish. There was no crime which he did not or could not commit. But he made good friends of the selectmen, served them with his best chop, when they supped at his house, and also with his honor the Judge, he was very cordial, grasping his hand. He introduced all the fiends, male and female, into the town, and united in his person the functions of bully, incendiary, swindler, bar-keeper, and burglar. He girdled the trees, and cut off the horses' tails of the temperance people, in the night. He led the 'rummies' and radicals in town-meeting with a speech. Meantime, he was civil, fat, and easy, in his house, and precisely the most public-spirited citizen. He was active in getting the roads repaired and planted with shade-trees; he subscribed for the fountains, the gas, and the telegraph; he introduced the new horse-rake, the new scraper, the baby-jumper, and what not, that Connecticut sends to the admiring citizens. He did this the easier, that the pedler stopped at his house, and paid his keeping, by setting up his new trap on the landlord's premises.

Whilst thus the energy for originating and executing work deforms itself by excess, and so our axe chops off our own fingers, — this evil is not without remedy. All the elements whose aid man calls in will sometimes become his masters, especially those of most subtle force. Shall he, then, renounce steam, fire, and electricity, or shall he learn to deal with them? The rule for this whole class of agencies is, — all *plus* is good; only put it in the right place.

Men of this surcharge of arterial blood cannot live on nuts, herb-tea, and elegies; cannot read novels, and play whist; cannot satisfy all their wants at the Thursday Lecture, or the Boston Athenæum. They pine for adventure, and must go to Pike's Peak; had rather die by the hatchet of a Pawnee, than sit all day and every day at a counting-room desk. They are made for war, for the sea, for mining, hunting, and clearing; for hair-breadth adventures, huge risks, and the joy of eventful living. Some men cannot endure an hour of calm at sea. I remember a poor Malay cook, on board a Liverpool packet, who, when the wind blew a gale, could not contain his joy;

"Blow!" he cried, "me do tell you, blow!" Their friends and governors must see that some vent for their explosive complexion is provided. The roisters who are destined for infamy at home, if sent to Mexico, will "cover you with glory," and come back heroes and generals. There are Oregons, Californias, and Exploring Expeditions enough appertaining to America, to find them in files to gnaw, and in crocodiles to eat. The young English are fine animals, full of blood, and when they have no wars to breathe their riotous valors in, they seek for travels as dangerous as war, diving into Maelstroms; swimming Hellesponts; wading up the snowy Himmaleh; hunting lion, rhinoceros, elephant, in South Africa; gypsying with Borrow in Spain and Algiers; riding alligators in South America with Waterton; utilizing Bedouin, Sheik, and Pacha, with Layard; yachting among the icebergs of Lancaster Sound; peeping into craters on the equator; or running on the creases of Malays in Borneo.

The excess of virility has the same importance in general history, as in private and industrial life. Strong race or strong individual rests at last on natural forces, which are best in the savage, who, like the beasts around him, is still in reception of the milk from the teats of Nature. Cut off the connection between any of our works, and this aboriginal source, and the work is shallow. The people lean on this, and the mob is not quite so bad an argument as we sometimes say, for it has this good side. "March without the people," said a French deputy from the tribune, "and you march into night: their instincts are a finger-pointing of providence, always turned toward real benefit. But when you espouse an Orleans party, or a Bourbon, or a Montalembert party, or any other but an organic party, though you mean well, you have a personality instead of a principle, which will inevitably drag you into a corner."

The best anecdotes of this force are to be had from savage life, in explorers, soldiers, and buccaneers. But who cares for fallings-out of assassins, and fights of bears, or grindings of icebergs? Physical force has no value, where there is nothing else. Snow in snow-banks, fire in volcanoes and solfataras is cheap. The luxury of ice is in tropical countries, and midsummer days. The luxury of fire is, to have a little on our hearth: and of electricity, not volleys of the charged cloud, but the manageable stream on the battery-wires. So of spirit, or energy; the rests or remains of it in the civil and moral man are worth all the cannibals in the Pacific.

In history, the great moment is, when the savage is just ceasing to be a savage, with all his hairy Pelasgic strength directed on his opening sense of beauty: — and you have Pericles and Phidias, — not yet passed over into the Corinthian civility. Everything good in nature and the world is in that moment of transition, when the swarthy juices still flow plentifully from nature, but their astringency or acridity is got out by ethics and humanity.

The triumphs of peace have been in some proximity to war. Whilst the hand was still familiar with the sword-hilt, whilst the habits of the camp were still visible in the port and complexion of the gentleman, his intellectual power culminated; the compression and tension of these stern conditions is a training for the finest and softest arts, and can rarely be compensated in tranquil times, except by some analogous vigor drawn from occupations as hardy as war.

We say that success is constitutional; depends on a *plus* condition of mind and body, on power of work, on courage; that it is of main efficacy in carrying on the world, and, though rarely found in the right state for an article of commerce, but oftener in the supersaturate or excess, which makes it dangerous and destructive, yet it cannot be spared, and must be had in that form, and absorbents provided to take off its edge.

The affirmative class monopolize the homage of mankind. They originate and execute all the great feats. What a force was coiled up in the skull of Napoleon! Of the sixty thousand men making his army at Eylau, it seems some thirty thousand were thieves and burglars. The men whom, in peaceful communities, we hold if we can, with iron at their legs, in prisons, under the muskets of sentinels, this man dealt with, hand to hand, dragged them to their duty, and won his victories by their bayonets.

This aboriginal might gives a surprising pleasure when it appears under conditions of supreme refinement, as in the proficients in high art. When Michel Angelo was forced to paint the Sistine Chapel in fresco, of which art he knew nothing, he went down into the Pope's gardens behind the Vatican, and with a shovel dug out ochres, red and yellow, mixed them with glue and water with his own hands, and having, after many trials, at last suited himself, climbed his ladders, and painted away, week after week, month after month, the sibyls and prophets. He surpassed his successors in rough vigor, as much as in purity of intellect and refinement. He was not crushed by his one picture left unfinished at last. Michel was wont to draw his figures first in skeleton, then to clothe them with flesh, and lastly to drape them. "Ah!" said a brave painter to me, thinking on these things, "if a man has failed, you will find he has dreamed instead of working. There is no way to success in our art, but to take off your coat, grind paint, and work like a digger on the railroad, all day and every day."

Success goes thus invariably with a certain *plus* or positive power: an ounce of power must balance an ounce of weight. And, though a man cannot return into his mother's womb, and be born with new amounts of vivacity, yet there are two economies, which are the best *succedanea* which the case admits. The first is, the stopping off decisively our miscellaneous activity, and concentrating our force on one or a few points; as the gardener, by severe pruning, forces the sap of the tree into one or two vigorous limbs, instead of suffering it to spindle into a sheaf of twigs.

"Enlarge not thy destiny," said the oracle: "endeavor not to do more than is given thee in charge." The one prudence in life is concentration; the one evil is dissipation: and it makes no difference whether our dissipations are coarse or fine; property and its cares, friends, and a social habit, or politics, or music, or feasting. Everything is good which takes away one plaything and delusion more, and drives us home to add one stroke of faithful work. Friends, books, pictures, lower duties, talents, flatteries, hopes, — all are distractions which cause oscillations in our giddy balloon, and make a good poise and a straight course impossible. You must elect your work; you shall take what your brain can, and drop all the rest. Only so, can that amount of vital force accumulate, which can make the step from knowing to doing. No matter how much faculty of idle seeing a man has, the step from knowing to doing is rarely taken. 'T is a step out of a chalk circle of imbecility into fruitfulness. Many an artist lacking this, lacks all: he sees the masculine Angelo or Cellini with despair. He, too, is up to Nature and the First Cause in his thought. But the spasm to collect and swing his whole being into one act, he has not. The poet Campbell said, that "a man accustomed to work was equal to any achievement he resolved on, and, that, for himself, necessity, not inspiration, was the prompter of his muse."

Concentration is the secret of strength in politics, in war, in trade, in short, in all management of human affairs. One of the high anecdotes of the world is the reply of Newton to the inquiry, "how he had been able to achieve his discoveries?" "By always intending my mind." Or if you will have a text from politics, take this from Plutarch: "There was, in the whole city, but one street in which Pericles was ever seen, the street which led to the market-place and the council-house. He declined all invitations to banquets, and all gay assemblies and company. During the whole period of his administration, he never dined at the table of a friend." Or if we seek an example from trade, — "I hope," said a good man to Rothschild, "your children are not too fond of money and business: I am sure you would not wish that." "I am sure I should wish that: I wish them to give mind, soul, heart, and body to business, — that is the way to be happy. It requires a great deal of boldness and a great deal of caution to make a great fortune, and when you have got it, it requires ten times as much wit to keep it. If I were to listen to all the projects proposed to me, I should ruin myself very soon. Stick to one business, young man. Stick to your brewery (he said this to young Buxton), and you will be the great brewer of London. Be brewer, and banker, and merchant, and manufacturer, and you will soon be in the Gazette."

Many men are knowing, many are apprehensive and tenacious, but they do not rush to a decision. But in our flowing affairs a decision must be made, — the best, if you can; but any is better than none. There are twenty ways of going to a point, and one is the shortest; but set out at once on one. A man who has that presence of mind which can bring to him on the instant all he knows, is worth for action a dozen men who know as much, but can only bring it to light slowly. The good Speaker in the House is not the man who knows the theory of parliamentary tactics, but the man who decides off-hand. The good judge is not he who does hair-splitting justice to every allegation, but who, aiming at substantial justice, rules something intelligible for the guidance of suitors. The good lawyer is not the man who has an eye to every side and angle of contingency, and qualifies all his qualifications, but who throws himself on your part so heartily, that he can get you out of a scrape. Dr. Johnson said, in one of his flowing sentences: "Miserable beyond all names of wretchedness is that unhappy pair, who are doomed to reduce beforehand to the principles of abstract reason all the details of each domestic day. There are cases where little can be said, and much must be done."

The second substitute for temperament is drill, the power of use and routine. The hack is a better roadster than the Arab barb. In chemistry, the galvanic stream, slow, but continuous, is equal in power to the electric spark, and is, in our arts, a better agent. So in human action, against the spasm of energy, we offset the continuity of drill. We spread the same amount of force over much time, instead of condensing it into a moment. 'T is the same ounce of gold here in a ball, and there in a leaf. At West Point, Col. Buford, the chief engineer, pounded with a hammer on the trunnions of a cannon, until he broke them off. He fired a piece of ordnance some hundred times in swift succession, until it burst. Now which stroke broke the trunnion? Every stroke. Which blast burst the piece? Every blast. "*Diligence passe sens,*" Henry VIII. was wont to say, or, great is drill. John Kemble said, that the worst provincial company of actors would go through a play better than the best amateur company. Basil Hall likes to show that the worst regular troops will beat the best volunteers. Practice is nine tenths. A course of mobs is good practice for orators. All the great speakers were bad speakers at first. Stumping it through England for seven years made Cobden a consummate debater. Stumping it through New England for twice seven trained Wendell Phillips. The way to learn German, is, to read the same dozen pages over and over a hundred times, till you know every word and particle in them and can pronounce and repeat them by heart. No genius can recite a ballad at first reading, so well as mediocrity can at the fifteenth or twentieth reading. The rule for hospitality and Irish 'help,' is, to have the same dinner every day throughout the year. At last, Mrs. O'Shaughnessy learns to cook it to a nicety, the host learns to carve it, and the guests are well served. A humorous friend of mine thinks, that the reason why Nature is so perfect in her art, and gets up such inconceivably fine sunsets, is, that she has learned how, at last, by dint of doing the same thing so very often. Cannot one converse better on a topic on which he has experience, than on one which is new? Men whose opinion is valued on 'Change, are only such as have a special experience, and off that ground their opinion is not valuable. "More are made good by exercitation, than by nature," said Democritus. The friction in nature is so enormous that we cannot spare any power. It is not question to express our thought, to elect our way, but to overcome resistances of the medium and material in everything we do. Hence the use of drill, and the worthlessness of amateurs to cope with practitioners. Six hours every day at the piano, only to give facility of touch; six hours a day at painting, only to give command of the odious materials, oil, ochres, and brushes. The masters say that they know a master in music, only by seeing the pose of the hands on the keys;— so difficult and vital an act is the command of the instrument. To have learned the use of the tools, by thousands of manipulations; to have learned the arts of reckoning, by endless adding and dividing, is the power of the mechanic and the clerk.

I remarked in England, in confirmation of a frequent experience at home, that, in literary circles, the men of trust and consideration, bookmakers, editors, university deans and professors, bishops, too, were by no means men of the largest literary talent, but usually of a low and ordinary intellectuality, with a sort of mercantile activity and working talent. Indifferent hacks and mediocrities tower, by pushing their forces to a lucrative point, or by working power, over multitudes of superior men, in Old as in New England.

I have not forgotten that there are sublime considerations which limit the value of talent and superficial success. We can easily overpraise the vulgar hero. There are sources on which we have not drawn. I know what I abstain from. I adjourn what I have to say on this topic to the chapters on Culture and Worship. But this force or spirit, being the means relied on by Nature for bringing the work of the day about,— as far as we attach importance to household life, and the prizes of the world, we must respect that. And I hold, that an economy may be applied to it; it is as much a subject of exact law and arithmetic as fluids and gases are; it may be husbanded, or wasted; every man is efficient only as he is a container or vessel of this force, and never was any signal act or achievement in history, but by this expenditure. This is not gold, but the gold-maker; not the fame, but the exploit.

If these forces and this husbandry are within reach of our will, and the laws of them can be read, we infer that all success, and all conceivable benefit for man, is also, first or last, within his reach, and has its own sublime economies by which it may be attained. The world is mathematical, and has no casualty, in all its vast and flowing curve. Success has no more eccentricity, than the gingham and muslin we weave in our mills. I know no more affecting lesson to our busy, plotting New England brains, than to go into one of the factories with which we have lined all the water-courses in the States. A man hardly knows how much he is a machine, until he begins to make telegraph, loom, press, and locomotive, in his own image. But in these, he is forced to leave out his follies and hindrances, so that when we go to the mill, the machine is more moral than we. Let a man dare go to a loom, and see if he be equal to it. Let machine confront machine, and see how they come out. The world-mill is more complex than the calico-mill, and the architect stooped less. In the gingham-mill, a broken thread or a shred spoils the web through a piece of a hundred yards, and is traced back to the girl that wove it, and lessens her wages. The stockholder, on being shown this, rubs his hands with delight. Are you so cunning, Mr. Profitloss, and do you expect to swindle your master and employer, in the web you weave? A day is a more magnificent cloth than any muslin, the mechanism that makes it is infinitely cunninger, and you shall not conceal the sleezy, fraudulent, rotten hours you have slipped into the piece, nor fear that any honest thread, or straighter steel, or more inflexible shaft, will not testify in the web.

III.

WEALTH.

Who shall tell what did befall,
Far away in time, when once,
Over the lifeless ball,
Hung idle stars and suns?
What god the element obeyed?
Wings of what wind the lichen bore,
Wafting the puny seeds of power,
Which, lodged in rock, the rock abrade?
And well the primal pioneer
Knew the strong task to it assigned
Patient through Heaven's enormous year
To build in matter home for mind.
From air the creeping centuries drew
The matted thicket low and wide,
This must the leaves of ages strew
The granite slab to clothe and hide,
Ere wheat can wave its golden pride.
What smiths, and in what furnace, rolled
(In dizzy æons dim and mute
The reeling brain can ill compute)
Copper and iron, lead, and gold?
What oldest star the fame can save
Of races perishing to pave
The planet with a floor of lime?
Dust is their pyramid and mole:
Who saw what ferns and palms were pressed
Under the tumbling mountain's breast,
In the safe herbal of the coal?
But when the quarried means were piled,
All is waste and worthless, till
Arrives the wise selecting will,
And, out of slime and chaos, Wit
Draws the threads of fair and fit.
Then temples rose, and towns, and marts,
The shop of toil, the hall of arts;
Then flew the sail across the seas
To feed the North from tropic trees;
The storm-wind wove, the torrent span,
Where they were bid the rivers ran;
New slaves fulfilled the poet's dream,
Galvanic wire, strong-shouldered steam.
Then docks were built, and crops were stored,
And ingots added to the hoard.
But, though light-headed man forget,
Remembering Matter pays her debt:
Still, through her motes and masses, draw
Electric thrills and ties of Law,
Which bind the strengths of Nature wild
To the conscience of a child.

WEALTH.

AS soon as a stranger is introduced into any company, one of the first questions which all wish to have answered, is, How does that man get his living? And with reason. He is no whole man until he knows how to earn a blameless livelihood. Society is barbarous, until every industrious man can get his living without dishonest customs.

Every man is a consumer, and ought to be a producer. He fails to make his place good in the world, unless he not only pays his debt, but also adds something to the common wealth. Nor can he do justice to his genius, without making some larger demand on the world than a bare subsistence. He is by constitution expensive, and needs to be rich.

Wealth has its source in applications of the mind to nature, from the rudest strokes of spade and axe, up to the last secrets of art. Intimate ties subsist between thought and all production; because a better order is equivalent to vast amounts of brute labor. The forces and the resistances are Nature's, but the mind acts in bringing things from where they abound to where they are wanted; in wise combining; in directing the practice of the useful arts, and in the creation of finer values, by fine art, by eloquence, by song or the reproductions of memory. Wealth is in applications of mind to nature; and the art of getting rich consists not in industry, much less in saving, but in a better order, in timeliness, in being at the right spot. One man has stronger arms, or longer legs; another sees by the course of streams, and growth of markets, where land will be wanted, makes a clearing to the river, goes to sleep, and wakes up rich. Steam is no stronger now, than it was a hundred years ago; but is put to better use. A clever fellow was acquainted with the expansive force of steam; he also saw the wealth of wheat and grass rotting in Michigan. Then he cunningly screws on the steam-pipe to the wheat-crop. Puff now, O Steam! The steam puffs and expands as before, but this time it is dragging all Michigan at its back to hungry New York and hungry England. Coal lay in ledges under the ground since the Flood, until a laborer with pick and windlass brings it to the surface. We may well call it black diamonds. Every basket is power and civilization. For coal is a portable climate. It carries the heat of the tropics to Labrador and the polar circle; and it is the means of transporting itself whithersoever it is wanted. Watt and Stephenson whispered in the ear of mankind their secret, that *a half-ounce of coal will draw two tons a mile*, and coal carries coal, by rail and by boat, to make Canada as warm as Calcutta, and with its comfort brings its industrial power.

When the farmer's peaches are taken from under the tree, and carried into town, they have a new look, and a hundredfold value over the fruit which grew on the same bough, and lies fulsomely on the ground. The craft of the merchant is this bringing a thing from where it abounds, to where it is costly.

Wealth begins in a tight roof that keeps the rain and wind out; in a good pump that yields you plenty of sweet water; in two suits of clothes, so to change your dress when you are wet; in dry sticks to burn; in a good double-wick lamp; and three meals; in a horse, or a locomotive, to cross the land; in a boat to cross the sea; in tools to work with; in books to read; and so, in giving, on all sides, by tolls and auxiliaries, the greatest possible extension to our powers, as if it added feet, and hands, and eyes, and blood, length to the day, and knowledge, and good-will.

Wealth begins with these articles of necessity. And here we must recite the iron law which Nature thunders in these northern climates. First, she requires that each man should feed himself. If, happily, his fathers have left him no inheritance, he must go to work, and by making his wants less, or his gains more, he must draw himself out of that state of pain and insult in which she forces the beggar to lie. She gives him no rest until this is done; she starves, taunts, and torments him, takes away warmth, laughter, sleep, friends, and daylight, until he has fought his way to his own loaf. Then, less peremptorily, but still with sting enough, she urges him to the acquisition of such things as belong to him. Every warehouse and shop-window, every fruit-tree, every thought of every hour, opens a new want to him, which it concerns his power and dignity to gratify. It is of no use to argue the wants down: the philosophers have laid the greatness of man in making his wants few; but will a man content himself with a hut and a handful of dried pease? He is born to be rich. He is thoroughly related; and is tempted out by his appetites and fancies to the conquest of this and that piece of nature, until he finds his well-being in the use of his planet, and of more planets than his own. Wealth requires, besides the crust of bread and the roof, — the freedom of the city, the freedom of the earth, travelling, machinery, the benefits of science, music, and fine arts, the best culture, and the best company. He is the rich man who can avail himself of all men's faculties. He is the richest man who knows how to draw a benefit from the labors of the greatest number of men, of men in distant countries, and in past times. The same correspondence that is between thirst in the stomach, and water in the spring, exists between the whole of man and the whole of nature. The elements offer their service to him. The sea, washing the equator and the poles, offers its perilous aid, and the power and empire that follow it, — day by day to his craft and audacity. 'Beware of me,' it says, 'but if you can hold me, I am the key to all the lands.' Fire offers, on its side, an equal power. Fire, steam, lightning, gravity, ledges of rock, mines of iron, lead, quicksilver, tin, and gold; forests of all woods; fruits of all climates; animals of all habits; the powers of tillage; the fabrics of his chemic laboratory; the webs of his loom; the masculine draught of his locomotive, the talismans of the machine-shop; all grand and subtile things, minerals, gases, ethers, passions, war, trade, government, are his natural playmates, and, according to the excellence of the machinery in each human being, is his attraction for the instruments he is to employ. The world is his tool-chest, and he is successful, or his education is carried on just so far, as is the marriage of his faculties with nature, or, the degree in which he takes up things into himself.

The strong race is strong on these terms. The Saxons are the merchants of the world; now, for a thousand years, the leading race, and by nothing more than their quality of personal independence, and, in its special modification, pecuniary independence. No reliance for bread and games on the government, no clanship, no patriarchal style of living by the revenues of a chief, no marrying-on, — no system of clientship suits them; but every man must pay his scot. The English are prosperous and peaceful, with their habit of considering that every man must take care of himself, and has himself to thank, if he do not maintain and improve his position in society.

The subject of economy mixes itself with morals, inasmuch as it is a peremptory point of virtue that a man's independence is secured. Poverty demoralizes. A man in debt is so far a slave; and Wall Street thinks it easy for a *millionnaire* to be a man of his word, a man of honor, but, that, in failing circumstances, no man can be relied on to keep his integrity. And when one observes in the hotels and palaces of our Atlantic capitals the habit of expense, the riot of the senses, the absence of bonds, clanship, fellow-feeling of any kind, he feels, that, when a man or a woman is driven to the wall, the chances of integrity are frightfully diminished, as if virtue were coming to be a luxury which few could afford, or, as Burke said, "at a market almost too high for humanity." He may fix his inventory of necessities and of enjoyments on what scale he pleases, but if he wishes the power and privilege of thought, the chalking out his own career, and having society on his own terms, he must bring his wants within his proper power to satisfy.

The manly part is to do with might and main what you can do. The world is full of fops who never did anything, and who have persuaded beauties and men of genius to wear their fop livery, and these will deliver the fop opinion, that it is not respectable to be seen earning a living; that it is much more respectable to spend without earning; and this doctrine of the snake will come also from the elect sons of light; for wise men are not wise at all hours, and will speak five times from their taste or their humor, to once from their reason. The brave workman, who might betray his feeling of it in his manners, if he do not succumb in his practice, must replace the grace or elegance forfeited, by the merit of the work done. No matter whether he make shoes, or statues, or laws. It is the privilege of any human work which is well done to invest the doer with a certain haughtiness. He can well afford not to conciliate, whose faithful work will answer for him. The mechanic at his bench carries a quiet heart and assured manners, and deals on even terms with men of any condition. The artist has made his picture so true, that it disconcerts criticism. The statue is so beautiful that it contracts no stain from the market, but makes the market a silent gallery for itself. The case of the young lawyer was pitiful to disgust, — a paltry matter of buttons or tweezer-cases; but the determined youth saw in it an aperture to insert his dangerous wedges, made the insignificance of the thing forgotten, and gave fame by his sense and energy to the name and affairs of the Tittleton snuff-box factory.

Society in large towns is babyish, and wealth is made a toy. The life of pleasure is so ostentatious, that a shallow observer must believe that this is the agreed best use of wealth, and, whatever is pretended, it ends in cosseting. But, if this were the main use of surplus capital, it would bring us to barricades, burned towns, and tomahawks, presently. Men of sense esteem wealth to be the assimilation of nature to themselves, the converting of the sap and juices of the planet to the incarnation and nutriment of their design. Power is what they want, — not candy, — power to execute their design, power to give legs and feet, form and actuality, to their thought, which, to a clear-sighted man, appears the end for which the Universe exists, and all its resources might be well applied. Columbus thinks that the sphere is a problem for practical navigation, as well as for closet geometry, and looks on all kings and peoples as cowardly landsmen, until they dare fit him out. Few men on the planet have more truly belonged to it. But he was forced to leave much of his map blank. His successors inherited his map, and inherited his fury to complete it.

So the men of the mine, telegraph, mill, map, and survey, — the monomaniacs, who talk up their project in marts, and offices, and entreat men to subscribe: — how did our factories get built? how did North America get netted with iron rails, except by the importunity of these orators, who dragged all the prudent men in? Is party the madness of many for the gain of a few? This *speculative* genius is the madness of few for the gain of the world. The projectors are sacrificed, but the public is the gainer. Each of these idealists, working after his thought, would make it tyrannical, if he could. He is met and antagonized by other speculators, as hot as he. The equilibrium is preserved by these counteractions, as one tree keeps down another in the forest, that it may not absorb all the sap in the ground. And the supply in nature of railroad presidents, copper-miners, grand-junctioners, smoke-burners, fire-annihilators, &c., is limited by the same law which keeps the proportion in the supply of carbon, of alum, and of hydrogen.

To be rich is to have a ticket of admission to the master-works and chief men of each race. It is to have the sea, by voyaging; to visit the mountains, Niagara, the Nile, the desert, Rome, Paris, Constantinople; to see galleries, libraries, arsenals, manufactories. The reader of Humboldt's "Cosmos" follows the marches of a man whose eyes, ears, and mind are armed by all the science, arts, and implements which mankind have anywhere accumulated, and who is using these to add to the stock. So is it with Denon, Beckford, Belzoni, Wilkinson, Layard, Kane, Lepsius, and Livingston. "The rich man," says Saadi, "is everywhere expected and at home." The rich take up something more of the world into man's life. They include the country as well as the town, the ocean-side, the White Hills, the Far West, and the old European homesteads of man, in their notion of available material. The world is his who has money to go over it. He arrives at the sea-shore, and a sumptuous ship has floored and carpeted for him the stormy Atlantic, and made it a luxurious hotel, amid the horrors of tempests. The Persians say, "'T is the same to him who wears a shoe, as if the whole earth were covered with leather."

Kings are said to have long arms, but every man should have long arms, and should pluck his living, his instruments, his power, and his knowing, from the sun, moon, and stars. Is not then the demand to be rich legitimate? Yet, I have never seen a rich man. I have never seen a man as rich as all men ought to be, or, with an adequate command of nature. The pulpit and the press have many commonplaces denouncing the thirst for wealth; but if men should take these moralists at their word, and leave off aiming to be rich, the moralists would rush to rekindle at all hazards this love of power in the people, lest civilization should be undone. Men are urged by their ideas to acquire the command over nature. Ages derive a culture from the wealth of Roman Cæsars, Leo Tenths, magnificent Kings of France, Grand Dukes of Tuscany, Dukes of Devonshire, Townleys, Vernons, and Peels, in England; or whatever great proprietors. It is the interest of all men, that there should be Vaticans and Louvres full of noble works of art; British museums, and French Gardens of Plants, Philadelphia Academies of Natural History, Bodleian, Ambrosian, Royal, Congressional Libraries. It is the interest of all that there should be Exploring Expeditions; Captain Cooks to voyage round the world, Rosses, Franklins, Richardsons, and

Kanes, to find the magnetic and the geographic poles. We are all richer for the measurement of a degree of latitude on the earth's surface. Our navigation is safer for the chart. How intimately our knowledge of the system of the Universe rests on that! — and a true economy in a state or an individual will forget its frugality in behalf of claims like these.

Whilst it is each man's interest, that, not only ease and convenience of living, but also wealth or surplus product should exist somewhere, it need not be in his hands. Often it is very undesirable to him. Goethe said well, "Nobody should be rich but those who understand it." Some men are born to own, and can animate all their possessions. Others cannot: their owning is not graceful; seems to be a compromise of their character: they seem to steal their own dividends. They should own who can administer; not they who hoard and conceal; not they who, the greater proprietors they are, are only the greater beggars, but they whose work carves out work for more, opens a path for all. For he is the rich man in whom the people are rich, and he is the poor man in whom the people are poor; and how to give all access to the masterpieces of art and nature, is the problem of civilization. The socialism of our day has done good service in setting men on thinking how certain civilizing benefits, now only enjoyed by the opulent, can be enjoyed by all. For example, the providing to each man the means and apparatus of science, and of the arts. There are many articles good for occasional use, which few men are able to own. Every man wishes to see the ring of Saturn, the satellites and belts of Jupiter and Mars; the mountains and craters in the moon: yet how few can buy a telescope! and of those, scarcely one would like the trouble of keeping it in order, and exhibiting it. So of electrical and chemical apparatus, and many the like things. Every man may have occasion to consult books which he does not care to possess, such as cyclopædias, dictionaries, tables, charts, maps, and public documents: pictures also of birds, beasts, fishes, shells, trees, flowers, whose names he desires to know.

There is a refining influence from the arts of Design on a prepared mind, which is as positive as that of music, and not to be supplied from any other source. But pictures, engravings, statues, and casts, beside their first cost, entail expenses, as of galleries and keepers for the exhibition; and the use which any man can make of them is rare, and their value, too, is much enhanced by the numbers of men who can share their enjoyment. In the Greek cities, it was reckoned profane, that any person should pretend a property in a work of art, which belonged to all who could behold it. I think sometimes, — could I only have music on my own terms; — could I live in a great city, and know where I could go whenever I wished the ablution and inundation of musical waves, — that were a bath and a medicine.

If properties of this kind were owned by states, towns, and lyceums, they would draw the bonds of neighborhood closer. A town would exist to an intellectual purpose. In Europe, where the feudal forms secure the permanence of wealth in certain families, those families buy and preserve these things, and lay them open to the public. But in America, where democratic institutions divide every estate into small portions, after a few years, the public should step into the place of these proprietors, and provide this culture and inspiration for the citizen.

Man was born to be rich, or, inevitably grows rich by the use of his faculties; by the union of thought with nature. Property is an intellectual production. The game requires coolness, right reasoning, promptness, and patience in the players. Cultivated labor drives out brute labor. An infinite number of shrewd men, in infinite years, have arrived at certain best and shortest ways of doing, and this accumulated skill in arts, cultures, harvestings, curings, manufactures, navigations, exchanges, constitutes the worth of our world to-day.

Commerce is a game of skill, which every man cannot play, which few men can play well. The right merchant is one who has the just average of faculties we call *common sense;* a man of a strong affinity for facts, who makes up his decision on what he has seen. He is thoroughly persuaded of the truths of arithmetic. There is always a reason, *in the man,* for his good or bad fortune, and so, in making money. Men talk as if there were some magic about this, and believe in magic, in all parts of life. He knows, that all goes on the old road, pound for pound, cent for cent, — for every effect a perfect cause, — and that good luck is another name for tenacity of purpose. He insures himself in every transaction, and likes small and sure gains. Probity and closeness to the facts are the basis, but the masters of the art add a certain long arithmetic. The problem is, to combine many and remote operations, with the accuracy and adherence to the facts, which is easy in near and small transactions; so to arrive at gigantic results, without any compromise of safety. Napoleon was fond of telling the story of the Marseilles banker, who said to his visitor, surprised at the contrast between the splendor of the banker's chateau and hospitality, and the meanness of the counting-room in which he had seen him: "Young man, you are too young to understand how masses are formed, — the true and only power, — whether composed of money, water, or men, it is all alike, — a mass is an immense centre of motion, but it must be begun, it must be kept up": — and he might have added, that the way in which it must be begun and kept up, is, by obedience to the law of particles.

Success consists in close appliance to the laws of the world, and, since those laws are intellectual and moral, an intellectual and moral obedience. Political Economy is as good a book wherein to read the life of man, and the ascendency of laws over all private and hostile influences, as any Bible which has come down to us.

Money is representative, and follows the nature and fortunes of the owner. The coin is a delicate metre of civil, social, and moral changes. The farmer is covetous of his dollar, and with reason. It is no waif to him. He knows how many strokes of labor it represents. His bones ache with the day's work that earned it. He knows how much land it represents; — how much rain, frost, and sunshine. He knows that, in the dollar, he gives you so much discretion and patience, so much hoeing and threshing. Try to lift his dollar; you must lift all that weight. In the city, where money follows the skit of a pen, or a lucky rise in exchange, it comes to be looked on as light. I wish the farmer held it dearer, and would spend it only for real bread; force for force.

The farmer's dollar is heavy, and the clerk's is light and nimble; leaps out of his pocket; jumps on to cards and faro-tables: but still more curious is its susceptibility to metaphysical changes. It is the finest barometer of social storms, and announces revolutions.

Every step of civil advancement makes every man's dollar worth more. In California, the country where it grew, — what would it buy? A few years since, it would buy a shanty, dysentery, hunger, bad company, and crime. There are wide countries, like Siberia, where it would buy little else to-day, than some petty mitigation of suffering. In Rome, it will buy beauty and magnificence. Forty years ago, a dollar would not buy much in Boston. Now it will buy a great deal more in our old town, thanks to railroads, telegraphs, steamers, and the contemporaneous growth of New York, and the whole country. Yet there are many goods appertaining to a capital city, which are not yet purchasable here, no, not with a mountain of dollars. A dollar in Florida is not worth a dollar in Massachusetts. A dollar is not value, but representative of value, and, at last, of moral values. A dollar is rated for the corn it will buy, or to speak strictly, not for the corn or house-room, but for Athenian corn, and Roman house-room, — for the wit, probity, and power, which we eat bread and dwell in houses to share and exert. Wealth is mental; wealth is moral. The value of a dollar is, to buy just things: a dollar goes on increasing in value with all the genius, and all the virtue of the world. A dollar in a university is worth more than a dollar in a jail; in a temperate, schooled, law-abiding community, than in some sink of crime, where dice, knives, and arsenic are in constant play.

The "Bank-Note Detector" is a useful publication. But the current dollar, silver or paper, is itself the detector of the right and wrong where it circulates. Is it not instantly enhanced by the increase of equity? If a trader refuses to sell his vote, or adheres to some odious right, he makes so much more equity in Massachusetts; and every acre in the State is more worth, in the hour of his action. If you take out of State Street the ten honestest merchants, and put in ten roguish persons, controlling the same amount of capital, — the rates of insurance will indicate it; the soundness of banks will show it: the highways will be less secure: the schools will feel it; the children will bring home their little dose of the poison: the judge will sit less firmly on the bench, and his decisions be less upright; he has lost so much support and constraint, — which all need; and the pulpit will betray it, in a laxer rule of life. An apple-tree, if you take out every day for a number of days, a load of loam, and put in a load of sand about its roots, will find it out. An apple-tree is a stupid kind of creature, but if this treatment be pursued for a short time, I think it would begin to mistrust something. And if you should take out of the powerful class engaged in trade a hundred good men, and put in a hundred bad, or, what is just the same thing, introduce a demoralizing institution, would not the dollar, which is not much stupider than an apple-tree, presently find it out? The value of a dollar is social, as it is created by society. Every man who removes into this city, with any purchasable talent or skill in him, gives to every man's labor in the city a new worth. If a talent is anywhere born into the world, the community of nations is enriched; and, much more, with a new degree of probity. The expense of crime, one of the principal charges of every nation, is so far stopped. In Europe, crime is observed to increase or abate with the price of bread. If the Rothschilds at Paris do not accept bills, the people at Manchester, at Paisley, at Birmingham, are forced into the highway, and landlords are shot down in Ireland. The police records attest it. The vibrations are presently felt in New York, New Orleans, and Chicago. Not much otherwise, the economical power touches the masses through the political lords. Rothschild refuses the Russian loan, and there is peace, and the harvests are saved. He takes it, and there is war, and an agitation through a large portion of mankind, with every hideous result, ending in revolution, and a new order.

Wealth brings with it its own checks and balances. The basis of political economy is non-interference. The only safe rule is found in the self-adjusting meter of demand and supply. Do not legislate. Meddle, and you snap the sinews with your sumptuary laws. Give no bounties: make equal laws: secure life and property, and you need not give alms. Open the doors of opportunity to talent and virtue, and they will do themselves justice, and property will not be in bad hands. In a free and just commonwealth, property rushes from the idle and imbecile, to the industrious, brave, and persevering.

The laws of nature play through trade, as a toy-battery exhibits the effects of electricity. The level of the sea is not more surely kept, than is the equilibrium of value in society, by the demand and supply; and artifice or legislation punishes itself by reactions, gluts, and bankruptcies. The sublime laws play indifferently through atoms and galaxies. Whoever knows what happens in the getting and spending of a loaf of bread and a pint of beer; that no wishing will change the rigorous limits of pints and penny loaves; that, for all that is consumed, so much less remains in the basket and pot; but what is gone out of these is not wasted, but well spent, if it nourish his body, and enable him to finish his task; — knows all of political economy that the budgets of empires can teach him. The interest of petty economy is this symbolization of the great economy; the way in which a house, and a private man's methods, tally with the solar system, and the laws of give and take, throughout nature; and however wary we are of the falsehoods and petty tricks which we suicidally play off on each other, every man has a certain satisfaction, whenever his dealing touches on the inevitable facts; when he sees that things themselves dictate the price, as they always tend to do, and, in large manufactures, are seen to do. Your paper is not fine or coarse enough, — is too heavy, or too thin. The manufacturer says, he will furnish you with just that thickness or thinness you want; the pattern is quite indifferent to him; here is his schedule; — any variety of paper, as cheaper or dearer, with the prices annexed. A pound of paper costs so much, and you may have it made up in any pattern you fancy.

There is in all our dealings a self-regulation that supersedes chaffering. You will rent a house, but must have it cheap. The owner can reduce the rent, but so he incapacitates himself from making proper repairs, and the tenant gets not the house he would have, but a worse one; besides, that a relation a little injurious is established between landlord and tenant. You dismiss your laborer, saying, 'Patrick, I shall send for you as soon as I cannot do without you.' Patrick goes off contented, for he knows that the weeds will grow with the potatoes, the vines must be planted, next week, and, however unwilling you may be, the cantelopes, crook-necks, and cucumbers will send for him. Who but must wish that all labor and value should stand on the same simple and surly market? If it is the best of its kind, it will. We must have joiner, locksmith, planter, priest, poet, doctor, cook, weaver, ostler; each in turn, through the year.

If a St. Michael's pear sells for a shilling, it costs a shilling to raise it. If, in Boston, the best securities offer twelve per cent for money, they have just six per cent of insecurity. You may not see that the fine pear costs you a shilling, but it costs the community so much. The shilling represents the number of enemies the pear has, and the amount of risk in ripening it. The price of coal shows the narrowness of the coal-field, and a compulsory confinement of the miners to a certain district. All salaries are reckoned on contingent, as well as on actual services. "If the wind were always southwest by west," said the skipper, "women might take ships to sea." One might say, that all things are of one price; that nothing is cheap or dear; and that the apparent disparities that strike us are only a shopman's trick of concealing the damage in your bargain. A youth coming into the city from his native New Hampshire farm, with its hard fare still fresh in his remembrance, boards at a first-class hotel, and believes he must somehow have outwitted Dr. Franklin and Malthus, for luxuries are cheap. But he pays for the one convenience of a better dinner, by the loss of some of the richest social and educational advantages. He has lost what guards! what incentives! He will perhaps find by and by, that he left the Muses at the door of the hotel, and found the Furies inside. Money often costs too much, and power and pleasure are not cheap. The ancient poet said, "The gods sell all things at a fair price."

There is an example of the compensations in the commercial history of this country. When the European wars threw the carrying-trade of the world, from 1800 to 1812, into American bottoms, a seizure was now and then made of an American ship. Of course, the loss was serious to the owner, but the country was indemnified; for we charged threepence a pound for carrying cotton, sixpence for tobacco, and so on; which paid for the risk and loss, and brought into the country an immense prosperity, early marriages, private wealth, the building of cities, and of states; and, after the war was over, we received compensation over and above, by treaty, for all the seizures. Well, the Americans grew rich and great. But the pay-day comes round. Britain, France, and Germany, which our extraordinary profits had impoverished, send out, attracted by the fame of our advantages, first their thousands, then their millions, of poor people, to share the crop. At first, we employ them, and increase our prosperity; but, in the artificial system of society and of protected labor, which we also have adopted and enlarged, there come presently checks and stoppages. Then we refuse to employ these poor men. But they will not so be answered. They go into the poor rates, and, though we refuse wages, we must now pay the same amount in the form of taxes. Again, it turns out that the largest proportion of crimes are committed by foreigners. The cost of the crime, and the expense of courts, and of prisons, we must bear, and the standing army of preventive police we must pay. The cost of education of the posterity of this great colony, I will not compute. But the gross amount of these costs will begin to pay back what we thought was a net gain from our Transatlantic customers of 1800. It is vain to refuse this payment. We cannot get rid of these people, and we cannot get rid of their will to be supported. That has become an inevitable element in our politics; and, for their votes, each of the dominant parties courts and assists them to get it executed. Moreover, we have to pay, not what would have contented them at home, but what they have learned to think necessary here; so that opinion, fancy, and all manner of moral considerations complicate the problem.

These were the prevalent opinions in 1850. Yet this result is no more final than the last. We have hardly time to study this adjustment and deplore these disadvantages, before the scale rights itself again, this time disclosing new and immense benefits. For this countless host of immigrants are now seen to be adding by their labor to the wealth of the country. They plant the wilderness with wheat and corn, work the mines for coal and lead and copper and gold, build roads and towns and states, create a market for the manufactures and commerce of either sea-coast, and swell by their taxes the national treasury.

There are a few measures of economy which will bear to be named without disgust; for the subject is tender, and we may easily have too much of it; and therein resembles the hideous animalcules of which our bodies are built up, — which, offensive in the particular, yet compose valuable and effective masses. Our nature and genius force us to respect ends, whilst we use means. We must use the means, and yet, in our most accurate using, somehow screen and cloak them, as we can only give them any beauty, by a reflection of the glory of the end. That is the good head, which serves the end, and commands the means. The rabble are corrupted by their means: the means are too strong for them, and they desert their end.

1. The first of these measures is that each man's expense must proceed from his character. As long as your genius buys, the investment is safe, though you spend like a monarch. Nature arms each man with some faculty which enables him to do easily some feat impossible to any other, and thus makes him necessary to society. This native determination guides his labor and his spending. He wants an equipment of means and tools proper to his talent. And to save on this point, were to neutralize the special strength and helpfulness of each mind. Do your work, respecting the excellence of the

work, and not its acceptableness. This is so much economy, that, rightly read, it is the sum of economy. Profligacy consists not in spending years of time or chests of money, — but in spending them off the line of your career. The crime which bankrupts men and states, is, job-work; — declining from your main design, to serve a turn here or there. Nothing is beneath you, if it is in the direction of your life: nothing is great or desirable, if it is off from that. I think we are entitled here to draw a straight line, and say, that society can never prosper, but must always be bankrupt, until every man does that which he was created to do.

Spend for your expense, and retrench the expense which is not yours. Allston, the painter, was wont to say, that he built a plain house, and filled it with plain furniture, because he would hold out no bribe to any to visit him, who had not similar tastes to his own. We are sympathetic, and, like children, want everything we see. But it is a large stride to independence, — when a man, in the discovery of his proper talent, has sunk the necessity for false expenses. As the betrothed maiden, by one secure affection, is relieved from a system of slaveries, — the daily inculcated necessity of pleasing all, — so the man who has found what he can do, can spend on that, and leave all other spending. Montaigne said: "When he was a younger brother, he went brave in dress and equipage, but afterward his chateau and farms might answer for him." Let a man who belongs to the class of nobles, those, namely, who have found out that they can do something, relieve himself of all vague squandering on objects not his. Let the realist not mind appearances. Let him delegate to others the costly courtesies and decorations of social life. The virtues are economists, but some of the vices are also. Thus, next to humility, I have noticed that pride is a pretty good husband. A good pride is, as I reckon it, worth from five hundred to fifteen hundred a year. Pride is handsome, economical: pride eradicates so many vices, letting none subsist but itself, that it seems as if it were a great gain to exchange vanity for pride. Pride can go without domestics, without fine clothes, can live in a house with two rooms, can eat potato, purslain, beans, lyed corn, can work on the soil, can travel afoot, can talk with poor men, or sit silent well-contented in fine saloons. But vanity costs money, labor, horses, men, women, health, and peace, and is still nothing at last, a long way leading nowhere. Only one drawback; proud people are intolerably selfish, and the vain are gentle and giving.

Art is a jealous mistress, and, if a man have a genius for painting, poetry, music, architecture, or philosophy, he makes a bad husband, and an ill provider, and should be wise in season, and not fetter himself with duties which will embitter his days, and spoil him for his proper work. We had in this region, twenty years ago, among our educated men, a sort of Arcadian fanaticism, a passionate desire to go upon the land, and unite farming to intellectual pursuits. Many effected their purpose, and made the experiment, and some became downright ploughmen; but all were cured of their faith that scholarship and practical farming (I mean, with one's own hands) could be united.

With brow bent, with firm intent, the pale scholar leaves his desk to draw a freer breath, and get a juster statement of his thought, in the garden-walk. He stoops to pull up a purslain, or a dock, that is choking the young corn, and finds there are two: close behind the last, is a third; he reaches out his hand to a fourth; behind that are four thousand and one. He is heated and untuned, and, by and by, wakes up from his idiot dream of chickweed and red-root, to remember his morning thought, and to find, that, with his adamantine purposes, he has been duped by a dandelion. A garden is like those pernicious machineries we read of, every month, in the newspapers, which catch a man's coat-skirt or his hand, and draw in his arm, his leg, and his whole body to irresistible destruction. In an evil hour he pulled down his wall, and added a field to his homestead. No land is bad, but land is worse. If a man own land, the land owns him. Now let him leave home, if he dare. Every tree and graft, every hill of melons, row of corn, or quickset hedge, all he has done, and all he means to do, stand in his way, like duns, when he would go out of his gate. The devotion to these vines and trees he finds poisonous. Long free walks, a circuit of miles, free his brain, and serve his body. Long marches are no hardship to him. He believes he composes easily on the hills. But this pottering in a few square yards of garden is dispiriting and drivelling. The smell of the plants has drugged him, and robbed him of energy. He finds a catalepsy in his bones. He grows peevish and poor-spirited. The genius of reading and of gardening are antagonistic, like resinous and vitreous electricity. One is concentrative in sparks and shocks: the other is diffuse strength; so that each disqualifies its workman for the other's duties.

An engraver whose hands must be of an exquisite delicacy of stroke should not lay stone-walls. Sir David Brewster gives exact instructions for microscopic observation: "Lie down on your back, and hold the single lens and object over your eye," &c., &c. How much more the seeker of abstract truth, who needs periods of isolation, and rapt concentration, and almost a going out of the body to think!

2. Spend after your genius, *and by system.* Nature goes by rule, not by sallies and saltations. There must be system in the economies. Saving and unexpensiveness will not keep the most pathetic family from ruin, nor will bigger incomes make free spending safe. The secret of success lies never in the amount of money, but in the relation of income to outgo; as if, after expense has been fixed at a certain point, then new and steady rills of income, though never so small, being added, wealth begins. But in ordinary, as means increase, spending increases faster, so that, large incomes, in England and elsewhere, are found not to help matters; — the eating quality of debt does not relax its voracity. When the cholera is in the potato, what is the use of planting larger crops? In England, the richest country in the universe, I was assured by shrewd observers, that great lords and ladies had no more guineas to give away than other people; that liberality with money is as rare, and as immediately famous a virtue as it is here. Want is a growing giant whom the coat of Have was never large enough to cover. I remember in Warwickshire, to have been shown a fair manor, still in the same name as in Shakespeare's time. The rent-roll, I was told, is some fourteen thousand pounds a year: but, when the second son of the late proprietor was born, the father was perplexed how to provide for him. The eldest son must inherit the manor; what to do with this supernumerary? He was advised to breed him for the Church, and to settle him in the rectorship, which was in the gift of the family; which was done. It is a general rule in that country, that bigger incomes do not help anybody. It is commonly observed, that a sudden wealth, like a prize drawn in a lottery, or a large bequest to a poor family, does not permanently enrich. They have served no apprenticeship to wealth, and, with the rapid wealth, come rapid claims: which they do not know how to deny, and the treasure is quickly dissipated.

A system must be in every economy, or the best single expedients are of no avail. A farm is a good thing when it begins and ends with itself, and does not need a salary, or a shop, to eke it out. Thus, the cattle are a main link in the chain-ring. If the non-conformist or æsthetic farmer leaves out the cattle, and does not also leave out the want which the cattle must supply, he must fill the gap by begging or stealing. When men now alive were born, the farm yielded everything that was consumed on it. The farm yielded no money, and the farmer got on without. If he fell sick, his neighbors came in to his aid : each gave a day's work ; or a half-day ; or lent his yoke of oxen, or his horse, and kept his work even : hoed his potatoes, mowed his hay, reaped his rye ; well knowing that no man could afford to hire labor, without selling his land. In autumn, a farmer could sell an ox or a hog, and get a little money to pay taxes withal. Now, the farmer buys almost all he consumes, — tin-ware, cloth, sugar, tea, coffee, fish, coal, railroad tickets, and newspapers.

A master in each art is required, because the practice is never with still or dead subjects, but they change in your hands. You think farm buildings and broad acres a solid property : but its value is flowing like water. It requires as much watching as if you were decanting wine from a cask. The farmer knows what to do with it, stops every leak, turns all the streamlets to one reservoir, and decants wine ; but a blunderhead comes out of Cornhill, tries his hand, and it all leaks away. So is it with granite streets, or timber townships, as with fruit or flowers. Nor is any investment so permanent, that it can be allowed to remain without incessant watching, as the history of each attempt to lock up an inheritance through two generations for an unborn inheritor may show.

When Mr. Cockayne takes a cottage in the country, and will keep his cow, he thinks a cow is a creature that is fed on hay, and gives a pail of milk twice a day. But the cow that he buys gives milk for three months ; then her bag dries up. What to do with a dry cow? who will buy her? Perhaps he bought also a yoke of oxen to do his work ; but they get blown and lame. What to do with blown and lame oxen? The farmer fats his after the spring work is done, and kills them in the fall. But how can Cockayne, who has no pastures, and leaves his cottage daily in the cars, at business hours, be pothered with fatting and killing oxen? He plants trees ; but there must be crops, to keep the trees in ploughed land. What shall be the crops? He will have nothing to do with trees, but will have grass. After a year or two, the grass must be turned up and ploughed: now what crops? Credulous Cockayne!

3. Help comes in the custom of the country, and the rule of *Impera parendo.* The rule is not to dictate, nor to insist on carrying out each of your schemes by ignorant wilfulness, but to learn practically the secret spoken from all nature, that things themselves refuse to be mismanaged, and will show to the watchful their own law. Nobody need stir hand or foot. The custom of the country will do it all. I know not how to build or to plant; neither how to buy wood, nor what to do with the house-lot, the field, or the wood-lot, when bought. Never fear; it is all settled how it shall be, long beforehand, in the custom of the country, whether to sand, or whether to clay it, when to plough, and how to dress, whether to grass, or to corn; and you cannot help or hinder it. Nature has her own best mode of doing each thing, and she has somewhere told it plainly, if we will keep our eyes and ears open. If not, she will not be slow in undeceiving us, when we prefer our own way to hers. How often we must remember the art of the surgeon, which, in replacing the broken bone, contents itself with releasing the parts from false position; they fly into place by the action of the muscles. On this art of nature all our arts rely.

Of the two eminent engineers in the recent construction of railways in England, Mr. Brunel went straight from terminus to terminus, through mountains, over streams, crossing highways, cutting ducal estates in two, and shooting through this man's cellar, and that man's attic window, and so arriving at his end, at great pleasure to geometers, but with cost to his company. Mr. Stephenson, on the contrary, believing that the river knows the way, followed his valley, as implicitly as our Western Railroad follows the Westfield River, and turned out to be the safest and cheapest engineer. We say the cows laid out Boston. Well, there are worse surveyors. Every pedestrian in our pastures has frequent occasion to thank the cows for cutting the best path through the thicket, and over the hills; and travellers and Indians know the value of a buffalo-trail, which is sure to be the easiest possible pass through the ridge.

When a citizen, fresh from Dock Square, or Milk Street, comes out and buys land in the country, his first thought is to a fine outlook from his windows; his library must command a western view: a sunset every day bathing the shoulder of Blue Hills, Wachusett, and the peaks of Monadnoc and Uncanoonuc. What, thirty acres, and all this magnificence for fifteen hundred dollars! It would be cheap at fifty thousand. He proceeds at once, his eyes dim with tears of joy, to fix the spot for his corner-stone. But the man who is to level the ground thinks it will take many hundred loads of gravel to fill the hollow to the road. The stone-mason who should build the well thinks he shall have to dig forty feet: the baker doubts he shall never like to drive up to the door: the practical neighbor cavils at the position of the barn; and the citizen comes to know that his predecessor the farmer built the house in the right spot for the sun and wind, the spring, and water-drainage, and the convenience to the pasture, the garden, the field, and the road. So Dock Square yields the point, and things have their own way. Use has made the farmer wise, and the foolish citizen learns to take his counsel. From step to step he comes at last to surrender at discretion. The farmer affects to take his orders; but the citizen says, You may ask me as often as you will, and in what ingenious forms, for an opinion concerning the mode of building my wall, or sinking my well, or laying out my acre, but the ball will rebound to you. These are matters on which I neither know, nor need to know anything. These are questions which you and not I shall answer.

Not less, within doors, a system settles itself paramount and tyrannical over master and mistress, servant and child, cousin and acquaintance. 'T is in vain that genius or virtue or energy of character strive and cry against it. This is fate. And 't is very well that the poor husband reads in a book of a new way of living, and resolves to adopt it at home: let him go home and try it, if he dare.

4. Another point of economy is to look for seed of the same kind as you sow: and not to hope to buy one kind with another kind. Friendship buys friendship; justice, justice; military merit, military success. Good husbandry finds wife, children, and household. The good merchant, large gains, ships, stocks, and money. The good poet, fame, and literary credit; but not either, the other. Yet there is commonly a confusion of expectations on these points. Hotspur lives for the moment; praises himself for it; and despises Furlong, that he does not. Hotspur, of course, is poor; and Furlong, a good provider. The old circumstance is, that Hotspur thinks it a superiority in himself, this improvidence, which ought to be rewarded with Furlong's lands.

I have not at all completed my design. But we must not leave the topic, without casting one glance into the interior recesses. It is a doctrine of philosophy, that man is a being of degrees; that there is nothing in the world, which is not repeated in his body; his body being a sort of miniature or summary of the world: then that there is nothing in his body, which is not repeated as in a celestial sphere in his mind: then, there is nothing in his brain, which is not repeated in a higher sphere, in his moral system.

5. Now these things are so in Nature. All things ascend, and the royal rule of economy is, that it should ascend also, or, whatever we do must have a higher aim. Thus it is a maxim, that money is another kind of blood, *Pecuniâ alter sanguis:* or, the estate of a man is only a larger kind of body, and admits of regimen analogous to his bodily circulations. So there is no maxim of the merchant, which does not admit of an extended sense, e. g. "The best use of money is to pay debts"; "Every business by itself"; "Best time is present time"; "The right investment is in tools of your trade"; and the like. The counting-room maxims liberally expounded are laws of the Universe. The merchant's economy is a coarse symbol of the soul's economy. It is, to spend for power, and not for pleasure. It is to invest income; that is to say, to take up particulars into generals; days into integral eras, —literary, emotive, practical, of its life, and still to ascend in its investment. The merchant has but one rule, *absorb and invest:* he is to be capitalist: the scraps and filings must be gathered back into the crucible; the gas and smoke must be burned, and earnings must not go to increase expense, but to capital again. Well, the man must be capitalist. Will he spend his income, or will he invest? His body and every organ is under the same law. His body is a jar, in which the liquor of life is stored. Will he spend for pleasure? The way to ruin is short and facile. Will he not spend, but hoard for power? It passes through the sacred fermentations, by that law of Nature whereby everything climbs to higher platforms, and bodily vigor becomes mental and moral vigor. The bread he eats is first strength and animal spirits; it becomes, in higher laboratories, imagery and thought; and in still higher results, courage and endurance. This is the right compound interest; this is capital doubled, quadrupled, centupled; man raised to his highest power.

The true thrift is always to spend on the higher plane; to

invest and invest, with keener avarice, that he may spend in spiritual creation, and not in augmenting animal existence. Nor is the man enriched, in repeating the old experiments of animal sensation, nor unless through new powers and ascending pleasures, he knows himself by the actual experience of higher good, to be already on the way to the highest.

IV.

CULTURE.

Can rules or tutors educate
The semigod whom we await ?
He must be musical,
Tremulous, impressional,
Alive to gentle influence
Of landscape and of sky,
And tender to the spirit-touch
Of man's or maiden's eye :
But, to his native centre fast,
Shall into Future fuse the Past,
And the world's flowing fates in his own mould recast.

CULTURE.

THE word of ambition at the present day is Culture. Whilst all the world is in pursuit of power, and of wealth as a means of power, culture corrects the theory of success. A man is the prisoner of his power. A topical memory makes him an almanac; a talent for debate, a disputant; skill to get money makes him a miser, that is, a beggar. Culture reduces these inflammations by invoking the aid of other powers against the dominant talent, and by appealing to the rank of powers. It watches success. For performance, Nature has no mercy, and sacrifices the performer to get it done; makes a dropsy or a tympany of him. If she wants a thumb, she makes one at the cost of arms and legs, and any excess of power in one part is usually paid for at once by some defect in a contiguous part.

Our efficiency depends so much on our concentration, that Nature usually in the instances where a marked man is sent into the world, overloads him with bias, sacrificing his symmetry to his working power. It is said, a man can write but one book; and if a man have a defect, it is apt to leave its impression on all his performances. If she creates a policeman like Fouché, he is made up of suspicions and of plots to circumvent them. "The air," said Fouché, "is full of poniards." The physician Sanctorius spent his life in a pair of scales, weighing his food. Lord Coke valued Chaucer highly, because the Canon Yeman's Tale illustrates the statute fifth *Hen. IV. Chap.* 4, against alchemy. I saw a man who believed the principal mischiefs in the English state were derived from the devotion to musical concerts. A freemason, not long since, set out to explain to this country, that the principal cause of the success of General Washington, was, the aid he derived from the freemasons.

But worse than the harping on one string, Nature has secured individualism, by giving the private person a high conceit of his weight in the system. The pest of society is egotists. There are dull and bright, sacred and profane, coarse and fine egotists. 'T is a disease that, like influenza, falls on all constitutions. In the distemper known to physicians as *chorea*, the patient sometimes turns round, and continues to spin slowly on one spot. Is egotism a metaphysical variety of this malady? The man runs round a ring formed by his own talent, falls into an admiration of it, and loses relation to the world. It is a tendency in all minds. One of its annoying forms is a craving for sympathy. The sufferers parade their miseries, tear the lint from their bruises, reveal their indictable crimes, that you may pity them. They like sickness, because physical pain will extort some show of interest from the bystanders, as we have seen children, who, finding themselves of no account when grown people come in, will cough till they choke, to draw attention.

This distemper is the scourge of talent, — of artists, inventors, and philosophers. Eminent spiritualists shall have an incapacity of putting their act or word aloof from them, and seeing it bravely for the nothing it is. Beware of the man who says, 'I am on the eve of a revelation.' It is speedily punished, inasmuch as this habit invites men to humor it, and by treating the patient tenderly, to shut him up in a narrower selfism, and exclude him from the great world of God's cheerful fallible men and women. Let us rather be insulted, whilst we are insultable. Religious literature has eminent examples, and if we run over our private list of poets, critics, philanthropists, and philosophers, we shall find them infected with this dropsy and elephantiasis, which we ought to have tapped.

This goitre of egotism is so frequent among notable persons, that we must infer some strong necessity in nature which it subserves; such as we see in the sexual attraction. The preservation of the species was a point of such necessity, that Nature has secured it at all hazards by immensely overloading the passion, at the risk of perpetual crime and disorder. So egotism has its root in the cardinal necessity by which each individual persists to be what he is.

This individuality is not only not inconsistent with culture, but is the basis of it. Every valuable nature is there in its own right, and the student we speak to must have a mother-wit invincible by his culture, which uses all books, arts, facilities, and elegancies of intercourse, but is never subdued and lost in them. He only is a well-made man who has a good determination. And the end of culture is not to destroy this, God forbid! but to train away all impediment and mixture, and leave nothing but pure power. Our student must have a style and determination, and be a master in his own specialty. But, having this, he must put it behind him. He must have a catholicity, a power to see with a free and disengaged look every object. Yet is this private interest and self so overcharged, that, if a man seeks a companion who can look at objects for their own sake, and without affection or self-reference, he will find the fewest who will give him that satisfaction; whilst most men are afflicted with a coldness, an incuriosity, as soon as any object does not connect with their self-love. Though they talk of the object before them, they are thinking of themselves, and their vanity is laying little traps for your admiration.

But after a man has discovered that there are limits to the interest which his private history has for mankind, he still converses with his family, or a few companions, — perhaps with half a dozen personalities that are famous in his neighborhood. In Boston, the question of life is the names of some eight or ten men. Have you seen Mr. Allston, Doctor Channing, Mr. Adams, Mr. Webster, Mr. Greenough? Have you heard Everett, Garrison, Father Taylor, Theodore Parker? Have you talked with Messieurs Turbinewheel, Summitlevel, and Lacofrupees? Then you may as well die. In New York, the question is of some other eight, or ten, or twenty. Have you seen a few lawyers, merchants, and brokers, — two or three scholars, two or three capitalists, two or three editors of newspapers? New York is a sucked orange. All conversation is at an end, when we have discharged ourselves of a dozen personalities, domestic or imported, which make up our American existence. Nor do we expect anybody to be other than a faint copy of these heroes.

Life is very narrow. Bring any club or company of intelligent men together again after ten years, and if the presence of some penetrating and calming genius could dispose them to frankness, what a confession of insanities would come up! The "causes" to which we have sacrificed, Tariff or Democracy, Whigism or Abolition, Temperance or Socialism, would show like roots of bitterness and dragons of wrath; and our talents are as mischievous as if each had been seized upon by some bird of prey, which had whisked him away from fortune, from truth, from the dear society of the poets, some zeal, some bias, and only when he was now gray and nerveless, was it relaxing its claws, and he awaking to sober perceptions.

Culture is the suggestion from certain best thoughts, that a man has a range of affinities, through which he can modulate the violence of any master-tones that have a droning preponderance in his scale, and succor him against himself. Culture redresses his balance, puts him among his equals and superiors, revives the delicious sense of sympathy, and warns him of the dangers of solitude and repulsion.

'T is not a compliment but a disparagement to consult a man only on horses, or on steam, or on theatres, or on eating, or on books, and, whenever he appears, considerately to turn the conversation to the bantling he is known to fondle. In the Norse heaven of our forefathers, Thor's house had five hundred and forty floors; and man's house has five hundred and forty floors. His excellence is facility of adaptation and of transition through many related points, to wide contrasts and extremes. Culture kills his exaggeration, his conceit of his village or his city. We must leave our pets at home, when we go into the street, and meet men on broad grounds of good meaning and good sense. No performance is worth loss of geniality. 'T is a cruel price we pay for certain fancy goods called fine arts and philosophy. In the Norse legend, Allfadir did not get a drink of Mimir's spring, (the fountain of wisdom,) until he left his eye in pledge. And here is a pedant that cannot unfold his wrinkles, nor conceal his wrath at interruption by the best, if their conversation do not fit his impertinency, — here is he to afflict us with his personalities. 'T is incident to scholars, that each of them fancies he is pointedly odious in his community. Draw him out of this limbo of irritability. Cleanse with healthy blood his parchment skin. You restore to him his eyes which he left in pledge at Mimir's spring. If you are the victim of your doing, who cares what you do? We can spare your opera, your gazetteer, your chemic analysis, your history, your syllogisms. Your man of genius pays dearly for his distinction. His head runs up into a spire, and instead of a healthy man, merry and wise, he is some mad dominie. Nature is reckless of the individual. When she has points to carry, she carries them. To wade in marshes and sea margins is the destiny of certain birds, and they are so accurately made for this, that they are imprisoned in those places. Each animal out of its *habitat* would starve. To the physician, each man, each woman, is an amplification of one organ. A soldier, a locksmith, a bank-clerk, and a dancer could not exchange functions. And thus we are victims of adaptation.

The antidotes against this organic egotism, are, the range and variety of attractions, as gained by acquaintance with the world, with men of merit, with classes of society, with travel, with eminent persons, and with the high resources of philosophy, art, and religion : books, travel, society, solitude.

The hardiest sceptic who has seen a horse broken, a pointer trained, or, who has visited a menagerie, or the exhibition of the Industrious Fleas, will not deny the validity of education. "A boy," says Plato, "is the most vicious of all wild beasts"; and, in the same spirit, the old English poet Gascoigne says, "A boy is better unborn than untaught." The city breeds one kind of speech and manners; the back country a different style; the sea, another; the army, a fourth. We know that an army which can be confided in, may be formed by discipline; that, by systematic discipline all men may be made heroes: Marshal Lannes said to a French officer, "Know, Colonel, that none but a poltroon will boast that he never was afraid." A great part of courage is the courage of having done the thing before. And, in all human action, those faculties will be strong which are used. Robert Owen said, "Give me a tiger and I will educate him." 'T is inhuman to want faith in the power of education, since to meliorate, is the law of nature; and men are valued precisely as they exert onward or meliorating force. On the other hand, poltroonery is the acknowledging a fault to be incurable.

Incapacity of melioration is the only mortal distemper. There are people who can never understand a trope, or any second or expanded sense given to your words, or any humor; but remain literalists, after hearing the music, and poetry, and rhetoric, and wit, of seventy or eighty years. They are past the help of surgeon or clergy. But even these can understand pitchforks and the cry of Fire! and I have noticed in some of this class a marked dislike of earthquakes.

Let us make our education brave and preventive. Politics is an after-work, a poor patching. We are always a little late. The evil is done, the law is passed, and we begin the uphill agitation for repeal of that of which we ought to have prevented the enacting. We shall one day learn to supersede politics by education. What we call our root-and-branch reforms of slavery, war, gambling, intemperance, is only medicating the symptoms. We must begin higher up, namely, in Education.

Our arts and tools give to him who can handle them much the same advantage over the novice, as if you extended his life ten, fifty, or a hundred years. And I think it the part of good sense to provide every fine soul with such culture, that it shall not, at thirty or forty years, have to say, 'This which I might do is made hopeless through my want of weapons.'

But it is conceded that much of our training fails of effect; that all success is hazardous and rare; that a large part of our cost and pains is thrown away. Nature takes the matter into her own hands, and, though we must not omit any jot of our system, we can seldom be sure that it has availed much, or, that as much good would not have accrued from a different system.

Books, as containing the finest records of human wit, must always enter into our notion of culture. The best heads that ever existed, Pericles, Plato, Julius Cæsar, Shakespeare, Goethe, Milton, were well-read, universally educated men, and quite too wise to undervalue letters. Their opinion has weight, because they had means of knowing the opposite opinion. We look that a great man should be a good reader, or, in proportion to the spontaneous power, should be the assimilating power. Good criticism is very rare, and always precious. I am always happy to meet persons who perceive the transcendent superiority of Shakespeare over all other writers. I like people who like Plato. Because this love does not consist with self-conceit.

But books are good only as far as a boy is ready for them. He sometimes gets ready very slowly. You send your child to the schoolmaster, but 't is the school-boys who educate him. You send him to the Latin class, but much of his tuition comes, on his way to school, from the shop-windows. You like the strict rules and the long terms; and he finds his best leading in a by-way of his own, and refuses any companions but of his choosing. He hates the grammar and *Gradus*, and loves guns, fishing-rods, horses, and boats. Well, the boy is right; and you are not fit to direct his bringing up, if your theory leaves out his gymnastic training. Archery, cricket, gun and fishing-rod, horse and boat, are all educators, liberalizers; and so are dancing, dress, and the street talk; and — provided only the boy has resources, and is of a noble and ingenuous strain — these will not serve him less than the books. He learns chess, whist, dancing, and theatricals. The father observes that another boy has learned algebra and geometry in the same time. But the first boy has acquired much more than these poor games along with them. He is infatuated for weeks with whist and chess; but presently will find out, as you did, that when he rises from the game too long played, he is vacant and forlorn, and despises himself. Thenceforward it takes place with other things, and has its due weight in his experience. These minor skills and accomplishments, for example, dancing, are tickets of admission to the dress-circle of mankind, and the being master of them enables the youth to judge intelligently of much, on which, otherwise, he would give a pedantic squint. Landor said, "I have suffered more from my bad dancing, than from all the misfortunes and miseries of my life put together." Provided always the boy is teachable, (for we are not proposing to make a statue out of punk,) football, cricket, archery, swimming, skating, climbing, fencing, riding, are lessons in the art of power, which it is his main business to learn; — riding, specially, of which Lord Herbert of Cherbury said, "A good rider on a good horse is as much above himself and others as the world can make him." Besides, the gun, fishing-rod, boat, and horse, constitute, among all who use them, secret freemasonries. They are as if they belonged to one club.

There is also a negative value in these arts. Their chief use to the youth, is, not amusement, but to be known for what they are, and not to remain to him occasions of heartburn. We are full of superstitions. Each class fixes its eyes on the advantages it has not; the refined, on rude strength, the democrat, on birth and breeding. One of the benefits of a college education is, to show the boy its little avail. I knew a leading man in a leading city, who, having set his heart on an education at the university, and missed it, could never quite feel himself the equal of his own brothers who had gone thither. His easy superiority to multitudes of professional men could never quite countervail to him this imaginary defect. Balls, riding, wine-parties, and billiards pass to a poor boy for something fine and romantic, which they are not; and a free admission to them on an equal footing, if it were possible, only once or twice, would be worth ten times its cost, by undeceiving them.

I am not much an advocate for travelling, and I observe that men run away to other countries, because they are not good in their own, and run back to their own, because they pass for nothing in the new places. For the most part, only the light characters travel. Who are you that have no task to keep you at home? I have been quoted as saying captious things about travel; but I mean to do justice. I think there is a restlessness in our people, which argues want of character. All educated Americans, first or last, go to Europe; perhaps, because it is their mental home, as the invalid habits of this country might suggest. An eminent teacher of girls said, "The idea of a girl's education, is, whatever qualifies her for going to Europe." Can we never extract this tapeworm of Europe from the brain of our countrymen? One sees very well what their fate must be. He that does not fill a place at home, cannot abroad. He only goes there to hide his insignificance in a larger crowd. You do not think you will find anything there which you have not seen at home? The stuff of all countries is just the same. Do you suppose, there is any country where they do not scald milkpans, and swaddle the infants, and burn the brushwood, and broil the fish? What is true anywhere is true everywhere. And let him go where he will, he can only find so much beauty or worth as he carries.

Of course, for some men, travel may be useful. Naturalists, discoverers, and sailors are born. Some men are made for couriers, exchangers, envoys, missionaries, bearers of despatches, as others are for farmers and workingmen. And if the man is of a light and social turn, and Nature has aimed to make a legged and winged creature, framed for locomotion, we must follow her hint, and furnish him with that breeding which gives currency, as sedulously as with that which gives worth. But let us not be pedantic, but allow to travel its full effect. The boy grown up on the farm, which he has never left, is said in the country to have had *no chance*, and boys and men of that condition look upon work on a railroad, or drudgery in a city, as opportunity. Poor country boys of Vermont and Connecticut formerly owed what knowledge they had to their peddling trips to the Southern States. California and the Pacific Coast is now the university of this class, as Virginia was in old times. 'To have *some chance*' is their word. And the phrase 'to know the world,' or to travel, is synonymous with all men's ideas of advantage and superiority. No doubt, to a man of sense, travel offers advantages. As many languages as he has, as many friends, as many arts and trades, so many times is he a man. A foreign country is a point of comparison, wherefrom to judge his own. One use of travel, is, to recommend the books and works of home, — for we go to Europe to be Americanized; and another, to find men. For, as Nature has put fruits apart in latitudes, a new fruit in every degree, so knowledge and fine moral quality she lodges in distant men. And thus, of the six or seven teachers whom each man wants among his contemporaries, it often happens that one or two of them live on the other side of the world.

Moreover, there is in every constitution a certain solstice, when the stars stand still in our inward firmament, and when there is required some foreign force, some diversion or alterative to prevent stagnation. And, as a medical remedy, travel seems one of the best. Just as a man witnessing the admirable effect of ether to lull pain, and meditating on the contingencies of wounds, cancers, lockjaws, rejoices in Dr. Jackson's benign discovery, so a man who looks at Paris, at Naples, or at London, says: 'If I should be driven from my own home, here, at least, my thoughts can be consoled by the most prodigal amusement and occupation which the human race in ages could contrive and accumulate.'

Akin to the benefit of foreign travel, the æsthetic value of railroads is to unite the advantages of town and country life, neither of which we can spare. A man should live in or near a large town, because, let his own genius be what it may, it will repel quite as much of agreeable and valuable talent as it draws, and, in a city, the total attraction of all the citizens is sure to conquer, first or last, every repulsion, and drag the most improbable hermit within its walls some day in the year. In town, he can find the swimming-school, the gymnasium, the dancing-master, the shooting-gallery, opera, theatre, and panorama; the chemist's shop, the museum of natural history; the gallery of fine arts; the national orators, in their turn; foreign travellers, the libraries, and his club. In the country, he can find solitude and reading, manly labor, cheap living, and his old shoes; moors for game, hills for geology, and groves for devotion. Aubrey writes: "I have heard Thomas Hobbes say, that, in the Earl of Devon's house, in Derbyshire, there was a good library and books enough for him, and his lordship

17*

stored the library with what books he thought fit to be bought. But the want of good conversation was a very great inconvenience, and, though he conceived he could order his thinking as well as another, yet he found a great defect. In the country, in long time, for want of good conversation, one's understanding and invention contract a moss on them, like an old paling in an orchard."

Cities give us collision. 'T is said, London and New York take the nonsense out of a man. A great part of our education is sympathetic and social. Boys and girls who have been brought up with well-informed and superior people show in their manners an inestimable grace. Fuller says, that "William, Earl of Nassau, won a subject from the King of Spain, every time he put off his hat." You cannot have one well-bred man, without a whole society of such. They keep each other up to any high point. Especially women; — it requires a great many cultivated women, — saloons of bright, elegant, reading women, accustomed to ease and refinement, to spectacles, pictures, sculpture, poetry, and to elegant society, in order that you should have one Madame de Staël. The head of a commercial house, or a leading lawyer or politician is brought into daily contact with troops of men from all parts of the country, and those too the driving-wheels, the business men of each section, and one can hardly suggest for an apprehensive man a more searching culture. Besides, we must remember the high social possibilities of a million of men. The best bribe which London offers to-day to the imagination, is, that, in such a vast variety of people and conditions, one can believe there is room for persons of romantic character to exist, and that the poet, the mystic, and the hero may hope to confront their counterparts.

I wish cities could teach their best lesson, — of quiet manners. It is the foible especially of American youth, — pretension. The mark of the man of the world is absence of pretension. He does not make a speech; he takes a low business-tone, avoids all brag, is nobody, dresses plainly, promises not at all, performs much, speaks in monosyllables, hugs his fact. He calls his employment by its lowest name, and so takes from evil tongues their sharpest weapon. His conversation clings to the weather and the news, yet he allows himself to be surprised into thought, and the unlocking of his learning and philosophy. How the imagination is piqued by anecdotes of some great man passing incognito, as a king in gray clothes, — of Napoleon affecting a plain suit at his glittering levee; of Burns, or Scott, or Beethoven, or Wellington, or Goethe, or any container of transcendent power, passing for nobody; of Epaminondas, "who never says anything, but will listen eternally"; of Goethe, who preferred trifling subjects and common expressions in intercourse with strangers, worse rather than better clothes, and to appear a little more capricious than he was. There are advantages in the old hat and box-coat. I have heard, that, throughout this country, a certain respect is paid to good broadcloth; but dress makes a little restraint: men will not commit themselves. But the box-coat is like wine; it unlocks the tongue and men say what they think. An old poet says,

> "Go far and go sparing,
> For you 'll find it certain,
> The poorer and the baser you appear,
> The more you 'll look through still." *

Not much otherwise Milnes writes, in the "Lay of the Humble,"

> "To me men are for what they are,
> They wear no masks with me."

'T is odd that our people should have, — not water on the brain, — but a little gas there. A shrewd foreigner said of the Americans, that, "whatever they say has a little the air of a speech." Yet one of the traits down in the books as distinguishing the Anglo-Saxon, is, a trick of self-disparagement. To be sure, in old, dense countries, among a million of good coats, a fine coat comes to be no distinction, and you find humorists. In an English party, a man with no marked manners or features, with a face like red dough, unexpectedly discloses wit, learning, a wide range of topics, and personal familiarity with good men in all parts of the world, until you think you have fallen upon some illustrious personage. Can it be that the American forest has refreshed some weeds of old Pictish barbarism just ready to die out, — the love of the scarlet feather, of beads, and tinsel? The Italians are fond of red clothes, peacock plumes, and embroidery; and I remember one rainy morning in the city of Palermo, the street was in a blaze with scarlet umbrellas. The English have a plain taste. The equipages of the grandees are plain. A gorgeous livery indicates new and awkward city wealth. Mr. Pitt, like Mr. Pym, thought the title of *Mister* good against

* Beaumont and Fletcher, *The Tamer Tamed.*

any king in Europe. They have piqued themselves on governing the whole world in the poor, plain, dark Committee-room which the House of Commons sat in, before the fire.

Whilst we want cities as the centres where the best things are found, cities degrade us by magnifying trifles. The countryman finds the town a chop-house, a barber's shop. He has lost the lines of grandeur of the horizon, hills and plains, and with them, sobriety and elevation. He has come among a supple, glib-tongued tribe, who live for show, servile to public opinion. Life is dragged down to a fracas of pitiful cares and disasters. You say the gods ought to respect a life whose objects are their own; but in cities they have betrayed you to a cloud of insignificant annoyances:

"Mirmidons, race féconde,
Mirmidons,
Enfin nous commandons;
Jupiter livre le monde
Aux mirmidons, aux mirmidons." *

'T is heavy odds
Against the gods,
When they will match with myrmidons.
We spawning, spawning myrmidons,
Our turn to-day! we take command,
Jove gives the globe into the hand
Of myrmidons, of myrmidons.

What is odious but noise, and people who scream and bewail? people whose vane points always east, who live to dine, who send for the doctor, who coddle themselves, who toast their feet on the register, who intrigue to secure a padded chair, and a corner out of the draught. Suffer them once to begin the enumeration of their infirmities, and the sun will go down on the unfinished tale. Let these trifles put us out of conceit with petty comforts. To a man at work, the frost is but a color: the rain, the wind, he forgot them when he came in. Let us learn to live coarsely, dress plainly, and lie hard. The least habit of dominion over the palate has certain good effects not easily estimated. Neither will we be driven into a quiddling abstemiousness. 'T is a superstition to insist on a special diet. All is made at last of the same chemical atoms.

A man in pursuit of greatness feels no little wants. How can you mind diet, bed, dress, or salutes or compliments, or the figure you make in company, or wealth, or even the bringing things to pass, when you think how paltry are the machinery and the workers? Wordsworth was praised to me, in

* Béranger.

Westmoreland, for having afforded to his country neighbors an example of a modest household where comfort and culture were secured, without display. And a tender boy who wears his rusty cap and outgrown coat, that he may secure the coveted place in college, and the right in the library, is educated to some purpose. There is a great deal of self-denial and manliness in poor and middle-class houses, in town and country, that has not got into literature, and never will, but that keeps the earth sweet; that saves on superfluities, and spends on essentials; that goes rusty, and educates the boy; that sells the horse, but builds the school; works early and late, takes two looms in the factory, three looms, six looms, but pays off the mortgage on the paternal farm, and then goes back cheerfully to work again.

We can ill spare the commanding social benefits of cities; they must be used; yet cautiously, and haughtily, — and will yield their best values to him who best can do without them. Keep the town for occasions, but the habits should be formed to retirement. Solitude, the safeguard of mediocrity, is to genius the stern friend, the cold, obscure shelter where moult the wings which will bear it farther than suns and stars. He who should inspire and lead his race must be defended from travelling with the souls of other men, from living, breathing, reading, and writing in the daily, time-worn yoke of their opinions. "In the morning, — solitude," said Pythagoras; that Nature may speak to the imagination, as she does never in company, and that her favorite may make acquaintance with those divine strengths which disclose themselves to serious and abstracted thought. 'T is very certain that Plato, Plotinus, Archimedes, Hermes, Newton, Milton, Wordsworth, did not live in a crowd, but descended into it from time to time as benefactors; and the wise instructor will press this point of securing to the young soul in the disposition of time and the arrangements of living, periods and habits of solitude. The high advantage of university life is often the mere mechanical one, I may call it, of a separate chamber and fire, — which parents will allow the boy without hesitation at Cambridge, but do not think needful at home. We say solitude, to mark the character of the tone of thought; but if it can be shared between two or more than two, it is happier, and not less noble. "We four," wrote Neander to his sacred friends, "will enjoy at Halle the inward blessedness of a *civitas Dei*, whose foundations are forever friendship. The more I know you, the more I dissatisfy and must dissatisfy all my wonted companions. Their very presence stupefies me. The common understanding withdraws itself from the one centre of all existence."

Solitude takes off the pressure of present importunities that more catholic and humane relations may appear. The saint and poet seek privacy to ends the most public and universal; and it is the secret of culture, to interest the man more in his public than in his private quality. Here is a new poem, which elicits a good many comments in the journals, and in conversation. From these it is easy, at last, to eliminate the verdict which readers passed upon it; and that is, in the main, unfavorable. The poet, as a craftsman, is only interested in the praise accorded to him, and not in the censure, though it be just. And the poor little poet hearkens only to that, and rejects the censure, as proving incapacity in the critic. But the poet *cultivated* becomes a stockholder in both companies, — say Mr. Curfew, — in the Curfew stock, and in the *humanity* stock; and, in the last, exults as much in the demonstration of the unsoundness of Curfew, as his interest in the former gives him pleasure in the currency of Curfew. For, the depreciation of his Curfew stock only shows the immense values of the humanity stock. As soon as he sides with his critic against himself, with joy, he is a cultivated man.

We must have an intellectual quality in all property and in all action, or they are naught. I must have children, I must have events, I must have a social state and history, or my thinking and speaking want body or basis. But to give these accessories any value, I must know them as contingent and rather showy possessions, which pass for more to the people than to me. We see this abstraction in scholars, as a matter of course; but what a charm it adds when observed in practical men. Bonaparte, like Cæsar, was intellectual, and could look at every object for itself, without affection. Though an egotist *à l'outrance*, he could criticise a play, a building, a character, on universal grounds, and give a just opinion. A man known to us only as a celebrity in politics or in trade gains largely in our esteem if we discover that he has some intellectual taste or skill; as when we learn of Lord Fairfax, the Long Parliament's general, his passion for antiquarian studies; or of the French regicide Carnot, his sublime genius in mathematics; or of a living banker, his success in poetry; or of a partisan journalist, his devotion to ornithology. So, if in travelling in the dreary wildernesses of Arkansas or Texas, we should observe on the next seat a man reading Horace, or Martial, or Calderon, we should wish to hug him. In callings that require roughest energy, soldiers, sea-captains, and civil engineers sometimes betray a fine insight, if only through a certain gentleness when off duty; a good-natured admission that there are illusions, and who shall say that he is not their sport? We only vary the phrase, not the doctrine, when we say that culture opens the sense of beauty. A man is a beggar who only lives to the useful, and, however he may serve as a pin or rivet in the social machine, cannot be said to have arrived at self-possession. I suffer, every day, from the want of perception of beauty in people. They do not know the charm with which all moments and objects can be embellished, the charm of manners, of self-command, of benevolence. Repose and cheerfulness are the badge of the gentleman, — repose in energy. The Greek battle-pieces are calm; the heroes, in whatever violent actions engaged, retain a serene aspect; as we say of Niagara, that it falls without speed. A cheerful, intelligent face is the end of culture, and success enough. For it indicates the purpose of Nature and wisdom attained.

When our higher faculties are in activity, we are domesticated, and awkwardness and discomfort give place to natural and agreeable movements. It is noticed, that the consideration of the great periods and spaces of astronomy induces a dignity of mind, and an indifference to death. The influence of fine scenery, the presence of mountains, appeases our irritations and elevates our friendships. Even a high dome, and the expansive interior of a cathedral, have a sensible effect on manners. I have heard that stiff people lose something of their awkwardness under high ceilings, and in spacious halls. I think sculpture and painting have an effect to teach us manners, and abolish hurry.

But, over all, culture must reinforce from higher influx the empirical skills of eloquence, or of politics, or of trade, and the useful arts. There is a certain loftiness of thought and power to marshal and adjust particulars, which can only come from an insight of their whole connection. The orator who has once seen things in their divine order, will never quite lose sight of this, and will come to affairs as from a higher ground, and, though he will say nothing of philosophy, he will have a certain mastery in dealing with them, and an incapableness of being dazzled or frighted, which will distinguish his handling from that of attorneys and factors. A man who stands on a good footing with the heads of parties at Washington, reads the rumors of the newspapers, and the guesses of provincial politicians, with a key to the right and wrong in each statement, and sees well enough where all this will end. Archimedes will look through your Connecticut machine, at a glance, and judge of its fitness. And much more, a wise man who knows not only what Plato, but what Saint John can show him, can easily raise the affair he deals with to a certain majesty. Plato says Pericles owed this elevation to the lessons of Anaxagoras. Burke descended from a higher sphere when he would influence human affairs. Franklin, Adams, Jefferson, Washington, stood on a fine humanity, before which the brawls of modern senates are but pot-house politics.

But there are higher secrets of culture, which are not for the apprentices, but for proficients. These are lessons only for the brave. We must know our friends under ugly masks. The calamities are our friends. Ben Jonson specifies in his address to the Muse : —

> "Get him the time's long grudge, the court's ill-will,
> And, reconciled, keep him suspected still,
> Make him lose all his friends, and, what is worse,
> Almost all ways to any better course;
> With me thou leav'st a better Muse than thee,
> And which thou brought'st me, blessed Poverty."

We wish to learn philosophy by rote, and play at heroism. But the wiser God says, Take the shame, the poverty, and the penal solitude, that belong to truth-speaking. Try the rough water as well as the smooth. Rough water can teach lessons worth knowing. When the state is unquiet, personal qualities are more than ever decisive. Fear not a revolution which will constrain you to live five years in one. Don't be so tender at making an enemy now and then. Be willing to go to Coventry sometimes, and let the populace bestow on you their coldest contempts. The finished man of the world must eat of every apple once. He must hold his hatreds also at arm's length, and not remember spite. He has neither friends nor enemies, but values men only as channels of power.

He who aims high must dread an easy home and popular manners. Heaven sometimes hedges a rare character about with ungainliness and odium, as the burr that protects the fruit. If there is any great and good thing in store for you, it will not come at the first or the second call, nor in the shape of fashion, ease, and city drawing-rooms. Popularity is for dolls. "Steep and craggy," said Porphyry, "is the path of the gods." Open your Marcus Antoninus. In the opinion of the ancients, he was the great man who scorned to shine, and who contested the frowns of fortune. They preferred the noble vessel too late for the tide, contending with winds and waves, dismantled and unrigged, to her companion borne into harbor with colors flying and guns firing. There is none of the social goods that may not be purchased too dear, and mere amiableness must not take rank with high aims and self-subsistency.

Bettine replies to Goethe's mother, who chides her disregard of dress, "If I cannot do as I have a mind, in our poor Frankfort, I shall not carry things far." And the youth must rate at its true mark the inconceivable levity of local opinion. The longer we live, the more we must endure the elementary existence of men and women; and every brave heart must treat society as a child, and never allow it to dictate.

"All that class of the severe and restrictive virtues," said Burke, "are almost too costly for humanity." Who wishes to be severe? Who wishes to resist the eminent and polite, in behalf of the poor, and low, and impolite? and who that dares do it, can keep his temper sweet, his frolic spirits? The high virtues are not debonair, but have their redress in being illustrious at last. What forests of laurel we bring, and the tears of mankind, to those who stood firm against the opinion of their contemporaries! The measure of a master is his success in bringing all men round to his opinion twenty years later.

Let me say here, that culture cannot begin too early. In talking with scholars, I observe that they lost on ruder companions those years of boyhood which alone could give imaginative literature a religious and infinite quality in their esteem. I find, too, that the chance for appreciation is much increased by being the son of an appreciator, and that these boys who now grow up are caught not only years too late, but two or three births too late, to make the best scholars of. And I think it a presentable motive to a scholar, that, as, in an old community, a well-born proprietor is usually found, after the first heats of youth, to be a careful husband, and to feel a habitual desire that the estate shall suffer no harm by his administration, but shall be delivered down to the next heir in as good condition as he received it; — so, a considerate man will reckon himself a subject of that secular melioration by which mankind is mollified, cured, and refined, and will shun every expenditure of his forces on pleasure or gain, which will jeopard this social and secular accumulation.

The fossil strata show us that Nature began with rudimental forms, and rose to the more complex, as fast as the earth was fit for their dwelling-place; and that the lower perish, as the higher appear. Very few of our race can be said to be yet finished men. We still carry sticking to us some remains of the preceding inferior quadruped organization. We call these millions men; but they are not yet men. Half engaged in the soil, pawing to get free, man needs all the music that can be brought to disengage him. If Love, red Love, with tears and joy; if Want with his scourge; if War with his cannonade; if Christianity with his charity; if Trade with its money; if Art with its portfolios; if Science with her telegraphs through the deeps of space and time; can set his dull nerves throbbing, and by loud taps on the tough chrysalis, can break its walls, and let the new creature emerge erect and free, — make way, and sing pæan! The age of the quadruped is to go out, — the age of the brain and of the heart is to come in. The time will come when the evil forms we have known can no more be organized. Man's culture can spare nothing, wants all the material. He is to convert all impediments into instruments, all enemies into power. The formidable mischief will only make the more useful slave. And if one shall read the future of the race hinted in the organic effort of Nature to mount and meliorate, and the corresponding impulse to the Better in the human being, we shall dare affirm that there is nothing he will not overcome and convert, until at last culture shall absorb the chaos and gehenna. He will convert the Furies into Muses, and the hells into benefit.

V.

BEHAVIOR.

Grace, Beauty, and Caprice
Build this golden portal;
Graceful women, chosen men
Dazzle every mortal:
Their sweet and lofty countenance
His enchanting food;
He need not go to them, their forms
Beset his solitude.
He looketh seldom in their face,
His eyes explore the ground,
The green grass is a looking-glass
Whereon their traits are found.
Little he says to them,
So dances his heart in his breast,
Their tranquil mien bereaveth him
Of wit, of words, of rest.
Too weak to win, too fond to shun
The tyrants of his doom,
The much deceived Endymion
Slips behind a tomb.

BEHAVIOR.

THE soul which animates Nature is not less significantly published in the figure, movement, and gesture of animated bodies, than in its last vehicle of articulate speech. This silent and subtile language is Manners; not *what*, but *how*. Life expresses. A statue has no tongue, and needs none. Good tableaux do not need declamation. Nature tells every secret once. Yes, but in man she tells it all the time, by form, attitude, gesture, mien, face, and parts of the face, and by the whole action of the machine. The visible carriage or action of the individual, as resulting from his organization and his will combined, we call manners. What are they but thought entering the hands and feet, controlling the movements of the body, the speech and behavior?

There is always a best way of doing everything, if it be to boil an egg. Manners are the happy ways of doing things; each once a stroke of genius or of love, — now repeated and hardened into usage. They form at last a rich varnish, with which the routine of life is washed, and its details adorned. If they are superficial, so are the dew-drops which give such a depth to the morning meadows. Manners are very communicable; men catch them from each other. Consuelo, in the romance, boasts of the lessons she had given the nobles in manners, on the stage; and, in real life, Talma taught Napoleon the arts of behavior. Genius invents fine manners, which the baron and the baroness copy very fast, and, by the advantage of a palace, better the instruction. They stereotype the lesson they have learned into a mode.

The power of manners is incessant, — an element as unconcealable as fire. The nobility cannot in any country be disguised, and no more in a republic or a democracy, than in a kingdom. No man can resist their influence. There are certain manners which are learned in good society, of that force, that, if a person have them, he or she must be considered, and is everywhere welcome, though without beauty, or wealth, or genius. Give a boy address and accomplishments, and you give him the mastery of palaces and fortunes where he goes. He has not the trouble of earning or owning them; they solicit him to enter and possess. We send girls of a timid, retreating disposition to the boarding-school, to the riding-school, to the ball-room, or wheresoever they can come into acquaintance and nearness of leading persons of their own sex; where they might learn address, and see it near at hand. The power of a woman of fashion to lead, and also to daunt and repel, derives from their belief that she knows resources and behaviors not known to them; but when these have mastered her secret, they learn to confront her, and recover their self-possession.

Every day bears witness to their gentle rule. People who would obtrude, now do not obtrude. The mediocre circle learns to demand that which belongs to a high state of nature or of culture. Your manners are always under examination, and by committees little suspected, — a police in citizens' clothes, — but are awarding or denying you very high prizes when you least think of it.

We talk much of utilities, — but 't is our manners that associate us. In hours of business, we go to him who knows, or has, or does this or that which we want, and we do not let our taste or feeling stand in the way. But this activity over, we return to the indolent state, and wish for those we can be at ease with; those who will go where we go, whose manners do not offend us, whose social tone chimes with ours. When we reflect on their persuasive and cheering force; how they recommend, prepare, and draw people together; how, in all clubs, manners make the members; how manners make the fortune of the ambitious youth; that, for the most part, his manners marry him, and, for the most part, he marries manners; when we think what keys they are, and to what secrets; what high lessons and inspiring tokens of character they convey; and what divination is required in us, for the reading of this fine telegraph, we see what range the subject has, and what relations to convenience, power, and beauty.

Their first service is very low, — when they are the minor morals: but 't is the beginning of civility, — to make us, I mean, endurable to each other. We prize them for their rough-plastic, abstergent force; to get people out of the quadruped state; to get them washed, clothed, and set up on end; to slough their animal husks and habits; compel them to be clean; overawe their spite and meanness, teach them to stifle the base, and choose the generous expression, and make them know how much happier the generous behaviors are.

Bad behavior the laws cannot reach. Society is infested with rude, cynical, restless, and frivolous persons who prey upon the rest, and whom, a public opinion concentrated into good manners, — forms accepted by the sense of all, — can reach: — the contradictors and railers at public and private tables, who are like terriers, who conceive it the duty of a dog of honor to growl at any passer-by, and do the honors of the house by barking him out of sight: — I have seen men who neigh like a horse when you contradict them, or say something which they do not understand: — then the overbold, who make their own invitation to your hearth; the persevering talker, who gives you his society in large, saturating doses; the pitiers of themselves, — a perilous class; the frivolous Asmodeus, who relies on you to find him in ropes of sand to twist; the monotones; in short, every stripe of absurdity; — these are social inflictions which the magistrate cannot cure or defend you from, and which must be intrusted to the restraining force of custom, and proverbs, and familiar rules of behavior impressed on young people in their school-days.

In the hotels on the banks of the Mississippi, they print, or used to print, among the rules of the house, that "no gentleman can be permitted to come to the public table without his coat"; and in the same country, in the pews of the churches, little placards plead with the worshipper against the fury of expectoration. Charles Dickens self-sacrificingly undertook the reformation of our American manners in unspeakable particulars. I think the lesson was not quite lost; that it held bad manners up, so that the churls could see the deformity. Unhappily, the book had its own deformities. It ought not to need to print in a reading-room a caution to strangers not to speak loud; nor to persons who look over fine engravings, that they should be handled like cobwebs and butterflies' wings; nor to persons who look at marble statues, that they shall not smite them with canes. But, even in the perfect civilization of this city, such cautions are not quite needless in the Athenæum and City Library.

Manners are factitious, and grow out of circumstance as well as out of character. If you look at the pictures of patricians and of peasants, of different periods and countries, you will see how well they match the same classes in our towns. The modern aristocrat not only is well drawn in Titian's Venetian doges, and in Roman coins and statues, but also in the pictures which Commodore Perry brought home of dignitaries in Japan. Broad lands and great interests not only arrive to such heads as can manage them, but form manners of power. A keen eye, too, will see nice gradations of rank, or see in the manners the degree of homage the party is wont to receive. A prince who is accustomed every day to be courted and deferred to by the highest grandees, acquires a corresponding expectation, and a becoming mode of receiving and replying to this homage.

There are always exceptional people and modes. English grandees affect to be farmers. Claverhouse is a fop, and, under the finish of dress, and levity of behavior, hides the terror of his war. But nature and Destiny are honest, and never fail to leave their mark, to hang out a sign for each and for every quality. It is much to conquer one's face, and perhaps the ambitious youth thinks he has got the whole secret when he has learned, that disengaged manners are commanding. Don't be deceived by a facile exterior. Tender men sometimes have strong wills. We had, in Massachusetts, an old statesman, who had sat all his life in courts and in chairs of state, without overcoming an extreme irritability of face, voice, and bearing: when he spoke, his voice would not serve him; it cracked, it broke, it wheezed, it piped; little cared he; he knew that it had got to pipe, or wheeze, or screech his argument and his indignation. When he sat down, after speaking, he seemed in a sort of fit, and held on to his chair with both hands: but underneath all this irritability was a puissant will, firm, and advancing, and a memory in which lay in order and method like geologic strata every fact of his history, and under the control of his will.

Manners are partly factitious, but, mainly, there must be capacity for culture in the blood. Else all culture is vain. The obstinate prejudice in favor of blood, which lies at the base of the feudal and monarchical fabrics of the Old World, has some reason in common experience. Every man — mathematician, artist, soldier, or merchant — looks with confidence for some traits and talents in his own child, which he would not dare to presume in the child of a stranger. The Orientalists are very orthodox on this point. "Take a thorn-bush," said the emir Abdel-Kader, "and sprinkle it for a whole year with water; it will yield nothing but thorns. Take a date-tree, leave it without culture, and it will always produce dates. Nobility is the date-tree, and the Arab populace is a bush of thorns."

A main fact in the history of manners is the wonderful expressiveness of the human body. If it were made of glass, or of air, and the thoughts were written on steel tablets within, it could not publish more truly its meaning than now. Wise men read very sharply all your private history in your look and gait and behavior. The whole economy of nature is bent on expression. The tell-tale body is all tongues. Men are like Geneva watches with crystal faces which expose the whole movement. They carry the liquor of life flowing up and down in these beautiful bottles, and announcing to the curious how it is with them. The face and eyes reveal what the spirit is doing, how old it is, what aims it has. The eyes indicate the antiquity of the soul, or, through how many forms it has already ascended. It almost violates the proprieties, if we say above the breath here, what the confessing eyes do not hesitate to utter to every street passenger.

Man cannot fix his eye on the sun, and so far seems imperfect. In Siberia, a late traveller found men who could see the satellites of Jupiter with their unarmed eye. In some respects the animals excel us. The birds have a longer sight, beside the advantage by their wings of a higher observatory. A cow can bid her calf, by secret signal, probably of the eye, to run away, or to lie down and hide itself. The jockeys say of certain horses, that "they look over the whole ground." The outdoor life, and hunting, and labor, give equal vigor to the human eye. A farmer looks out at you as strong as the horse ; his eye-beam is like the stroke of a staff. An eye can threaten like a loaded and levelled gun, or can insult like hissing or kicking ; or, in its altered mood, by beams of kindness, it can make the heart dance with joy.

The eye obeys exactly the action of the mind. When a thought strikes us, the eyes fix, and remain gazing at a distance ; in enumerating the names of persons or of countries, as France, Germany, Spain, Turkey, the eyes wink at each new name. There is no nicety of learning sought by the mind, which the eyes do not vie in acquiring. "An Artist," said Michel Angelo, "must have his measuring tools not in the hand, but in the eye" ; and there is no end to the catalogue of its performances, whether in indolent vision, (that of health and beauty,) or in strained vision, (that of art and labor.)

Eyes are bold as lions, — roving, running, leaping, here

and there, far and near. They speak all languages. They wait for no introduction; they are no Englishmen; ask no leave of age or rank; they respect neither poverty nor riches, neither learning nor power, nor virtue, nor sex, but intrude, and come again, and go through and through you, in a moment of time. What inundation of life and thought is discharged from one soul into another, through them! The glance is natural magic. The mysterious communication established across a house between two entire strangers, moves all the springs of wonder. The communication by the glance is in the greatest part not subject to the control of the will. It is the bodily symbol of identity of nature. We look into the eyes to know if this other form is another self, and the eyes will not lie, but make a faithful confession what inhabitant is there. The revelations are sometimes terrific. The confession of a low, usurping devil is there made, and the observer shall seem to feel the stirring of owls, and bats, and horned hoofs, where he looked for innocence and simplicity. 'T is remarkable, too, that the spirit that appears at the windows of the house does at once invest himself in a new form of his own, to the mind of the beholder.

The eyes of men converse as much as their tongues, with the advantage, that the ocular dialect needs no dictionary, but is understood all the world over. When the eyes say one thing, and the tongue another, a practised man relies on the language of the first. If the man is off his centre, the eyes show it. You can read in the eyes of your companion, whether your argument hits him, though his tongue will not confess it. There is a look by which a man shows he is going to say a good thing, and a look when he has said it. Vain and forgotten are all the fine offers and offices of hospitality, if there is no holiday in the eye. How many furtive inclinations avowed by the eye, though dissembled by the lips! One comes away from a company, in which, it may easily happen, he has said nothing, and no important remark has been addressed to him, and yet, if in sympathy with the society, he shall not have a sense of this fact, such a stream of life has been flowing into him, and out from him, through the eyes. There are eyes, to be sure, that give no more admission into the man than blueberries. Others are liquid and deep, — wells that a man might fall into; — others are aggressive and devouring, seem to call out the police, take all too much notice, and require crowded Broadways, and the security of millions, to protect individuals against them. The military eye I meet, now darkly sparkling under clerical, now under rustic brows. 'T is the city of Lacedæmon; 't is a stack of bayonets. There are asking eyes, asserting eyes, prowling eyes; and eyes full of fate, — some of good, and some of sinister omen. The alleged power to charm down insanity, or ferocity in beasts, is a power behind the eye. It must be a victory achieved in the will, before it can be signified in the eye. 'T is very certain that each man carries in his eye the exact indication of his rank in the immense scale of men, and we are always learning to read it. A complete man should need no auxiliaries to his personal presence. Whoever looked on him would consent to his will, being certified that his aims were generous and universal. The reason why men do not obey us, is because they see the mud at the bottom of our eye.

If the organ of sight is such a vehicle of power, the other features have their own. A man finds room in the few square inches of the face for the traits of all his ancestors; for the expression of all his history, and his wants. The sculptor, and Winckelmann, and Lavater, will tell you how significant a feature is the nose; how its forms express strength or weakness of will, and good or bad temper. The nose of Julius Cæsar, of Dante, and of Pitt suggest "the terrors of the beak." What refinement, and what limitations, the teeth betray! "Beware you don't laugh," said the wise mother, "for then you show all your faults."

Balzac left in manuscript a chapter, which he called "*Théorie de la démarche*," in which he says: "The look, the voice, the respiration, and the attitude or walk, are identical. But, as it has not been given to man, the power to stand guard, at once over these four different simultaneous expressions of his thought, watch that one which speaks out the truth, and you will know the whole man."

Palaces interest us mainly in the exhibition of manners, which in the idle and expensive society dwelling in them are raised to a high art. The maxim of courts is that manner is power. A calm and resolute bearing, a polished speech, an embellishment of trifles, and the art of hiding all uncomfortable feeling, are essential to the courtier; and Saint Simon, and Cardinal de Retz, and Rœderer, and an encyclopædia of *Memoires*, will instruct you, if you wish, in those potent secrets. Thus, it is a point of pride with kings, to remember faces and names. It is reported of one prince, that his head had the air of leaning downwards, in order not to humble the crowd. There are people who come in ever like a child with a piece of good news. It was said of the late Lord Holland, that he always came down to breakfast with the air of a man who had just met with some signal good-fortune. In "*Notre Dame,*" the grandee took his place on the dais, with the look of one who is thinking of something else. But we must not peep and eavesdrop at palace-doors.

Fine manners need the support of fine manners in others. A scholar may be a well-bred man, or he may not. The enthusiast is introduced to polished scholars in society, and is chilled and silenced by finding himself not in their element. They all have somewhat which he has not, and, it seems, ought to have. But if he finds the scholar apart from his companions, it is then the enthusiast's turn, and the scholar has no defence, but must deal on his terms. Now they must fight the battle out on their private strengths. What is the talent of that character so common, — the successful man of the world, — in all marts, senates, and drawing-rooms? Manners: manners of power; sense to see his advantage, and manners up to it. See him approach his man. He knows that troops behave as they are handled at first; — that is his cheap secret; just what happens to every two persons who meet on any affair, one instantly perceives that he has the key of the situation, that his will comprehends the other's will, as the cat does the mouse; and he has only to use courtesy, and furnish good-natured reasons to his victim to cover up the chain, lest he be shamed into resistance.

The theatre in which this science of manners has a formal importance is not with us a court, but dress-circles, wherein, after the close of the day's business, men and women meet at leisure, for mutual entertainment, in ornamented drawing-rooms. Of course, it has every variety of attraction and merit: but, to earnest persons, to youths or maidens who have great objects at heart, we cannot extol it highly. A well-dressed, talkative company, where each is bent to amuse the other, — yet the high-born Turk who came hither fancied that every woman seemed to be suffering for a chair; that all the talkers were brained and exhausted by the deoxygenated air: it spoiled the best persons: it put all on stilts. Yet here are the secret biographies written and read. The aspect of that man is repulsive; I do not wish to deal with him. The other is irritable, shy, and on his guard. The youth looks humble and manly: I choose him. Look on this woman. There is not beauty, nor brilliant sayings, nor distinguished power to serve you; but all see her gladly; her whole air and impression are healthful. Here come the sentimentalists, and the invalids. Here is Elise, who caught cold in coming into the world, and has always increased it since. Here are creep-mouse manners; and thievish manners. "Look at Northcote," said Fuseli; "he looks like a rat that has seen a cat." In the shallow company, easily excited, easily tired, here is the columnar Bernard: the Alleghanies do not express more repose than his behavior. Here are the sweet following eyes of Cecile: it seemed always that she demanded the heart. Nothing can be more excellent in kind than the Corinthian grace of Gertrude's manners, and yet Blanche, who has no manners, has better manners than she; for the movements of Blanche are the sallies of a spirit which is sufficient for the moment, and she can afford to express every thought by instant action.

Manners have been somewhat cynically defined to be a contrivance of wise men to keep fools at a distance. Fashion is shrewd to detect those who do not belong to her train, and seldom wastes her attentions. Society is very swift in its instincts, and, if you do not belong to it, resists and sneers at you; or quietly drops you. The first weapon enrages the party attacked; the second is still more effective, but is not to be resisted, as the date of the transaction is not easily found. People grow up and grow old under this infliction, and never suspect the truth, ascribing the solitude which acts on them very injuriously to any cause but the right one.

The basis of good manners is self-reliance. Necessity is the law of all who are not self-possessed. Those who are not self-possessed obtrude and pain us. Some men appear to feel that they belong to a Pariah caste. They fear to offend, they bend and apologize, and walk through life with a timid step. As we sometimes dream that we are in a well-dressed company without any coat, so Godfrey acts ever as if he suffered from some mortifying circumstance. The hero should find himself at home, wherever he is; should impart comfort by his own security and good-nature to all beholders. The hero is suffered to be himself. A person of strong mind comes to perceive that for him an immunity is secured so long as he renders to society that service which is native and proper to him, —an immunity from all the observances, yea, and duties, which society so tyrannically imposes on the rank and file of its members. "Euripides," says Aspasia, "has not the fine manners of Sophocles: but," she adds good-humoredly, "the movers and masters of our souls have surely a right to throw out their limbs as carelessly as they please, on the world that belongs to them, and before the creatures they have animated." *

Manners require time, as nothing is more vulgar than haste. Friendship should be surrounded with ceremonies and respects, and not crushed into corners. Friendship requires more time than poor busy men can usually command. Here comes to me Roland, with a delicacy of sentiment leading and inwrapping him like a divine cloud or holy ghost. 'T is a great destitution to both that this should not be entertained with large leisures, but contrariwise should be balked by importunate affairs.

But through this lustrous varnish, the reality is ever shining. 'T is hard to keep the *what* from breaking through this pretty painting of the *how.* The core will come to the surface. Strong will and keen perception overpower old manners, and create new; and the thought of the present moment has a greater value than all the past. In persons of character, we do not remark manners, because of their instantaneousness. We are surprised by the thing done, out of all power to watch the way of it. Yet nothing is more charming than to recognize the great style which runs through the actions of such. People masquerade before us in their fortunes, titles, offices, and connections, as academic or civil presidents, or senators, or professors, or great lawyers, and impose on the frivolous, and a good deal on each other, by these fames. At least, it is a point of prudent good manners to treat these reputations tenderly, as if they were merited. But the sad realist knows these fellows at a glance, and they know him; as when in Paris the chief of the police enters a ball-room, so many diamonded pretenders shrink and make themselves as inconspicuous as they can, or give him a supplicating look as they pass. "I had received," said a sibyl, — "I had received at birth the fatal gift of penetration"; and these Cassandras are always born.

Manners impress as they indicate real power. A man who is sure of his point, carries a broad and contented expression, which everybody reads. And you cannot rightly train one to an air and manner, except by making him the kind of man of whom that manner is the natural expression. Nature forever puts a premium on reality. What is done for effect, is seen

* Landor, *Pericles and Aspasia.*

to be done for effect; what is done for love, is felt to be done for love. A man inspires affection and honor, because he was not lying in wait for these. The things of a man for which we visit him, were done in the dark and the cold. A little integrity is better than any career. So deep are the sources of this surface-action, that even the size of your companion seems to vary with his freedom of thought. Not only is he larger, when at ease, and his thoughts generous, but everything around him becomes variable with expression. No carpenter's rule, no rod and chain, will measure the dimensions of any house or house-lot: go into the house: if the proprietor is constrained and deferring, 't is of no importance how large his house, how beautiful his grounds, — you quickly come to the end of all: but if the man is self-possessed, happy, and at home, his house is deep-founded, indefinitely large and interesting, the roof and dome buoyant as the sky. Under the humblest roof, the commonest person in plain clothes sits there massive, cheerful, yet formidable like the Egyptian colossi.

Neither Aristotle, nor Leibnitz, nor Junius, nor Champollion has set down the grammar-rules of this dialect, older than Sanscrit; but they who cannot yet read English, can read this. Men take each other's measure, when they meet for the first time, — and every time they meet. How do they get this rapid knowledge, even before they speak, of each other's power and dispositions? One would say, that the persuasion of their speech is not in what they say, — or, that men do not convince by their argument, — but by their personality, by who they are, and what they said and did heretofore. A man already strong is listened to, and everything he says is applauded. Another opposes him with sound argument, but the argument is scouted, until by and by it gets into the mind of some weighty person; then it begins to tell on the community.

Self-reliance is the basis of behavior, as it is the guaranty that the powers are not squandered in too much demonstration. In this country, where school education is universal, we have a superficial culture, and a profusion of reading and writing and expression. We parade our nobilities in poems and orations, instead of working them up into happiness. There is a whisper out of the ages to him who can understand it, — 'whatever is known to thyself alone has always very great value.' There is some reason to believe, that, when a man does not write his poetry, it escapes by other vents through him, instead of the one vent of writing; clings to his form and manners, whilst poets have often nothing poetical about them except their verses. Jacobi said, that "when a man has fully expressed his thought, he has somewhat less possession of it." One would say, the rule is, — What a man is irresistibly urged to say, helps him and us. In explaining his thought to others, he explains it to himself: but when he opens it for show, it corrupts him.

Society is the stage on which manners are shown; novels are their literature. Novels are the journal or record of manners; and the new importance of these books derives from the fact, that the novelist begins to penetrate the surface, and treat this part of life more worthily. The novels used to be all alike, and had a quite vulgar tone. The novels used to lead us on to a foolish interest in the fortunes of the boy and girl they described. The boy was to be raised from a humble to a high position. He was in want of a wife and a castle, and the object of the story was to supply him with one or both. We watched sympathetically, step by step, his climbing, until, at last, the point is gained, the wedding-day is fixed, and we follow the gala procession home to the bannered portal, when the doors are slammed in our face, and the poor reader is left outside in the cold, not enriched by so much as an idea, or a virtuous impulse.

But the victories of character are instant, and victories for all. Its greatness enlarges all. We are fortified by every heroic anecdote. The novels are as useful as Bibles, if they teach you the secret, that the best of life is conversation, and the greatest success is confidence, or perfect understanding between sincere people. 'T is a French definition of friendship, *rien que s'entendre*, good understanding. The highest compact we can make with our fellow, is, — 'Let there be truth between us two forevermore.' That is the charm in all good novels, as it is the charm in all good histories, that the heroes mutually understand, from the first, and deal loyally, and with a profound trust in each other. It is sublime to feel and say of another, I need never meet, or speak, or write to him: we need not reinforce ourselves, or send tokens of remembrance: I rely on him as on myself: if he did thus or thus, I know it was right.

In all the superior people I have met, I notice directness, truth spoken more truly, as if everything of obstruction of malformation, had been trained away. What have they to conceal? What have they to exhibit? Between simple and noble persons, there is always a quick intelligence: they recognize at sight, and meet on a better ground than the talents and skills they may chance to possess, namely, on sincerity and uprightness. For, it is not what talents or genius a man has, but how he is to his talents, that constitutes friendship and character. The man that stands by himself, the universe stands by him also. It is related of the monk Basle, that, being excommunicated by the Pope, he was, at his death, sent in charge of an angel to find a fit place of suffering in hell; but, such was the eloquence and good-humor of the monk, that, wherever he went he was received gladly, and civilly treated, even by the most uncivil angels: and, when he came to discourse with them, instead of contradicting or forcing him, they took his part, and adopted his manners: and even good angels came from far, to see him, and take up their abode with him. The angel that was sent to find a place of torment for him attempted to remove him to a worse pit, but with no better success; for such was the contented spirit of the monk, that he found something to praise in every place and company, though in hell, and made a kind of heaven of it. At last the escorting angel returned with his prisoner to them that sent him, saying, that no phlegethon could be found that would burn him; for that, in whatever condition, Basle remained incorrigibly Basle. The legend says, his sentence was remitted, and he was allowed to go into heaven, and was canonized as a saint.

There is a stroke of magnanimity in the correspondence of Bonaparte with his brother Joseph, when the latter was King of Spain, and complained that he missed in Napoleon's letters the affectionate tone which had marked their childish correspondence. "I am sorry," replies Napoleon, "you think you shall find your brother again only in the Elysian Fields. It is natural, that at forty, he should not feel towards you as he did at twelve. But his feelings towards you have greater truth and strength. His friendship has the features of his mind."

How much we forgive in those who yield us the rare spectacle of heroic manners! We will pardon them the want of books, of arts, and even of the gentler virtues. How tenaciously we remember them! Here is a lesson which I brought along with me in boyhood from the Latin School, and which ranks with the best of Roman anecdotes. Marcus Scaurus was accused by Quintus Varius Hispanus, that he had excited the allies to take arms against the Republic. But he, full of firmness and gravity, defended himself in this manner: "Quintus Varius Hispanus alleges that Marcus Scaurus, President of the Senate, excited the allies to arms: Marcus Scaurus, President of the Senate, denies it. There is no witness. Which do you believe, Romans?" "*Utri creditis, Quirites?*" When he had said these words, he was absolved by the assembly of the people.

I have seen manners that make a similar impression with personal beauty; that give the like exhilaration, and refine us like that; and, in memorable experiences, they are suddenly better than beauty, and make that superfluous and ugly. But they must be marked by fine perception, the acquaintance with real beauty. They must always show self-control: you shall not be facile, apologetic, or leaky, but king over your word; and every gesture and action shall indicate power at rest. Then they must be inspired by the good heart. There is no beautifier of complexion, or form, or behavior, like the wish to scatter joy and not pain around us. 'T is good to give a stranger a meal, or a night's lodging. 'T is better to be hospitable to his good meaning and thought, and give courage to a companion. We must be as courteous to a man as we are to a picture, which we are willing to give the advantage of a good light. Special precepts are not to be thought of: the talent of well-doing contains them all. Every hour will show a duty as paramount as that of my whim just now; and yet I will write it, — that there is one topic peremptorily forbidden to all well-bred, to all rational mortals, namely, their distempers. If you have not slept, or if you have slept, or if you have headache, or sciatica, or leprosy, or thunder-stroke, I beseech you, by all angels, to hold your peace, and not pollute the morning, to which all the housemates bring serene and pleasant thoughts, by corruption and groans. Come out of the azure. Love the day. Do not leave the sky out of your landscape. The oldest and the most deserving person should come very modestly into any newly awaked company, respecting the divine communications, out of which all must be presumed to have newly come. An old man who added an elevating culture to a large experience of life, said to me: "When you come into the room, I think I will study how to make humanity beautiful to you."

As respects the delicate question of culture, I do not think that any other than negative rules can be laid down. For positive rules, for suggestion, Nature alone inspires it. Who dare assume to guide a youth, a maid, to perfect manners? — the golden mean is so delicate, difficult, — say frankly, unattainable. What finest hands would not be clumsy to sketch the genial precepts of the young girl's demeanor? The chances seem infinite against success; and yet success is continually attained. There must not be secondariness, and 'tis a thousand to one that her air and manner will at once betray that she is not primary, but that there is some other one or many of her class, to whom she habitually postpones herself. But Nature lifts her easily, and without knowing it, over these impossibilities, and we are continually surprised with graces and felicities not only unteachable, but undescribable.

VI.

WORSHIP.

This is he, who, felled by foes,
Sprung harmless up, refreshed by blows:
He to captivity was sold,
But him no prison-bars would hold:
Though they sealed him in a rock,
Mountain chains he can unlock:
Thrown to lions for their meat,
The crouching lion kissed his feet:
Bound to the stake, no flames appalled,
But arched o'er him an honoring vault.
This is he men miscall Fate,
Threading dark ways, arriving late,
But ever coming in time to crown
The truth, and hurl wrongdoers down.
He is the oldest, and best known,
More near than aught thou call'st thy own,
Yet, greeted in another's eyes,
Disconcerts with glad surprise.
This is Jove, who, deaf to prayers,
Floods with blessings unawares.
Draw, if thou canst, the mystic line,
Severing rightly his from thine,
Which is human, which divine.

WORSHIP.

SOME of my friends have complained, when the preceding papers were read, that we discussed Fate, Power, and Wealth, on too low a platform; gave too much line to the evil spirit of the times; too many cakes to Cerberus; that we ran Cudworth's risk of making, by excess of candor, the argument of atheism so strong, that he could not answer it. I have no fears of being forced in my own despite to play, as we say, the devil's attorney. I have no infirmity of faith; no belief that it is of much importance what I or any man may say: I am sure that a certain truth will be said through me, though I should be dumb, or though I should try to say the reverse. Nor do I fear scepticism for any good soul. A just thinker will allow full swing to his scepticism. I dip my pen in the blackest ink, because I am not afraid of falling into my inkpot. I have no sympathy with a poor man I knew, who, when suicides abounded, told me he dared not look at his razor. We are of different opinions at different hours, but we always may be said to be at heart on the side of truth.

I see not why we should give ourselves such sanctified airs. If the Divine Providence has hid from men neither disease, nor deformity, nor corrupt society, but has stated itself out in passions, in war, in trade, in the love of power and pleasure, in hunger and need, in tyrannies, literatures, and arts, — let us not be so nice that we cannot write these facts down coarsely as they stand, or doubt but there is a counter-statement as ponderous, which we can arrive at, and which, being put, will make all square. The solar system has no anxiety about its reputation, and the credit of truth and honesty is as safe; nor have I any fear that a sceptical bias can be given by leaning hard on the sides of fate, of practical power, or of trade, which the doctrine of Faith cannot down-weigh. The strength of that principle is not measured in ounces and pounds; it tyrannizes at the centre of Nature. We may well give scepticism as much line as we can. The spirit will return and fill us. It drives the drivers. It counterbalances any accumulations of power.

"Heaven kindly gave our blood a moral flow."

We are born loyal. The whole creation is made of hooks and eyes, of bitumen, of sticking-plaster, and whether your community is made in Jerusalem or in California, of saints or of wreckers, it coheres in a perfect ball. Men as naturally make a state, or a church, as caterpillars a web. If they were more refined, it would be less formal, it would be nervous like that of the Shakers, who, from long habit of thinking and feeling together, it is said, are affected in the same way, at the same time, to work and to play, and as they go with perfect sympathy to their tasks in the field or shop, so are they inclined for a ride or a journey at the same instant, and the horses come up with the family carriage unbespoken to the door.

We are born believing. A man bears beliefs, as a tree bears apples. A self-poise belongs to every particle; and a rectitude to every mind, and is the Nemesis and protector of every society. I and my neighbors have been bred in the notion, that, unless we came soon to some good church, — Calvinism, or Behmenism, or Romanism, or Mormonism, — there would be a universal thaw and dissolution. No Isaiah or Jeremy has arrived. Nothing can exceed the anarchy that has followed in our skies. The stern old faiths have all pulverized. 'T is a whole population of gentlemen and ladies out in search of religions. 'T is as flat anarchy in our ecclesiastic realms, as that which existed in Massachusetts, in the Revolution, or which prevails now on the slope of the Rocky Mountains or Pike's Peak. Yet we make shift to live. Men are loyal. Nature has self-poise in all her works; certain proportions in which oxygen and azote combine, and, not less a harmony in faculties, a fitness in the spring and the regulator.

The decline of the influence of Calvin, or Fenelon, or Wesley, or Channing, need give us no uneasiness. The builder of heaven has not so ill constructed his creature as that the religion, that is, the public nature, should fall out: the public and the private element, like north and south, like inside and outside, like centrifugal and centripetal, adhere to every soul, and cannot be subdued, except the soul is dissipated. God builds his temple in the heart on the ruins of churches and religions.

In the last chapters, we treated some particulars of the question of culture. But the whole state of man is a state of culture; and its flowering and completion may be described as Religion, or Worship. There is always some religion, some hope and fear extended into the invisible, — from the blind boding which nails a horseshoe to the mast or the threshold, up to the song of the Elders in the Apocalypse. But the religion cannot rise above the state of the votary. Heaven always bears some proportion to earth. The god of the cannibals will be a cannibal, of the crusaders a crusader, and of the merchants a merchant. In all ages, souls out of time, extraordinary, prophetic, are born, who are rather related to the system of the world, than to their particular age and locality. These announce absolute truths, which, with whatever reverence received, are speedily dragged down into a savage interpretation. The interior tribes of our Indians, and some of the Pacific-Islanders, flog their gods, when things take an unfavorable turn. The Greek poets did not hesitate to let loose their petulant wit on their deities also. Laomedon, in his anger at Neptune and Apollo, who had built Troy for him, and demanded their price, does not hesitate to menace them that he will cut their ears off.* Among our Norse forefathers, King Olaf's mode of converting Eyvind to Christianity was to put a pan of glowing coals on his belly, which burst asunder. "Wilt thou now, Eyvind, believe in Christ?" asks Olaf, in excellent faith. Another argument was an adder put into the mouth of the reluctant disciple Rand, who refused to believe.

Christianity, in the romantic ages, signified European culture, — the grafted or meliorated tree in a crab forest. And to marry a pagan wife or husband was to marry Beast, and voluntarily to take a step backwards towards the baboon.

"Hengist had verament,
A daughter both fair and gent,
But she was heathen Sarazine,
And Vortigern for love fine
Her took to fere and to wife,
And was cursed in all his life;
For he let Christian wed heathen,
And mixed our blood as flesh and mathen." †

What Gothic mixtures the Christian creed drew from the pagan sources, Richard of Devizes's chronicle of Richard I.'s crusade, in the twelfth century, may show. King Richard taunts God with forsaking him: "O fie! O how unwilling should I be to

* Iliad, Book xxi. l. 455.

† Moths or worms.

forsake thee, in so forlorn and dreadful a position, were I thy lord and advocate, as thou art mine. In sooth, my standards will in future be despised, not through my fault, but through thine ; in sooth, not through any cowardice of my warfare, art thou thyself, my king and my God, conquered this day, and not Richard thy vassal." The religion of the early English poets is anomalous, so devout and so blasphemous, in the same breath. Such is Chaucer's extraordinary confusion of heaven and earth in the picture of Dido.

> " She was so fair,
> So young, so lusty, with her eyen glad,
> That if that God that heaven and earthe made
> Would have a love for beauty and goodness,
> And womanhede, truth, and seemliness,
> Whom should he loven but this lady sweet?
> There n' is no woman to him half so meet."

With these grossnesses, we complacently compare our own taste and decorum. We think and speak with more temperance and gradation, — but is not indifferentism as bad as superstition ?

We live in a transition period, when the old faiths which comforted nations, and not only so, but made nations, seem to have spent their force. I do not find the religions of men at this moment very creditable to them, but either childish and insignificant, or unmanly and effeminating. The fatal trait is the divorce between religion and morality. Here are know-nothing religions, or churches that prescribe intellect ; scortatory religions ; slave-holding and slave-trading religions ; and, even in the decent populations, idolatries wherein the whiteness of the ritual covers scarlet indulgence. The lover of the old religion complains that our contemporaries, scholars as well as merchants, succumb to a great despair, — have corrupted into a timorous conservatism, and believe in nothing. In our large cities, the population is godless, materialized, — no bond, no fellow-feeling, no enthusiasm. These are not men, but hungers, thirsts, fevers, and appetites walking. How is it people manage to live on, — so aimless as they are ? After their peppercorn aims are gained, it seems as if the lime in their bones alone held them together, and not any worthy purpose. There is no faith in the intellectual, none in the moral universe. There is faith in chemistry, in meat, and wine, in wealth, in machinery, in the steam-engine, galvanic battery, turbine-wheels, sewing machines, and in public opinion, but not in divine causes. A silent revolution has loosed the tension of the old religious sects, and, in place of the gravity and permanence of those societies of opinion, they run into freak and extravagance. In creeds never was such levity; witness the heathenisms in Christianity, the periodic "revivals," the Millennium mathematics, the peacock ritualism, the retrogression to Popery, the maundering of Mormons, the squalor of Mesmerism, the deliration of rappings, the rat and mouse revelation, thumps in table-drawers, and black art. The architecture, the music, the prayer, partake of the madness: the arts sink into shift and make-believe. Not knowing what to do, we ape our ancestors; the churches stagger backward to the mummeries of the Dark Ages. By the irresistible maturing of the general mind, the Christian traditions have lost their hold. The dogma of the mystic offices of Christ being dropped, and he standing on his genius as a moral teacher, 't is impossible to maintain the old emphasis of his personality; and it recedes, as all persons must, before the sublimity of the moral laws. From this change, and in the momentary absence of any religious genius that could offset the immense material activity, there is a feeling that religion is gone. When Paul Leroux offered his article "*Dieu*" to the conductor of a leading French journal, he replied, "*La question de Dieu manque d'actualité.*" In Italy, Mr. Gladstone said of the late King of Naples, "It has been a proverb, that he has erected the negation of God into a system of government." In this country, the like stupefaction was in the air, and the phrase "higher law" became a political jibe. What proof of infidelity, like the toleration and propagandism of slavery? What, like the direction of education? What, like the facility of conversion? What, like the externality of churches that once sucked the roots of right and wrong, and now have perished away till they are a speck of whitewash on the wall? What proof of scepticism like the base rate at which the highest mental and moral gifts are held? Let a man attain the highest and broadest culture that any American has possessed, then let him die by sea-storm, railroad collision, or other accident, and all America will acquiesce that the best thing has happened to him; that, after the education has gone far, such is the expensiveness of America, that the best use to put a fine person to, is, to drown him to save his board.

Another scar of this scepticism is the distrust in human virtue. It is believed by well-dressed proprietors that there is no more virtue than they possess; that the solid portion of society exist for the arts of comfort: that life is an affair to put somewhat between the upper and lower mandibles. How prompt the suggestion of a low motive! Certain patriots in England devoted themselves for years to creating a public opinion that should break down the corn-laws and establish free trade. 'Well,' says the man in the street, 'Cobden got a stipend out of it.' Kossuth fled hither across the ocean to try if he could rouse the New World to a sympathy with European liberty. 'Ay,' says New York, 'he made a handsome thing of it, enough to make him comfortable for life.'

See what allowance vice finds in the respectable and well-conditioned class. If a pickpocket intrude into the society of gentlemen, they exert what moral force they have, and he finds himself uncomfortable, and glad to get away. But if an adventurer go through all the forms, procure himself to be elected to a post of trust, as of senator, or president, — though by the same arts as we detest in the house-thief, — the same gentlemen who agree to discountenance the private rogue, will be forward to show civilities and marks of respect to the public one: and no amount of evidence of his crimes will prevent them giving him ovations, complimentary dinners, opening their own houses to him, and priding themselves on his acquaintance. We were not deceived by the professions of the private adventurer, — the louder he talked of his honor, the faster we counted our spoons; but we appeal to the sanctified preamble of the messages and proclamations of the public sinner, as the proof of sincerity. It must be that they who pay this homage have said to themselves, On the whole, we don't know about this that you call honesty; a bird in the hand is better.

Even well-disposed, good sort of people are touched with the same infidelity, and for brave, straightforward action, use half-measures and compromises. Forgetful that a little measure is a great error, forgetful that a wise mechanic uses a sharp tool, they go on choosing the dead men of routine. But the official men can in no wise help you in any question of to-day, they deriving entirely from the old dead things. Only those can help in counsel or conduct who did not make a party pledge to defend this or that, but who were appointed by God Almighty, before they came into the world, to stand for this which they uphold.

It has been charged that a want of sincerity in the leading men is a vice general throughout American society. But the multitude of the sick shall not make us deny the existence of health. In spite of our imbecility and terrors, and "universal decay of religion," &c., &c., the moral sense reappears to-day with the same morning newness that has been from of old the fountain of beauty and strength. You say, there is no religion now. 'T is like saying in rainy weather, there is no sun, when at that moment we are witnessing one of his superlative effects. The religion of the cultivated class now, to be sure, consists in an avoidance of acts and engagements which it was once their religion to assume. But this avoidance will yield spontaneous forms in their due hour. There is a principle which is the basis of things, which all speech aims to say, and all action to evolve, a simple, quiet, undescribed, undescribable presence, dwelling very peacefully in us, our rightful lord; we are not to do, but to let do; not to work, but to be worked upon; and to this homage there is a consent of all thoughtful and just men in all ages and conditions. To this sentiment belong vast and sudden enlargements of power. 'T is remarkable that our faith in ecstasy consists with total inexperience of it. It is the order of the world to educate with accuracy the senses and the understanding; and the enginery at work to draw out these powers in priority, no doubt, has its office. But we are never without a hint that these powers are mediate and servile, and that we are one day to deal with real being, — essences with essences. Even the fury of material activity has some results friendly to moral health. The energetic action of the times develops individualism, and the religious appear isolated. I esteem this a step in the right direction. Heaven deals with us on no representative system. Souls are not saved in bundles. The Spirit saith to the man, 'How is it with thee? thee personally? is it well? is it ill?' For a great nature, it is a happiness to escape a religious training, — religion of character is so apt to be invaded. Religion must always be a crab fruit: it cannot be grafted and keep its wild beauty. "I have seen," said a traveller who had known the extremes of society, — "I have seen human nature in all its forms, it is everywhere the same, but the wilder it is, the more virtuous."

We say, the old forms of religion decay, and that a scepticism devastates the community. I do not think it can be cured or stayed by any modification of theologic creeds, much less by theologic discipline. The cure for false theology is motherwit. Forget your books and traditions, and obey your moral perceptions at this hour. That which is signified by the words "moral" and "spiritual" is a lasting essence, and, with whatever illusions we have loaded them, will certainly bring back the words, age after age, to their ancient meaning. I know no words that mean so much. In our definitions, we grope after the *spiritual* by describing it as invisible. The true meaning of *spiritual* is *real;* that law which executes itself, which works without means, and which cannot be conceived as not existing. Men talk of "mere morality," — which is much as if one should say, 'Poor God, with nobody to help him.' I find the omnipresence and the almightiness in the reaction of every atom in Nature. I can best indicate by examples those reactions by which every part of Nature replies to the purpose of the actor, — beneficently to the good, penally to the bad. Let us replace sentimentalism by realism, and dare to uncover those simple and terrible laws, which, be they seen or unseen, pervade and govern.

Every man takes care that his neighbor shall not cheat him. But a day comes when he begins to care that he do not cheat his neighbor. Then all goes well. He has changed his market-cart into a chariot of the sun. What a day dawns, when we have taken to heart the doctrine of faith! to prefer, as a better investment, being to doing; being to seeming; logic to rhythm and to display; the year to the day; the life to the year; character to performance; — and have come to know that justice will be done us; and, if our genius is slow, the term will be long.

'T is certain that worship stands in some commanding relation to the health of man, and to his highest powers, so as to be, in some manner, the source of intellect. All the great ages have been ages of belief. I mean, when there was any extraordinary power of performance, when great national movements began, when arts appeared, when heroes existed, when poems were made, the human soul was in earnest, and had fixed its thoughts on spiritual verities, with as strict a grasp as that of the hands on the sword, or the pencil, or the trowel. It is true that genius takes its rise out of the mountains of rectitude; that all beauty and power which men covet are somehow born out of that Alpine district; that any extraordinary degree of beauty in man or woman involves a moral charm. Thus, I think, we very slowly admit in another man a higher degree of moral sentiment than our own, — a finer conscience, more impressionable, or, which marks minuter degrees; an ear to hear acuter notes of right and wrong, than we can. I think we listen suspiciously and very slowly to any evidence to that point. But, once satisfied of such superiority, we set no limit to our expectation of his genius. For such persons are nearer to the secret of God than others; are bathed by sweeter waters; they hear notices, they see visions, where others are vacant. We believe that holiness confers a certain insight, because not by our private, but by our public force, can we share and know the nature of things.

There is an intimate interdependence of intellect and morals. Given the equality of two intellects, — which will form the most reliable judgments, the good, or the bad hearted? "The heart has its arguments, with which the understanding is not acquainted." For the heart is at once aware of the state of health or disease, which is the controlling state, that is, of sanity or of insanity, prior, of course, to all question of the ingenuity of arguments, the amount of facts, or the elegance of rhetoric. So intimate is this alliance of mind and heart, that talent uniformly sinks with character. The bias of errors of principle carries away men into perilous courses, as soon as their will does not control their passion or talent. Hence the extraordinary blunders, and final wrong head, into which men spoiled by ambition usually fall. Hence the remedy for all blunders, the cure of blindness, the cure of crime, is love. "As much love, so much mind," said the Latin proverb. The superiority that has no superior; the redeemer and instructor of souls, as it is their primal essence, is love.

The moral must be the measure of health. If your eye is on the eternal, your intellect will grow, and your opinions and actions will have a beauty which no learning or combined advantages of other men can rival. The moment of your loss of faith, and acceptance of the lucrative standard, will be marked in the pause, or solstice of genius, the sequent retrogression, and the inevitable loss of attraction to other minds. The vulgar are sensible of the change in you, and of your descent, though they clap you on the back, and congratulate you on your increased common sense.

Our recent culture has been in natural science. We have learned the manners of the sun and of the moon, of the rivers and the rains, of the mineral and elemental kingdoms, of plants and animals. Man has learned to weigh the sun, and its weight neither loses nor gains. The path of a star, the moment of an eclipse, can be determined to the fraction of a second. Well, to him the book of history, the book of love, the lures of passion, and the commandments of duty are opened; and the next lesson taught, is, the continuation of the inflexible law of matter into the subtile kingdom of will, and of thought; that, if, in sidereal ages, gravity and projection keep their craft, and the ball never loses its way in its wild path through space, — a secreter gravitation, a secreter projection, rule not less tyrannically in human history, and keep the balance of power from age to age unbroken. For, though the new element of freedom and an individual has been admitted, yet the primordial atoms are prefigured and predetermined to moral issues, are in search of justice, and ultimate right is done. Religion or worship is the attitude of those who see this unity, intimacy, and sincerity; who see that, against all appearances, the nature of things works for truth and right forever.

'T is a short sight to limit our faith in laws to those of gravity, of chemistry, of botany, and so forth. Those laws do not stop where our eyes lose them, but push the same geometry and chemistry up into the invisible plane of social and rational life, so that, look where we will, in a boy's game, or in the strifes of races, a perfect reaction, a perpetual judgment keeps watch and ward. And this appears in a class of facts which concerns all men, within and above their creeds.

Shallow men believe in luck, believe in circumstances: It was somebody's name, or he happened to be there at the time, or, it was so then, and another day it would have been otherwise. Strong men believe in cause and effect. The man was born to do it, and his father was born to be the father of him and of this deed, and, by looking narrowly, you shall see there was no luck in the matter, but it was all a problem in arithmetic, or an experiment in chemistry. The curve of the flight of the moth is preordained, and all things go by number, rule, and weight.

Scepticism is unbelief in cause and effect. A man does not see, that, as he eats, so he thinks: as he deals, so he is, and so he appears; he does not see, that his son is the son of his thoughts and of his actions; that fortunes are not exceptions but fruits; that relation and connection are not somewhere and sometimes, but everywhere and always; no miscellany, no exemption, no anomaly, — but method, and an even web; and what comes out, that was put in. As we are, so we do; and as we do, so is it done to us; we are the builders of our fortunes; cant and lying and the attempt to secure a good which does not belong to us, are, once for all, balked and vain. But, in the human mind, this tie of faith is made alive. The law is the basis of the human mind. In us, it is inspiration; out there in Nature, we see its fatal strength. We call it the moral sentiment.

We owe to the Hindoo Scriptures a definition of Law, which compares well with any in our Western books. "Law it is, which is without name, or color, or hands, or feet; which is smallest of the least, and largest of the large; all, and knowing all things; which hears without ears, sees without eyes, moves without feet, and seizes without hands."

If any reader tax me with using vague and traditional phrases, let me suggest to him, by a few examples, what kind of a trust this is, and how real. Let me show him that the dice are loaded; that the colors are fast, because they are the native colors of the fleece; that the globe is a battery, because every atom is a magnet; and that the police and sincerity of the Universe are secured by God's delegating his divinity to every particle; that there is no room for hypocrisy, no margin for choice.

The countryman leaving his native village, for the first time, and going abroad, finds all his habits broken up. In a new nation and language, his sect, as Quaker, or Lutheran, is lost. What! it is not then necessary to the order and existence of society? He misses this, and the commanding eye of his neighborhood, which held him to decorum. This is the peril of New York, of New Orleans, of London, of Paris, to young men. But after a little experience, he makes the discovery that there are no large cities, — none large enough to hide in; that the censors of action are as numerous and as near in Paris, as in Littleton or Portland; that the gossip is as prompt and vengeful. There is no concealment, and, for each offence, a several vengeance; that, reaction, or *nothing for nothing*, or, *things are as broad as they are long*, is not a rule for Littleton or Portland, but for the Universe.

We cannot spare the coarsest muniment of virtue. We are disgusted by gossip; yet it is of importance to keep the angels in their proprieties. The smallest fly will draw blood, and gossip is a weapon impossible to exclude from the privatest, highest, selectest. Nature created a police of many ranks. God has delegated himself to a million deputies. From these low external penalties, the scale ascends. Next come the resentments, the fears, which injustice calls out; then, the false relations in which the offender is put to other men; and the reaction of his fault on himself, in the solitude and devastation of his mind.

You cannot hide any secret. If the artist succor his flagging spirits by opium or wine, his work will characterize itself as the effect of opium or wine. If you make a picture or a statue, it sets the beholder in that state of mind you had, when you made it. If you spend for show, on building, or gardening, or on pictures, or on equipages, it will so appear. We are all physiognomists and penetrators of character, and things themselves are detective. If you follow the suburban fashion in building a sumptuous-looking house for a little money, it will appear to all eyes as a cheap dear house. There is no privacy that cannot be penetrated. No secret can be kept in the civilized world. Society is a masked ball, where every one hides his real character, and reveals it by hiding. If a man wish to conceal anything he carries, those whom he meets know that he conceals somewhat, and usually know what he conceals. Is it otherwise if there be some belief or some purpose he would bury in his breast? 'T is as hard to hide as fire. He is a strong man who can hold down his opinion. A man cannot utter two or three sentences, without disclosing to intelligent ears precisely where he stands in life and thought, namely, whether in the kingdom of the senses and the understanding, or, in that of ideas and imagination, in the realm of intuitions and duty. People seem not to see that their opinion of the world is also a confession of character. We can only see what we are, and if we misbehave we suspect others. The fame of Shakespeare or of Voltaire, of Thomas à Kempis, or of Bonaparte, characterizes those who give it. As gaslight is found to be the best nocturnal police, so the universe protects itself by pitiless publicity.

Each must be armed, — not necessarily with musket and pike. Happy, if, seeing these, he can feel that he has better muskets and pikes in his energy and constancy. To every creature is his own weapon, however skilfully concealed from himself, a good while. His work is sword and shield. Let him accuse none, let him injure none. The way to mend the bad world is to create the right world. Here is a low political economy plotting to cut the throat of foreign competition, and establish our own; excluding others by force, or making war on them; or, by cunning tariffs, giving preference to worse wares of ours. But the real and lasting victories are those of peace, and not of war. The way to conquer the foreign artisan, is, not to kill him, but to beat his work. And the Crystal Palaces and World Fairs, with their committees and prizes on all kinds of industry, are the result of this feeling. The American workman who strikes ten blows with his hammer, whilst the foreign workman only strikes one, is as really vanquishing that foreigner, as if the blows were aimed at and told on his person. I look on that man as happy, who, when there is question of success, looks into his work for a reply, not into the market, not into opinion, not into patronage. In every variety of human employment, in the mechanical and in the fine arts, in navigation, in farming, in legislating, there are among the numbers who do their task perfunctorily, as we say, or just to pass, and as badly as they dare, — there are the workingmen, on whom the burden of the business falls, — those who love work, and love to see it rightly done, who finish their task for its own sake; and the state and the world is happy, that has the most of such finishers. The world will always do justice at last to such finishers: it cannot otherwise. He who has acquired the ability may wait securely the occasion of making it felt and appreciated, and know that it will not loiter. Men talk as if victory were something fortunate. Work is victory. Wherever work is done, victory is obtained. There is no chance, and no blanks. You want but one verdict: if you have your own, you are secure of the rest. And yet, if witnesses are wanted, witnesses are near. There was never a man born so wise or good, but one or more companions came into the world with him, who delight in his faculty and report it. I cannot see without awe, that no man thinks alone, and no man acts alone, but the divine assessors who came up with him into life, — now under one disguise, now under another, — like a police in citizens' clothes, walk with him, step for step, through the kingdom of time.

This reaction, this sincerity, is the property of all things. To make our word or act sublime, we must make it real. It is our system that counts, not the single word or unsupported action. Use what language you will, you can never say anything but what you are. What I am, and what I think, is conveyed to you, in spite of my efforts to hold it back. What I am has been secretly conveyed from me to another, whilst I was vainly making up my mind to tell him it. He has heard from me what I never spoke.

As men get on in life, they acquire a love for sincerity, and somewhat less solicitude to be lulled or amused. In the progress of the character, there is an increasing faith in the moral sentiment, and a decreasing faith in propositions. Young people admire talents, and particular excellences. As we grow older, we value total powers and effects, as the spirit, or quality of the man. We have another sight, and a new standard; an insight which disregards what is done *for* the eye, and pierces to the doer; an ear which hears not what men say, but hears what they do not say.

There was a wise, devout man who is called, in the Catholic Church, St. Philip Neri, of whom many anecdotes touching his discernment and benevolence are told at Naples and Rome. Among the nuns in a convent not far from Rome, one had appeared, who laid claim to certain rare gifts of inspiration and prophecy, and the abbess advised the Holy Father, at Rome, of the wonderful powers shown by her novice. The Pope did not well know what to make of these new claims, and Philip coming in from a journey, one day, he consulted him. Philip undertook to visit the nun, and ascertain her character. He threw himself on his mule, all travel-soiled as he was, and hastened through the mud and mire to the distant convent. He told the abbess the wishes of his Holiness, and begged her to summon the nun without delay. The nun was sent for, and, as soon as she came into the apartment, Philip stretched out his leg all bespattered with mud, and desired her to draw off his boots. The young nun, who had become the object of much attention and respect, drew back with anger, and refused the office: Philip ran out of doors, mounted his mule, and returned instantly to the Pope: "Give yourself no uneasiness, Holy Father, any longer: here is no miracle, for here is no humility."

We need not much mind what people please to say, but what they must say; what their natures say though their busy, artful, Yankee understandings try to hold back, and choke that word, and to articulate something different. If we will sit quietly, — what they ought to say is said, with their will, or against their will. We do not care for you, let us pretend what we will; — we are always looking through you to the dim dictator behind you. Whilst your habit or whim chatters, we civilly and impatiently wait until that wise superior shall speak again. Even children are not deceived by the false reasons which their parents give in answer to their questions, whether touching natural facts, or religion, or persons. When the parent, instead of thinking how it really is, puts them cff with a traditional or a hypocritical answer, the children perceive that it is traditional or hypocritical. To a sound constitution the defect of another is at once manifest; and the marks of it are only concealed from us by our own dislocation. An anatomical observer remarks, that the sympathies of the chest, abdomen, and pelvis tell at last on the face, and on all its features. Not only does our beauty waste, but it leaves word how it went to waste. Physiognomy and phrenology are not new sciences, but declarations of the soul that it is aware of certain new sources of information. And now sciences of broader scope are starting up behind these. And so for ourselves, it is really of little importance what blunders in statement we make, so only we make no wilful departures from the truth. How a man's truth comes to mind, long after we have forgotten all his words! How it comes to us in silent hours, that truth is our only armor in all passages of life and death! Wit is cheap, and anger is cheap; but if you cannot argue or explain yourself to the other party, cleave to the truth against me, against thee, and you gain a station from which you cannot be dislodged. The other party will forget the words that you spoke, but the part you took continues to plead for you.

Why should I hasten to solve every riddle which life offers me? I am well assured that the Questioner, who brings me so many problems, will bring the answers also in due time. Very rich, very potent, very cheerful Giver that he is, he shall have it all his own way for me. Why should I give up my thought, because I cannot answer an objection to it? Consider only, whether it remains in my life the same it was. That only which we have within, can we see without. If we meet no gods, it is because we harbor none. If there is grandeur in you, you will find grandeur in porters and sweeps. He only is rightly immortal, to whom all things are immortal. I have read somewhere, that none is accomplished, so long as any are incomplete; that the happiness of one cannot consist with the misery of any other.

The Buddhists say, "No seed will die": every seed will grow. Where is the service which can escape its remuneration? What is vulgar, and the essence of all vulgarity, but the avarice of reward? 'T is the difference of artisan and artist, of talent and genius, of sinner and saint. The man whose eyes are nailed not on the nature of his act, but on the wages, whether it be money, or office, or fame, — is almost equally low. He is great, whose eyes are opened to see that the reward of actions cannot be escaped, because he is transformed into his action, and taketh its nature, which bears its own fruit, like every other tree. A great man cannot be hindered of the effect of his act, because it is immediate. The genius of life is friendly to the noble, and in the dark brings them friends from far. Fear God, and where you go, men shall think they walk in hallowed cathedrals.

And so I look on those sentiments which make the glory of the human being, love, humility, faith, as being also the intimacy of Divinity in the atoms; and, that, as soon as the man is right, assurances and previsions emanate from the interior of his body and his mind; as, when flowers reach their ripeness, incense exhales from them, and, as a beautiful atmosphere is generated from the planet by the averaged emanations from all its rocks and soils.

Thus man is made equal to every event. He can face danger for the right. A poor, tender, painful body, he can run into flame or bullets or pestilence, with duty for his guide. He feels the insurance of a just employment. I am not afraid of accident, as long as I am in my place. It is strange that superior persons should not feel that they have some better resistance against cholera, than avoiding green peas and salads. Life is hardly respectable, — is it? if it has no generous, guaranteeing task, no duties or affections, that constitute a necessity of existing. Every man's task is his life-preserver. The conviction that his work is dear to God and cannot be spared, defends him. The lightning-rod that disarms the cloud of its threat is his body in its duty. A high aim reacts on the means, on the days, on the organs of the body. A high aim is curative, as well as arnica. "Napoleon," says Goethe, "visited those sick of the plague, in order to prove that the man who could vanquish fear, could vanquish the plague also; and he was right. 'T is incredible what force the will has in such cases: it penetrates the body, and puts it in a state of activity, which repels all hurtful influences; whilst fear invites them."

It is related of William of Orange, that, whilst he was besieging a town on the continent, a gentleman sent to him on public business came to his camp, and, learning that the King was before the walls, he ventured to go where he was. He found him directing the operation of his gunners, and, having explained his errand, and received his answer, the King said: "Do you not know, sir, that every moment you spend here is at the risk of your life?" "I run no more risk," replied the gentleman, "than your Majesty." "Yes," said the King, "but my duty brings me here, and yours does not." In a few minutes, a cannon-ball fell on the spot, and the gentleman was killed.

Thus can the faithful student reverse all the warnings of his early instinct, under the guidance of a deeper instinct. He learns to welcome misfortune, learns that adversity is the prosperity of the great. He learns the greatness of humility. He shall work in the dark, work against failure, pain, and ill-will. If he is insulted, he can be insulted; all his affair is not to insult. Hafiz writes: —

> At the last day, men shall wear
> On their heads the dust,
> As ensign and as ornament
> Of their lowly trust.

The moral equalizes all; enriches, empowers all. It is the coin which buys all, and which all find in their pocket. Under the whip of the driver, the slave shall feel his equality with saints and heroes. In the greatest destitution and calamity, it surprises man with a feeling of elasticity which makes nothing of loss.

I recall some traits of a remarkable person whose life and discourse betrayed many inspirations of this sentiment. Benedict was always great in the present time. He had hoarded nothing from the past, neither in his cabinets, neither in his memory. He had no designs on the future, neither for what he should do to men, nor for what men should do for him. He said: 'I am never beaten until I know that I am beaten. I meet powerful brutal people to whom I have no skill to reply. They think they have defeated me. It is so published in society, in the journals; I am defeated in this fashion, in all men's sight, perhaps on a dozen different lines. My leger may show that I am in debt, cannot yet make my ends meet, and vanquish the enemy so. My race may not be prospering: we are sick, ugly, obscure, unpopular. My children may be worsted. I seem to fail in my friends and clients, too. That is to say, in all the encounters that have yet chanced, I have not been weaponed for that particular occasion, and have been historically beaten; and yet, I know, all the time, that I have never been beaten; have never yet fought, shall certainly fight, when my hour comes, and shall beat.' "A man," says the Vishnu Sarma, "who having well compared his own strength or weakness with that of others, after all doth not know the difference, is easily overcome by his enemies."

'I spent,' he said, 'ten months in the country. Thick-starred Orion was my only companion. Wherever a squirrel or a bee can go with security, I can go. I ate whatever was set before me; I touched ivy and dogwood. When I went abroad, I kept company with every man on the road, for I knew that my evil and my good did not come from these, but from the Spirit, whose servant I was. For I could not stoop to be a circumstance, as they did, who put their life into their fortune and their company. I would not degrade myself by casting about in my memory for a thought, nor by waiting for one. If the thought come, I would give it entertainment. It should, as it ought, go into my hands and feet; but if it come not spontaneously, it comes not rightly at all. If it can spare me, I am sure I can spare it. It shall be the same with my friends. I will never woo the loveliest. I will not ask any friendship or favor. When I come to my own, we shall both know it. Nothing will be to be asked or to be granted.' Benedict went out to seek his friend, and met him on the way; but he expressed no surprise at any coincidences. On the other hand, if he called at the door of his friend, and he was not at home, he did not go again; concluding that he had misinterpreted the intimations.

He had the whim not to make an apology to the same individual whom he had wronged. For this, he said, was a piece of personal vanity; but he would correct his conduct in that respect in which he had faulted, to the next person he should meet. Thus, he said, universal justice was satisfied.

Mira came to ask what she should do with the poor Genesee woman who had hired herself to work for her, at a shilling a day, and, now sickening, was like to be bedridden on her hands. Should she keep her, or should she dismiss her? But Benedict said, 'Why ask? One thing will clear itself as the thing to be done, and not another, when the hour comes. Is it a question, whether to put her into the street. Just as much whether to thrust the little Jenny on your arm into the street. The milk and meal you give the beggar will fatten Jenny. Thrust the woman out, and you thrust your babe out of doors, whether it so seem to you or not.'

In the Shakers, so called, I find one piece of belief, in the doctrine which they faithfully hold, that encourages them to open their doors to every wayfaring man who proposes to come among them; for, they say, the Spirit will presently manifest to the man himself, and to the society, what manner of person he is, and whether he belongs among them. They do not receive him, they do not reject him. And not in vain have they worn their clay coat, and drudged in their fields, and shuffled in their bruin dance, from year to year, if they have truly learned thus much wisdom.

Honor him whose life is perpetual victory; him, who, by sympathy with the invisible and real, finds support in labor, instead of praise: who does not shine, and would rather not. With eyes open, he makes the choice of virtue, which outrages the virtuous; of religion, which churches stop their discords to burn and exterminate: for the highest virtue is always against the law.

Miracle comes to the miraculous, not to the arithmetician. Talent and success interest me but moderately. The great class, they who affect our imagination, the men who could not make their hands meet around their objects, the rapt, the lost, the fools of ideas, — they suggest what they cannot execute. They speak to the ages, and are heard from afar. The Spirit does not love cripples and malformations. If there ever was a good man, be certain there was another, and will be more.

And so in relation to that future hour, that spectre clothed with beauty at our curtain by night, at our table by day, — the apprehension, the assurance of a coming change. The race of mankind have always offered at least this implied thanks for the gift of existence, — namely, the terror of its being taken away; the insatiable curiosity and appetite for its continuation. The whole revelation that is vouchsafed us, is, the gentle trust, which, in our experience we find, will cover also with flowers the slopes of this chasm.

Of immortality, the soul, when well employed, is incurious. It is so well, that it is sure it will be well. It asks no questions of the Supreme Power. The son of Antiochus asked his father, when he would join battle. "Dost thou fear," replied the King, "that thou only in all the army wilt not hear the trumpet?" 'T is a higher thing to confide, that, if it is best we should live, we shall live, — 't is higher to have this conviction than to have the lease of indefinite centuries and millenniums and æons. Higher than the question of our duration is the question of our deserving. Immortality will come to such as are fit for it, and he who would be a great soul in future, must be a great soul now. It is a doctrine too great to rest on any legend, that is, on any man's experience but our own. It must be proved, if at all, from our own activity and designs, which imply an interminable future for their play.

What is called religion effeminates and demoralizes. Such as you are, the gods themselves could not help you. Men are too often unfit to live, from their obvious inequality to their own necessities, or, they suffer from politics, or bad neighbors, or from sickness, and they would gladly know that they were to be dismissed from the duties of life. But the wise instinct asks, 'How will death help them?' These are not dismissed when they die. You shall not wish for death out of pusillanimity. The weight of the Universe is pressed down on the shoulders of each moral agent to hold him to his task. The only path of escape known in all the worlds of God is performance. You must do your work, before you shall be released. And as far as it is a question of fact respecting the government of the Universe, Marcus Antoninus summed the whole in a word: "It is pleasant to die, if there be gods; and sad to live, if there be none."

And so I think that the last lesson of life, the choral song which rises from all elements and all angels, is, a voluntary obedience, a necessitated freedom. Man is made of the same atoms as the world is, he shares the same impressions, predispositions, and destiny. When his mind is illuminated, when his heart is kind, he throws himself joyfully into the sublime order, and does, with knowledge, what the stones do by structure.

The religion which is to guide and fulfil the present and coming ages, whatever else it be, must be intellectual. The scientific mind must have a faith which is science. "There are two things," said Mahomet, "which I abhor, the learned in his infidelities, and the fool in his devotions." Our times are impatient of both, and specially of the last. Let us have nothing now which is not its own evidence. There is surely enough for the heart and imagination in the religion itself. Let us not be pestered with assertions and half-truths, with emotions and snuffle.

There will be a new church founded on moral science, at first cold and naked, a babe in a manger again, the algebra and mathematics of ethical law, the church of men to come, without shawms, or psaltery, or sackbut; but it will have heaven and earth for its beams and rafters; science for symbol and illustration; it will fast enough gather beauty, music, picture, poetry. Was never stoicism so stern and exigent as this shall be. It shall send man home to his central solitude, shame these social, supplicating manners, and make him know that much of the time he must have himself to his friend. He shall expect no co-operation, he shall walk with no companion. The nameless Thought, the nameless Power, the superpersonal Heart, — he shall repose alone on that. He needs only his own verdict. No good fame can help, no bad fame can hurt him. The Laws are his consolers, the good Laws themselves are alive, they know if we have kept them, they animate him with the leading of great duty, and an endless horizon. Honor and fortune exist to him who always recognizes the neighborhood of the great, always feels himself in the presence of high causes.

VII.

CONSIDERATIONS BY THE WAY.

Hear what British Merlin sung,
Of keenest eye and truest tongue.
Say not, the chiefs who first arrive
Usurp the seats for which all strive;
The forefathers this land who found
Failed to plant the vantage-ground;
Ever from one who comes to-morrow
Men wait their good and truth to borrow.
But wilt thou measure all thy road,
See thou lift the lightest load.
Who has little, to him who has less, can spare,
And thou, Cyndyllan's son! beware
Ponderous gold and stuffs to bear,
To falter ere thou thy task fulfil, —
Only the light-armed climb the hill.
The richest of all lords is Use,
And ruddy Health the loftiest Muse.
Live in the sunshine, swim the sea,
Drink the wild air's salubrity:
Where the star Canope shines in May,
Shepherds are thankful, and nations gay.
The music that can deepest reach,
And cure all ill, is cordial speech:
Mask thy wisdom with delight,
Toy with the bow, yet hit the white.
Of all wit's uses, the main one
Is to live well with who has none.
Cleave to thine acre; the round year
Will fetch all fruits and virtues here:
Fool and foe may harmless roam,
Loved and lovers bide at home.
A day for toil, an hour for sport,
But for a friend is life too short.

CONSIDERATIONS BY THE WAY.

ALTHOUGH this garrulity of advising is born with us, I confess that life is rather a subject of wonder, than of didactics. So much fate, so much irresistible dictation from temperament and unknown inspiration enters into it, that we doubt we can say anything out of our own experience whereby to help each other. All the professions are timid and expectant agencies. The priest is glad if his prayers or his sermon meet the condition of any soul; if of two, if of ten, 't is a signal success. But he walked to the church without any assurance that he knew the distemper, or could heal it. The physician prescribes hesitatingly out of his few resources, the same tonic or sedative to this new and peculiar constitution, which he has applied with various success to a hundred men before. If the patient mends, he is glad and surprised. The lawyer advises the client, and tells his story to the jury, and leaves it with them, and is as gay and as much relieved as the client, if it turns out that he has a verdict. The judge weighs the arguments, and puts a brave face on the matter, and, since there must be a decision, decides as he can, and hopes he has done justice, and given satisfaction to the community; but is only an advocate after all. And so is all life a timid and unskilful spectator. We do what we must, and call it by the best names. We like very well to be praised for our action, but our conscience says, "Not unto us." 'T is little we can do for each other. We accompany the youth with sympathy, and manifold old sayings of the wise, to the gate of the arena, but 't is certain that not by strength of ours, or of the old sayings, but only on strength of his own, unknown to us or to any, he must stand or fall. That by which a man conquers in any passage, is a profound secret to every other being in the world, and it is only as he turns his back on us and all men, and draws on this most private wisdom, that any good can come to him. What we have, therefore, to say of life, is rather description, or, if you please, celebration, than available rules.

Yet vigor is contagious, and whatever makes us either think or feel strongly, adds to our power and enlarges our field of action. We have a debt to every great heart, to every fine genius; to those who have put life and fortune on the cast of an act of justice; to those who have added new sciences; to those who have refined life by elegant pursuits. 'T is the fine souls who serve us, and not what is called fine society. Fine society is only a self-protection against the vulgarities of the street and the tavern. Fine society, in the common acceptation, has neither ideas nor aims. It renders the service of a perfumery, or a laundry, not of a farm or factory. 'T is an exclusion and a precinct. Sidney Smith said, "A few yards in London cement or dissolve friendship." It is an unprincipled decorum; an affair of clean linen and coaches, of gloves, cards, and elegance in trifles. There are other measures of self-respect for a man, than the number of clean shirts he puts on every day. Society wishes to be amused. I do not wish to be amused. I wish that life should not be cheap, but sacred. I wish the days to be as centuries, loaded, fragrant. Now we reckon them as bank-days, by some debt which is to be paid us, or which we are to pay, or some pleasure we are to taste. Is all we have to do to draw the breath in, and blow it out again? Porphyry's definition is better: "Life is that which holds matter together." The babe in arms is a channel through which the energies we call fate, love, and reason, visibly stream. See what a cometary train of auxiliaries man carries with him, of animals, plants, stones, gases, and imponderable elements. Let us infer his ends from this pomp of means. Mirabeau said: "Why should we feel ourselves to be men, unless it be to succeed in everything, everywhere. You must say of nothing, *That is beneath me*, nor feel that anything can be out of your power. Nothing is impossible to the man who can will. *Is that necessary? That shall be:* — this is the only law of success." Whoever said it, this is in the right key. But this is not the tone and genius of the men in the street. In the streets, we grow cynical. The men we meet are coarse and torpid. The finest wits have their sediment. What quantities of fribbles, paupers, invalids, epicures, antiquaries, politicians, thieves, and triflers of both sexes, might be advantageously spared! Mankind divides itself into two classes, — benefactors and malefactors. The second class is vast, the first a handful. A person seldom falls sick, but the bystanders are animated with a faint hope that he will die: — quantities of poor lives; of distressing invalids; of cases for a gun. Franklin said: "Mankind are very superficial and dastardly: they begin upon a thing, but, meeting with a difficulty, they fly from it discouraged: but they have capacities, if they would employ them." Shall we then judge a country by the majority, or by the minority? By the minority, surely. 'T is pedantry to estimate nations by the census, or by square miles of land, or other than by their importance to the mind of the time.

Leave this hypocritical prating about the masses. Masses are rude, lame, unmade, pernicious in their demands and influence, and need not to be flattered but to be schooled. I wish not to concede anything to them, but to tame, drill, divide, and break them up, and draw individuals out of them. The worst of charity is, that the lives you are asked to preserve are not worth preserving. Masses! the calamity is the masses. I do not wish any mass at all, but honest men only, lovely, sweet, accomplished women only, and no shovel-handed, narrow-brained, gin-drinking million stockingers or lazzaroni at all. If government knew how, I should like to see it check, not multiply the population. When it reaches its true law of action, every man that is born will be hailed as essential. Away with this hurrah of masses, and let us have the considerate vote of single men spoken on their honor and their conscience. In old Egypt, it was established law, that the vote of a prophet be reckoned equal to a hundred hands. I think it was much underestimated. "Clay and clay differ in dignity," as we discover by our preferences every day. What a vicious practice is this of our politicians at Washington pairing off! as if one man who votes wrong, going away, could excuse you, who mean to vote right, for going away; or, as if your presence did not tell in more ways than in your vote. Suppose the three hundred heroes at Thermopylæ had paired off with three hundred Persians: would it have been all the same to Greece, and to history? Napoleon was called by his men *Cent Mille.* Add honesty to him, and they might have called him Hundred Million.

Nature makes fifty poor melons for one that is good, and shakes down a tree full of gnarled, wormy, unripe crabs, before you can find a dozen dessert apples; and she scatters nations of naked Indians, and nations of clothed Christians, with two or three good heads among them. Nature works very hard, and only hits the white once in a million throws. In mankind, she is contented if she yields one master in a century. The more difficulty there is in creating good men, the more they are used when they come. I once counted in a little neighborhood, and found that every able-bodied man had, say from twelve to fifteen persons dependent on him for material aid, — to whom he is to be for spoon and jug, for backer and sponsor, for nursery and hospital, and many functions beside: nor does it seem to make much difference whether he is bachelor or patriarch; if he do not violently decline the duties that fall to him, this amount of helpfulness will in one way or another be brought home to him. This is the tax which his abilities pay. The good men are employed for private centres of use, and for larger influence. All revelations, whether of mechanical or intellectual or moral science, are made, not to communities, but to single persons. All the marked events of our day, all the cities, all the colonizations, may be traced back to their origin in a private brain. All the feats which make our civility were the thoughts of a few good heads.

Meantime, this spawning productivity is not noxious or needless. You would say, this rabble of nations might be spared, But no, they are all counted and depended on. Fate keeps everything alive so long as the smallest thread of public necessity holds it on to the tree. The coxcomb and bully and thief class are allowed as proletaries, every one of their vices being the excess or acridity of a virtue. The mass are animal, in pupilage, and near chimpanzee. But the units, whereof this mass is composed are neuters, every one of which may be grown to a queen-bee. The rule is, we are used as brute atoms, until we think: then, we use all the rest. Nature turns all malfaisance to good. Nature provided for real needs. No sane man at last distrusts himself. His existence is a perfect answer to all sentimental cavils. If he is, he is wanted, and has the precise properties that are required. That we are here, is proof we ought to be here. We have as good right, and the same sort of right to be here, as Cape Cod or Sandy Hook have to be there.

To say then, the majority are wicked, means no malice, no bad heart in the observer, but, simply, that the majority are unripe, and have not yet come to themselves, do not yet know their opinion. *That*, if they knew it, is an oracle for them and for all. But in the passing moment, the quadruped interest is very prone to prevail: and this beast-force, whilst it makes the discipline of the world, the school of heroes, the glory of martyrs, has provoked in every age the satire of wits, and the tears of good men. They find the journals, the clubs, the governments, the churches, to be in the interest, and the pay of the Devil. And wise men have met this obstruction in their times, like Socrates, with his famous irony; like Bacon, with life-long dissimulation; like Erasmus, with his book "The Praise of Folly"; like Rabelais, with his satire rending the nations. "They were the fools who cried against me, you will say," wrote the Chevalier de Boufflers to Grimm; "ay, but the fools have the advantage of numbers, and 't is that which decides. 'T is of no use for us to make war with them: we shall not weaken them; they will always be the masters. There will not be a practice or an usage introduced, of which they are not the authors."

In front of these sinister facts, the first lesson of history is the good of evil. Good is a good doctor, but Bad is sometimes a better. 'T is the oppressions of William the Norman, savage forest-laws, and crushing despotism, that made possible the inspirations of *Magna Charta* under John. Edward I. wanted money, armies, castles, and as much as he could get. It was necessary to call the people together by shorter, swifter ways, — and the House of Commons arose. To obtain subsidies, he paid in privileges. In the twenty-fourth year of his reign, he decreed, "that no tax should be levied without consent of Lords and Commons"; — which is the basis of the English Constitution. Plutarch affirms that the cruel wars which followed the march of Alexander, introduced the civility, language, and arts of Greece into the savage East; introduced marriage; built seventy cities: and united hostile nations under one government. The barbarians who broke up the Roman empire did not arrive a day too soon. Schiller says, the Thirty Years' War made Germany a nation. Rough, selfish despots serve men immensely, as Henry VIII. in the contest with the Pope; as the infatuations no less than the wisdom of Cromwell; as the ferocity of the Russian czars; as the fanaticism of the French regicides of 1789. The frost which kills the harvest of a year, saves the harvests of a century, by destroying the weevil or the locust. Wars, fires, plagues, break up immovable routine, clear the ground of rotten races, and dens of distemper, and open a fair field to new men. There is a tendency in things to right themselves, and the war or revolution or bankruptcy that shatters a rotten system, allows things to take a new and natural order. The sharpest evils are bent into that periodicity which makes the errors of planets, and the fevers and distempers of men, self-limiting. Nature is upheld by antagonism. Passions, resistance, danger, are educators. We acquire the strength we have overcome. Without war, no soldier; without enemies, no hero. The sun were insipid, if the universe were not opaque. And the glory of character is in affronting the horrors of depravity, to draw thence new nobilities of power: as Art lives and thrills in new use and combining of contrasts, and mining into the dark evermore for blacker pits of night. What would painter do, or what would poet or saint, but for crucifixions and hells? And evermore in the world in this marvellous balance of beauty and disgust, magnificence and rats. Not Antoninus, but a poor washerwoman said: "The more trouble, the more lion; that 's my principle."

I do not think very respectfully of the designs or the doings of the people who went to California, in 1849. It was a rush and a scramble of needy adventurers, and, in the western country, a general jail-delivery of all the rowdies of the rivers. Some of them went with honest purposes, some with very bad ones, and all of them with the very commonplace wish to find a short way to wealth. But Nature watches over all, and turns this malfaisance to good. California gets peopled and subdued, — civilized in this immoral way, — and, on this fiction, a real prosperity is rooted and grown. 'T is a decoy-duck; 't is tubs thrown to amuse the whale: but real ducks, and whales that yield oil, are caught. And out of Sabine rapes, and out of robbers' forays, real Romes and their heroisms come in fulness of time.

In America, the geography is sublime, but the men are not: the inventions are excellent, but the inventors one is sometimes ashamed of. The agencies by which events so grand as the opening of California, of Texas, of Oregon, and the junction of the two oceans, are effected, are paltry, — coarse selfishness, fraud, and conspiracy: and most of the great results of history are brought about by discreditable means.

The benefaction derived in Illinois, and the great West, from railroads, is inestimable, and vastly exceeding any intentional philanthropy on record. What is the benefit done by a good King Alfred, or by a Howard, or Pestalozzi, or Elizabeth Fry, or Florence Nightingale, or any lover, less or larger, compared with the involuntary blessing wrought on nations by the selfish capitalists who built the Illinois, Michigan, and the network of the Mississippi valley roads, which have evoked not only all the wealth of the soil, but the energy of millions of men. 'T is a sentence of ancient wisdom, "that God hangs the greatest weights on the smallest wires."

What happens thus to nations, befalls every day in private houses. When the friends of a gentleman brought to his notice the follies of his sons, with many hints of their danger, he replied, that he knew so much mischief when he was a boy, and had turned out on the whole so successfully, that he was not alarmed by the dissipation of boys; 't was dangerous water, but, he thought, they would soon touch bottom, and then swim to the top. This is bold practice, and there are many failures to a good escape. Yet one would say, that a good understanding would suffice as well as moral sensibility to keep one erect; the gratifications of the passions are so quickly seen to be damaging, and — what men like least — seriously lowering them in social rank. Then all talent sinks with character.

"*Croyez moi, l'erreur aussi a son mérite*," said Voltaire. We see those who surmount, by dint of some egotism or infatuation, obstacles from which the prudent recoil. The right partisan is a heady narrow man, who, because he does not see many things, sees some one thing with heat and exaggeration, and, if he falls among other narrow men, or on objects which have a brief importance, as some trade or politics of the hour, he prefers it to the universe, and seems inspired, and a godsend to those who wish to magnify the matter, and carry a point. Better, certainly, if we could secure the strength and fire which rude, passionate men bring into society, quite clear of their vices. But who dares draw out the linchpin from the wagon-wheel? 'T is so manifest, that there is no moral deformity but is a good passion out of place; that there is no man who is not indebted to his foibles; that, according to the old oracle, "the Furies are the bonds of men"; that the poisons are our principal medicines, which kill the disease, and save the life. In the high prophetic phrase, *He causes the wrath of man to praise him*, and twists and wrenches our evil to our good. Shakespeare wrote, —

> "'T is said, best men are moulded of their faults";

and great educators and lawgivers, and especially generals, and leaders of colonies, mainly rely on this stuff, and esteem men of irregular and passional force the best timber. A man of sense and energy, the late head of the Farm School in Boston Harbor said to me: "I want none of your good boys, — give me the bad ones." And this is the reason, I suppose, why, as soon as the children are good, the mothers are scared, and think they are going to die. Mirabeau said: "There are none but men of strong passions capable of going to greatness; none but such capable of meriting the public gratitude." Passion, though a bad regulator, is a powerful spring. Any absorbing passion has the effect to deliver from the little coils and cares of every day: 't is the heat which sets our human atoms spinning, overcomes the friction of crossing thresholds, and first addresses in society, and gives us a good start and speed, easy to continue, when once it is begun. In short, there is no man who is not at some time indebted to his vices, as no plant that is not fed from manures. We only insist that the man meliorate, and that the plant grow upward, and convert the base into the better nature.

The wise workman will not regret the poverty or the solitude which brought out his working talents. The youth is charmed with the fine air and accomplishments of the children of fortune: but all great men come out of the middle classes. 'T is better for the head; 't is better for the heart. Marcus Antoninus says, that Fronto told him, "that the so-called high-born are for the most part heartless"; whilst nothing is so indicative of deepest culture as a tender consideration of the ignorant. Charles James Fox said of England: "The history of this country proves, that we are not to expect from men in affluent circumstances the vigilance, energy, and exertion without which the House of Commons would lose its greatest force and weight. Human nature is prone to indulgence, and the most meritorious public services have always been performed by persons in a condition of life removed from opulence." And yet what we ask daily, is to be conventional. Supply, most kind gods! this defect in my address, in my form, in my fortunes, which puts me a little out of the ring: supply it, and let me be like the rest whom I admire, and on good terms with them. But the wise gods say, No, we have better things for thee. By humiliations, by defeats, by loss of sympathy, by gulfs of disparity, learn a wider truth and humanity than that of a fine gentleman. A

Fifth-Avenue landlord, a West-End householder, is not the highest style of man; and, though good hearts and sound minds are of no condition, yet he who is to be wise for many, must not be protected. He must know the huts where poor men lie, and the chores which poor men do. The first-class minds, Homer, Æsop, Socrates, Alfred, Cervantes, Shakespeare, Franklin, had the poor man's feeling and mortification. A rich man was never insulted in his life; but this man must be stung. A rich man was never in danger from cold, or hunger, or war, or ruffians, and you can see he was not, from the moderation of his ideas. 'T is a fatal disadvantage to be cockered, and to eat too much cake. What tests of manhood could he stand? Take him out of his protections. He is a good book-keeper; or he is a shrewd adviser in the insurance office: perhaps he could pass a college examination, and take his degrees: perhaps he can give wise counsel in a court of law. Now plant him down among farmers, firemen, Indians, and emigrants. Set a dog on him: set a highwayman on him: try him with a course of mobs: send him to Kansas, to Pike's Peak, to Oregon: and, if he have true faculty, this may be the element he wants, and he will come out of it with broader wisdom and manly power. Æsop, Saadi, Cervantes, Regnard, have been taken by corsairs, left for dead, sold for slaves, and know the realities of human life.

Bad times have a scientific value. These are occasions a good learner would not miss. As we go gladly to Faneuil Hall, to be played upon by the stormy winds and strong fingers of enraged patriotism, so is a fanatical persecution, civil war, national bankruptcy, or revolution, more rich in the central tones than languid years of prosperity. What had been, ever since our memory, solid continent, yawns apart, and discloses its composition and genesis. We learn geology the morning after the earthquake, on ghastly diagrams of cloven mountains, upheaved plains, and the dry bed of the sea.

In our life and culture, everything is worked up and comes in use, — passion, war, revolt, bankruptcy, and not less, folly and blunders, insult, ennui, and bad company. Nature is a rag-merchant, who works up every shred and ort and end into new creations; like a good chemist, whom I found, the other day, in his laboratory, converting his old shirts into pure white sugar. Life is a boundless privilege, and when you pay for your ticket, and get into the car, you have no guess what good company you shall find there. You buy much that is not rendered in the bill. Men achieve a certain greatness unawares, when working to another aim.

If now in this connection of discourse, we should venture on laying down the first obvious rules of life, I will not here repeat the first rule of economy, already propounded once and again, that every man shall maintain himself, — but I will say, get health. No labor, pains, temperance, poverty, nor exercise, that can gain it, must be grudged. For sickness is a cannibal which eats up all the life and youth it can lay hold of, and absorbs its own sons and daughters. I figure it as a pale, wailing, distracted phantom, absolutely selfish, heedless of what is good and great, attentive to its sensations, losing its soul, and afflicting other souls with meanness and mopings, and with ministration to its voracity of trifles. Dr. Johnson said severely, "Every man is a rascal as soon as he is sick." Drop the cant, and treat it sanely. In dealing with the drunken, we do not affect to be drunk. We must treat the sick with the same firmness, giving them, of course, every aid, — but withholding ourselves. I once asked a clergyman in a retired town, who were his companions? what men of ability he saw? he replied, that he spent his time with the sick and the dying. I said, he seemed to me to need quite other company, and all the more that he had this: for if people were sick and dying to any purpose, we would leave all and go to them, but, as far as I had observed, they were as frivolous as the rest, and sometimes much more frivolous. Let us engage our companions not to spare us. I knew a wise woman who said to her friends, "When I am old, rule me." And the best part of health is fine disposition. It is more essential than talent, even in the works of talent. Nothing will supply the want of sunshine to peaches, and, to make knowledge valuable, you must have the cheerfulness of wisdom. Whenever you are sincerely pleased, you are nourished. The joy of the spirit indicates its strength. All healthy things are sweet-tempered. Genius works in sport, and goodness smiles to the last; and, for the reason, that whoever sees the law which distributes things does not despond, but is animated to great desires and endeavors. He who desponds betrays that he has not seen it.

'T is a Dutch proverb, that "paint costs nothing," such are its preserving qualities in damp climates. Well, sunshine costs less, yet is finer pigment. And so of cheerfulness, or a good temper, the more it is spent, the more of it remains. The latent heat of an ounce of wood or stone is inexhaustible. You may rub the same chip of pine to the point of kindling, a hundred times; and the power of happiness of any soul is not to be computed or drained. It is observed that a depression of spirits develops the germs of a plague in individuals and nations.

It is an old commendation of right behavior, "*Aliis lætus, sapiens sibi,*" which our English proverb translates, "Be merry *and* wise." I know how easy it is to men of the world to look grave and sneer at your sanguine youth, and its glittering dreams. But I find the gayest castles in the air that were ever piled, far better for comfort and for use, than the dungeons in the air that are daily dug and caverned out by grumbling, discontented people. I know those miserable fellows, and I hate them, who see a black star always riding through the light and colored clouds in the sky overhead: waves of light pass over and hide it for a moment, but the black star keeps fast in the zenith. But power dwells with cheerfulness; hope puts us in a working mood, whilst despair is no muse, and untunes the active powers. A man should make life and Nature happier to us, or he had better never been born. When the political economist reckons up the unproductive classes, he should put at the head this class of pitiers of themselves, cravers of sympathy, bewailing imaginary disasters. An old French verse runs, in my translation: —

Some of your griefs you have cured,
  And the sharpest you still have survived;
But what torments of pain you endured
  From evils that never arrived!

There are three wants which never can be satisfied: that of the rich, who wants something more; that of the sick, who wants something different; and that of the traveller, who says: 'Anywhere but here.' The Turkish cadi said to Layard, "After the fashion of thy people, thou hast wandered from one place to another, until thou art happy and content in none." My countrymen are not less infatuated with the *rococo* toy of Italy. All America seems on the point of embarking for Europe. But we shall not always traverse seas and lands with light purposes, and for pleasure, as we say. One day we shall cast out the passion for Europe, by the passion for America. Culture will give gravity and domestic rest to those who now travel only as not knowing how else to spend money. Already, who provoke pity like that excellent family party just arriving in their well-appointed carriage, as far from home and any honest end as ever? Each nation has asked successively, 'What are they here for?' until at last the party are shamefaced, and anticipate the question at the gates of each town.

Genial manners are good, and power of accommodation to any circumstance, but the high prize of life, the crowning fortune of a man is to be born with a bias to some pursuit, which finds him in employment and happiness, — whether it be to make baskets, or broadswords, or canals, or statutes, or songs. I doubt not this was the meaning of Socrates, when he pronounced artists the only truly wise, as being actually, not apparently so.

In childhood, we fancied ourselves walled in by the horizon, as by a glass bell, and doubted not, by distant travel, we should reach the baths of the descending sun and stars. On experiment, the horizon flies before us, and leaves us on an endless common, sheltered by no glass bell. Yet 't is strange how tenaciously we cling to that bell-astronomy, of a protecting domestic horizon. I find the same illusion in the search after happiness, which I observe, every summer, recommenced in this neighborhood, soon after the pairing of the birds. The young people do not like the town, do not like the sea-shore, they will go inland; find a dear cottage deep in the mountains, secret as their hearts. They set forth on their travels in search of a home: they reach Berkshire; they reach Vermont; they look at the farms; — good farms, high mountain-sides; but where is the seclusion? The farm is near this; 't is near that; they have got far from Boston, but 't is near Albany, or near Burlington, or near Montreal. They explore a farm, but the house is small, old, thin; discontented people lived there, and are gone: — there 's too much sky, too much outdoors; too public. The youth aches for solitude. When he comes to the house, he passes through the house. That does not make the deep recess he sought. 'Ah! now, I perceive,' he says, 'it must be deep with persons; friends only can give depth.' Yes, but there is a great dearth, this year, of friends; hard to find, and hard to have when found: they are just going away: they too are in the whirl of the flitting world, and have engagements and necessities. They are just starting for Wisconsin; have letters from Bremen: — see you again, soon. Slow, slow to learn the lesson, that there is but one depth, but one interior, and that is, — his purpose. When joy or calamity or genius shall show him it, then woods, then farms, then city shopmen and cab-drivers, indifferently with prophet or friend, will mirror back to him its unfathomable heaven, its populous solitude.

The uses of travel are occasional, and short; but the best fruit it finds, when it finds it, is conversation; and this is a main function of life. What a difference in the hospitality of minds! Inestimable is he to whom we can say what we cannot say to ourselves. Others are involuntarily hurtful to us, and bereave us of the power of thought, impound and imprison us. As, when there is sympathy, there needs but one wise man in a company, and all are wise, — so a blockhead makes a blockhead of his companion. Wonderful power to benumb possesses this brother. When he comes into the office or public room, the society dissolves; one after another slips out, and the apartment is at his disposal. What is incurable but a frivolous habit? A fly is as untamable as a hyena. Yet folly in the sense of fun, fooling, or dawdling can easily be borne; as Talleyrand said, "I find nonsense singularly refreshing"; but a virulent, aggressive fool taints the reason of a household. I have seen a whole family of quiet, sensible people unhinged and beside themselves, victims of such a rogue; for the steady wrongheadedness of one perverse person irritates the best: since we must withstand absurdity. But resistance only exasperates the acrid fool, who believes that Nature and gravitation are quite wrong, and he only is right. Hence all the dozen inmates are soon perverted, with whatever virtues and industries they have, into contradictors, accusers, explainers, and repairers of this one malefactor; like a boat about to be overset, or a carriage run away with, — not only the foolish pilot or driver, but everybody on board is forced to assume strange and ridiculous attitudes, to balance the vehicle and prevent the upsetting. For remedy, whilst the case is yet mild, I recommend phlegm and truth: let all the truth that is spoken or done be at the zero of indifferency, or truth itself will be folly. But, when the case is seated and malignant, the only safety is in amputation; as seamen say, you shall cut and run. How to live with unfit companions? — for, with such, life is for the most part spent: and experience teaches little better than our earliest instinct of self-defence, namely, not to engage, not to mix yourself in any manner with them; but let their madness spend itself unopposed.

Conversation is an art in which a man has all mankind for his competitors, for it is that which all are practising every day while they live. Our habit of thought — take men as they rise — is not satisfying; in the common experience, I fear, it is poor and squalid. The success which will content them is a bargain, a lucrative employment, an advantage gained over a competitor, a marriage, a patrimony, a legacy, and the like. With these objects, their conversation deals with surfaces: politics, trade, personal defects, exaggerated bad news, and the rain. This is forlorn, and they feel sore and sensitive. Now, if one comes who can illuminate this dark house with thoughts, show them their native riches, what gifts they have, how indispensable each is, what magical powers over nature and men; what access to poetry, religion, and the powers which constitute character; he wakes in them the feeling of worth, his suggestions require new ways of living, new books, new men, new arts and sciences, — then we come out of our egg-shell existence into the great dome, and see the zenith over and the nadir under us. Instead of the tanks and buckets of knowledge to which we are daily confined, we come down to the shore of the sea, and dip our hands in its miraculous waves. 'T is wonderful the effect on the company. They are not the men they were. They have all been to California, and all have come back millionnaires. There is no book and no pleasure in life comparable to it. Ask what is best in our experience, and we shall say, a few pieces of plain-dealing with wise people. Our conversation once and again has apprised us that we belong to better circles than we have yet beheld; that a mental power invites us, whose generalizations are more worth for joy and for effect than anything that is now called philosophy or literature. In excited conversation, we have glimpses of the Universe, hints of power native to the soul, far-darting lights and shadows of an Andes landscape, such as we can hardly attain in lone meditation. Here are oracles sometimes profusely given, to which the memory goes back in barren hours.

Add the consent of will and temperament, and there exists the covenant of friendship. Our chief want in life, is, somebody who shall make us do what we can. This is the service of a friend. With him we are easily great. There is a sublime attraction in him to whatever virtue is in us. How he flings wide the doors of existence! What questions we ask of him! what an understanding we have! how few words are needed! It is the only real society. An Eastern poet, Ali Ben Abu Taleb, writes with sad truth: —

"He who has a thousand friends has not a friend to spare,
And he who has one enemy shall meet him everywhere."

But few writers have said anything better to this point than Hafiz, who indicates this relation as the test of mental health: "Thou learnest no secret until thou knowest friendship, since to the unsound no heavenly knowledge enters." Neither is life long enough for friendship. That is a serious and majestic affair, like a royal presence, or a religion, and not a postilion's dinner to be eaten on the run. There is a pudency about friendship, as about love, and though fine souls never lose sight of it, yet they do not name it. With the first class of men our friendship or good understanding goes quite behind all accidents of estrangement, of condition, of reputation. And yet we do not provide for the greatest good of life. We take care of our health; we lay up money; we make our roof tight, and our clothing sufficient; but who provides wisely that he shall not be wanting in the best property of all, — friends? We know that all our training is to fit us for this, and we do not take the step towards it. How long shall we sit and wait for these benefactors?

It makes no difference, in looking back five years, how you have been dieted or dressed; whether you have been lodged on the first floor or the attic; whether you have had gardens and baths, good cattle and horses, have been carried in a neat equipage, or in a ridiculous truck: these things are forgotten so quickly, and leave no effect. But it counts much whether we have had good companions, in that time, — almost as much as what we have been doing. And see the overpowering importance of neighborhood in all association. As it is marriage, fit or unfit, that makes our home, so it is who lives near us of equal social degree, — a few people at convenient distance, no matter how bad company, — these, and these only, shall be your life's companions: and all those who are native, congenial, and by many an oath of the heart, sacramented to you, are gradually and totally lost. You cannot deal systematically with this fine element of society, and one may take a good deal of pains to bring people together, and to organize clubs and debating societies, and yet no result come of it. But it is certain that there is a great deal of good in us that does not know itself, and that a habit of union and competition brings people up and keeps them up to their highest point; that life would be twice or ten times life, if spent with wise and fruitful companions. The obvious inference is, a little useful deliberation and preconcert, when one goes to buy house and land.

But we live with people on other platforms; we live with dependents, not only with the young whom we are to teach all we know, and clothe with the advantages we have earned, but also with those who serve us directly, and for money. Yet the old rules hold good. Let not the tie be mercenary, though the service is measured by money. Make yourself necessary to somebody. Do not make life hard to any. This point is acquiring new importance in American social life. Our domestic service is usually a foolish fracas of unreasonable demand on one side, and shirking on the other. A man of wit was asked, in the train, what was his errand in the city? He replied, "I have been sent to procure an angel to do cooking." A lady complained to me, that, of her two maidens, one was absent-minded, and the other was absent-bodied. And the evil increases from the ignorance and hostility of every ship-load of the immigrant population swarming into houses and farms. Few people discern that it rests with the master or the mistress what service comes from the man or the maid; that this identical hussy was a tutelar spirit in one house, and a haridan in the other. All sensible people are selfish, and nature is tugging at every contract to make the terms of it fair. If you are proposing only your own, the other party must deal a little hardly by you. If you deal generously, the other, though selfish and unjust, will make an exception in your favor, and deal truly with you. When I asked an iron-master about the slag and cinder in railroad iron, — "O," he said, "there's always good iron to be had: if there's cinder in the iron, 't is because there was cinder in the pay."

But why multiply these topics, and their illustrations, which are endless? Life brings to each his task, and, whatever art you select, algebra, planting, architecture, poems, commerce, politics, — all are attainable, even to the miraculous triumphs, on the same terms, of selecting that for which you are apt; begin at the beginning, proceed in order, step by step. 'T is as easy to twist iron anchors, and braid cannons, as to braid straw, to boil granite as to boil water, if you take all the steps in order. Wherever there is failure, there is some giddiness, some superstition about luck, some step omitted, which Nature never pardons. The happy conditions of life may be had on the same terms. Their attraction for you is the pledge that they are within your reach. Our prayers are prophets. There must be fidelity, and there must be adherence. How respectable the life that clings to its objects! Youthful aspirations are fine things, your theories and plans of life are fair and commendable : — but will you stick? Not one, I fear, in that Common full of people, or, in a thousand, but one : and when you tax them with treachery, and remind them of their high resolutions, they have forgotten that they made a vow. The individuals are fugitive, and in the act of becoming something else, and irresponsible. The race is great, the ideal fair, but the men whiffling and unsure. The hero is he who is immovably centred. The main difference between people seems to be, that one man can come under obligations on which you can rely, — is obligable; and another is not. As he has not a law within him, there 's nothing to tie him to.

'T is inevitable to name particulars of virtue, and of condition, and to exaggerate them. But all rests at last on that integrity which dwarfs talent, and can spare it. Sanity consists in not being subdued by your means. Fancy prices are paid for position, and for the culture of talent, but to the grand interests, superficial success is of no account. The man, — it is his attitude, — not feats, but forces, — not on set days and public occasions, but at all hours, and in repose alike as in energy, still formidable, and not to be disposed of. The populace says, with Horne Tooke, "If you would be powerful, pretend to be powerful." I prefer to say, with the old prophet, "Seekest thou great things? seek them not" : — or, what was said of a Spanish prince, "The more you took from him, the greater he looked." *Plus on lui ôte, plus il est grand.*

The secret of culture is to learn, that a few great points steadily reappear, alike in the poverty of the obscurest farm, and in the miscellany of metropolitan life, and that these few are alone to be regarded, — the escape from all false ties; courage to be what we are; and love of what is simple and beautiful; independence, and cheerful relation, these are the essentials, — these, and the wish to serve, — to add somewhat to the well-being of men.

VIII.

BEAUTY.

Was never form and never face
So sweet to SEYD as only grace
Which did not slumber like a stone
But hovered gleaming and was gone.
Beauty chased he everywhere,
In flame, in storm, in clouds of air.
He smote the lake to feed his eye
  With the beryl beam of the broken wave;
He flung in pebbles well to hear
  The moment's music which they gave.
Oft pealed for him a lofty tone
From nodding pole and belting zone.
He heard a voice none else could hear
From centred and from errant sphere.
The quaking earth did quake in rhyme,
Seas ebbed and flowed in epic chime.
In dens of passion, and pits of woe,
He saw strong Eros struggling through,
To sun the dark and solve the curse,
And beam to the bounds of the universe.
While thus to love he gave his days
In loyal worship, scorning praise,
How spread their lures for him, in vain,
Thieving Ambition and paltering Gain!
He thought it happier to be dead,
To die for Beauty, than live for bread.

BEAUTY.

THE spiral tendency of vegetation infects education also. Our books approach very slowly the things we most wish to know. What a parade we make of our science, and how far off, and at arm's length, it is from its objects! Our botany is all names, not powers: poets and romancers talk of herbs of grace and healing; but what does the botanist know of the virtues of his weeds? The geologist lays bare the strata, and can tell them all on his fingers: but does he know what effect passes into the man who builds his house in them? what effect on the race that inhabits a granite shelf? what on the inhabitants of marl and of alluvium?

We should go to the ornithologist with a new feeling, if he could teach us what the social birds say, when they sit in the autumn council, talking together in the trees. The want of sympathy makes his record a dull dictionary. His result is a dead bird. The bird is not in its ounces and inches, but in its relations to Nature; and the skin or skeleton you show me is no more a heron, than a heap of ashes or a bottle of gases into which his body has been reduced, is Dante or Washington. The naturalist is led *from* the road by the whole distance of his fancied advance. The boy had juster views when he gazed at the shells on the beach, or the flowers in the meadow, unable to call them by their names, than the man in the pride of his nomenclature. Astrology interested us, for it tied man to the system. Instead of an isolated beggar, the farthest star felt him, and he felt the star. However rash and however falsified by pretenders and traders in it, the hint was true and divine, the soul's avowal of its large relations, and that climate, century, remote natures, as well as near, are part of its biography. Chemistry takes to pieces, but it does not construct. Alchemy which sought to transmute one element into another, to prolong life, to arm with power, — that was in the right direction. All our science lacks a human side. The tenant is more than the house. Bugs and stamens and spores, on which we lavish so many years, are not finalities, and man, when his powers unfold in order, will take Nature along with him, and emit light into all her recesses. The human heart concerns us more than the poring into miscroscopes, and is larger than can be measured by the pompous figures of the astronomer.

We are just so frivolous and sceptical. Men hold themselves cheap and vile: and yet a man is a fagot of thunderbolts. All the elements pour through his system: he is the flood of the flood, and fire of the fire; he feels the antipodes and the pole, as drops of his blood: they are the extension of his personality. His duties are measured by that instrument he is; and a right and perfect man would be felt to the centre of the Copernican system. 'T is curious that we only believe as deep as we live. We do not think heroes can exert any more awful power than that surface-play which amuses us. A deep man believes in miracles, waits for them, believes in magic, believes that the orator will decompose his adversary; believes that the evil eye can wither, that the heart's blessing can heal; that love can exalt talent; can overcome all odds. From a great heart secret magnetisms flow incessantly to draw great events. But we prize very humble utilities, a prudent husband, a good son, a voter, a citizen, and deprecate any romance of character; and perhaps reckon only his money value, — his intellect, his affection, as a sort of bill of exchange, easily convertible into fine chambers, pictures, music, and wine.

The motive of science was the extension of man, on all sides, into Nature, till his hands should touch the stars, his eyes see through the earth, his ears understand the language of beast and bird, and the sense of the wind; and, through his sympathy, heaven and earth should talk with him. But that is not our science. These geologies, chemistries, astronomies, seem to make wise, but they leave us where they found us. The invention is of use to the inventor, of questionable help to any other. The formulas of science are like the papers in your pocket-book, of no value to any but the owner. Science in England, in America, is jealous of theory, hates the name of love and moral purpose. There 's a revenge for this inhumanity. What manner of man does science make? The boy is not attracted. He says, I do not wish to be such a kind of man as my professor is. The collector has dried all the plants in his herbal, but he has lost weight and humor. He has got all snakes and lizards in his phials, but science has done for him also, and has put the man into a bottle. Our reliance on the physician is a kind of despair of ourselves. The clergy have bronchitis, which does not seem a certificate of spiritual health. Macready thought it came of the *falsetto* of their voicing. An Indian prince, Tisso, one day riding in the forest, saw a herd of elk sporting. "See how happy," he said, "these browsing elks are! Why should not priests, lodged and fed comfortably in the temples, also amuse themselves?" Returning home, he imparted this reflection to the king. The king, on the next day, conferred the sovereignty on him, saying, "Prince, administer this empire for seven days: at the termination of that period, I shall put thee to death." At the end of the seventh day, the king inquired, "From what cause hast thou become so emaciated?" He answered, "From the horror of death." The monarch rejoined: "Live, my child, and be wise. Thou hast ceased to take recreation, saying to thyself, In seven days I shall be put to death. These priests in the temple incessantly meditate on death; how can they enter into healthful diversions?" But the men of science or the doctors or the clergy are not victims of their pursuits, more than others. The miller, the lawyer, and the merchant dedicate themselves to their own details, and do not come out men of more force. Have they divination, grand aims, hospitality of soul, and the equality to any event, which we demand in man, or only the reactions of the mill, of the wares, of the chicane?

No object really interests us but man, and in man only his superiorities; and though we are aware of a perfect law in Nature, it has fascination for us only through its relation to him, or, as it is rooted in the mind. At the birth of Winckelmann, more than a hundred years ago, side by side with this arid, departmental, *post-mortem* science, rose an enthusiasm in the study of Beauty; and perhaps some sparks from it may yet light a conflagration in the other. Knowledge of men, knowledge of manners, the power of form, and our sensibility to personal influence, never go out of fashion. These are facts of a science which we study without book, whose teachers and subjects are always near us.

So inveterate is our habit of criticism, that much of our

knowledge in this direction belongs to the chapter of pathology. The crowd in the street oftener furnishes degradations than angels or redeemers; but they all prove the transparency. Every spirit makes its house; and we can give a shrewd guess from the house to the inhabitant. But not less does Nature furnish us with every sign of grace and goodness. The delicious faces of children, the beauty of school-girls, "the sweet seriousness of sixteen," the lofty air of well-born, well-bred boys, the passionate histories in the looks and manners of youth and early manhood, and the varied power in all that well-known company that escort us through life, — we know how these forms thrill, paralyze, provoke, inspire, and enlarge us.

Beauty is the form under which the intellect prefers to study the world. All privilege is that of beauty; for there are many beauties; as, of general nature, of the human face and form, of manners, of brain, or method, moral beauty, or beauty of the soul.

The ancients believed that a genius or demon took possession at birth of each mortal, to guide him; that these genii were sometimes seen as a flame of fire partly immersed in the bodies which they governed; — on an evil man, resting on his head; in a good man, mixed with his substance. They thought the same genius, at the death of its ward, entered a new-born child, and they pretended to guess the pilot, by the sailing of the ship. We recognize obscurely the same fact, though we give it our own names. We say, that every man is entitled to be valued by his best moment. We measure our friends so. We know, they have intervals of folly, whereof we take no heed, but wait the reappearings of the genius, which are sure and beautiful. On the other side, everybody knows people who appear bedridden, and who, with all degrees of ability, never impress us with the air of free agency. They know it too, and peep with their eyes to see if you detect their sad plight. We fancy, could we pronounce the solving word, and disenchant them, the cloud would roll up, the little rider would be discovered and unseated, and they would regain their freedom. The remedy seems never to be far off, since the first step into thought lifts this mountain of necessity. Thought is the pent air-ball which can rive the planet, and the beauty which certain objects have for him is the friendly fire which expands the thought, and acquaints the prisoner that liberty and power await him.

The question of Beauty takes us out of surfaces, to thinking of the foundations of things. Goethe said: "The beautiful is a manifestation of secret laws of Nature, which, but for this appearance, had been forever concealed from us." And the working of this deep instinct makes all the excitement — much of it superficial and absurd enough — about works of art, which leads armies of vain travellers every year to Italy, Greece, and Egypt. Every man values every acquisition he makes in the science of beauty, above his possessions. The most useful man in the most useful world, so long as only commodity was served, would remain unsatisfied. But, as fast as he sees beauty, life acquires a very high value.

I am warned by the ill fate of many philosophers not to attempt a definition of Beauty. I will rather enumerate a few of its qualities. We ascribe beauty to that which is simple; which has no superfluous parts; which exactly answers its end; which stands related to all things; which is the mean of many extremes. It is the most enduring quality, and the most ascending quality. We say love is blind, and the figure of Cupid is drawn with a bandage round his eyes. Blind: — yes, because he does not see what he does not like; but the sharpest-sighted hunter in the universe is Love, for finding what he seeks, and only that; and the mythologists tell us, that Vulcan was painted lame, and Cupid blind, to call attention to the fact, that one was all limbs, and the other, all eyes. In the true mythology, Love is an immortal child, and Beauty leads him as a guide: nor can we express a deeper sense than when we say, Beauty is the pilot of the young soul.

Beyond their sensuous delight, the forms and colors of Nature have a new charm for us in our perception, that not one ornament was added for ornament, but each is a sign of some better health, or more excellent action. Elegance of form in bird or beast, or in the human figure, marks some excellence of structure: or beauty is only an invitation from what belongs to us. 'T is a law of botany, that in plants, the same virtues follow the same forms. It is a rule of largest application, true in a plant, true in a loaf of bread, that in the construction of any fabric or organism, any real increase of fitness to its end, is an increase of beauty.

The lesson taught by the study of Greek and of Gothic art, of antique and of Pre-Raphaelite painting, was worth all the research, — namely, that all beauty must be organic;

that outside embellishment is deformity. It is the soundness of the bones that ultimates itself in a peach-bloom complexion: health of constitution that makes the sparkle and the power of the eye. 'T is the adjustment of the size and of the joining of the sockets of the skeleton, that gives grace of outline and the finer grace of movement. The cat and the deer cannot move or sit inelegantly. The dancing-master can never teach a badly built man to walk well. The tint of the flower proceeds from its root, and the lustres of the sea-shell begin with its existence. Hence our taste in building rejects paint, and all shifts, and shows the original grain of the wood: refuses pilasters and columns that support nothing, and allows the real supporters of the house honestly to show themselves. Every necessary or organic action pleases the beholder. A man leading a horse to water, a farmer sowing seed, the labors of haymakers in the field, the carpenter building a ship, the smith at his forge, or, whatever useful labor, is becoming to the wise eye. But if it is done to be seen, it is mean. How beautiful are ships on the sea! but ships in the theatre, — or ships kept for picturesque effect on Virginia Water, by George IV., and men hired to stand in fitting costumes at a penny an hour! — What a difference in effect between a battalion of troops marching to action, and one of our independent companies on a holiday! In the midst of a military show, and a festal procession gay with banners, I saw a boy seize an old tin pan that lay resting under a wall, and poising it on the top of a stick, he set it turning, and made it describe the most elegant imaginable curves, and drew away attention from the decorated procession by this startling beauty.

Another text from the mythologists. The Greeks fabled that Venus was born of the foam of the sea. Nothing interests us which is stark or bounded, but only what streams with life, what is in act or endeavor to reach somewhat beyond. The pleasure a palace or a temple gives the eye, is, that an order and method has been communicated to stones, so that they speak and geometrize, become tender or sublime with expression. Beauty is the moment of transition, as if the form were just ready to flow into other forms. Any fixedness, heaping, or concentration on one feature, — a long nose, a sharp chin, a hump-back, — is the reverse of the flowing, and therefore deformed. Beautiful as is the symmetry of any form, if the form can move, we seek a more excellent symmetry. The interruption of equilibrium stimulates the eye to desire the restoration of symmetry, and to watch the steps through which it is attained. This is the charm of running water, sea-waves, the flight of birds, and the locomotion of animals. This is the theory of dancing, to recover continually in changes the lost equilibrium, not by abrupt and angular, but by gradual and curving movements. I have been told by persons of experience in matters of taste, that the fashions follow a law of gradation, and are never arbitrary. The new mode is always only a step onward in the same direction as the last mode; and a cultivated eye is prepared for and predicts the new fashion. This fact suggests the reason of all mistakes and offence in our own modes. It is necessary in music, when you strike a discord, to let down the ear by an intermediate note or two to the accord again: and many a good experiment, born of good sense, and destined to succeed, fails, only because it is offensively sudden. I suppose, the Parisian milliner who dresses the world from her imperious boudoir, will know how to reconcile the Bloomer costume to the eye of mankind, and make it triumphant over Punch himself, by interposing the just gradations. I need not say how wide the same law ranges; and how much it can be hoped to effect. All that is a little harshly claimed by progressive parties may easily come to be conceded without question, if this rule be observed. Thus the circumstances may be easily imagined, in which woman may speak, vote, argue causes, legislate, and drive a coach, and all the most naturally in the world, if only it come by degrees. To this streaming or flowing belongs the beauty that all circular movement has; as, the circulation of waters, the circulation of the blood, the periodical motion of planets, the annual wave of vegetation, the action and reaction of Nature; and, if we follow it out, this demand in our thought for an ever-onward action is the argument for the immortality.

One more text from the mythologists is to the same purpose, — *Beauty rides on a lion.* Beauty rests on necessities. The line of beauty is the result of perfect economy. The cell of the bee is built at that angle which gives the most strength with the least wax; the bone or the quill of the bird gives the most alar strength with the least weight. "It is the purgation of superfluities," said Michel Angelo. There is not a particle to spare in natural structures. There is a compelling reason in the uses of the plant, for every novelty of color or form: and our art saves material, by more skilful arrangement, and reaches beauty by taking every superfluous ounce that can be spared from a wall, and keeping all its strength in the poetry of columns. In rhetoric, this art of omission is a chief secret of power, and, in general, it is proof of high culture, to say the greatest matters in the simplest way.

Veracity first of all, and forever. *Rien de beau que le vrai.* In all design, art lies in making your object prominent, but there is a prior art in choosing objects that are prominent. The fine arts have nothing casual, but spring from the instincts of the nations that created them.

Beauty is the quality which makes to endure. In a house that I know, I have noticed a block of spermaceti lying about closets and mantel-pieces, for twenty years together, simply because the tallow-man gave it the form of a rabbit; and, I suppose, it may continue to be lugged about unchanged for a century. Let an artist scrawl a few lines or figures on the back of a letter, and that scrap of paper is rescued from danger, is put in portfolio, is framed and glazed, and, in proportion to the beauty of the lines drawn, will be kept for centuries. Burns writes a copy of verses, and sends them to a newspaper, and the human race take charge of them that they shall not perish.

As the flute is heard farther than the cart, see how surely a beautiful form strikes the fancy of men, and is copied and reproduced without end. How many copies are there of the Belvedere Apollo, the Venus, the Psyche, the Warwick Vase, the Parthenon, and the Temple of Vesta? These are objects of tenderness to all. In our cities, an ugly building is soon removed, and is never repeated, but any beautiful building is copied and improved upon, so that all masons and carpenters work to repeat and preserve the agreeable forms, whilst the ugly ones die out.

The felicities of design in art, or in works of Nature, are shadows or forerunners of that beauty which reaches its perfection in the human form. All men are its lovers. Wherever it goes, it creates joy and hilarity, and everything is permitted to it. It reaches its height in woman. "To Eve," say the Mahometans, "God gave two thirds of all beauty." A beautiful woman is a practical poet, taming her savage mate, planting tenderness, hope, and eloquence in all whom she approaches. Some favors of condition must go with it, since a certain serenity is essential, but we love its reproofs and superiorities. Nature wishes that woman should attract man, yet she often cunningly moulds into her face a little sarcasm, which seems to say, 'Yes, I am willing to attract, but to attract a little better kind of man than any I yet behold.' French *mémoires* of the fifteenth century celebrate the name of Pauline de Viguiere, a virtuous and accomplished maiden, who so fired the enthusiasm of her contemporaries, by her enchanting form, that the citizens of her native city of Toulouse obtained the aid of the civil authorities to compel her to appear publicly on the balcony at least twice a week, and, as often as she showed herself, the crowd was dangerous to life. Not less, in England, in the last century, was the fame of the Gunnings, of whom Elizabeth married the Duke of Hamilton; and Maria, the Earl of Coventry. Walpole says: "The concourse was so great, when the Duchess of Hamilton was presented at court, on Friday, that even the noble crowd in the drawing-room clambered on chairs and tables to look at her. There are mobs at their doors to see them get into their chairs, and people go early to get places at the theatres, when it is known they will be there." "Such crowds," he adds, elsewhere, "flock to see the Duchess of Hamilton, that seven hundred people sat up all night, in and about an inn, in Yorkshire, to see her get into her post-chaise next morning."

But why need we console ourselves with the fames of Helen of Argos, or Corinna, or Pauline of Toulouse, or the Duchess of Hamilton? We all know this magic very well, or can divine it. It does not hurt weak eyes to look into beautiful eyes never so long. Women stand related to beautiful Nature around us, and the enamored youth mixes their form with moon and stars, with woods and waters, and the pomp of summer. They heal us of awkwardness by their words and looks. We observe their intellectual influence on the most serious student. They refine and clear his mind; teach him to put a pleasing method into what is dry and difficult. We talk to them and wish to be listened to; we fear to fatigue them, and acquire a facility of expression which passes from conversation into habit of style.

That Beauty is the normal state, is shown by the perpetual effort of Nature to attain it. Mirabeau had an ugly face on a handsome ground; and we see faces every day which have a good type, but have been marred in the casting: a proof that we are all entitled to beauty, should have been beautiful, if our ancestors had kept the laws, — as every lily and every rose is well. But our bodies do not fit us, but caricature and satirize us. Thus, short legs, which constrain to short, mincing steps, are a kind of personal insult and contumely to the owner; and long stilts, again, put him at perpetual disadvantage, and force him to stoop to the general level of mankind. Martial ridicules a gentleman of his day whose countenance resembled the face of a swimmer seen under water. Saadi describes a schoolmaster "so ugly and crabbed, that a sight of him would derange the ecstasies of the orthodox." Faces are rarely true to any ideal type, but are a record in sculpture of a thousand anecdotes of whim and folly. Portrait painters say that most faces and forms are irregular and unsymmetrical; have one eye blue, and one gray; the nose not straight; and one shoulder higher than another; the hair unequally distributed, etc. The man is physically as well as metaphysically a thing of shreds and patches, borrowed unequally from good and bad ancestors, and a misfit from the start.

A beautiful person, among the Greeks, was thought to betray by this sign some secret favor of the immortal gods; and we can pardon pride, when a woman possesses such a figure, that wherever she stands, or moves, or throws a shadow on the wall, or sits for a portrait to the artist, she confers a favor on the world. And yet — it is not beauty that inspires the deepest passion. Beauty without grace is the hook without the bait. Beauty, without expression, tires. Abbé Ménage said of the President Le Bailleul, "that he was fit for nothing but to sit for his portrait." A Greek epigram intimates that the force of love is not shown by the courting of beauty, but when the like desire is inflamed for one who is ill-favored. And petulant old gentlemen, who have chanced to suffer some intolerable weariness from pretty people, or who have seen cut flowers to some profusion, or who see, after a world of pains have been successfully taken for the costume, how the least mistake in sentiment takes all the beauty out of your clothes, — affirm, that the secret of ugliness consists not in irregularity, but in being uninteresting.

We love any forms, however ugly, from which great qualities shine. If command, eloquence, art, or invention exist in the most deformed person, all the accidents that usually displease, please, and raise esteem and wonder higher. The great orator was an emaciated, insignificant person, but he was all brain. Cardinal De Retz says of De Bouillon, "With the physiognomy of an ox, he had the perspicacity of an eagle." It was said of Hooke, the friend of Newton, "He is the most, and promises the least, of any man in England." "Since I am so ugly," said Du Guesclin, "it behooves that I be bold." Sir Philip Sidney, the darling of mankind, Ben Jonson tells us, "was no pleasant man in countenance, his face being spoiled with pimples, and of high blood, and long." Those who have ruled human destinies, like planets, for thousands of years, were not handsome men. If a man can raise a small city to be a great kingdom, can make bread cheap, can irrigate deserts, can join oceans by canals, can subdue steam, can organize victory, can lead the opinions of mankind, can enlarge knowledge, 'tis no matter whether his nose is parallel to his spine, as it ought to be, or whether he has a nose at all; whether his legs are straight, or whether his legs are amputated; his deformities will come to be reckoned ornamental and advantageous on the whole. This is the triumph of expression, degrading beauty, charming us with a power so fine and friendly and intoxicating, that it makes admired persons insipid, and the thought of passing our lives with them insupportable. There are faces so fluid with expression, so flushed and rippled by the play of thought, that we can hardly find what the mere features really are. When the delicious beauty of lineaments loses its power, it is because a more delicious beauty has appeared; that an interior and durable form has been disclosed. Still, Beauty rides on her lion, as before. Still, "it was for beauty that the world was made." The lives of the Italian artists, who established a despotism of genius amidst the dukes and kings and mobs of their stormy epoch, prove how loyal men in all times are to a finer brain, a finer method, than their own. If a man can cut such a head on his stone gate-post as shall draw and keep a crowd about it all day, by its grace, good-nature, and inscrutable meaning; — if a man can build a plain cottage with such symmetry, as to make all the fine palaces look cheap and vulgar; can take such advantage of Nature that all her powers serve him; making use of geometry, instead of expense; tapping a mountain for his water-jet; causing the sun and moon to seem only the decorations of his estate; this is still the legitimate dominion of beauty.

The radiance of the human form, though sometimes astonishing, is only a burst of beauty for a few years or a few months, at the perfection of youth, and in most, rapidly declines. But we remain lovers of it, only transferring our interest to interior excellence. And it is not only admirable in singular and salient talents, but also in the world of manners.

But the sovereign attribute remains to be noted. Things are pretty, graceful, rich, elegant, handsome, but, until they speak to the imagination, not yet beautiful. This is the reason why beauty is still escaping out of all analysis. It is not yet possessed, it cannot be handled. Proclus says, "It swims on the light of forms." It is properly not in the form, but in the mind. It instantly deserts possession, and flies to an object in the horizon. If I could put my hand on the north star, would it be as beautiful? The sea is lovely, but when we bathe in it, the beauty forsakes all the near water. For the imagination and senses cannot be gratified at the same time. Wordsworth rightly speaks of "a light that never was on sea or land," meaning, that it was supplied by the observer, and the Welsh bard warns his countrywomen, that

"Half of their charms with Cadwallon shall die."

The new virtue which constitutes a thing beautiful is a certain cosmical quality, or, a power to suggest relation to the whole world, and so lift the object out of a pitiful individuality. Every natural feature — sea, sky, rainbow, flowers, musical tone — has in it somewhat which is not private, but universal, speaks of that central benefit which is the soul of Nature, and thereby is beautiful. And, in chosen men and women, I find somewhat in form, speech, and manners, which is not of their person and family, but of a humane, catholic, and spiritual character, and we love them as the sky. They have a largeness of suggestion, and their face and manners carry a certain grandeur, like time and justice.

The feat of the imagination is in showing the convertibility of everything into every other thing. Facts which had never before left their stark common sense suddenly figure as Eleusinian mysteries. My boots and chair and candlestick are fairies in disguise, meteors and constellations. All the facts in Nature are nouns of the intellect, and make the grammar of the eternal language. Every word has a double, treble, or centuple use and meaning. What! has my stove and pepper-pot a false bottom! I cry you mercy, good shoe-box! I did not know you were a jewel-case. Chaff and dust begin to sparkle, and are clothed about with immortality. And there is a joy in perceiving the representative or symbolic character of a fact, which no bare fact or event can ever give. There are no days in life so memorable as those which vibrated to some stroke of the imagination.

The poets are quite right in decking their mistresses with the spoils of the landscape, flower-gardens, gems, rainbows, flushes of morning, and stars of night, since all beauty points at identity, and whatsoever thing does not express to me the sea and sky, day and night, is somewhat forbidden and wrong. Into every beautiful object there enters somewhat immeasurable and divine, and just as much into form bounded by outlines, like mountains on the horizon, as into tones of music, or depths of space. Polarized light showed the secret architecture of bodies ; and when the *second-sight* of the mind is opened, now one color or form or gesture, and now another, has a pungency, as if a more interior ray had been emitted, disclosing its deep holdings in the frame of things.

The laws of this translation we do not know, or why one feature or gesture enchants, why one word or syllable intoxicates, but the fact is familiar that the fine touch of the eye, or a grace of manners, or a phrase of poetry, plants wings at our shoulders ; as if the Divinity, in his approaches, lifts away mountains of obstruction, and deigns to draw a truer line, which the mind knows and owns. This is that haughty force of beauty, "*vis superba formæ*," which the poets praise, — under calm and precise outline, the immeasurable and divine : Beauty hiding all wisdom and power in its calm sky.

All high beauty has a moral element in it, and I find the antique sculpture as ethical as Marcus Antoninus : and the beauty ever in proportion to the depth of thought. Gross and obscure natures, however decorated, seem impure shambles ; but character gives splendor to youth, and awe to wrinkled skin and gray hairs. An adorer of truth we cannot choose but obey, and the woman who has shared with us the moral sentiment, — her locks must appear to us sublime. Thus there is a climbing scale of culture, from the first agreeable sensation which a sparkling gem or a scarlet stain affords the eye, up through fair outlines and details of the landscape, features of the human face and form, signs and tokens of thought and character in manners, up to the ineffable mysteries of the intellect. Wherever we begin, thither our steps tend : an ascent from the joy of a horse in his trappings, up to the perception of Newton, that the globe on which we ride is only a larger apple falling from a larger tree ; up to the perception of Plato, that globe and universe are rude and early expressions of an all-dissolving Unity, — the first stair on the scale to the temple of the Mind.

IX.

ILLUSIONS.

Flow, flow the waves hated,
Accursed, adored,
The waves of mutation:
No anchorage is.
Sleep is not, death is not;
Who seem to die live.
House you were born in,
Friends of your spring-time,
Old man and young maid,
Day's toil and its guerdon,
They are all vanishing,
Fleeing to fables,
Cannot be moored.
See the stars through them,
Through treacherous marbles.
Know, the stars yonder,
The stars everlasting,
Are fugitive also,
And emulate, vaulted,
The lambent heat-lightning,
And fire-fly's flight.

When thou dost return
On the wave's circulation,
Beholding the shimmer,
The wild dissipation,
And, out of endeavor
To change and to flow,
The gas becomes solid,
And phantoms and nothings
Return to be things,
And endless imbroglio
Is law and the world, —
Then first shalt thou know,
That in the wild turmoil,
Horsed on the Proteus,
Thou ridest to power,
And to endurance.

ILLUSIONS.

SOME years ago, in company with an agreeable party, I spent a long summer day in exploring the Mammoth Cave in Kentucky. We traversed, through spacious galleries affording a solid masonry foundation for the town and county overhead, the six or eight black miles from the mouth of the cavern to the innermost recess which tourists visit, — a niche or grotto made of one seamless stalactite, and called, I believe, Serena's Bower. I lost the light of one day. I saw high domes, and bottomless pits; heard the voice of unseen waterfalls; paddled three quarters of a mile in the deep Echo River, whose waters are peopled with the blind fish; crossed the streams "Lethe" and "Styx"; plied with music and guns the echoes in these alarming galleries; saw every form of stalagmite and stalactite in the sculptured and fretted chambers, — icicle, orange-flower, acanthus, grapes, and snowball. We shot Bengal lights into the vaults and groins of the sparry cathedrals, and examined all the masterpieces which the four combined engineers, water, limestone, gravitation, and time, could make in the dark.

The mysteries and scenery of the cave had the same dignity that belongs to all natural objects, and which shames the fine things to which we foppishly compare them. I remarked, especially, the mimetic habit, with which Nature, on new instruments, hums her old tunes, making night to mimic day, and chemistry to ape vegetation. But I then took notice, and still chiefly remember, that the best thing which the cave had to offer was an illusion. On arriving at what is called the "Star-Chamber," our lamps were taken from us by the guide, and extinguished or put aside, and, on looking upwards, I saw or seemed to see the night heaven thick with stars glimmering more or less brightly over our heads, and even what seemed a comet flaming among them. All the party were touched with astonishment and pleasure. Our musical friends sung with much feeling a pretty song, "The stars are in the quiet sky," &c., and I sat down on the rocky floor to enjoy the serene picture. Some crystal specks in the black ceiling high overhead, reflecting the light of a half-hid lamp, yielded this magnificent effect.

I own, I did not like the cave so well for eking out its sublimities with this theatrical trick. But I have had many experiences like it, before and since; and we must be content to be pleased without too curiously analyzing the occasions. Our conversation with Nature is not just what it seems. The cloud-rack, the sunrise and sunset glories, rainbows and northern lights, are not quite so spheral as our childhood thought them; and the part our organization plays in them is too large. The senses interfere everywhere, and mix their own structure with all they report of. Once, we fancied the earth a plane, and stationary. In admiring the sunset, we do not yet deduct the rounding, co-ordinating, pictorial powers of the eye.

The same interference from our organization creates the most of our pleasure and pain. Our first mistake is the belief that the circumstance gives the joy which we give to the circumstance. Life is an ecstasy. Life is sweet as nitrous oxide; and the fisherman dripping all day over a cold pond, the switchman at the railway intersection, the farmer in the field, the negro in the rice-swamp, the fop in the street, the hunter in the woods, the barrister with the jury, the belle at the ball, all ascribe a certain pleasure to their employment, which they themselves give it. Health and appetite impart the sweetness to sugar, bread, and meat. We fancy that our civilization has got on far, but we still come back to our primers.

We live by our imaginations, by our admirations, by our sentiments. The child walks amid heaps of illusions, which he does not like to have disturbed. The boy, how sweet to him is his fancy! how dear the story of barons and battles! What a hero he is, whilst he feeds on his heroes! What a debt is his to imaginative books! He has no better friend or influence, than Scott, Shakespeare, Plutarch, and Homer. The man lives to other objects, but who dare affirm that they are more real? Even the prose of the streets is full of refractions. In the life of the dreariest alderman, fancy enters into all details, and colors them with rosy hue. He imitates the air and actions of people whom he admires, and is raised in his own eyes. He pays a debt quicker to a rich man than to a poor man. He wishes the bow and compliment of some leader in the state, or in society; weighs what he says; perhaps he never comes nearer to him for that, but dies at last better contented for this amusement of his eyes and his fancy.

The world rolls, the din of life is never hushed. In London, in Paris, in Boston, in San Francisco, the carnival, the masquerade, is at its height. Nobody drops his domino. The unities, the fictions of the piece, it would be an impertinence to break. The chapter of fascinations is very long. Great is paint; nay, God is the painter; and we rightly accuse the critic who destroys too many illusions. Society does not love its unmaskers. It was wittily, if somewhat bitterly, said by D'Alembert, "*qu'un état de vapeur était un état très fâcheux, parcequ'il nous faisait voir les choses comme elles sont.*" I find men victims of illusion in all parts of life. Children, youths, adults, and old men, all are led by one bawble or another. Yoganidra, the goddess of illusion, Proteus, or Momus, or Gylfi's Mocking, — for the Power has many names, — is stronger than the Titans, stronger than Apollo. Few have overheard the gods, or surprised their secret. Life is a succession of lessons which must be lived to be understood. All is riddle, and the key to a riddle is another riddle. There are as many pillows of illusion as flakes in a snow-storm. We wake from one dream into another dream. The toys, to be sure, are various, and are graduated in refinement to the quality of the dupe. The intellectual man requires a fine bait; the sots are easily amused. But everybody is drugged with his own frenzy, and the pageant marches at all hours, with music and banner and badge.

Amid the joyous troop who give in to the charivari comes now and then a sad-eyed boy, whose eyes lack the requisite refractions to clothe the show in due glory, and who is afflicted with a tendency to trace home the glittering miscellany of fruits and flowers to one root. Science is a search after identity, and the scientific whim is lurking in all corners. At the State Fair, a friend of mine complained that all the varieties of fancy pears in our orchards seem to have been selected by somebody who had a whim for a particular kind of pear, and only cultivated such as had that perfume; they were all alike. And I remember the quarrel of another youth with the confectioners, that, when he racked his wit to choose the best comfits in the shops, in all the endless varieties of sweetmeat he could only find three flavors, or two. What then? Pears and cakes are good for something; and because you, unluckily, have an eye or nose too keen, why need you spoil the comfort which the rest of us find in them? I knew a humorist, who, in a good deal of rattle, had a grain or two of sense. He shocked the company by maintaining that the attributes of God were two, — power and risibility; and that it was the duty of every pious man to keep up the comedy. And I have known gentlemen of great stake in the community, but whose sympathies were cold, — presidents of colleges, and governors, and senators, — who held themselves bound to sign every temperance pledge, and act with Bible societies, and missions, and peacemakers, and cry *Hist-a-boy!* to every good dog. We must not carry comity too far, but we all have kind impulses in this direction. When the boys come into my yard for leave to gather horse-chestnuts, I own I enter into Nature's game, and affect to grant the permission reluctantly, fearing that any moment they will find out the imposture of that showy chaff. But this tenderness is quite unnecessary; the enchantments are laid on very thick. Their young life is thatched with them. Bare and grim to tears is the lot of the children in the hovel I saw yesterday; yet not the less they hung it round with frippery romance, like the children of the happiest fortune, and talked of "the dear cottage where so many joyful hours had flown." Well, this thatching of hovels is the custom of the country. Women, more than all, are the element and kingdom of illusion. Being fascinated, they fascinate. They see through Claude-Lorraines. And how dare any one, if he could, pluck away the *coulisses*, stage effects, and ceremonies, by which they live? Too pathetic, too pitiable, is the region of affection, and its atmosphere always liable to *mirage*.

We are not very much to blame for our bad marriages. We live amid hallucinations; and this especial trap is laid to trip up our feet with, and all are tripped up first or last. But the mighty Mother who had been so sly with us, as if she felt that she owed us some indemnity, insinuates into the Pandora-box of marriage some deep and serious benefits, and some great joys. We find a delight in the beauty and happiness of children, that makes the heart too big for the body. In the worst-assorted connections there is ever some mixture of true marriage. Teague and his jade get some just relations of mutual respect, kindly observation, and fostering of each other, learn something, and would carry themselves wiselier, if they were now to begin.

'T is fine for us to point at one or another fine madman, as if there were any exempts. The scholar in his library is none. I, who have all my life heard any number of orations and debates, read poems and miscellaneous books, conversed with many geniuses, am still the victim of any new page; and, if Marmaduke, or Hugh, or Moosehead, or any other, invent a new style or mythology, I fancy that the world will be all brave and right, if dressed in these colors, which I had not thought of. Then at once I will daub with this new paint; but it will not stick. 'T is like the cement which the pedler sells at the door; he makes broken crockery hold with it, but you can never buy of him a bit of the cement which will make it hold when he is gone.

Men who make themselves felt in the world avail themselves of a certain fate in their constitution, which they know how to use. But they never deeply interest us, unless they lift a corner of the curtain, or betray never so slightly their penetration of what is behind it. 'T is the charm of practical men, that outside of their practicality are a certain poetry and play, as if they led the good horse Power by the bridle, and preferred to walk, though they can ride so fiercely. Bonaparte is intellectual, as well as Cæsar; and the best soldiers, sea-captains, and railway men, have a gentleness, when off duty; a good-natured admission that there are illusions, and who shall say that he is not their sport? We stigmatize the cast-iron fellows, who cannot so detach themselves, as "dragon-ridden," "thunder-stricken," and fools of fate, with whatever powers endowed.

Since our tuition is through emblems and indirections, 't is well to know that there is method in it, a fixed scale, and rank above rank in the phantasms. We begin low with coarse masks, and rise to the most subtle and beautiful. The red men told Columbus, "they had an herb which took away fatigue"; but he found the allusion of "arriving from the east at the Indies" more composing to his lofty spirit than any tobacco. Is not our faith in the impenetrability of matter more sedative than narcotics? You play with jack-straws, balls, bowls, horse and gun, estates and politics; but there are finer games before you. Is not time a pretty toy? Life will show you masks that are worth all your carnivals. Yonder mountain must migrate into your mind. The fine star-dust and nebulous blur in Orion, "the portentous year of Mizar and Alcor," must come down and be dealt with in your household thought. What if you shall come to discern that the play and playground of all this pompous history are radiations from yourself, and that the sun borrows his beams? What terrible questions we are learning to ask! The former men believed in magic, by which temples, cities, and men were swallowed up, and all trace of them gone. We are coming on the secret of a magic which sweeps out of men's minds all vestige of theism and beliefs which they and their fathers held and were framed upon.

There are deceptions of the senses, deceptions of the passions, and the structural, beneficent illusions of sentiment and of the intellect. There is the illusion of love, which attributes to the beloved person all which that person shares with his or her family, sex, age, or condition, nay with the human mind itself. 'T is these which the lover loves, and Anna Matilda gets the credit of them. As if one shut up always in a tower, with one window, through which the face of heaven and earth could be seen, should fancy that all the marvels he beheld belonged to that window. There is the illusion of time, which is very deep; who has disposed of it? or come to the conviction that what seems the *succession* of thought is only the distribution of wholes into causal series? The intellect sees that every atom carries the whole of Nature; that the mind opens to omnipotence; that, in the endless striving and ascents, the metamorphosis is entire, so that the soul doth not know itself in its own act, when that act is perfected. There is illusion that shall deceive even the elect. There is illusion that shall deceive even the performer of the miracle. Though he make his body, he denies that he makes it. Though the world exist from thought, thought is daunted in presence of the world. One after the other we accept the mental laws, still resisting those which follow, which however must be accepted. But all our concessions only compel us to new profusion. And what avails it that science has come to treat space and time as simply forms of thought, and the material world as hypothetical, and withal our pretension of *property* and even of selfhood are fading with the rest, if, at last, even our thoughts are not finalities; but the incessant flowing and ascension reach these also, and each thought which yesterday was a finality, to-day is yielding to a larger generalization?

With such volatile elements to work in, 't is no wonder if our estimates are loose and floating. We must work and affirm, but we have no guess of the value of what we say or do. The cloud is now as big as your hand, and now it covers a county. That story of Thor, who was set to drain the drinking-horn in Asgard, and to wrestle with the old woman, and to run with the runner Lok, and presently found that he had been drinking up the sea, and wrestling with Time, and racing with Thought, describes us who are contending, amid these seeming trifles, with the supreme energies of Nature. We fancy we have fallen into bad company and squalid condition, low debts, shoe-bills, broken glass to pay for, pots to buy, butcher's meat, sugar, milk, and coal. 'Set me some great task, ye gods! and I will show my spirit.' 'Not so,' says the good Heaven; 'plod and plough, vamp your old coats and hats, weave a shoestring; great affairs and the best wine by and by.' Well, 't is all phantasm; and if we weave a yard of tape in all humility, and as well as we can, long hereafter we shall see it was no cotton tape at all, but some galaxy which we braided, and that the threads were Time and Nature.

We cannot write the order of the variable winds. How can we penetrate the law of our shifting moods and susceptibility? Yet they differ as all and nothing. Instead of the firmament of yesterday, which our eyes require, it is to-day an eggshell which coops us in; we cannot even see what or where our stars of destiny are. From day to day, the capital facts of human life are hidden from our eyes. Suddenly the mist rolls up, and reveals them, and we think how much good time is gone, that might have been saved, had any hint of these things been shown. A sudden rise in the road shows us the system of mountains, and all the summits, which have been just as near us all the year, but quite out of mind. But these alternations are not without their order, and we are parties to our various fortune. If life seem a succession of dreams, yet poetic justice is done in dreams also. The visions of good men are good; it is the undisciplined will that is whipped with bad thoughts and bad fortunes. When we break the laws, we lose our hold on the central reality. Like sick men in hospitals, we change only from bed to bed, from one folly to another; and it cannot signify much what becomes of such castaways, — wailing, stupid, comatose creatures, — lifted from bed to bed, from the nothing of life to the nothing of death.

In this kingdom of illusions we grope eagerly for stays and

foundations. There is none but a strict and faithful dealing at home, and a severe barring out of all duplicity or illusion there. Whatever games are played with us, we must play no games with ourselves, but deal in our privacy with the last honesty and truth. I look upon the simple and childish virtues of veracity and honesty as the root of all that is sublime in character. Speak as you think, be what you are, pay your debts of all kinds. I prefer to be owned as sound and solvent, and my word as good as my bond, and to be what cannot be skipped, or dissipated, or undermined, to all the *éclat* in the universe. This reality is the foundation of friendship, religion, poetry, and art. At the top or at the bottom of all illusions, I set the cheat which still leads us to work and live for appearances, in spite of our conviction, in all sane hours, that it is what we really are that avails with friends, with strangers, and with fate or fortune.

One would think from the talk of men, that riches and poverty were a great matter; and our civilization mainly respects it. But the Indians say, that they do not think the white man with his brow of care, always toiling, afraid of heat and cold, and keeping within doors, has any advantage of them. The permanent interest of every man is, never to be in a false position, but to have the weight of Nature to back him in all that he does. Riches and poverty are a thick or thin costume; and our life — the life of all of us — identical. For we transcend the circumstance continually, and taste the real quality of existence; as in our employments, which only differ in the manipulations, but express the same laws; or in our thoughts, which wear no silks, and taste no ice-creams. We see God face to face every hour, and know the savor of Nature.

The early Greek philosophers Heraclitus and Xenophanes measured their force on this problem of identity. Diogenes of Apollonia said, that unless the atoms were made of one stuff, they could never blend and act with one another. But the Hindoos, in their sacred writings, express the liveliest feeling, both of the essential identity, and of that illusion which they conceive variety to be. "The notions, '*I am*,' and '*This is mine*,' which influence mankind, are but delusions of the mother of the world. Dispel, O Lord of all creatures! the conceit of knowledge which proceeds from ignorance." And the beatitude of man they hold to lie in being freed from fascination.

The intellect is stimulated by the statement of truth in a

trope, and the will by clothing the laws of life in illusions. But the unities of Truth and of Right are not broken by the disguise. There need never be any confusion in these. In a crowded life of many parts and performers, on a stage of nations, or in the obscurest hamlet in Maine or California, the same elements offer the same choices to each new-comer, and, according to his election, he fixes his fortune in absolute Nature. It would be hard to put more mental and moral philosophy than the Persians have thrown into a sentence: —

> "Fooled thou must be, though wisest of the wise:
> Then be the fool of virtue, not of vice."

There is no chance, and no anarchy, in the universe. All is system and gradation. Every god is there sitting in his sphere. The young mortal enters the hall of the firmament; there is he alone with them alone, they pouring on him benedictions and gifts, and beckoning him up to their thrones. On the instant, and incessantly, fall snow-storms of illusions. He fancies himself in a vast crowd which sways this way and that, and whose movement and doings he must obey: he fancies himself poor, orphaned, insignificant. The mad crowd drives hither and thither, now furiously commanding this thing to be done, now that. What is he that he should resist their will, and think or act for himself? Every moment, new changes, and new showers of deceptions, to baffle and distract him. And when, by and by, for an instant, the air clears, and the cloud lifts a little, there are the gods still sitting around him on their thrones, — they alone with him alone.

THE END.

Cambridge: Electrotyped and Printed by Welch, Bigelow, & Co.

www.ingramcontent.com/pod-product-compliance
Lightning Source LLC
LaVergne TN
LVHW020917110826
845150LV00004B/695

* 9 7 8 1 4 2 5 5 5 5 6 6 5 *